LIST OF PLATES

Photograph

E A

THE MACMILLAN COMPANY
1910

Set up and electrotyped. Published October, 1910.

ILLUSTRATIONS IN TEXT

INTRODUCTION

INTRODUCTION

THE car comes to a stop. After several years of absence I am in Poland again. The sun sheds upon the snow myriads of sparks, which glisten like so many precious gems; a purple strip of mist rises above the distant forest of dark, pointed pines, which form a background to white, humble huts, throbbing with lives of patience and toil, under the iron hand of the ruler. . . . I feel a mysterious glow penetrating into the very depth of my heart, tears rise to my eyes; I humbly bow my head and whisper, "Hail, beloved . . ." "Einsteigen, meine Herrschaften," shouts the metallic voice of the conductor, waking me from my revery, and by his sudden cry in a foreign language brutally recalling to my mind the misfortunes of my country.

As we proceed further through German Poland we look in vain for any outward sign of the nationality of the inhabitants; there is none. No Polish inscriptions, no Polish names of the stations, no railroad employees allowed to speak Polish; yet crowds of peasants and workingmen hurrying to the fourth-class cars speak only the vernacular. Strange to say, there is one thing that all the efforts of the repressive governmental system cannot destroy, and that is the deep-rooted patriotism of the people, nor can they make of no avail their heroic struggle to preserve their mother-tongue.

It was almost dark when we reached a station with a name evidently Polish, but so distorted by the Germanizing process that we could not make it out. Here our train stopped. We had been delayed and had missed the connection. The prospect of spending the night in some awful inn in this out-of-the-way place appeared most unpleasant. My husband tried to charter a special train to Oswiecim (the Austrian frontier station), thirty miles away, where we could make connection for Cracow, but there was not the slightest chance of getting such a luxury in that small place.

While we were still holding council on the course to take, the station-master, a jovial, good-natured German, proposed to us to go this short distance by a freight-train; and laughing, he invited us to the conductor's box. In Germany they have no regular caboose on the freight-train, but at the end of the rear car there is a kind of covered box or cage perched near the roof where the conductor remains confined between stations.

My American friend, Miss L. B. F., who, prompted by the extravagant idea of visiting the land of "Thaddeus of Warsaw," had joined us in our travels, was elated with the station-master's suggestion. With all the vigor of youth, good health, and good humor, she hastily climbed the steep, ladder-like stairs conducting to the box. We followed more leisurely. There we sat, five of us, my buoyant American, my husband, my grumbling maid, the conductor, and I, on very narrow seats, in a very tight place, and in an overheated, suffocating atmosphere, making the best of our queer situation.

The conductor, a young man with a pale, sad face, seeing us nearly smothered with rugs and furs, from which we tried in vain to extricate ourselves, speaks with a strangely patient and sympathetic voice, marked by a foreign accent. Evidently he is a Pole, but does not dare to address us in Polish, lest he lose his position. . . . I happened to complain in Polish of the heat; the conductor, without a word, puts his pencil behind his ear and opens the window. It is dark and foggy. The earth and sky are both the same dull gray, — like the background of a picture, — upon which the breath of the engine disgorges clouds of white smoke, studded with millions of red sparks, glittering like dancing, leaping, floating stars. Some of them shoot high in the air, only to fall down with the same speed, and to die in the snow; others, less ambitious, keep lower above ground and disappear in the wallowing clouds of smoke. Poor evanescent stars!

The fog is so dense that it is impossible to distinguish the earth from the sky, the whole seeming a sombre immensity of space and smoke. For a while I imagine myself embarked on some fantastic journey in an airship, and indulge in fanciful dreams, admiring the wonderful performance of those artificial clouds which with such unearthly speed rush through the air, furiously pushing and destroying each other, until they gradually melt away, and vanish in the mist of the night. The train stops. "Fallen Sie nicht, meine Damen" ("Do not fall, ladies"), says the patient voice of the conductor, who offers his slender hand to lead us down the steep steps, and for which I give him a German "Ich danke." He smiles faintly, and whispers "Dobranoc" in Polish.[1]

Oswiecim! This is the frontier between Prussia and Austria, and we enter that part of Poland which is named Galitzia and Lodomeria, and which is ruled by the kind-hearted Kaiser Franz Joseph, so unlike his ancestor, who joined hands with Katherine of Russia and Frederick the king of Prussia to crush the Poles.

We are taken to the Custom House. Here the employees are all Poles. Some of them recognized and greeted us with friendliness. Our trunks pass through a courteous and speedy inspection, very unlike the finicking, rummaging, and prying scrutiny which the passengers are subjected to at the New York docks.

[1] Good-night.

After the inspection of our trunks, we go to the refreshment room for a cup of coffee, and there, to my great delight, we meet Count A. W., who, with three of his friends, is returning from a hunt. They are all clad in immense furs, all tall, about six feet or above, all laughing and greeting us with effusion, which so delights Miss L. B. F. that she surprises them with a Polish sentence she learned from me, and which sounds more like Volapuk than anything else, but it is nevertheless welcomed with shouts.

After parting with our friends, we are led to a reserved compartment in the slow local train. Here the usual railroad notices are in three languages, Polish, German, and Czech (Bohemian). Every employee speaks Polish. We feel at home. A few stations more, and we shall be in Cracow, my native city.

Some fifteen miles separate us yet from the old Polish capital. How shall I spend that time, so that it may not seem an eternity? Oh! I want to be there at once; I have a wild desire to open the window and shriek, "Hurry up!" and to strike the lazy engine with my fists. One more station. This is awful; I sink into my seat and try to be patient. Patience is sister to pain. I sit and suffer. At last the train moves a little faster; the engine, possibly to make a fine stage entrance, gives a few lively jerks just before coming into the city, the white pillars of the depot pass before our eyes, the wheels jangle, the engine gives a piercing whistle, and the train stops.

"Cracow!" This is really Cracow — my cradle, my nurse, my mentor and master. Here I was born and bred. Here trees and stars taught me to think. From the green meadows with their wild flowers I took lessons of harmony in color, the nightingales with their longing songs made me dream of love and beauty. The famous "Zygmunt" bell of the cathedral, with its deep and rich sound, reminded me of the glorious past of Poland; the organs in the churches spoke of God and His Angels; stained windows, statues, and altars suggested art — its importance, its dignity.

At the depot the usual crowd of idlers as well as many friends wait for us. Faces not seen for years, faithful eyes and friendly, smiling lips, shaking of hands, words of hearty welcome, — all this fills me with joy, warms me, intoxicates me. The lapse of years spent far away from the country shrinks into nothingness; I am again with my own people as of old, and they are the same, unchanged and true! I am happy!

Next morning I dress hastily, wake my American friend, and leaving Mr. Chlapowski with his cigarettes and piles of newspapers, we start out in the streets of Cracow.

The day is glorious, the sun shines brightly, the snow creaks under our feet, the sleigh-bells jingle their melodious tunes; my soul is filled with rapture, and I feel as light as a feather.

Miss L. B. F. loves the snow, and plans a long drive in one of those diminutive sliding conveyances, in which young women look so pretty wrapped in furs from head to foot, their rosy cheeks and bright eyes peeping from beneath the fur-trimmed characteristic "Kolpaks." [1]

From time to time, as these sleighs rush along the street, a sweet face leans out, uttering a surprised "Ah," and sends a kiss or wave of hand to me. This amuses my friend, who is one of the most exhilarating persons I know, always ready to enjoy even the slightest glimpse of brightness in life. She bows back to the ladies, and says, "Bon jour," and laughing merrily, asks me who they are. To this I can scarcely answer. "Oh! I understand," she exclaims, "they are the public! How lovely!"

Ah! the dear old walls, worn by so many centuries! We enter the church of the Virgin Mary (Panna Marya). It is

[1] A fur toque with an aigrette.

Church of Panna Marya, Cracow.

encumbered with high scaffolding, reaching to the ceiling. Matejko reigns there again. According to his plans, the old walls, the arched ceiling, the pillars and altars, are restored and repainted in their old original glory. The work on the main altar, covered with the carved statuary of the great "Wit Stwos," a sculptor of the fifteenth century, and one part of the centre nave, is already finished. We stand awhile admiring. It is a marvellous restoration. The walls are covered with most vivid colors, yet the whole is harmonious, soft, and beautiful. The character remains purely mediæval, full of color, glowing, inspiring, a true temple of God, for the people.

"Show me the house you were born in," says my friend.

"I can show you the place, not the house; it was burned down in the conflagration of 1850," I answered. We walk a short distance, and now we are standing before the new house built on the spot where my mother's old home had stood. I pointed to Miss L. B. F. the location of two windows on the third floor, behind which I spent the first ten years of my life. Dim memories, sweet as old lullabies, spread their charm over my being; but soon other recollections, full of the anxieties of the past, alight on my brain like a swarm of gnats. I turn my head away. At the other side of Szeroka Street stands an old house which miraculously escaped the Austrian bomb as well as the flames, intact in its clumsiness, with squatty, sprawling walls and small square windows. At the angle of it, in a shallow niche provided with a small, protecting tin roof, a statue of the Virgin is placed. Ten golden stars surround her head, ornamented with most elaborate puffs and curls, a golden belt imprisons her waist, a blue cloak fastened with a gold buckle falls in graceful folds down to her feet. Her right hand is extended as in blessing over the people who pass beneath her. Her eyes are turned toward heaven, and her feet repose lightly on a silver crescent. In a word, a true relic of baroque style. Seeing me smiling tenderly at the statue, Miss L. B. F. asks:—

"What are you thinking about?"

"I am thinking what an important part this image of the Virgin played in my childhood."

"What! That ugly thing!"

"It was not ugly to me then. It was the most wonderful incarnation of virtue, grace, and motherhood. It brought into my little brain marvellous dreams of angels and saints. I firmly believed that she loved me, and many a time I related to her long stories of my childish grievances, in a whisper. I knew she heard me, in spite of the wide street between us, and every morning and evening I said my prayers, kneeling by the window on a chair, so that I might behold her lovely countenance!"

"You were a superstitious child, I see."

"I suppose I was, but I am still infinitely grateful for those glimpses into the land of wonders, which left an everlasting impression on my soul."

"Oh! you are such a baby still!" This Miss L. B. F. uttered, smiling broadly, and showing two rows of marvellous white teeth. I laughed and answered:—

"This time I will forgive you that absurd nickname you apply to me, a nickname of young America, given to those brought up by centuries of traditions and idealistic training." Upon which we both laugh and proceed on our way.

The Royal Castle is the next thing I want my friend to see. One part of the castle is restored and turned into Austrian barracks, but the old portion of the edifice, ragged, with moss-covered roof, is still there, looking down on the city, with its small grated windows and huge stone gate. One would say, a very old and lonesome man, with weak eyes and open mouth, brooding over his past. He has witnessed horrors of war, crime, lust, victories, pride, conceit, honors, as well as inexpressible sorrows, great Christian virtues, monstrous injustice, and finally the downfall of the noble race.

We postpone until another day our visit to the picture galleries, museums, and private studios; and conversing on the subjects of national grievances and art, we enter slowly the long avenue of old chestnut-trees which encircles the city, meeting in the neighborhood of the Royal Castle.

THE ROYAL PALACE, CRACOW.

This avenue, called the "Planty," is the favorite promenade of the people during the warm season of the year, but even in winter it is not deserted; students of the different schools find always a pretext to walk on the fresh snow of their beloved "Planty." In fact, everybody frequents the avenue. I remember when I was a young aspirant for dramatic honors, I used to rise at five o'clock in the morning, take my part with me, and walk up and down in the shade of the wide-branched trees, studying my lines. At eight o'clock I had to return, for fear of being exposed to the jests of the students.

While in Cracow I gave a series of performances, the total ceipts of which I placed in the hands of the mayor of the ty, as the beginning of a fund for the building of a new .eatre. With this first money as an inducement, he opened collection. Generous offers followed, and a few years .ter a handsome theatre was built, in a large square, standig alone. A lawn, shrubs, and flowers lent to it a refreshig grace. The interior is ornamented with pictures and ;atues, and our late great artist, Siemiradzki, painted curtain and offered it as a gift to the city. This curtain s an object of admiration to all who visit Cracow. As a rule ery little attention is paid to a curtain, but this one is an mportant ornament. It strikes a noble note, and fills the uditorium with an artistic atmosphere.

* * * * * * *

These few pages I wrote some years ago; I have not lestroyed them, because this return to my native country, after a long absence, inspired me with the idea of writing my reminiscences. It was at this time that I commenced making notes, collecting such material as I thought necessary, with the firm project of describing my own personal experiences, as well as some characteristics of the prominent people I have met during my stage career.

PART I

CHILDHOOD AND YOUTH

While in Cracow I gave a series of performances, the total receipts of which I placed in the hands of the mayor of the city, as the beginning of a fund for the building of a new theatre. With this first money as an inducement, he opened a collection. Generous offers followed, and a few years later a handsome theatre was built, in a large square, standing alone. A lawn, shrubs, and flowers lent to it a refreshing grace. The interior is ornamented with pictures and statues, and our late great artist, Siemiradzki, painted a curtain and offered it as a gift to the city. This curtain is an object of admiration to all who visit Cracow. As a rule very little attention is paid to a curtain, but this one is an important ornament. It strikes a noble note, and fills the auditorium with an artistic atmosphere.

* * * * * * *

These few pages I wrote some years ago; I have not destroyed them, because this return to my native country, after a long absence, inspired me with the idea of writing my reminiscences. It was at this time that I commenced making notes, collecting such material as I thought necessary, with the firm project of describing my own personal experiences, as well as some characteristics of the prominent people I have met during my stage career.

PART I

CHILDHOOD AND YOUTH

CHAPTER I

SOME of the events and surroundings among which I was brought up come back to my mind with the clearness of a silhouette, perfect in its outline; and since I have to tell the story of my life, it is just as well to begin at the very beginning. Yet I beg my readers to believe that I have not undertaken this task for the mere pleasure of speaking of myself or boasting of my triumphs. I only write because I cannot help thinking that this work, though deficient in many points, may yet interest some people, or be of some use to others.

It is impossible to write a biography leaving out entirely one's wretched "I," yet I shall be as discreet as possible, as there is nothing I dread more than a touch of "pseudologia-fantastica-madness," to which much stronger natures than my own are often subjected.

Born on the 12th of October, 1840, I was one of ten children at home, and being a member of such a numerous family, I could not claim the exclusive attention of my mother, who, besides many domestic duties, had the management of her property on her shoulders. Therefore my younger sister Josephine and myself were left entirely in the care of my great-aunt Teresa, who loved us dearly, who was very careful of our health, but whose attempts in developing our little souls were limited to the scrupulous reciting with us of our morning and evening prayers.

In consequence, I grew up mostly under the influence of Nature, among the incidents of life and national calamities, free, unrestrained, forming my own judgment of things blindly, innocently, adorning and magnifying them with my vivid imagination, catching eagerly snatches of heroic songs, poems, or religious hymns, memorizing and repeating them, and thus unconsciously building up my character as well as laying the foundation for my artistic future.

Talent is born with us, but the influence of surroundings shapes, develops, or subdues it. That sweet sadness, which for the most part exists in Polish melodies and poems and which is the outcome of the whole nation's sufferings, that limitless tenderness and longing, unconsciously rooted itself in my soul from my very childhood, in spite of the fiery and stormy temperament I brought with me into the world —presumably an inheritance from a Hungarian great-grandmother. That note of tenderness always predominated both in my nature and my work, in which often flashes of inborn vivacity and passion were overshadowed by that touch of Slavonic *Tesknota,* a word quite untranslatable into a foreign language, which may be best interpreted by the following verse of Longfellow: —

> "A feeling of sadness and longing
> That is not akin to pain,
> And resembles sorrow only
> As the mist resembles rain."

When I follow closely my childhood I see distinctly the logical evolution of my destiny. As far as I can remember, I did not find much pleasure in the society of other children, who often left my company, branding me with nicknames, such as: "Princess of the Sea Foam" or "Lady with Long Nails"; sometimes they called me "a Fury," or "a Weeping Willow," sometimes again "Laughing Magpie," on account of my occasional uncontrollable fits of laughter.

It seems that I was not one of the most amiable of children, and all these nicknames my brothers used to christen me with fitted my behavior.

Misfortunes, fires, the hissing of cannon-balls, the crash

of bursting bombs, the march of armies, men killed and lying in their blood, — these are never-forgotten impressions which thrilled my childish soul through and through, shaping it into an untimely maturity and awakening in it inclination for heroism, thirst for greatness, for sacrifice; in a word, the necessity of attaining the unattainable, the upward start in quest of high ideals.

Alas! it was not my destiny to die for my country, as was my cherished dream, but instead of becoming a heroine I had to be satisfied with acting heroines, exchanging the armor for tinsel, and the weapon for words.

My father, Michael Opid, was a student of philology and a teacher in one of the high schools in Cracow. Born in the Carpathian Mountains, he brought with him to the valley a warm, unsophisticated heart, a most vivid imagination, and a great love for music. He also was very fond of children; I remember him during long winter evenings, sitting by the fireside, holding me and my sister on his knees; near him, my mother knitting, and the boys, together with neighbors' children, scattered on the floor, watching him with glistening, curious eyes, and listening attentively to his stories. They were wonderful stories that touched us with pity or thrilled us with joy. Some of them were taken from national legends or from the mountaineer folk-lore, some were his own invention, or subjects taken from his cherished books. His favorite story was Homer's "Iliad," extracts of which he told us in his simple language. I do not know how much I understood then of the famous epic poem, but when I read it some fifteen years later, many famous scenes came back vividly to my mind, and the picture of my father rose from the remote past, filling my eyes with tears.

Music was his passion. He played on several instruments, mostly on the flute, which instrument was then in fashion, and almost every week he arranged quartets in his rooms.

On such occasions the children were allowed to enter his "sanctum sanctorum." He played with great feeling, and often during the tender passages I burst into a loud wail, after the fashion of dogs, which resulted in my being taken out of the room and unjustly punished. My mother did not, could not, know that this disgraceful behavior was the effect of the music, and that my tears were a genuine tribute to my father's art. I understood, however, that this loud crying disturbed the music, and I used to creep into the remotest corner of the room, where I could hide my smothered demonstrations and avoid the vigilant eye of the maternal authority.

Those who knew my father say that he was a man of great kindness — kindness verging on weakness — a man of great feeling and few words, keeping the doors of his inner self closely shut. He died at the age of forty-three, of consumption, caused by a severe cold contracted while searching for his drowned brother's body. At last the body was found, but my father returned home with high fever and pneumonia. A few months later he died in the mountains, to which he was transported at his ardent request. I was at that time about seven years old.

In contrast to my father's gentle nature, my mother was a person of great energy, great activity, very quick and outspoken, very generous, but rash in judgment, and often regretting her hasty words and actions. She possessed good health and a merry heart. Some of her old friends spoke of her great beauty. My mother never knew her own father, also a mining engineer, who perished in an attempt to rescue workingmen entombed in a burning mine. She was born a few weeks after his death. A year later her mother was married again, and followed her second husband to Russian Poland, leaving her little daughter in the care of her old widowed mother, Mrs. von Goltz. When my mother was seven years old, my great-grandmother was killed by lightning, and then one of her friends, the wife of Senator R., brought up the little granddaughter.

At nineteen she married a wealthy citizen of Cracow, Mr. Simon Benda, who was ennobled for the numerous services he had rendered the city. He was a widower, and nearly thirty years older than his young wife. When he died, he left her several sons, and a fortune somewhat compromised by his liberalities. In consequence, my poor mother had her hands full; but in a few years, thanks to her industry, economy, and energy she had paid off all debts, and established a perfect order in her affairs. A few years later my father appeared; and this time it was a love match.

CHAPTER II

In the early spring of 1848 the people of Cracow were greatly excited. The young men talked a great deal, their enthusiasm was immense; they were merry, they sang derisive couplets on Metternich and General Castiglione. The girls were busy sewing the red and white and blue cockades and scarfs for the National Guards.[1]

I remember with what delight I handed thread and ribbons to Miss Apollonia, our young neighbor from the third floor, who, while ardently stitching the inspiring ornaments, recited patriotic verses or sang sentimental love-songs. One of those songs began with the words, "Here is the brook and the meadow where my lover waits for me." The next one was very long, composed of four stanzas, of which the first three ended with the words, "No, no, I cannot and I will not," and the last one was concluded with: "Yes, yes, I can and I will — I love — I love — tra la la, tra la la." I never knew why she changed her mind, but I admired Miss Apollonia's delivery of the songs. She sang them with tender, melting voice, which pleased me, but my half-brother, Simon Benda, teased her, saying that her nose was not suited to sentimental or tragic poetry, being but an

[1] In 1815 Cracow, with its surroundings, was proclaimed a free city by the Congress of Vienna, with the agreement of the powers, Russia, Prussia, and Austria. Notwithstanding the stipulations of those monarchs, and contrary to their pledges, Cracow was annexed by Austria in October, 1846. During the same year Metternich's policy created a new "Jacquerie" in Galitzia, sending out his agents to rouse the peasants against the nobles, and a terrible massacre ensued. Cracow people naturally were indignant against the new régime, and when, in 1848, the revolution broke out in Vienna, they were awakened to their old hopes of independence. The Austrians crushed these hopes by the bombardment of the city.

upturned little bit of a nose, and so highly uplifted in the air that her profile looked very much like the profile of a coffee-pot.

In spite of this slight defect, for which she was not responsible at all, Miss Apollonia was very patriotic. It was she who informed me that all Russians, and Austrians in particular, were scoundrels and cowards who deserved to be hanged one after another until none of them were left on earth. One morning she told me in a whisper that there would be war, that the young Cracovians were learning to drill, and would fight like tigers, upon which she changed the subject and told me a fairy story:—

"One morning a handsome young prince saw a pretty green frog looking at him with pitiful eyes. He picked it up and took it to his palace. He placed the poor creature in a separate room, and fed it every morning with flies and honey. The frog was happy, and danced and croaked and began to grow wonderfully. In a week it was as large as a big rat, in another week it came up to the size of a cat, then later on it grew as big as a lamb, until at last it measured five feet and six inches. One morning the prince heard beautiful singing in the frog's room. He opened the door, and there was Miss Croaky standing on her hind legs, singing. When the last sounds of the beautiful air died away, the monstrous animal shut its mouth, took a long breath, and puffed itself to such an extent that it looked like a large round balloon. Then it burst suddenly with a fearful noise, filling the room with a delicious perfume, and out of the repulsive hide of the monster stepped the most beautiful princess, in a wedding gown covered all over with pearls and diamonds." . . . Here she stopped for a while; I listened to the story breathlessly, and when I was just asking her nervously: "What happened next, please?—what happened next?"—the distant report of a gun was heard, then another and again another. Miss Apollonia, with outstretched arms, cried: "It is the war — the war! Did I not tell you!"

One morning my mother entered the room; she was quite pale; then all my brothers rushed in, very much excited, and all talked together about the National Guard, the exiles, the Austrians. The names of Baron Krieg and General Castiglione were mentioned, and while they were talking, a murmur of voices was heard approaching nearer and nearer, until an unusual clamor filled the streets, and in the midst of it a cry, "Build barricades!" Then all the houses disgorged their inhabitants, who carried beds, mattresses, chairs, sofas, throwing them into a large heap until a barricade was raised across the street. We counted one, two, three barricades, the last one at the end of our street; and leaning out of the window, we could see the Austrians' bayonets in the distance. Our maidservants worked with spirit, carrying heavy pieces of furniture, kitchen utensils, etc., and placing them on top of the shaky structure. Every time they climbed up they called to the Austrian soldiers, shaking their red fists at them and giving them funny and uncomplimentary names. The whole scene seemed rather amusing. My brother Simon, then fourteen years old, jumping down off the barricade, rushed into the house, then into the room where we were all assembled, shouting:—

"Give me a sword, a pistol, anything! Give me a spit! a spit! and I will stick that General with a cockade on his casque, and roast him like a chicken!" which speech provoked merry laughter from the hearers. Mother, fearing the lad might get into mischief, seized his two hands, pushed him into the adjoining room, and locked the door. We heard him stamping and shrieking:—

"I want to kill him! Let me out! I must kill him!"

My sister and myself were highly interested in looking at the National Guards arranging themselves behind protective barricades, when we were peremptorily ordered by my mother to keep away from the window. We obeyed, and crept into the next room, where stood my mother's stately bed, supported by four carved and painted little negroes. We soon forgot what was going on, absorbed in touching the large eyeballs, red lips, and gold ornaments of the queer dark fellows with whom we planned a long journey to the tropics, where pepper grows, when suddenly a loud report of a cannon made us spring up, run to mother, and cling to her dress. She cried:—

"Great God! They are bombarding the city! Aunt Teresa, call the boys and servants, and let us go to the cellar — and please tell them to bring some bedding, as we must pass the night there, if they do not stop!" . . . She unlocked the door where my poor brother was imprisoned, and ordered him to go first. Cooled off from his first excitement, he meekly submitted. Then, taking my sister by the hand, our imposing mamma turned to me and said briefly:—

"Follow me!" . . . But I stood where she left me. Was it fright or curiosity? I cannot tell; but I did not move. I heard her descending the stairs; I knew it was naughty to stay when she had ordered me to follow her, and when she was sure that I was walking behind her. I knew all that — and yet — I stood where she left me.

My youngest and my own brother, Adolphe Opid, three years older than myself, tearing himself away from Aunt Teresa's protecting arms, came up to me dishevelled, and with an expression of wild passion in his face he said:—

"I will not go to the cellar! I want to see!" On the instant a tremendous crash shook the house to its foundations. Something unnaturally heavy struck the wall, followed by something equally heavy falling with a clang against the stone pavement. I began to cry aloud. My brother grew very pale. His lips were trembling. He ran to the window, and leaning out with half of his body, he said excitedly:—

"A bomb tore away half of the iron balcony, and made a big hole in the wall!" The cannon reports still continued, the streets were filled with the clamors and cries of the people, and then, with a noise like the snapping of whips, the rifles began their work. Louder and louder grew the shooting, and with it the crash of broken window-panes falling to the floor together with the bullets. Adolphe, who, during that time, ran from one room to another, picking up the bullets, came back, and taking me by the hand pulled me with him to the corner room, the one most exposed to the projectiles of the Austrian carabines.

"Hide in that corner," he cried, pushing me forward, and then added, with unhidden pleasure, "There will be more bullets." And there were more. This time bullets and shots together like hail fell through the window. . . . "I told you so! hold up your apron!" and picking the leaden toys up from the floor, he threw them into my apron, which I obediently lifted up,—not altogether displeased with the contents.

"Pretty little things—round and heavy, too," he repeated, weighing them one by one in his hand. "When I grow up I will make different bullets to kill the 'cow's feet.'[1] They will be pointed, that they may go deep into their accursed flesh!"

The shooting ceased for a while and we went to the window. There a picture met my eyes. On the opposite side of the street a man lies on his back on the pavement; his shirt is open, in the middle of his breast gapes a red wound. A woman kneels by him, trying to stop the blood, which drips on the pavement and congeals. The face of the man is white, the eyes staring wide open. In the middle of the

[1] A name for Austrian soldiers, caused presumably by the gaiters they wore, made of the undressed hide of that harmless animal.

street a boy of ten or twelve lies, his face to the ground. Oh! the pity of it! Oh! the sight of murder and death for a child's eyes! The marring of the fresh bloom of a little soul with such a tinge of sadness and horror! Clinging close to my brother, I cry. He is pale and silent, but a nervous shiver runs through his frame. . . . Some other wounded men are carried away. The street is alive with wailing, lamenting people, and we sit by the window and look and look, taking in every detail of that sad, never-to-be-forgotten picture. . . . My mother's desperate call, "Helcia![1] Adolphe!" makes us leave the window. We rush out of the room and down to the cellar.

By the dim light of a lantern and a few candles the interior of our large cellar looks more picturesque than pleasant. The odor of dampness is unwelcome to the nostrils, the stone walls glisten with drops of moisture, and the cold, cavernous air chills me through. An immense quantity of bedding is heaped in one corner, and the maids, under my mother's direction, are making beds on the floor. My sister's plump little body is reposing on cushions, her beautiful golden hair forming an aureole about her fair round face. My two half-brothers, Simon and Felix, are quarrelling; Simon calls Felix "Metternich," which is such an insult that Felix springs up to fight with his brother, but mother's authoritative voice brings order into the ranks of the fiery youngsters. Miss Apollonia, half reclining on a mattress, turns her large eyes and little nose up to the ceiling and sighs, murmuring:—

"God will punish them,—you will see," and then with an inspired voice she adds, "Poland is not lost yet!" Her mother sits on a barrel saying her rosary, and Adolphe plays with bullets.

Slowly silence begins to reign (in our subterranean dwell-

[1] Helcia is a Polish diminutive for Helena.

ing), and we only hear the distant shooting and faint cries of the people. Mother sits on her improvised bed, with her head in her hands. Aunt Teresa undresses me, and I kneel to say my evening prayers. After a while we hear outside of the door the clang of a sword against the stone stairs, and then the sound of steps approaching our cellar. In an instant my mother turns the huge key of the iron door. Some one tries the knob, then there is a knock, and then silence. Finally the gentle voice of my eldest half-brother, Joseph, is heard.

"It is I, mamma; please open." Mother gives a sigh of relief and lets him in.

There he stands, in the fine uniform of the National Guard, with a sword at his belt, and by his side a beautiful creature leaning on his arm. I learned years afterwards that she was an actress nicknamed "Cornflower" (Blawatka), on account of her wonderful blue eyes. Her popularity was great, especially among young men, who admired her beauty and light-heartedness. . . . Mother, seeing "that person" (as she called her), grew pale with anger. She did not say a word, however, but looked straight into my brother's eyes.

"Please, mamma," said Joseph, "be so kind as to give shelter to this lady." She answered:—

"No one can refuse shelter to those in danger, and the young lady may stay with us; but you" — turning to my brother — "what are you doing here? The Austrians kill men and children like game, and you are here, sane and safe. Go back where your duty calls you!" And when Joseph obediently retired, she said to Cornflower in a softer tone of voice, "Sit down, young lady, and rest." Then, seeing that I was sitting with eyes wide open, she came to me, kissed my forehead, and whispered: —

"Lie down and sleep; shut your eyes; you have seen too much to-day. Good-night." I did as she told me; but behind my closed eyelids I saw a streak of red, a pale face, and the wide-open eyes of a dying man who stared at me.

* * * * * * *

Three days afterwards, on the large square, "Rynek," opposite St. Mary's Church, I stand with my mother. On the square, crowds and crowds of people wait for the funeral

THE "RYNEK," CRACOW.

procession of the victims killed on the day of the bombardment. The sound of organs reaches our ears. The church is overflowed. Many kneel outside on the pavement, and at the call of the great "Zygmunt" bell more and more people come streaming by. The whole city is out. Then a long, plaintive wail of the people is heard, and the coffins appear, carried on the shoulders of men and women, and the long chain of victims proceeds to the final resting-place.

CHAPTER III

Be it from the shock of the tragic events I mentioned in the last chapter, or from some organic defect, shortly after the bombardment, my youngest brother, Adolphe, then eleven years old, began to show signs of somnambulism. On nights when the moon was full he would rise from his bed, walk with staggering steps, yet rapidly, to the window, and stand there with his eyes wide open, laughing softly and stretching his arms towards the moon. After a while he would open the window and try to jump out, which would have been sure death. But usually our guardian angel, in a white nightcap and a long white robe, our dear Aunt Teresa, appeared in time to rescue the boy from his dangerous position and bring him back to bed, screening off the moonlight from him. Every time my brother had one of those fits, I could not fall asleep again. I used to creep softly out of my couch, go to the window, and look down. The street, half white from the flood of moonlight, and half black with mysterious shadows, was a great attraction to me. Leaning a little forward I could see the Franciscan square and a corner of the church. That part of the square always inspired me with a sort of awe. Often on the days of funerals I have seen emerging from the church door the brotherhood of St. Francis, of dreadful appearance, with which people used to frighten children. The members of that society are dressed in black cassocks, painted all over with skulls, bones, and flames. They wear black cowls drawn over their faces, falling in a V-shape below the chin, and looking like masks with round holes for the eyes. This institution is a relic from mediæval times, and

I believe that even at the present time the brotherhood appears at some church ceremonies.

The Franciscan square had yet another attraction: the old tradition was that during some terrible epidemics the authorities, not being able to bury all the people, threw them pell-mell into the church vaults. My brother told me that one of those vaults was here in the corner of the church; I also heard some awful ghost stories connected with it. The ghosts were not kind enough to appear, but at night, out of the corner, two huge century-old owls used to appear and walk in the moonlight, throwing long shadows behind them, which made them seem three times their own length. These uncanny creatures moved very slowly, with silent steps, spreading their wings from time to time in a vain effort to fly; but, unable to lift their old clumsy bodies above the ground, they dropped their feathered arms in despair, dragging them on the pavement. The phantom birds, I imagined, were some penitent souls, creeping in the dust and begging for mercy. They made me shiver with fright, and yet I could not turn my eyes away from them, but sat there in the warmth of a summer moonlight, fascinated, hypnotized. What thoughts passed across my little brain then I cannot remember, but many years later, when I studied the part of Juliet, the tomb of the Capulets brought back vividly to my mind those childhood impressions of the Franciscan church, the mysterious vault, and the phantom owls.

CHAPTER IV

As far back as my memory can reach, I remember that I loved to be in church. To be there, kneeling on the marble floor, looking at the altars, and listening to the organ music, was sufficient to make me happy; and when I prayed during the Mass, a deep sense of beauty and holy peace spread over me, and the church seemed filled with angels. Often I closed my eyes, and with face upturned, waited, hoping that one of those holy spirits floating in the air would touch my forehead with its wings. I would remain there motionless, all absorbed by some unutterable thoughts and the perfect bliss of the moment.

At the end of our short and wide street, about one block from our house, and in the opposite direction from the Franciscans, stands the Dominican church, a point of great attraction to me. The naves of that church are singularly narrow, and their arches drawn up so high that they seem to be out of proportion, — a regular old Gothic structure. Not knowing anything about architecture then, I supposed that this church was built in imitation of two hands joined for prayer, with the finger-tips meeting and relaxed above the wrists, as in some of the pictures of praying Madonnas whose hands form an arch not unlike the entrance to a Gothic church. My favorite amusement after the evening prayers was to join my hands in the same way; holding them against the light, I imagined I had a little chapel of my own, with three arches, a door, and a window in the background.

The Dominican church has a basement with widely spread arches of graceful design. That was my favorite place.

I liked to go there during the summer months. In the winter the unheated church, with its stone floor, was too chilly, but it was a delight to be there during the warm weather, so cool, so quiet, with no sound except the twitter of the sparrows in the yard. How often I used to steal away from the house and stay there for hours. How often I would lie down, with my face to the ground, in imitation of our peasant women, with arms outstretched in the shape of a cross, kissing the floor, and praying fervently to God for a miracle, for a glimpse of an angel or of some saint.

One afternoon, when I was in one of my ecstasies, I heard muffled steps near the door. Some one was coming towards me very softly, nearer and nearer. "A miracle!" I thought. "My prayer is granted! It is an angel who comes, or a saint!" and thrilled with mysterious joy, I even imagined I felt the waft of a heavenly garment or wings, like a cooling breeze upon my neck, when suddenly a strong grasp clutched at the belt of my frock, lifted me up, and with one turn of the hand put me on my feet, forcing me to face my angel in the shape of a distressed old maid. The dear Aunt Teresa, looking for me in vain for more than an hour, had come upon my track at last, and fearing I might catch cold, was determined to use even force in order to bring me out into the sun.

After that time I was watched more closely, and soon after this capture my sister and I were taken to Mrs. R., in whose house we were to receive our first education. That charming lady was my mother's old friend. She had two highly educated daughters, Salomea and Ludwina, who at my mother's urgent request had consented to be our teachers. I was taught to read at the age of four, and at seven I read fluently. To any modern mother it may seem absurd to teach a child so early, but in the days of my childhood and youth girls were taught to read at four, and were ready for matrimonial duties at fifteen.

The stories which Miss Ludwina gave me had developed in me quite a passion for reading, and I read everything I could find, my brother's school books as well as the sentimental love stories which Miss Apollonia rented from a circulating library. In fact, I read long before I could understand what I read.

Opposite Mrs. R.'s house stood a large building, with boxed-up windows. It was a provisory jail for political prisoners. One morning I saw Miss Salomea sitting by an open window, with a sheet of paper before her and a pencil, looking intensely at the house opposite, as if watching or waiting for something to see. After a while she began to sing a plaintive Polish song. As soon as she finished the first verse, a large white hand appeared in one of the windows of the jail, over the boxed casement, and began to trace with the forefinger some letters in the air. At once Miss Salomea wrote down some words, and raising her eyes again, she watched the hand and wrote down what the prisoner communicated. She was doing that for many days, and what she wrote down she read in a whisper to her mother and sister, and after some consultation they usually sent Felix on some errand, and then some visitors called and they shut themselves in the parlor. That was all I noticed. I racked my little brain in vain to find out what was the meaning of it all, when one day Miss Salomea, seeing me watching her, explained to me that the man opposite was a dear friend, whom the Austrians kept unjustly in prison, and whom she and her family were trying to release.

"And mind, Helenka," she added, "you must not tell any one what you saw." I promised, and never betrayed the secret, proud of the confidence placed in me, and more strongly than ever confirmed in my adverse feelings towards Poland's enemies.

"I do hate the Austrians," I repeated mentally on my

way home, and I was so deeply impressed by Miss Salomea's words that I wrote "I hate the Austrians" several times on the copy-book of my grammar exercise.

I do not recollect the exact program of our studies, but my favorite subjects were grammar, Polish history, and French, and it seemed that I made some progress in my studies as well as in my behavior, for my mother came one day and expressed her gratitude to our teachers, Mrs. R. and her daughters, for the good influence they exerted over me, assuring them that they had corrected many deficiencies in my character. To which Mrs. R. replied, that though I seemed to improve, yet there were two things in my character she could not cure me of: my stubbornness and my bashfulness. Oh, that horrible, shrinking shyness, which stood in my way so often, which sent all the blood to my cheeks and made me look like a boiled lobster at the least provocation. That awful timidity which many times, even in my days of maturity, prevented me from asserting my own value in the face of impudent ignorance! How often I loathed that unwelcome defect without being able to overcome it! Even my long stage career did not cure me entirely of this disease, which our Polish poet, Asnyk, an old and indulgent friend of mine, called "fits of modesty."

Mrs. R. often received visitors, and those reception days were real trials to me. The more I tried to be "a good girl, and answer the questions addressed to me," the more awkward I felt, and when I saw everybody smiling at my behavior, I simply ran out of the room, and would not come back for anything in the world. In the meantime, my little sister placidly occupied the field of action, and, handed from one charming lady to another, was filled with candy and cakes. When she told me of her triumphs, I was very angry with my own stupidity, but the next time I fell into the same blunder.

Mrs. R. and her daughters were very fond of the theatre,

and one afternoon, together with my mother, they planned to take a box, to hear the new soprano, Miss Studzinska. Miss Ludwina, always kind and thoughtful of others, begged my mother to take Josephine and me with them, the box being large enough for six.

The play was "The Daughter of the Regiment," followed by a one-act ballet entitled, "The Siren of Dniestr." Miss Studzinska was the heroine of the opera, and little Josephine Hofmann,[1] dressed as a butterfly, had the prominent dancing part in the ballet. It was my first visit to a theatre, and the whole evening was a dream of joy and enchantment to me. My mother told me, years afterwards, that I was so absorbed in the play that I became perfectly oblivious to the surroundings. I was blind, mute, and deaf, and she could not get a sign from me. I went to bed with a high fever, and for weeks afterwards I tried to imitate the butterfly dance, and sang some airs, accompanying them with gestures, exciting the derision of my brothers, who had spied me on the sly.

Every child tries to imitate actresses seen on the stage, — there is nothing wonderful in that! and there is no indication of talent in such demonstrations. Still, I know mothers of little girls who think that their daughters must one day be great actresses because they are naturally graceful and fond of pretty frocks and dances. It is rather dangerous to encourage that sort of thing, and mark out a career for a child who, were it not for the constant flattery, would perhaps choose another more suitable occupation. The stage is overcrowded with young persons without talent, possessing only some adaptability and the usual ability for imitation. They prosper sometimes as long as they are young, and then are pushed aside to make room for younger and more attractive women. Thus is formed quite an army of disappointed, discontented, poor struggling creatures,

[1] Josef Hofmann's aunt.

who, had they chosen differently, would occupy more dignified positions in life. I cannot be grateful enough to my dear mother for never encouraging my inclination to the stage, and never exciting my vanity by flattering or praising me to my face. I became an actress because I think it was my destiny to be an artist of some kind, and as the stage was the most accessible of all branches of art, I chose it.

But, returning to "The Daughter of the Regiment," my mother, seeing my excitement, decided that children ought to stay away from the theatre. And she kept her word; but we found compensation in concerts given at our house by some friends and artists. Madame Majeranowska, née Hofmann,[1] then a young and very talented woman, who later was a well-known opera-singer, and Bogucki, a splendid basso profundo, gave us many never-forgotten moments of delight.

It is sometimes difficult for parents to keep their children away from their cherished attractions. My three older brothers were crazy about the stage, and asked mother for the permission to give private theatricals at home. Wearied with their incessant pleadings, she consented at last, probably to keep them out of mischief. And it happened, to my great delight, that we had regular performances every month. Joseph, the eldest, though married, painted the scenery; Simon took care of the music and songs; and Felix was the leading man. With four or five young students they formed a company. Girls were not admitted to this histrionic circle, but boys assumed female parts. I remember still a young red-headed and freckled youth, by the name of Jahnsen, dressed in a white muslin gown, and white stockings in place of shoes, probably to make his steps light and fairy-like, reciting dramatic verses, which called forth

[1] The elder aunt of Josef Hofmann, who by marriage was connected with the Benda family.

many enthusiastic bravos. He and Felix were the best actors of the troup.

We had many of these performances, and many friends came to see them. They praised or blamed according to the value of the performer, and these were the first lessons I received in dramatic art. Who knows if this childish enthusiasm for the theatre did not decide my fate, and also the fate of my sister and my two brothers. All four of us went on the stage.

CHAPTER V

In July, 1850, on Sunday at noon, the heat was intense. After returning from church, Aunt Teresa undressed my sister and me to the skin, and throwing on our bare backs long gingham blouses, and putting slippers on our feet, she ordered a bath for us. Suddenly some one opens the door of the adjoining room, shouting:—

"The lower mills are on fire!" Aunt Teresa looks frightened. The maid who appears at the door, with hot water for our bath, nearly drops the buckets, and placing them where she stands in the very entrance, rushes downstairs for further information. I hear my mother's voice calling my brothers, but all of them are already on their way to the burning mills, eager to see the sight,—always so attractive to boys, young and old. No more than half an hour later we see flames on the roof of the bishops' palace on Franciscan Street, and almost simultaneously the red tongues of fire are licking the roof of a house opposite ours on Grodzka Street.

Czas,[1] the Cracow newspaper, describes the conflagration in the following words: "The panic was indescribable. People were maddened with fright. We heard their cries: 'Golembia Street is on fire!' then 'the Wielopolski's palace! Prince Jablonowski's house! Four churches burning at once!' It seemed as if the whole city were one flame. A strong wind blew, the air was full of smoke and cinders, and not one fire-engine, not even a ladder—nothing! All was left to the mercy of the destructive element."

My poor mother, left only with Aunt Teresa and one ser-

[1] Time.

vant for help, is at a loss what to do first; but before all, she wants to see Josephine and me in a safe place, and hurriedly tells Aunt Teresa to take us to St. Sebastian's meadow, which is situated on the other side of the Chestnut Alley, and to wait there until she shall be able to join us. I obey promptly, and taking under my arm the life of St. Genevieve, a book I have just begun to read, holding my sister's hand, I start — without waiting for Aunt Teresa — straight to the designated spot.

We both are so excited that we run ahead without looking under our feet, and in consequence do not see the drainage canal, filled with water and overgrown with vegetation. In one instant Josephine disappears under the green, slimy crust of the ditch, and I, following her closely, find myself up to my chest in the water. Happily I feel Josephine's fingers on my arm. I grasp her hand, and retracing my steps, pull her up to the dry land; at the same time I inspect my precious book, anxious to see if it has not been destroyed by the immersion, but it seems that I held it so tightly under my arm that only the cover and the edges are a little wet. This unexpected bath has a cooling effect upon us. Having wrung out our scanty clothes as soon as we can, we begin to feel anxious, and look for Aunt Teresa, but she is not there. Behind the trees of the avenue the sky is red, covered with smoke and sparks, the sun is fierce, and our blouses are steaming under his hot touch.

Crowds of men, women, and children scatter on the meadow, bringing with them such articles as they have been able to save from the flames. Men are going back and forth, carrying furniture, bedding, and clothing, piling them up in different camps. Evidently they intend to spend the night there. People, horses, cattle, dogs, birds in cages, and cats — all are mixed up. Alone, among strangers, we are on the point of bursting into tears, when at last we perceive our dear, perspiring, tired, panting Aunt Teresa, carrying on one arm a large feather quilt, and with the other arm pressing tenderly to her bosom my large doll. That is all she thought, in her confusion, worth saving.

We hasten to meet her. Seeing us, she drops the quilt to the ground, sits on it, and then — a flood of words, which could only be compared to a rushing mountain stream, or the bursting of a cloud, falls on our heads, protesting, grumbling, scolding us for our independence and the unkind spirit which prompted us to leave her side and to run so fast that she could not possibly keep pace with us. While she is talking, her dark brown eyes and black, frowning brows look so angry that their aspect chills us through; but suddenly she stops. She touches our wet clothes, and Josephine tells her of our narrow escape from "drowning." In an instant her countenance changes. Her voice becomes soft, and kissing us, she falls into another extreme, giving us sweet names, stroking our cheeks, and scolding herself for being rude. Dearest old Aunt Teresa!

After a while we learn from her that mother changed her plan and decided that we should go to the hills, called "Krzemionki," and ask the hospitality of Mrs. X., my aunt's old acquaintance. The hills are about three miles from Cracow. We mount the hill, and at sunset we reach Mrs. X.'s modest villa. After a frugal meal, which we finish almost in total darkness, we all go to the top of the hill to look at the burning city.

Heavens! What a sight! The whole town is on fire. Flames, black and white smoke, sparks shooting high in the air, and — O God! such a red, red sky! It is terrifying but also beautiful! I cannot help admiring the picture. I clap my hands and exclaim, "Oh, how glorious!" My outburst of enthusiasm is interrupted by a painful slap on the back, accompanied by Aunt Teresa's voice, which rings in my ears like an archangel's trumpet.

"You ungodly child! Hundreds and hundreds of people's

homes are turning to ashes, and you rejoice over it! Kneel down and pray God to forgive you for your sin." And she pushes me by the shoulders towards the house. But here shame, distraction, anger, take hold of me; I strike, bite, scratch, and altogether behave like a wild animal, until, exhausted, I fall in a fit of violent sobbing, followed by an acute cramp around my heart. The next thing I remember is a small parlor, myself lying on a sofa, the dear Aunt Teresa's face bending over me, and behind her the disgusted countenance of Mrs. X, who looks harshly at me, saying these memorable words to my aunt: —

"Why do you take so much trouble with her? She will not die. 'Les mauvaises herbes poussent toujours.'"[1] Years afterwards I recalled that woman's words.

Dressed in one of Mrs. X.'s nightgowns, a huge garment in which I feel lost, I kneel at my prayers, sad, meek, full of contrition. I am put into a strange bed for the first time in my life, and as I lie down, looking at the walls covered with pictures and daguerreotypes of unknown persons, I sadly realize that I have lost my home forever.

The conflagration lasted ten days. During that time there was not one night that was not brightened by flames, not one day without a new alarm. Every breeze revived the fire smouldering under the ashes, creating a new panic. The calamity was complete. During that time mother tried to find lodgings, but failed. Every remaining house, every attic, even cellars, being crowded with homeless families. At last Dr. Schantzer[2] offered us two rooms until we should be able to rent a flat or a house.

During those days spent in Dr. Schantzer's house I was left entirely to myself, every one having their hands full, and I used my freedom in the most pleasant way I could.

[1] Weeds always grow.

[2] The father of Miss Schantzer, a well-known actress in Germany. She married Hans von Bülow after his divorce from his first wife, Cosima.

Hidden behind baskets and bundles of clothes, I gave myself entirely to the reading and re-reading of the life of my favorite saint, the sweet Genevieve. At moments I felt quite consoled for the loss of home; for could we not go to the woods, as she did, and live on herbs and roots, until we should meet a polite doe who would yield her milk to us?

We had not fallen to such extremities, but dark days came upon our lives. Days of sorrow for my mother, sleepless nights, nights of tears and sighs of regret for the past happier hours, and heavy cares for the morrow. My mother lost in the fire almost everything she possessed. Her two houses were bringing her a fine income. The houses were highly insured, but by some fatal stroke of fate the payment of the next year's insurance was not remitted in time. She was just ten days behind. The walls of the houses as well as the grounds were sold. With that money, and certain sums she had among the people, we had to live until the brothers were able to help.

Seeing every day my mother's tears, and the thousand unpleasant experiences she was exposed to, I ripened quickly, my mind developed prematurely, and I became unusually serious and sensitive.

CHAPTER VI

Two months after the conflagration, mother, prompted by economy, inscribed Josephine and me as day scholars at St. John's convent. We lived now in a different part of the city, and four times a day, accompanied by a maid, Josephine and I had to cross, there and back, the fashionable sidewalk, usually called line A. B., of the large square "Rynek." This was a kind of distraction to us and a new experience. I remember meeting almost daily several characteristic types I never could forget. One of them, or rather two of them, were the brothers M., two middle-aged bachelors, dressed entirely alike, in long, whitish, tight-fitting coats, tall hats, and immaculate frilled shirt-fronts. They both wore small side-whiskers à la Byron, and when they lifted their hats, which they did frequently before promenading ladies, I noticed their high, elaborate *toupées*, firm and glossy at the top of their heads.

Next were two rich, aristocratic young ladies, two sisters with very blond hair, and such large hoops and so many flounces on their dresses that when they walked side by side people were obliged to step off the sidewalk, or to flatten themselves against the houses, to make room for them; but it was a peculiar pleasure for us to go right through between them, though we were nearly smothered by falbalas and the odor of musk. It was equal to an adventure.

The funny street urchins, with their sallies and gambols, so distressing, yet so amusing, and the crazy Paul (Pawelek) were also interesting. Poor, silly Pawelek, who offered to kiss every pretty girl he saw, without regard to their station in life; for that innocent desire he had been many times seized by the collar and given into the hands of an unromantic policeman.

The last and most entertaining type I remember was a person called Aunt Pumpkin, given this surname on account of her enormous rotundity, in contrast with her face. It was a benevolent, shiny, flushed, crab-apple face, framed in a large poke bonnet, smiling kindly at the world. Her small head was rhythmically wagging on a long, slender neck, while she carried on her swift, waddling legs the huge, seemingly artificial abdomen, which lifted her dress in front about ten inches above ground, exhibiting her white stockings and her low, black, cross-bandaged shoes. She never could appear in the street without being followed by a crowd of guying boys, yet she had means of disarming their malicious remarks by a pleasant smile, a kind word, and dry plums, which she carried in her large green reticule. Poor Aunt Pumpkin! We laughed at her, and she died of dropsy.

At first I did not like the convent. There were so many girls in my class, and only a few congenial ones. The comparison between the crowded, stuffy schoolroom and the quiet, refined atmosphere of Mrs. R.'s library, drew frequent tears from my eyes, but I soon learned to love the sisters, who seemed pleased with my application in the lessons of Polish history, grammar, and catechism, and liked my way of reciting verses as well as my utter disdain for the German language. The sisters of St. John were known as great patriots. I remember how they shielded me on the examination days, when the Austrian school inspector was present, and how they always managed not to let him ask me any German questions.

Our mother did not neglect our education in spite of adverse fortune, and we had additional French hours at the convent, music at home, and a few dancing lessons. Our health was also taken care of. In spring, accompanied by three of our brothers, every morning at half-past five o'clock we were sent on a two-mile walk to a country place, where we had a glass of milk and a slice of bread. Then we returned home for breakfast and school, by the longest way on the shore of the river, where the boys usually performed gymnastic feats, walking on the top of barriers erected for protection of people against possible falls into the whirlpool, in which exercises they made me take part. It was at the same spot where my uncle, the priest, was drowned, and I was afraid to comply with their wishes, which sounded like orders. To avoid the name of coward, I obeyed, in spite of the imminent danger looking up at me from the dark, mysterious waters.

It was in the autumn of 1850 that my brother Joseph introduced to my mother Mr. Gustave Modjeski.[1] I was ten years old; he was nearly thirty then. He soon became a friend of the family, and offered to teach us children German, which we hated in every way, but which became obligatory in public schools and convents. My sister and myself tried to get out of these lessons, but we were held fast to them by Mr. Modjeski's stern behavior. It took quite a long time for us to get used to him, but we ended by liking him quite well, especially when, during the long winter evenings, he read aloud to us some wonderful stories. It was he who established in our house the custom of reading aloud in the evenings. Every one had to take turns, and while my mother and Aunt Teresa were knitting, and we children were dressing or stitching clothes for our dolls, one of my brothers, or any one who would volunteer to do so, would read aloud. These were very delightful, never-to-be-forgotten evenings.

A few years later my three brothers were scattered in the world. Joseph Benda, after his wife's death, leaving his two-year-old daughter in my mother's care, went to

[1] His full name was Gustave Sinnmayer Modrzejewski.

Russian Poland, where he joined a theatrical company. Simon Benda, my musical half-brother, went to Vienna to a conservatory of music. Felix Benda, at nineteen years of age, became an actor, and was engaged at the Cracow theatre, but soon went with the company on a provincial tour. Our household became very quiet, and something had to be done to enliven it. My brother Adolphe[1] suggested that, as we were now "grown up" (he was fifteen and I twelve), we could give performances as the big brothers did, and for that purpose we wrote a play together. We had no stage, no scenery, but that did not matter. We found a plot in a magazine, and shaped it into a drama in one act, I writing two female parts, and he supplying his own speeches. It was a fierce tragedy, with the scene laid in Greece. A jealous sweetheart was waiting for her lover, who was hundreds of miles away on some secret patriotic mission. He had sworn to be back on such a day, at such an hour. In case he failed to return in time, his affianced lady swore on her part to take poison, which the ladies of that nation were supposed always to carry about their frail bodies, in rings, medallions, even in scapularies.

The bill read as follows:—

Sophronia, an aristocratic Grecian lady .	Helena Opid.
Ismena, her companion	Josephine Opid.
Hector, the young patriot	Adolphe Opid.

At the opening scene, dressed in Aunt Teresa's black gown, tucked and pinned to make it suit my size, with a black lace mantilla on her head, Sophronia walks up and down, excitedly wringing her hands. Suddenly she stops, and looking at the clock, exclaims:—

"Ten o'clock, and he is not here!" Then a short dialogue between herself and her plump duenna, whose long dress is dreadfully in her way.

[1] The youngest boy, and my own brother, Adolphe Opid.

"Twelve! Heavens! Now it is time to die!" and she pours the poison into a tin cup. She lifts it to her lips, when at once: Oh, rapture! Oh, joy! Footsteps are heard: "Yes, it is he!" and with a laugh of joy she nestles on her hero's breast. But, alas! poor Hector, after a short explanation, falls down and dies from exhaustion and a neglected wound. The heroine's joy turns into a desperate speech and a convulsive sob over the dead lover's body. Curtain! The dear Aunt Teresa was wiping her eyes, but mother looked stern. She took me aside and said I had made a poor exhibition before the neighboring children, playing such a play and in this absurd manner. Then she concluded with an imperative "No more theatricals!" I received the blow with tears. My brother and Josephine both laughed. So much work for nothing! I had studied my part so thoroughly, not only the speeches, but also the gestures and poses, which was a rather difficult task, for we had no looking-glass in our room.

I had often asked Aunt Teresa why, when all the girls I knew had mirrors in their rooms, we had none. But she replied that it was a dangerous thing to look in them, especially after dark, because then a girl, instead of her own face, may suddenly see a horrid mask with horns, or a skull. The evil spirits, being very malicious, play awful tricks on silly girls. Instead of a mirror, I used to place a lamp in the middle of the room, and standing in between it and the white wall, I could see distinctly the silhouette of my whole body, which I twisted in all sorts of impossible poses. I had great difficulty in managing my arms, and I did not like the appearance of my rather short-fingered hands; they did not look a bit like those I saw in pictures and statues. I came to the conclusion that the best way of managing them was to keep the fingers close together, as in some of the archaic pictures I saw in churches. In spite of all these attempts at what is now called "Physical Culture" (we have such scientific names for everything nowadays) — in spite of all that, when I was before our modest audience (composed of a few children and their nurses, my mother, and Aunt Teresa), I forgot my hands and arms and poses, and thought only of the miseries of my heroine. And mother did not like it, while I only tried to please *her* above all the people in the room. Tears rose to my eyes. I took the manuscript and tore it up in little pieces, which I threw into the fire, watching until the last scrap was consumed, then knelt to my prayers, with a feeling of sacrifice accomplished.

There was nothing left in the way of pleasures during the long winter evenings but books, crochet, and fairy stories. But in summer there were excursions; first, the Rocks of the Virgins, where lilies of the valley grow wild; then Bielany, with its monastery of Camaldule brothers, built on a high hill amidst centenarian oaks, the most picturesque edifice, inhabited by equally picturesque monks in white robes and cloaks. We also visited, though rarely, the Dragon's Cave; for Poland, too, has the myth of a dragon killed by the first chief of the Poles, Krakus, from whom the name of Cracow is derived. Most often we went to Kosciuszko's mound, raised by the people, who carried with their own hands the earth to the spot until they erected a hill in his memory.

Besides the excursions, we attended faithfully the numerous festivities. The most important of them is the Corpus Christi procession. Early in the morning, at the sound of the Great "Zygmunt" bell, crowds of peasants from the neighboring villages stream in from all the streets and stop at the Rynek, where provisory altars are built at almost every corner. These altars are called stations. When the large square is filled with people, it is hard to describe the wonderful display of costumes. Each village wears different garbs in shape and color. There are the white, blue, green, gray, and brown coats of the men, — some plain, some embroidered and spangled, with tassels, strings of brass rings hanging from their belts, sleeveless vests with red lapels, high boots, and striped, loose, wide trousers. Women in rich brocade or velvet-spangled waists and jackets, with turbans of embroidered lawn and lace. Girls with artificial wreaths and ribbons and strings of coral ornamenting their throats and breasts. All these people come in quietly, modestly, with their prayer books and rosaries, deeply impressed by the occasion. Then marches in a regiment of Austrian soldiers in their handsome uniforms; then, city people in their best clothes, a string of girls in white, with garlands on their heads, carrying the images of saints on their shoulders, priests, brotherhoods, monks, banners of all kinds, etc. They all crowd the Rynek, and that mass of human beings forms the most gorgeous harmony of color, spotted here and there by a dark modern coat or the black crape of a widow.

The service begins at the first altar, and when the benediction bell rings, military trumpets send forth a peal of victorious melody, repeated three times and accompanied by a muffled roll of drums, and all the banners bend down over the heads of the prostrate people.

There is also the so-called "Konik" (little horse). A peasant, accompanied by pipes and drums, appears riding a hobby horse. He is armed with an imitation mace, stuffed with straw, with which he hits every one who comes in his way, making funny remarks, allusions, and altogether behaving without respect or regard to his fellow-men. The only way of stopping his tongue and his blows is to give him a few coins, for which he usually returns graceful thanks, unless some features, dress, gesture, or walk of the giver excites his sense of humor. Then his thanks are followed by such awful wishes and remarks that his benefactor soon regrets his kindness, and runs away from the persecutor, amidst the uproarious laughter of the crowd. This ludicrous custom was established after one of the Tartar invasions, in memory of a peasant by the name of Micinski, who saved Cracow by galloping at night to the city and warning the authorities of the approaching hordes. Since that time the privilege of this pageant was granted to him and his descendants, which in Poland's happy days, when the great lords of the city were lavish in their gifts, proved very profitable to the Micinski family.

At present "Konik" makes but a poor show, though it called forth loud laughter from the youthful Emperor Franz Joseph at his first visit to Cracow.

Of all the festivities I loved best the "Wianki" (the Wreaths). On St. John's day crowds and crowds of people come to a certain spot upon the bank of the Vistula. They begin to come in the afternoon, though the festivity opens only at dark. Slowly, one after another, small boats, trimmed with foliage and flowers, appear on the rippling waters of the river. Some are rowed by a single young man, some contain three or four men. At last a large raft filled with students, vocalists, makes its triumphant entrance amidst hearty applause.

On the bank, a little higher up the stream, is a group of young girls. Each of them holds a wreath of flowers, tied with ribbons on a square board, with a small wax lamp or candle in the centre. Each of these wreaths is marked with a different color in ribbon. With nightfall, at a given signal, the girls launch their lighted wreaths on the water, and let them go with the stream. Dear little garlands! Each of them carries a thought, a pang, or a sigh, a hope or a wish, towards an imaginary lover or the chosen one, and by two, by three, by four, hunting each other, spreading apart or huddling together, they advance on the dark current to their unknown fate. Simultaneously with the appearance of these fluttering messages the young men begin a chase for them. Steering adroitly with their swift, small boats among those diminutive floating, flowery islands, they try to catch them without putting out the lights. This requires a certain degree of agility. Often two boatmen will aim at the same wreath, and then a fight ensues, usually fatal to the object of their desire. This creates great excitement among the girls, who watch the game anxiously. Voices are heard: "It is Wanda's wreath, what a shame! Poor, poor Wanda!" These sad ejaculations are easily explained. There is a superstitious belief that the girl whose wreath is caught safely, with its light burning, will soon be married happily; but the one whose wreath is drowned, or its light put out, is condemned to celibacy if not to early death.

When the game is over, the choral song of the students hushes the animated crowd. People become suddenly silent, listening with delight to the fresh, youthful voices whose notes ring out with that clearness and magic beauty which music produces in the stillness of the night. After several songs, a dazzling Bengal light floods the boats, the old castle, and the distant group of peasants on the opposite shore of the Vistula, and then, as a finale, the National Hymn is heard. Oh, that hymn, full of tears, supplications, and revenge! The people join in the chorus, and when the last note dies away, they return home with heavy hearts, pondering on the helpless tragedy of their country.

CHAPTER VII

AT the age of fourteen I had finished the highest grade at the convent school, and then my literary education began. I read frantically our own poets first of all. First, our great poet Mickiewicz, then Krasinski, Slowacki, that incomparable master of poetic language, and Bohdan Zaleski, called the nightingale of "Ukraina," and many other poets. In the winter evenings the sole pleasure of our small circle consisted in reading aloud, and we made the acquaintance of Walter Scott, Dickens, Bulwer, Madame George Sand, and of course of Dumas, père, the idol of young people. We never liked to read Russian or German stories, such was the resentment we cherished in our hearts toward those nations; but one evening we were invited by Mr. Modjeski to see the German troupe playing at that time in our city. By the wish of the government it was decided that Polish and German companies should play alternately at the Cracow theatre. I had not been at the theatre since I was seven years old, and the temptation was great. Mother hesitated, but Mr. Modjeski suggested to her that it would be a great help in my study to see a German play, and might encourage me to learn that language, so sadly neglected by me at school. The argument was convincing, and she accepted the invitation.

I dressed in a hurry, and was so fidgety and afraid of being late that I made mother start three-quarters of an hour before the beginning, and when we arrived the lights were not yet up. I remember with what respect, almost reverence, I entered "the temple." For it was a real temple to me, a place where human hearts beat quicker at a word from the stage, where one sentence of the author, or one magic touch of the actor's art, makes the audience laugh or cry; where, . . . well, I do not remember exactly what thoughts whirled in my brain at my entrance to the theatre, but I know that my whole being was filled with a kind of rapturous awe.

Schiller's "Kabale und Liebe" ("Intrigue and Love") was the play, and it fascinated me completely. I sat like one petrified, drinking in the words I did not understand, and feasting my eyes on the somewhat stiff and ponderous players. In the dramatic passages, however, their actions were impressive and clear. By the force of the acting, and the help of Mr. Modjeski, who translated to me several scenes, I succeeded in understanding the plot. When we returned home, I sat at the tea-table without a word, ruminating over the wonderful masterpiece I had just seen, until, jeered at as a lunatic, I was sent to bed.

That evening created a revulsion of feeling in me. I thought better of Germans. Next morning I did not rest until I had bought a printed copy of "Kabale und Liebe," which I read from cover to cover with a dictionary. It was very slow work, and it lasted several days, but I was not discouraged, and in this same toilsome way I read almost all Schiller's plays. By the time I came to "Mary Stuart" I understood German quite well.

The more I read, the more I admired that great poet. I actually fell in love with him; I bought a little statuette representing him in a graceful, quiet pose, with his sad, beautiful face slightly inclined towards his great heart. I gazed at it so often that I fell into the habit of holding my head in the same way exactly, looking wistfully into space; and when, many years afterwards, I met in London the "Æsthetics," a semi-artistic circle of people who tried to fashion themselves after Dante Rossetti's and Burne-Jones's pictures, their poses reminded me of those fanciful days of my girlhood. When I compared Schiller with our poets, he was not at all superior to them in ideas or sentiment, but I suppose it was the dramatic form which took such strong hold on me. Our dear old poets were almost a part of me; I had heard of them since my childhood. I loved and worshipped them, and laid at their feet my soul and my patriotic heart. Schiller was only a lover, and, as it sometimes happens to lovers, was in time put into the shade by another, a mightier one, of whom I shall speak later.

Since the evening of "Kabale und Liebe," mother, who loved to go to Polish plays, often took Josephine and me with her. We saw several performances that season, some melodramas very much in fashion then, and also some Polish plays, brilliant because of gorgeous costumes, and touching because of the patriotic sentiment.

There were not many remarkable actors at that time in Cracow. My brother and the young leading lady pleased me the best. Felix [1] played a romping, jolly, rude peasant, just as well as a refined young marquis, and I regarded him, in all his parts, as the perfection of grace and boyish beauty. Mrs. R. H., the character actress and heavy lead, was considered very fine, but I cannot remember her acting; all I know of it is that she walked with great dignity, and that she pulled her long train of velvet and ermine with a sort of jerk. Josephine and I drew her picture many times; it was easy to draw ermine, and we did not care how the face looked, as we had never seen her except over the footlights, which, in the fifties, were not so brilliant as they are now. We did not even know if she was old or young. There were no reporters to describe every feature, handsome or otherwise, and the witty or silly talk of the actors and actresses. The public knew very little of their personalities except what they chose to show in their acting. A hero was a hero; a lover was a lover; a villain a villain. The

[1] Felix Benda, my half-brother and a popular actor.

stage was surrounded with a kind of mystery which lent to performances a charm of which they are deprived in these days. I would have hated any one who had told me that the hero was a married man of fifty with seven children; or that the pure maiden, our juvenile lady, was engaged every season to another man. I even was not curious enough to read their family names on the program;—the names of the characters were sufficient. Yet, as it often happens that we obtain a thing we do not care for, so at the end of the season I was brought face to face with the owner of the black velvet and ermine.

One afternoon, thinking that no one but my sister was listening to me, I recited a snatch from the poem "Maria," by Malczewski. When I finished, I saw Felix standing in the door and smiling. I was terrified, as if I had been caught in some naughtiness, but he asked quietly:—

"Who taught you to recite?"

"Nobody," I murmured.

"Would you like to go on the stage?" he asked. "He mocks me," I thought, and said nothing. But he continued:—

"I am not jesting; if you wish to become an actress, I can help you." Saying this, he left me; left me with a whirl in my thoughts.

"What did he say? I to become an actress!" I exclaimed, and looked at my sister, who giggled, saying:—

"He, he, he! How funny you will look in black velvet and ermine!"

"How can I be an actress? How shall I ever dare to appear before a crowd, when I am too shy to speak before a single stranger?" I was neither happy nor unhappy at the idea of devoting my life to the stage, and only when I looked at Schiller's statuette a great joy, a vague hope, filled my heart.

"I may, if I succeed, act in his plays." I re-read the

lines of Louise, the heroine of Schiller's play, "Intrigue and Love," kissed the statuette, and had a long talk with it.

Next day I was walking with Felix on the line A. B. towards Madame R. H.'s lodgings. I had to recite before her that she might decide whether I had any ability for the stage or not. After a short walk, trembling with fear and anticipation, I stood before my oracle. A thin, middle-aged lady; oh, so unlike the handsome, rosy-looking heroine of velvet and ermine, sat before an embroidery frame and did not rise when we entered, but offered her long-fingered hand to my brother, who kissed it respectfully. She smiled with her pale, thin lips, and pointed a seat to me, while my brother was introducing me. She looked at me attentively from head to feet, and I blushed "all over" under her scrutinizing gaze. I hated my blushes, and was angry at myself. Indeed, I must have looked foolish, for she asked my brother how old I was.

"Sixteen," he answered.

"Already? I should not have thought so." Then she added, "Since she is sixteen, it would be time to prepare her for the stage, if . . ."—here she turned to my brother—"if her mother has nothing against it," and "if" . . . and so on, until she asked me to recite. My brother excused himself, and left the room, sending me an encouraging smile. How I ever dared to say my lines before this stately authority I do not know, but I did so. She said nothing, still bent over her work; then, after a few moments of torturing silence, she asked me if I could sing.

"No; I never took singing lessons," I said, but she insisted, saying she only wanted to know if I had any voice. I had to submit.

I think and I believe every young girl will agree with me that it is a dreadful ordeal to stand in the middle of the room and warble, without preparation and without accompaniment. I told her I should never dare to do it, especially while she was looking at me.

"Oh, is that so? Then you may stand in the recess of that window and hide behind the curtains, and I will resume my embroidery, since my eyes disturb you." She said this with a ring of sarcasm in her voice, which fell upon my ears like a slap; but I did as she told me. For a long time I was at a loss what to sing. I was ashamed, confused; I could not remember the words of any of the pretty songs I knew, but, instead of them, one most unsuited to the circumstances came to my mind, over and over with the obstinacy of a fly — a rude and jolly peasant song I had heard during one of our excursions in the fields. Some mischievous spirit whispered in my ear, "Sing it, sing it!" and I obeyed the imp. In order to assume a peasant's voice, I made mine sound very deep and as harsh as possible, and I sang this thing with the desperate effort of a gambler who has lost all he possessed, and throws his last coin on the table with the firm conviction of ruin.

Through the lace curtains I watched the effect. The madame was highly amused; happily my brother was not in the room. It was a fizzle — I knew it. I dared not leave the window. Madame R. H., mastering her merriment, asked me politely to come down, then rose from her seat, went to a small book shelf, and giving me a booklet covered with marbled paper, said: —

"Take this home and learn the part marked with a red pencil. The day after to-morrow come here, and I will give you your first lesson." I left her. What a relief! She gave me a part; evidently she thought I had some ability. I pressed the precious treasure to my heart, and walked very fast, anxious to reach home as soon as possible and give myself entirely to this new, glorious task. But alas, what a disappointment! The title of the play was already discouraging: "Our Grandmother's Parrots." I read the short play, and it seemed to me idiotic. Here is the plot: —

A grandmother, who suffered in her youth from man's treachery, brings up two girls, her orphan granddaughter and her foster-sister, in strict confinement, not allowing them ever to see a man. The girls were ignorant even of the existence of Adam's descendants, when one day two young scapegraces appear on the wall of their garden and talk to them; the simpletons ask their grandmother what sort of animals they are. "Parrots" is the answer of the wise ancestor. At the end of the play, marriage, of course.

To study such a play! Oh, shades of the sublime poets! Oh, Mickiewicz! Oh, Schiller!

After my first lesson, madame told my brother that it was useless to teach me. She could not discover any trace of talent in me. She said that I laughed all through my part, and seemed to be amused instead of taking it seriously, as I ought to. Then she advised my mother to keep me at home, instead of condemning me to become a mediocre actress; this cruel sentence was repeated to me by my dear mother, who seemed rather pleased with the decree. But my heart was sore, and this time my ambition for the stage was crushed forever, or so I thought.

CHAPTER VIII

THE next year happened the incident which turned, in no small degree, my heart from Schiller. The German manager, in order to attract the Polish public, which obstinately kept away from the German theatre, used to engage different stars from Vienna and Berlin for what is called "Gast Rollen," equivalent to "Star Engagement." After the financial failure of several stars, a bill appeared at the corners of the street, announcing Fritz Devrient in the part of Hamlet. I had heard of Shakespeare, but never had read or seen any of his plays, and naturally enough my curiosity was aroused.

Hamlet made an overwhelming impression on me, and I worshipped at once the great masterwork of that powerful man born and buried somewhere on the British Islands centuries ago. That mysterious spirit ruling over human souls, the wonderful wizard, reading human hearts and God's nature, the great inimitable Shakespeare. He became my master then and there, and remained so through my theatrical career. I never took better lessons in acting than those Hamlet gives to the players; I never enjoyed acting more than when I played those wayward, sweet, passionate, proud, tender, jolly, or cruel and sad heroines of Shakespeare's dramas.

I lived weeks afterwards in continual enchantment. The translations of Shakespeare were scarce, but Mr. Modjeski succeeded in getting Hamlet in Polish translation and also "Two Gentlemen of Verona," "The Merchant of Venice," and "Simon of Athens," which I read greedily.

Fritz Devrient, who played Hamlet, was a young man,

blond and graceful. He was the nephew of Emil Devrient, one of the most celebrated German actors of that time, and played the part with a great deal of dignity and in a most natural way. A glorious future lay before him, but he died young, leaving behind the most flattering memory of his great talent. His acting made a tremendous impression on me, and the longing for the stage work was aroused again. I spent a sleepless night, and had to use all my strength of will in order to crush down in my soûl that wild desire. I succeeded, and the result of Devrient's Hamlet manifested itself only in a long poem, written in secret, read and re-read and finally destroyed. The vision of his art, however, lived with me for years, linked in some way with my worship of Shakespeare.

My ambition to become a priestess of Melpomene and Thalia was nipped in the bud by Madame R. H.'s verdict, and I gave up all aspirations in the direction of the stage. But my desire for achieving a name for myself had never left me, and I thought for a while I might gain it as a writer. Poems were manufactured in secret, and psychological studies, as well as sketches of different incidents. I tried to adopt a certain style in writing, but this was a vain desire; I felt I was ignorant, and being too shy to confide my ambitious hopes to some one who could give me good advice, I burned my lucubrations as soon as I wrote them. The only person in whom I placed my confidence was my brother, Simon Benda, who lived in Vienna, and to whom I wrote letters in rhyme. But though he was pleased by my facility in rhyming, he never gave it a serious thought, and never encouraged my aspirations.

At the same time my good mother wanted me to pass a teacher's examination, believing in self-support for women. I began to study history, mathematics, and everything else I had been told to study. To me learning was the highest pleasure. Endowed as I was with an exceptionally strong memory, it did not cost me any effort; I enjoyed it. Some of the studies, algebra, for instance, seemed a little tedious, but no matter in what shape knowledge was presented to me, I grasped it eagerly, and was still crying with Goethe, "Light! more light!" Who could have believed, then, that all these studies were only preparing and smoothing my way to the stage? Since my failure in "Our Grandmother's Parrots" and the victory over myself after Devrient's Hamlet, I had no desire of becoming an actress, yet owing to a mere incident I nearly became an opera-singer. It was at that time I formed a friendship with a young actress, Ptaszynska. Engaged in the Polish stock company, she had to play divers parts very often not suited to her abilities. In one of those parts she had to sing the grand aria from the opera "Hernani." My friend sang a little, but not well enough to execute this difficult piece of music, and the management sent her a teacher, the well-known and excellent master, Mr. Mirecki, whose task was to transform this modest little actress into a prima donna.

One morning when I called on her she was just taking her lesson. Hearing her exercising, I quietly entered her bedroom and waited. She was singing the great aria. I heard a man's voice correcting her. She went over and over the same passage, but could not get it right; then the old master grew impatient, and sang for her the whole aria. After a while he took leave. As soon as he left the room, I strolled in, and in joke, began to sing the same aria, trying as near as possible to get his expression and accent, accompanying it with extravagant gestures, when suddenly the door opened, and the dear old master, the celebrated Mirecki, appeared before us! In an instant I was under the piano, afraid that he would scold me for imitating him. His eyesight was very weak, and he wore a green shade over his eyes. He did not see me, but he asked abruptly, with, I thought then, an angry ring in his voice:—

"Who sang here, just now?" My friend, pointing to me crouching under the piano, said:—

"There she is!" then, turning to the master, added, in the way of mocking introduction, "Miss Helena Opid, Felix Benda's half-sister." . . . There was no remedy. I had to come out from my hiding-place and face the master, who, lifting his shade, looked at me with scrutinizing, bloodshot gaze; but what was my astonishment when, instead of scolding me, he said that I had a good voice, that I must come to his class and he would teach me for nothing. I was so overcome and so surprised that I could not say a word of thanks, even; I bowed my head and stood motionless until he left the room. But as soon as he departed I nearly screamed with joy. I took my friend by the waist, and we started on a wild dance around the room. She was as happy as I, for there was no jealousy in her nature. She put on her hat and went home with me to tell mother the happy news. This time there was no objection on mother's part, and I went steadily to Mr. Mirecki's music school for three months. My only ambition and desire then was to become one day a church and concert singer, but the master insisted on making me a prima donna, and again the vision of my treading the stage boards stood before me by day and by night. Alas! It was not to be. The dear old man died in a few months, and I never took another lesson.

Again one of my cherished dreams was dispelled, but among the numerous occupations at home and my studies I soon forgot this mischance. Memorizing verses was one of my dearest pastimes. After having learned a few scores of Polish poems, I read one day Schiller's "Kinder Moderin," and was so deeply struck by the dramatic pathos that I learned and recited it before Mr. Modjeski. When he heard it, he told me, to my great surprise, he thought that, in spite of Mademoiselle R. H.'s verdict, I might make a success as an actress, but he would not advise me to go on the Polish stage, where there was only a small field and very few opportunities, but suggested the German stage. A few days later Mr. Modjeski introduced to us Herr Axtman, who then was one of the best actors in the Cracow German stock company. I learned with him Louise in "Kabale und Liebe," Gretchen in "Faust," Klärchen Marchen in "Egmont," and Lessing's "Kätchen von Heilbrun."

A pathetic incident is connected with my dramatic lessons. Herr Axtman had a fine voice, and played on the guitar, which instrument I also cultivated at that time. The most beautiful thing he sang was Schubert's serenade ("Ständchen"). One afternoon he seemed to be very tired, his face was drawn and pale. I thought I would not trouble him with too much rehearsing. I stopped in the middle of my part, took the guitar, and sang a jolly Polish air, thinking I might dispel his sadness; then, handing him the instrument, I asked him to sing the "Ständchen." He sighed deeply, and his face wore an expression of distress, but he struck a few chords and began to sing. He scarcely sang two lines when the guitar slipped from his hands, his body bent forward, and he fell to the ground in a dead faint. It seems that my dear teacher had had scarcely any nourishment for two days, and had fainted from sheer hunger. I mentioned before what bad business the German managers were doing in Cracow. Mr. Axtman and his friend stayed in Cracow with the hope of making some money by teaching until they obtained a good engagement in Germany. They were, however, reduced to utter poverty.

In spite of this extreme need, Herr Axtman never wanted to accept any remuneration for my lessons, saying that my success on the stage would be his best reward. This looks like a fancy story, but it is nevertheless the perfect truth. We often find among artists such natures, full of pride, recklessness, and abnegation. Shortly afterwards, Herr Axtman and his friend, having obtained the desired engagement, left Cracow, to my great regret, which was, however, relieved by the hope of a better existence for the kind artist whose memory still lives in my heart.

Among my papers I have found the following letter I wrote about that time to my brother Simon, who was studying music in Vienna, and also a scrap of paper to which I confided a few of my impressions: —

"Dear Brother,

"I would have written to you oftener, but I was and am very busy all the time. You ask me what I am doing. First of all, I help mamma in the house, for we have no servant, only old Kazimierzowa comes twice a day to wash the dishes. She also does our laundry, but ironing belongs to mother and me.

"Aunt Teresa is still very ill. The doctor says she has a cancer. She scarcely leaves her bed now, and of course we have to look after her. Dear — poor Aunt Teresa, she suffers awful pains.

"I have also to help Stasia[1] with her lessons. We have a good deal of trouble with her, for she constantly runs into the street, and is as wild as a boy. Mamma took her shoes off one day and locked them in a closet, but the imp crept barefoot out of the kitchen window and went to the neighboring garden, where she ate so many berries that she was quite ill afterwards. . . . I am the only one that can manage her, because she loves me, and I talk to her as to a grown person.

"All my days are taken up with sewing, studies, and a thousand little things. The evenings I spend in reading, sometimes prolonged until three o'clock in the morning.

"And now I have very important news for you, but I am afraid you will scream. Yet I am going to tell you, for I have more courage to write than to speak — I am to become an actress! This is not all. I am to become a German actress. Please do not swear! Mr. Gustave [Modjeski] says I shall have better opportunities on the German stage, and though I do not like the idea, yet, — I think I have to please him. You see, dear brother, I

[1] My niece, Joseph Benda's daughter, whom he left in my mother's care before leaving for Russian Poland.

want to do something in the world, and though I may not get an engagement, yet I study, study, and study. It may be useful to me some day, and if not, well, — at least it gives me a great deal of comfort at present.

"I know you will say that I always live in the clouds. Alas, it is so. And I think I shall never have peace until I am really up there among the clouds. I feel great strength in me, sometimes, and then again at times I am so weak that I am afraid of my own shadow.

"Mr. Gustave says I am nervous and need rest and change of air. He always brings me books. A few weeks ago he brought me Buchner's 'Kraft und Stoff.' It is a philosophical work in which the author tries to prove that there is no God, and that the world created itself out of a spark and accumulation of matter, etc. I am curious to know who made the spark, because he does not tell that. No, no, I shall never cease to believe in God, to love Christ and his Holy Mother. I am now reading Kochanowski's poems, 'Treny.' They are beautiful because they are so infinitely sad.

"You know already that Adolphe works at some house-building, and gives mamma every month thirty florins. He lives with us, and we spend Sundays in excursions on foot or in 'furki.'[1] Aunt Teresa, though she does not love Adolphe very much because he used to tease me and Josephine when we were children, and now is 'torturing' Stasia, yet she says that he is the only one in the family who will become a man.[2] Which means that neither you nor Felix nor Joseph have become 'men,' because you are all artists, and art does not pay. . . . 'Dixi.'

"I wish spring were here! But it is only autumn now, and a long, heavy winter is coming. Adieu. Mr. Gustave sends hearty greetings to you. Mamma, Josephine, and myself send you a thousand kisses. Your loving sister,

"HELENA.

"P.S. Felix is going on a tour with his wife. The company is going to play in small towns and pleasure resorts during the summer months. You should see Felix on the stage. He is simply wonderful! Ah! When shall we be together again? Do write often and long."

A scrap found among my papers:—

"The days do not belong to me, but the nights are mine. When all are asleep I go to the window, open it, and look out into the moon-

[1] A sort of peasant basket wagon.

[2] In Polish, the word "man" is the same as a man of means, used in this sense.

light, into the starlight night. I stretch my arms and breathe deeply. The nightingale's song, the perfume of the acacias, fill me with unspeakable delight and sadness. I wish to have wings and to fly into the endless space. Why am I so moved? Does the idea of becoming an actress fill me with joy? I do not know, though I feel happy at the thought, yet a mysterious pang is connected with it. I do not know what ails me. I have to leave my country, go on the German stage, among strangers. Ha! If it must be, I will go! Why do I not speak English? I would play Ophelia — Portia — Juliet. Gradually peace comes over me. I think of the parts I shall most likely perform. Half closing my eyes, I see among the trees and shrubs, Louise, wringing her hands and shedding tears, Ophelia with her vacant stare, Marguerite in the arms of Faust, Klärchen addressing the mob in desperate accents, Portia in a lawyer's gown, and sweet Julia of the 'Gentlemen of Verona' reading her lover's letter. All these phantoms, though unlike each other, have one and the same face, changed only by the expression, and it is mine. I send my thoughts into the vague future and see myself on the stage. I hear the applause of the people. I see their tears and smiles. I know I make them feel what I feel. This is power! . . . Ah, no, no, this is all a dream, a delusion. What does my miserable life amount to? Where am I going, and what will become of me?"

About that time happened the great event of my life: Mr. G. S. Modjeski, knowing my great love for reading, always provided me with books. I read with him Goethe, Wieland, and Lessing. He also made me memorize selected verses from Nibelungen Saga. It was during those readings that one day he asked me to become his wife. I answered "Yes" without hesitation, because he had already become as dear to me as my own brothers; and besides, my imagination had adorned him with the attributes of all the possible and impossible heroes I read about in poetry or prose. I believed him to be a man who could fight to death, kill a lion or a dragon for my sake, or, like Werther, commit suicide if I rejected him; for I truly believed he loved me with all the intensity of that most unhappy of Goethe's lovers.

PART II

POLAND

CHAPTER IX

In 1861, in the month of May, Mr. Modjeski, my little son Rudolphe, then four months old, and myself were living in Bochnia, where my mother and my little niece had moved previously. The dear Aunt Teresa was not with us any more. She died in the early part of January.

Bochnia is a small town of two or three thousand inhabitants in that part of Poland which belongs to Austria, and which is called the Kingdom of Galitzia. It lies about fifty miles east of Cracow. In old times Bochnia was a place of note, celebrated for its salt mines. At present the mines are nearly exhausted, and cannot compare with those of Wieliczka, the latter being probably the largest in the world. Buildings half ruined and miserable huts now stand in place of old historic castles, and instead of brilliant knights and rich noblemen, you see on the muddy streets merely poor peasants, shabby Jews, and only a few decently dressed men and women. In short, Bochnia to-day is a very uninteresting spot, except for the legend of the twelfth century clinging to its name.[1]

At the present time little remains in Bochnia of the marvels of its past, or its glorious associations, and I would not have mentioned the little town at all had it not been closely connected with my stage career.

One day at a May festival, while the young men and girls of Bochnia were trying their feet in a quadrille on the uneven ground of a meadow, Mr. Modjeski and I perceived the figure of a man in a summer suit and blue cravat coming

[1] This legend has been already printed in *The Arena* of February, 1890, in an article of mine entitled, "Reminiscences of Débuts in Many Lands."

toward us with dancing steps, smiling all over and waving his hat in repeated greetings. We did not recognize him at first, but when he came nearer, we both exclaimed:—

"Mr. Loboiko! What are you doing here?" Upon which he told us that Cracow, being overcrowded with photographic studios, he had come to Bochnia to establish one, and also to give dancing lessons.

One afternoon he brought news of an unfortunate accident at the salt mines, causing the death of several men, who left widows and orphans without any means of support. We felt very badly about it, and decided to arrange an amateur performance for the benefit of the bereaved families, the receipts of which we had no doubt would be considerable, for Bochnia had no theatre of its own, and the travelling companies never stopped there on their tours.

This prospect transported me into the seventh heaven. The poor would be relieved, and moreover I should act on a real stage. Mr. Loboiko at once offered his services as instructor and artistic director. He went to a book-store and returned with several booklets containing short plays, which he left with us, and which I devoured one after the other, with the hunger of a beggar deprived for days of nourishing food.

Our artistic mentor, being also a very practical man, obtained at once the Casino Hall, in which he built a stage about ten feet deep. Then he manufactured some scenery out of wall-paper and canvas, and made a curtain of red calico, painted all over with golden stars. We went to the Casino every morning to see him, with apron and tucked-up sleeves, working on the paraphernalia.

Our company was composed of two men: Mr. Loboiko, the leading man; Mr. Bauman, our director's dancing pupil; Miss Josephine Kossowska (my sister's stage name); myself as leading lady; and my eleven-year-old niece, Stasia, as prompter,—five in all. The difficulties standing in the way of regular charitable performances did not trouble us much. We had a hall in the Casino gratis. As to advertisements, there was no newspaper in town, so it was impossible to advertise, and the few bills posted on the corners of the streets were done at small expense by a hand printing-press, used commonly for announcements of deaths or public balls.

We selected two plays for the performance: "The White Camelia," comedy in one act, and the "Prima Donna," or "A Foster-sister," a play with songs, in two acts. We had eight rehearsals, and the actors were, speaking in theatrical slang, "dead-letter perfect." Yet, when I heard the curtain bell I nearly fainted. I tried to recollect the first lines of my part, but could not. My hands became cold as ice, thrilling acute shivers ran up and down my spinal column, and all together I had a feeling of sinking slowly into the ground. I do not recollect how I found myself on the stage, but once before the footlights I recovered my presence of mind, and never made a mistake or forgot one word of my part. Toward the middle of the performance I was so much at ease that, when just at the beginning of a long soliloquy, my niece in the prompter's box dropped the manuscript, the leaves went scattering on the floor and the poor child began to cry, asking me in a desperate whisper: —

"What shall I do now?" I answered composedly, "Pick up the leaves," and continued my part. My inborn shyness had totally disappeared when at work, and it only came back to me the next morning after the performance.

The audience was more numerous than we expected. All the authorities of the district and city, several country gentlemen of the neighborhood with their families, a few occasional visitors to the town, the teachers and the local schools, in fact, everybody who dressed in Occidental fashion, and even a thin scattering of Jews in their long silk gaberdines, filled the Casino Hall, and represented what is called, in the American theatrical language, "a full house." I do not remember very well the details of the reception, but I suppose that our achievement must have been a genuine success, because two more performances were given, each with a change of bill. We played several new pieces, rehearsing the whole week each time, and playing Saturdays.

In one of these plays — a farce — I was cast for a man's part. It was necessity that prompted our stage director to give it to me. The personages of the farce did not exceed four, which was exactly the number of our company, but unfortunately they represented three men and one woman, whilst our dramatic organization was composed of two men and two women. To meet this difficulty I was cast for the part of a young, "saucy lackey," whose chief performance consisted in stealing a pair of boots from a shoe store. Mr. Modjeski, afraid that I would appear ungainly in the part, and also to counteract my shyness, ordered at once a suit of boy's clothes for me, and every evening he took me out for long walks, so that, on the night of the performance, I almost forgot the strange garment I had on, and played my part with ease.

The preceding piece that night was a drama in two acts, entitled, "A Window on the First Floor," by Korzeniowski, where I had to play a very dramatic part — that of a wife, who, on the point of being unfaithful to her husband, is saved by the cry of her sick baby.

The success was great, and the audience called the company several times before the curtain. The unsophisticated public of that time loved plays with a healthy sentiment and a moral. It was before the times of Ibsen, D'Annunzio, or the French decadents. They always wanted virtue to be rewarded, and wickedness to fall into the depth of misery. They were very old-fashioned, but they had one good point:

they paid most strict attention to the words and to the acting, which was a great comfort to a beginner like me. I knew that nothing would escape the critical eye or ear of that little crowd of provincials, and I took the same pains for them as if I were playing before the swells and sages of a metropolis. The farce following the drama was also well received, and I was not recognized in my boy's dress.

The chief event of the evening consisted in the visit of a stranger who came behind the scenes after the performance. He was very pleasant, and rather amused at my "childish appearance," as he called it. He asked me, nevertheless, how long I had been on the stage, which I considered a flattering mistake.

"I never was on the stage," I answered, "and I am not an actress. We only act for our pleasure, and we are only amateurs, except Mr. Loboiko." It was Mr. Chencinski,[1] a well-known actor on the Warsaw stage, a stage manager as well as a humorous dramatic author. He said something complimentary which I do not remember, and then concluded, taking leave of me:—

"I hope to see you in Warsaw soon." These words engraved themselves in my memory, and turned my head completely. All the doubts concerning my abilities were dispelled. I knew now that I had talent. I knew I had to become an actress or to die! And I wanted to be, not a German, but a Polish, actress; and go one day to Warsaw to play at the Imperial theatre before a brilliant audience, poets, artists, learned men and refined women, and with great actors and actresses.

In a few hours it was decided that my little experience had opened the way to a career, and Mr. Modjeski advised Mr. Loboiko to go to Cracow and obtain a license for a travelling company, which was easily granted to actors; and thus we started on the road under Mr. Loboiko's management.

[1] Read Hencinski.

In a short time, however, he handed over the direction to Mr. Modjeski, who had more experience and leisure to attend to the business part of the concern. Loboiko's name was on the posters and programs, but he was only a member of the company and stage director; while Mr. Modjeski was "de facto" the business head of our new-born company.

After leaving my baby in my dear mother's care, we started on our way towards New Soncz (New Sandec), on a mountaineer's large three-seated wagon covered with white canvas, looking very much like those prairie schooners the Argonauts of 1849 used in crossing the plains on their way to the gold hills of California. We were six all together: the company of four members, the manager, and the driver. Behind us waddled a little one-horse cart filled with our famous paper scenery and the trunks.

The picture of this first professional trip stands vividly before my eyes. The weather was glorious! From the road, which led uphill almost all the time, we saw villages with luxuriant orchards, golden fields, and diminutive white huts, all flooded with warm sunlight, and far ahead of us the Carpathian Mountains! My soul was filled with enchantment and delight. The joy was so great that I sang. My sister caught the tune, and the others followed. Absorbed by our own merriment, we did not notice that we were crossing a village, until our wagon stopped and we saw peasants gathered around us, — girls with pink cheeks looking at us from the windows and from the garden gates, and little Jews yelling, "Circus! Circus!" Amidst laughter and jokes we descended from our Noah's Ark at an inn. The horses had to rest an hour before we could proceed farther.

"It is now twelve o'clock, and the repast is ready." So says the handsome stout Jewess inviting us to the dining room. Her husband stands in the doorway looking at us. He is not handsome. On both sides of his cheeks hang the two traditional curls, which this time happen to be of a bright red hue. He wears a black skull cap, breeches, white stockings, slippers, and a sort of vest with several strings hanging around it. I noticed that seeing us he kissed one of the strings, and then again another.[1] He is not hospitable either, but lets his wife play the part of kind hostess, which she does to perfection, in spite of the five small children who hang around her, pulling her right and left, wiping their noses on her gown, and making faces at each other. We enter the whitewashed room, adorned by a few cheap prints and the inevitable swarm of flies, and we order a dinner.

"Everything is ready," says the landlady. We shall have to wait "only half an hour," our plump beauty assures us. We have to submit, since there is no other inn in the village.

While waiting for the young chickens, which had to be killed first and fried afterwards, we take a stroll in the village. It is an hour of rest, and the whole village is eating. Some of the peasants are taking their meals in the huts and some in the open air, under the shade of a large apple or cherry tree. Our peasants are almost all vegetarians by necessity. They are poor, and can only very seldom afford the luxury of meat; yet they are strong, vigorous, indefatigable workmen, with ruddy cheeks, excellent humor, always singing while at work. Their songs are for the most part improvisations; they are often witty and always melodious. These people can no more help singing than the birds. They set all their feelings to music: love, tears,

[1] The orthodox Jews in our country wear those vests with strings. They lift one of those strings from time to time and kiss it, and probably for that reason they call them in Yiddish "Tzitsele," which sounds euphonic enough. There is a saying among the Christian peasants that these strings represent the Ten Commandments, and every time the Jew trespasses on one of them, or is tempted to do so, he amends the offence by kissing the "Tzitsele," and by this act of devotion drives the evil spirits away.

joy, despair, oppression, — all are expressed in the various songs of these illiterate poets whose only learning consists of prayers and Nature's own inspirations. We return to the inn just in time, and the dinner is excellent.

Provided with food — and fleas! — we take leave of our hospitable Rebecca, and mount the high grades of our wagon. She and her five offspring, augmented by the addition of a sucking baby at her breast, which evidently was asleep when we arrived, are sitting on the porch. She waves her hand to us, smiles with her white teeth, and says: "Do widzenia!" Her husband stands frowning at the door. We bow to him, but he only nods slightly and kisses the "Tzitsele."

Our trip to New Sandec was delightful. We were young, full of spirit and hope, the day was beautiful, and the country enchanting. We made plans for future work, we rode on the clouds, building Spanish castles. We were free as birds and happy as young dogs.

When we were established in New Sandec, Mr. Loboiko wrote to several actors and actresses, who soon joined us. Some of them came even without being invited, so that, at the end of three weeks, we had a company of nineteen members. The success was great, and soon we were able to buy decent scenery and costumes.

I was the star from the beginning, but I wanted to play parts of various kinds in order to gain experience, and I made several hits in episodical small parts. One evening I played a hysterical, comical old lady, and made the public laugh. I was ready to play even a few lines in pieces where there was no good part for me. Work was a delight to me. Even now when I think of my enthusiasm of those days, I am thrilled with the recollection. We lived in rooms which were barely furnished. We had to sit on boxes and all sorts of improvised seats. I had but two dresses, one black and the other white, with two tunics, which I used to transform by addition of black or pink ruches; our meals were frugal, but I could see from the porch fields of wild flowers, trees, and mountains; above all, I had my parts. Walking up and down on the veranda, I studied them, to the accompaniment of the birds' songs, and I felt as proud and wealthy as the richest woman. To live in the imaginary world of my heroines, to speak their poetic language, to render different sentiments, to work out a character, were the most cherished delights of my existence.

The rendering of the part was not so attractive as the study of it, and I never was satisfied with the applause when I was not quite pleased with myself. Even at that early stage of my career I had a habit of calling before my mind a picture of the person I had to represent, and then filling it with my own self. When I could not see the vision in my mind from head to foot, even to the garment and gestures, when I could not hear my own voice ringing in the accents of my vision, I rejected the part, for I knew I could not play it to my satisfaction.

At the end of August we left New Sandec, where, owing to the generosity of the public, we had become of some importance. In order to prove our gratitude to the town, we called our company "The New Sandec Combination."

CHAPTER X

After leaving New Sandec we went to Krynica, a fashionable health resort, greatly in favor with Warsaw people, who used to spend summers among the pines and rocks of that picturesque nook in the Carpathian Mountains. We found the place in alarm. The news had come from Warsaw that several men and women had been killed in the streets by the Russian soldiers.

It was in February of 1861 that the Poles began their demonstrations, singing hymns and national songs in public places, gathering in churches and walking in processions. All these demonstrations had seemingly a religious character, but they were in fact the forerunners of the Insurrection of 1863.[1]

[1] The uprising of the Poles bore from the start a mystic character. In June, 1861, there was a rumor which ran like an electric current through all the country, that in great forests near Warsaw strange men appeared, dressed in peasant garbs or blouses. They seldom came out of their hiding-places, but when they were seen, they behaved with modesty and piety. Some people saw them at a forester's abandoned house; some girls gathering wild berries met them, and were greeted with courtesy. Here and there they bought milk and eggs from the peasant women; they paid royally, talked gently, and with a kind of mystic inspiration. They soon won the respect of the people. When they were asked who they were and what they wanted, they answered with allegories; they called themselves men who came through their own sufferings to redeem the sufferings of their fellow-men. The peasants thought they were hermits seeking a refuge where they could freely repent of their sins, but the city people and the governmental spheres saw in them secret revolutionary agents.

The first cause of the dissatisfaction of the people was the peasant question. The Poles desired to emancipate the peasants. This was opposed by Alexander II, on the ground that this action would establish the popularity of the nobles. He preferred to be himself the originator of the idea, which he brought to life afterwards, and for which he gained the name of "White Czar." This measure of absolutism against the praiseworthy endeavors of the Polish nobility was the first spark thrown into

In the presence of the tragic news from Warsaw it was impossible to give performances in Krynica. We returned to Bochnia, where we rested awhile; then, taking with us our baby boy and his nurse, we started on our further tour. It was absolutely necessary to stop a day in Cracow on account of scenery and luggage, which had to be unloaded and transferred to the railroad cars. The aspect of the city was unspeakably sad.

Already in February, 1861, after the first demonstration and the first victims in Warsaw, the women began to dress in black, but now mourning was recommended by ecclesiastic authorities, and the whole country — all the three parts of Poland remaining under three different governments — wore black. When we travelled through the country, the black dresses of city people were often relieved by bright costumes of peasants, but in Cracow there was not one person dressed in colors. Even the few German women and officers' wives were obliged to wear black dresses, lest they should be molested by street urchins, or jeered at and remonstrated with by the people.

The interiors of the churches were covered with mortuary palls; groups of men gathered at the corners of the streets or on the "Planty," talking with animation but in low tones of voice. All the faces bore the same serious and anxious expression. In the evening, black crowds knelt down in the Rynek before the picture of the Virgin; and the National Hymn, in accents of desperate complaint, was rising slowly up to heaven!

a heap of combustibles. The whole nation caught the fever. Many unpleasant complications followed. Men, women, and even children, were killed in the streets while singing religious hymns, or following funerals. The government, at first lenient and undecided what course to take against praying and singing crowds, finished by a terrible repression. Cossacks were camping in the streets of Warsaw, outraging the inhabitants and committing all sorts of cruelties. The Poles threw themselves recklessly into the Insurrection which broke out in 1863 with all the fierceness of a long-suffering and injured people.

Next day we left Cracow, after having taken a large provision of books, and we started "on the road," travelling from one town to another, and staying in each at least two weeks, and often longer. In Rzeszow we stayed three months, and played to good houses all the time.

Our company grew rapidly. In April, 1862, it contained thirty-six members, and our equipment and staff were considerable. There were no regular salaries, however, in our combination; but we shared the income according to the importance and abilities of the actors. Not being in the cast did not exclude the actor from his right to a share. This system had one good point. The actors, being interested in the income, tried their best to help the success. It happened often that small parts were played by those who would never have condescended to accept them under an individual management. When we played national plays or dramas requiring a great number of people, all actors who were not in the cast appeared in mute parts as leaders of the supernumeraries. The result of this loyal spirit of the company was that the performances were smooth and artistic, and soon the reputation of the "New Sandec Combination" reached the ears of Mr. Nowakowski, one of the managers of the endowed theatre in Lwów (Lemberg),[1] who came to Sambor to see our performance.

We played "Sluby Panienskie" ("Maiden's Vows"), by Fredro, our Polish Molière. The play, written in verse, is one of his best and most popular comedies, and I played the subtle and spirited part of Clara. Mr. Nowakowski was pleased; he paid many compliments to the company and to me, and said he would surely remember me. In case I should get tired of travelling and wish an engagement in the Lemberg theatre, the doors would be opened for me. His gracious words, however, did not result at once in any material form, and we went on our further travels.

[1] The capital of the southeastern part of Poland called Galitzia.

I became a favorite of our provincial public, and the evenings on which I did not appear the "houses" were smaller. It was more flattering than comfortable, because the company wanted to have my name continually on the bill, no matter if my health permitted it or not; and so it happened that my daughter Marylka was born two hours after a five-act tragedy in which I played the principal rôle, and ten days afterwards I had to appear again on the stage. Another time, being seriously ill, I stayed in bed two weeks. One of our ladies came and told me that the public would not come if they did not see my name in the cast. Could I make an effort and appear in a one-act play, just to have my name on the bills? I made an effort, played my part, fainted after the performance, stayed in bed two days, then played again and went to bed.

I recovered, however with the help of youth and country air, and in April, 1862, we visited Lemberg. As soon as we came, my first desire, of course, was to go to the theatre. I was very anxious to see how the great city actors played.

The old theatre, built by Count Skarbek, and endowed by him, is a very large building occupying a square block. The stage, scenery, and auditorium seemed to me very handsome then. The play was "Marie Tudor," by Victor Hugo, and when the curtain rose I was all eyes and ears. Madame Ashberger, the leading lady, in the title rôle, made a powerful impression on me, but the others did not seem to me great. They were commonplace, though correct, but they wore very handsome costumes.

After the performance I could not sleep for a long while. I was thinking what a comfort it must be to act on a stage like that, to have appropriate lights, good orchestra, fine audience, and experienced, solid support, and I was determined to get there. At that time I was reading a little book called "The Hygiene of the Soul," by Feuchtersleben. In this book the author tries to prove that everything we wish can be obtained if we only wish it strongly.[1] Obedient to the spirit of this Utopian, I rose from the bed, and stamping the floor, I exclaimed, "Well, then, I must and I will!" This woke up my nurse, and the baby began to cry, so I crept back to bed, dreaming of future laurels.

Feuchtersleben, however, did not help, and we went on our further provincial tour.

In the meantime the news from Warsaw was stirring the whole nation and filling all hearts with sad apprehensions. Even to the farthest corners of the country the echo of Warsaw outrages came, magnified by distance and casting a gloom over all. People, however, did not cease to go to the theatre, but even there they were reminded of the ills of the country.

We performed many Polish historical plays then, and besides, popular pieces were placed on the bill every week, — plays with songs and dances, in which I also took part. Sad songs and desperate dances indeed; at every patriotic word or suggestion of the present state of the country, the people in front wiped their eyes, and the actors on the stage danced with tears rolling down their cheeks.

In 1862 the spring was beautiful, the business very prosperous, and, in consequence, the company was pleased, and everybody looked bright in spite of the sad events in Russian Poland. I am mistaken; not everybody looked bright. There were among them those who were in love, and they looked very unhappy, and there were many of both sexes in our company who were touched with that disease which spring sends to the world with the first waft of her breath. I watched those poor victims. Ah! those killing, desperate looks, the sighs, the nonsense, written and spoken, so full of charm or ridicule

There were Romeos ready to use daggers against their

[1] It seems that he failed in his theories, for a few years later he committed suicide.

lives, and Juliets on the point of being buried alive. Some of them were young and some of them were old, but they were all romantic to excess. Our juvenile lady, who was desperately in love with a young student, failing to obtain her mother's consent to the marriage, tried to poison herself by drinking a bottle of the white liquid with which she painted her neck and hands for the stage. This attempt on her youthful life resulted in seasickness and total awakening from her dream. Another young lady tried to jump out of the window, but screamed so loud before the fatal leap that her sister had ample time to rescue her. The young men were not so rash in taking such decided leaps into the next world; their usual demonstrations consisted in slight cuts in their flesh, using their own blood instead of ink for writing ardent messages to their sweethearts.

During the season 1862, from February till September, besides many parts in Polish dramas, I played Amelia in Schiller's "Die Räuber," Lady Teazle in Sheridan's "School for Scandal," and also the leading parts in French melodramas: "Thirty Years of a Gambler's Life," "The Pearl of Savoy," "Life in Dream," etc. It is impossible to remember all the plays, and I have no records of that year.

In September, 1862, we arrived in Brody, a town in which the Jewish population predominated. And we did not expect great success among this mixed population. Civilized Hebrews as a rule are very constant theatre-goers and patrons of art, but Brody, for the most part, was inhabited by orthodox Jews, who keep strictly to their religion, and do not indulge often in worldly entertainments. The Israelites of Brody were for the most part very moral in their home life, and so exclusive that they did not like their girls to be seen by "goys,"[1] but kept them at home at their housework until their marriage. To these grave people, deeply engaged in pursuits of fortune or religious rites, the

[1] Yiddish for Christians.

theatre was no attraction; therefore we could not at all count upon their support. However, being in town, we spread our camp. Lodgings were found, and the theatre rented.

A few days later, on a bright afternoon, we strolled around the town in company with our juvenile lady, my sister, and some young actors. As the day was very fine, some one suggested an excursion to the next village. On the road we met a band of gypsies, and among them an old woman, who, as soon as we approached the camp, offered to tell our fortunes. My companions were eager to let the old lady have her way. They all had their fortunes read, and when my turn came I hesitated, but the old witch looked so intently at me with her piercing black eyes that I succumbed to her fascination and extended my hand towards her. After a moment of scrutiny with which she observed the lines of my hand, she raised her head, and looking straight in my face, she said in Little Russian: —"

"After to-morrow you will be in Lwów." We all laughed, and I answered that it was impossible because we had just settled down for two or three weeks. She frowned and repeated: —

"After to-morrow you will be in Lwów," and then proceeded with her mind-reading. We returned to town, very much amused by the various prophecies and nonsense we had heard, but very soon we realized that the gypsy woman's words were true, after all.

The very next night I was awakened by a glare of flames and an alarm bell. I looked out. The roof of the house opposite to ours was on fire, shooting sparks and sending them on the neighboring houses. I had enough presence of mind to pack our trunks without wakening up any one for fear of confusion, and when this was done, I woke my husband, the nurse, and the babies, whom he dressed in a hurry, and, having succeeded in transporting our trunks out of the reach of the flames, we waited until daylight in the open. The whole city seemed to be on fire, and we soon learned that the theatre was burning, too. There was nothing to do but to leave the town as soon as possible. We caught the morning train for Lemberg, and the gypsy's prophecy was fulfilled.

In September of 1862 Mr. Modjeski saw the managers in Lemberg, who consented to give me a trial, and selected three plays in which I had to appear. Thus by mere accident my dream of appearing on the Lemberg stage was realized.

The first of the plays selected for my début was a drama called "Domy Polskie" ("Polish Homes") by Majeranowski. My part was strong, very dramatic and heroic, but also full of tenderness and love. It suited me, I thought; and, strange to say, I was not at all afraid of playing on that large stage. There is a great deal of courage, even boldness, in youth and inexperience. Timidity comes with responsibility, when we are afraid of falling down from the pedestal on which the audience and the critics have placed us.

I passed happily through the verdict of the audience, in spite of a slight incident which happened at the close of one of the acts. I had to shoot from my castle at the attacking enemies, and was supposed to kill a man. We had four rehearsals, and I thought that everything went smoothly. But it seems that the supernumerary man who had to fall at my shot sent a substitute for the next rehearsal, and the substitute sent another for the third rehearsal, and this one being awkward, was replaced by an old man belonging to the theatre. At the night of the performance the first "super" and his two substitutes came, and all together, with the old man who rehearsed the last, appeared in the mob. The result is easily foreseen — all four of them fell at my single shot. This, of course, put the public for a while in a hilarious mood, but I was called before the curtain repeatedly, and when the play was over, I had no doubt of having made a favorable impression.

Next was the part of an *ingénue*, demure, shy, and clinging, very unlike the heroine in "Domy Polskie"; and the third play which the management selected was "The Primrose Farm," from the English, a sort of "Bluette," with songs and dances. I had to dance a hornpipe! A hornpipe! I had never seen, not even heard of such a dance! I was in despair, and while I was trying to persuade the stage manager to leave out the dance, Mademoiselle de Fontlief, who was crossing the stage, stopped and listened to my desperate appeal. Then she came right to me and said that if I wanted, she would teach me the dance, as she had played the part in "Primrose Farm" before. She took me to her dressing-room and showed me the steps, then invited me to her lodgings and rehearsed with me several times, playing the tune of the dance for me until I was quite at ease in it.

Mademoiselle de Fontlief was leaving the Polish stage at that time. She accepted an engagement in Vienna, where she made a great success at Carl's Theatre in modern French plays. She left the stage to marry Prince Turn und Taxis, who was related to the imperial family. She left one of the sweetest impressions on my soul. I admired not only her talent but also her great kind heart.

CHAPTER XI

After my trial performances I was almost sure of an engagement, especially when I realized how useful I could be to the management.

The favorite of the audience was then a talented and very beautiful young woman, Madame X, to whom the parts of ingénues belonged exclusively. She was greatly admired by the public in the part of "La Petite Fadette," the play which Madame Birch Pfeifer adapted for the stage from George Sand's novel. This beautiful actress was rather capricious. Her spontaneous success went to her head, and she enjoyed imposing her sweet will upon the management. Several times she sent a message to the stage manager just before the performance, declaring that, being indisposed, she would not play. Sometimes she refused parts assigned to her. In a word, she caused some annoyance to both managers.

When I came, they saw in me a sort of antidote agains her whims, and proposed to engage me, on the absurd salar of forty florins a month, to play the parts she rejected, an also to be her understudy. Mr. Modjeski advised me t accept the engagement. I played all sorts of parts. was in one play a great lady, in the next a page, a Venetia courtesan or a Hungarian dancing boy, a gypsy or a fair queen, a shy *ingénue* or a rattling singing soubrette in a operetta! I also understudied all Madame X.'s parts.

All went well and smoothly until one evening I came in collision with the capricious favorite. One morning t management sent for me to rehearse one of her parts.

knew the lines well, and the stage manager was satisfied, and said: —

"Madame X. is ill, and will not be able to play to-night; as you know her part, you must play for her." Then very kindly he went over the business with me. I came to the theatre early that night and dressed. Just as I was leaving my room, I saw Madame X., standing in the wing waiting for her entrance. As she lived in the theatre building, she came all dressed and made up, and without reporting to the stage manager, appeared behind the scenes just in time for her cue. When she saw me she looked at me in utter disdain, and exclaimed: —

"What does this mean? What are you going to play to-night?" I explained that the management called for me to play her part because she was supposed to be ill. "My dear, they were joking," she answered, with a three-cornered smile, and shrugging her shoulders, she turned her back on me. That was not the only humiliation I had to stand from the ladies of the theatre. Most of the numerous *personnel* of that endowed theatre were very kind and charitable, especially Madame Ashberger, the leading lady, who took me under her protective wing from the start, and whenever a difficult or unsuitable part fell to my share, she asked me to come to her room, and talked to me about it, and sometimes even read the lines for me. She also gave me designs for costumes I had to wear in my various parts. This favor she conferred on me created more enmity then ever in the ranks of my adversaries. One evening two of the three antagonistic goddesses were so incensed against me that they would not allow me even a corner in the large dressing-room, where four could dress comfortably, and where I occupied a dressing-table by right. These spirited and not over-kind priestesses of art arranged their costumes and baskets in such a way that, when I came in, not the least space was left for me among them. Not being satisfied with the trick they played on the provincial strolling actress, they began to sting me with their silly remarks, until I was boiling all over with anger. I was just about to lift a beautiful spangled gown off my table to make room *coûte que coûte,* when I heard a clear musical voice:—

"Madame Modjeska, come to my room, please." It was Madame Ashberger's voice, who, from her dressing-room, separated only by a partition, had heard every word of the conflict. I was so touched by this new proof of that dear woman's kindness that I could not speak. I only kissed her hand, and hot tears fell from my eyes.

"Do not cry," she whispered to me. "It would give them a great satisfaction to know that you took their silly talk to heart. Be calm! Think of your part, and do not mind them."

The play that night was "Balladyna," by Slowacki,—entirely new to me; for, though I had read and memorized many of his poems, I was not well acquainted with his plays. My part was that of an imp, a sort of "Puck." Madame Ashberger gave me a design for the costume, and I executed it to the best of my ability. The tunic was composed of strips of shaded brown gauze folded thickly over yellow silk, which was intended to produce the effect of a beetle. My dress was short in contrast to the conventional long skirts actresses then wore on the stage even in boy's parts. I wore brown and gold wings and fleshings! Horrors! Each of the goddesses passing before me said aloud:—

"Shame! Outrageous! She is naked!" And Madame Ashberger only laughed, and said to me:—

"Never mind, never mind. You are all right!" But in spite of her kind, encouraging words, I experienced one of those terrific fits of stage fright which makes the voice sound hollow and paralyzes the gestures. The dreadful remarks of the trio resounded in my ears, they burned, they scorched, until I became conscious of my scanty dress, which, when I tried it on first, seemed to me rather pretty and characteristic. I crossed my arms over my chest, and did not unfold them until the end of the scene. I was awkward and felt the ground slipping from under my feet, and only after I had delivered one of the speeches I had particularly studied, and received recognition from the public, did I begin to be my own self again. The language of Slowacki is so beautiful that it was a delight to speak the lines. I soon forgot all the bitterness I was fed on that evening, and gave myself up entirely to my part and the fairyland in which the author made me live for a while.

After a few weeks of my uncertain engagement on that miserable salary, I received a more serious proposal from the management. A high-spirited and absurd letter I wrote at that time to my mother gives the description of that incident:—

NOVEMBER 9th, 1862.

"DEAR MAMECZKA (little mother),

"Although I have just written to you, the event which happened here lately compels me to write again, for it is only my duty to enlighten you, dear mamma, as well as all big and small members of the family upon the subject:—

"I have actually signed the contract with the management of the Lemberg theatre for one year and a half. The following official act will best describe this important fact:—

"To all present, etc.—

"It happened in Lemberg on the 6th of November, 1862d. year, in the following manner:—

"At eight o'clock in the morning came to the lodgings of the undersigned a certain female in a straw hat, a red shawl, a green dress [without hoops], and a large wicker bag on her arm. Judging by her face, she could be more or less between thirty and fifty years old. Her Christian name is Justyna, and after her husband she is called Urbanska, and she is the wife of the property man of the theatre.

"She entered the bedroom without knocking, and found all the family in bed, and Mr. Modjeski in deep negligée. A vivid scarlet tint spread over the unbeautiful face and the beet-root nose of Pani Justina, and a sigh escaped through the wide-open lips, — a sigh of indignation over the sad realities of the world, — such at least was the supposition of the undersigned. After that deep and expressive sigh, she delivered a statement to Mr. Modjeski and the undersigned, in which she declared that the gentlemen managers wished to speak with them.

"Mr. Modjeski and the undersigned dressed immediately and went to the managers' office, asking for the reason of the summons. They only found one manager in the office, Mr. S.; John the Spendthrift, so called for his great economy, was not there. Manager N. sent for him, however, and when he arrived we were shown into the rehearsal hall. He took Mr. Modjeski and the undersigned aside and declared in soft tones of voice that, prompted by the noble feelings of a thoughtful father, he desired to raise the salary of the undersigned and wished to sign a contract with her. Mr. Modjeski asked what salary he would be willing to offer me, and John the Spendthrift answered:—

"'I raise her salary to fifty-five florins a month.' To which both Mr. Modjeski and the undersigned agreed.

"What was the reason of this wastefulness, unheard of in Lemberg theatre history, no one knows, but the current of whispers brought to our ears the intimation that Majeranowska, who was until now a member of the Lemberg Stock Company, had obtained a more lucrative engagement in Warsaw, and will not likely return. The management was then in need of an operetta singer, and, having no one at hand, they have destined the undersigned to that position.

"How it happened, no matter; but it happened. Besides the raising of the salary, the contract allows travelling expenses for the undersigned and family, as well as hotel expenses, should the company go on the road.

"The hearing of which arrangements is granted to each person concerned in the matter, as well as to all present and absent members of the family.

"This act has been composed and written in the presence of two trustworthy witnesses, who, by their own signatures, affirm its authority. The names of the witnesses: Rudolphe S. Modjeski, age twenty-one months, citizen of Lemberg, born in Cracow;

Marie S. Modjeska,[1] thirty weeks old, spinster, born in Sambor, inhabitant of Lemberg.

"LEMBERG, November 9th, 1862d. year.

"×RUDOLPHE S. MODJESKI
as witness.
"×MARIE S. MODJESKA
as witness.

"(The witnesses, not knowing how to write, put down a sign of the cross.)

"From the official act you may, dear little mother, judge how our affairs stand."

* * * * * * *

I suppress the end of the letter, as it only contained some very intimate details about the babies and people which could not possibly be of any interest to the readers.

[1] The last vowel of the name in Polish changes according to the sex, "i" for men, "a" for women.

CHAPTER XII

IN the second part of January, 1863, the Insurrection broke out. The Poles, encouraged by a few successful encounters with the Russians, threw themselves blindly into the whirl of battle. Their courage, their intense love of the country, their devotion to the cause, and their undaunted spirit aroused the admiration of our neighbors.

For a long time they were under the delusion that the emperor of France, Napoleon III, would help them, but that hope, like so many others, was vain.

The poor Poles were left alone, with no sympathy save in words, and no help but what they received secretly in ammunition, arms, and money from different parts of the world. These means were soon exhausted, and nothing was left but their own courage to depend upon. They fought desperately. Thousands of young men — even boys under sixteen — enlisted under the national flag. Every day brought tears and mourning into the Polish homes.

The greatest misfortune of this uprising was that not all our peasants were in sympathy with those who fought for independence. If the whole nation could have risen like one man, then there might have been some hope for the nation; but this division was fatal, and the Insurrection was rapidly progressing to its hopeless end.

Oh, the painful recollections of those horrible times! From the April of 1861 (when the first five men were sacrificed), when women and children were killed in the streets for singing hymns, the whole people, even those who had but a few drops of Polish blood in their veins, were penetrated with a most acute feeling of great wrongs and pity for the victims. The whole nation was palpitating with pain and desire for revenge, the atmosphere was full of something combustible, something which made all the nerves vibrate at the slightest news from the battle-field.

In spite of the tension of pain, this pit of horror and despair in which the poor country was precipitated, the theatres were kept open, and it was the right thing to do, for the unfortunate young men who were going to fight found there at least a few moments' pleasure before they went to sacrifice their young lives for the country.

One never-forgotten performance comes to my mind. The youth of Lemberg had just finished their enlisting. The newly enlisted regiment was about to start. On the eve of departure the theatre was crowded. All the young insurgents were there. The play was a Polish melodrama, with national costumes and songs. In the last act almost every actor in the play had to sing a "couplet" suited to the occasion, the words of which were pencilled in a hurry in the dressing-rooms during the play. The manager read the compositions, approving or correcting them. They were words of farewell and good wishes, or appeals full of patriotic meaning, spurring the young men to brave deeds. The youthful volunteers cheered at every verse; the actors sung, choking with tears, and there was such a bond of sympathy between the audience and the stage that were it not for the footlights they would have all joined in one embrace.

There was something grand, inspiring, and heartrending in the aspect of all these young, eager faces, many of them mere boys, with no trace of hair on their upper lips or chins, mad enthusiasts who threw themselves blindly into the whirl of battle, never doubting that the deliverance depended on their courage alone, and that the dawn of liberty was near at hand. No one could look at them with dry eyes, and we all cried. When the curtain fell, the company was called again and again, and new cheers and farewells were exchanged, until the exhausted actors refused to appear, and the audience was reduced to a few enthusiasts, who would not leave the theatre until the lights were put out.

I did not stay in Lemberg until the expiration of my contract. The salary was really too small to live and dress upon, and my enthusiasm received many shocks from the constant conflict with the "trio" and also from the "fatherly" managers, who put all the parts no one wanted to my care. But, poor souls, they were forced to do so. When on one particular occasion they gave me a really good part of a pathetic, patriotic boy of fourteen, because that boy had to sing, and none of the trio had any voice, and when Mr. Lozinski, the prominent critic, declared that I possessed an unmistakable talent, the trio made so much ado, accusing the dear old managers of patronizing a "pretty face," that they never even tried to repeat the experience, and I continued playing pages, gypsies, servant-girls, peasant women, mysterious countesses in French melodramas, etc. I sang and danced, laughed and cried, and always tried to play even the smallest part to the satisfaction of my best friend, Madame Ashberger, who allowed me to recite in her presence, and many a time corrected me during rehearsals. I had worked hard and always with the hope of rising some day, and though I saw no chance of the realization of my hopes in the near future, still I plodded on my way patiently. It was discouraging, yet that year's experience did me a great deal of good; and though I did not seem to advance in my art, yet I was unconsciously working towards development, acquiring versatility and originality, for I had to use a good deal of observation to play so many various characters.

But playing two or three new parts every week, rehearsing, and making my own costumes at night, nearly exhausted me. I looked thin and pale, and my health was visibly failing. Even Madame Ashberger ceased to encourage me, and advised me to take the engagement offered me by one of the provincial managers, who promised me leading parts and a good salary.

CHAPTER XIII

AFTER a few weeks of a "star" engagement in small towns of Galitzia, we settled down in Czerniowce, where Mr. Modjeski rented the city theatre and established a stock company. Soon afterwards all my three half-brothers Benda — Joseph, Felix, and Simon — joined us; and also a very talented actor, Ortynski. We also had in our company Wincenty Rapacki (who became famous a few years later) and his wife Josephine Hofmann. My sister and her husband, Tomaszewicz, were also in our company. Being over twenty in number, we played a very imposing repertoire: comedies, classic and modern, tragedies and dramas, melodramas and operettas, of which my brother Simon, who had just returned from the Vienna conservatory, was the leader.

WINCENTY RAPACKI.

In order to satisfy the authorities, Mr. Modjeski had to engage a German company to alternate with the Polish performances. The German actors and actresses used to come to our plays, and I received great encouragement from them. They advised me to study for the German stage, and persuaded Mr. Modjeski that the field of the Polish stage was too small for me, that I needed a larger space in order to "spread out my wings" (the phrase is theirs, not mine).

My husband looked to it at once. He brought to our house Herr Neugebauer, the high school professor of German literature, who undertook to instruct me in his native tongue. Though I was not a novice in the language, yet I was deficient in pronunciation, emphasis, and enunciation.

After a few months of study, however, I was ready to appear with the German company in a one-act play called "On Water and Bread" (Bei Wasser und Brod). It was a very modest beginning, but Mr. Modjeski did not want me to appear in any of the responsible parts in a language with which I was not thoroughly acquainted as yet. The rehearsals were called, and a bill in large type announcing my first appearance on the German stage was placed at the theatre entrance.

It was only then — only when I saw that unfortunate announcement — that I realized what I was doing, and a sense of shame filled me at the meanness of my deserting the Polish stage just at the time when the poor country was fighting desperately for independence, with but a slight hope of winning the cause. My spirits fell to the lowest degree of temperature at the last rehearsal, and when, on leaving the theatre, I perceived several students before my bill frowning as they read aloud my name in German type, I ran home with my head down, not daring to lift my eyes for fear of meeting glances of reproach or contempt.

I ate my midday meal in silence and without the slightest appetite. Mr. Modjeski was chatting merrily, asked me if I had my costume ready, and how it looked, etc.

"And mind, read your part again in the afternoon," he added, "or else you may get confused." I wanted to scream at the top of my voice, "I shall never play in German!" But I dared not disappoint him, and besides, I knew well that he would treat this outburst as a caprice not worthy of a sensible person. I stifled my feelings, and went to the garden with my part. I sat there motionless, brooding over my misery, and forming all sorts of arguments to justify my appearance on the German stage, or to get out of it entirely, when, suddenly, like an answer called forth by some magic power, the sound of a passing military band struck my ears, my breast, my whole being, with unspeakable exultation and pain.[1] I listened for a while, then, flinging my part away, I fell on my knees, and burying my face in my hands, I sobbed convulsively, repeating:—

"No, no! I will never be a renegade! Never! Never!" Mr. Modjeski found me in that state, and lifting me up, took me to my room. I do not remember what happened next, but one detail is still in my mind: I shook with fever, my nails were blue, and my mother was sitting at the foot of my bed. My dear, sweet mother, who had travelled so many miles to come and live with us, poured many comforting words into my ears, words which acted as balm to my overstrung nerves, soothing the pain and restoring me to my own self again. How it happened I do not know. There was no more question of my going on the German stage. I continued to play in Polish.

We produced "Angelo Malipieri," by Victor Hugo. This was my first attempt at tragedy. I also played Louise in "Kabale und Liebe," in "Wilhelm Tell," in all the French melodramas, and in a great many patriotic Polish plays. Offenbach was also in our repertoire, and I played

[1] The Austrian under the reign of the Emperor Franz Joseph was liberal, and the national music was not excluded from the military band's program.

in "Fortunio," "Enchanted Violin," "Wedding by Lanterns," and in several other musical plays, besides the Polish comic operas; when, on one occasion, during the finale, I had to keep the high C during four full bars, my uncultivated voice broke, and I could sing no more. I ought not to have sung high soprano parts, for my voice was a decided mezzo, but we had no one else to sing those high notes except Madame Hofmann Rapacka, and she being ill at the time, I had to take her place. The loss of my voice was not very important, for I never liked my singing parts. Light operas did not appeal to me. I was anxious to make a repertoire of serious dramas and comedies.

Neither did I like my parts in French melodramas; but I had to play them, as in those days nothing was so highly appreciated and enjoyed by the audience as a good melodrama. I recollect an amusing incident connected with one of these popular plays: —

We had in our company a young, very talented actor, who was an ardent follower of the French melodrama. He had tendencies for writing, and in one of his happy, or unhappy, moods he wrote a play based on the French novel, "Le Bossu" (The Hunchback). The hero's object in the play was to appear as a hunchback in the first three acts, by way of disguising his real personality; then, at the supreme moment, to straighten himself up to the full height of six feet, in order to confound the villains and destroy their wicked plots.

This young actor thought that the mere stooping and bending of his body was not sufficient to represent the appearance of a man with a hump on his back, and in order to give his figure a realistic touch (every one had to be realistic at that time) he contrived a peculiar scheme: he bought a bladder which he filled with air, and placed it on his right shoulder under the coat. Previous to the performance he made the stage carpenter place a strong wooden board braced by iron clasps behind the painted pillar, so that he could lean against it. He imagined that by pressing the right shoulder against the pillar the air would escape from the bladder, and by this action he would complete a marvellous change from a hunchback to the straight, tall, h ndsome fellow he was normally.

He forgot, however, one of the eternal laws of the stage: "Before you let the audience see you, you must see yourself," which means the rehearsing of every point of the part. When the culminating point of the play arrived, and the villain was about to obtain the victory, our hero pressed his shoulder against the prepared pillar, but instead of flattening the hump he bounced back with a jerk which made him sway from one side to the other. Determined to execute his purpose, he again braced himself with all his strength against the supporting board, but with no result.

I played that night the unhappy girl who wore a wedding gown, being about to marry a hated man. I noticed our hero's struggle with the pillar, not understanding, however, the object of his exertions, when suddenly I saw him taking out of his pocket a penknife which he quickly opened. The audience could not see this action because he was shielded by the mob of supers, and only his head and shoulders were visible. I became most interested in his movements. I knew he was in terrible trouble about something, but could not for the world understand what it was all about, when he turned toward me with the expression of a hunted animal, and handing me the knife, whispered desperately:—

"Please cut my bladder!"

"What?" I exclaimed in surprise.

"Cut the bladder on my shoulder," he added, impatiently, yet still in a whisper. Then the whole situation dawned on me, and with the willingness common among actors of helping the fellow-artist out of his trouble, I approached him, took the knife, and concealing my action as much as I could, I plunged the small weapon even to the hilt. But oh! what happened next was simply dreadful! When I drew out the knife, the air escaped from the artificial hump with a gentle and prolonged whistle!

This unexpected sound put me almost into a convulsion of laughter. The audience did not notice anything, but I wanted to shriek when I saw my hero's expression and his set teeth, with a suppressed curse behind them. Hearing my cue, I drew the veil over my face and advanced to the footlights, with eyes cast down and a handkerchief pressed to my lips. Fearing to speak lest I should choke with laughter, I pretended to faint, and fell flat on the floor, shaking with unwonted merriment.

The curtain fell. The hero was applauded. My fainting was taken for granted as belonging to the play, and one critic even said that I had quite an original fall. You may imagine how amused I was when I read the following lines:—

". . . she turned her back to the audience, but every one could see the great suffering shaking the whole frame of her slender body; then, covering her face with her veil, she fell flat to the ground, still quivering with emotion."

CHAPTER XIV

In 1863 Mr. Modjeski took a vacation, and we both went to Vienna, in order to see a little of the world, and mostly for the sake of my instruction. I was very anxious to see the best actors of the great city, and my delight was very great indeed when Mr. Modjeski bought two tickets for the Burg Theatre.

The play was "Don Carlos." I still remember Sonnenthal's impressive figure, even the voice in which he uttered the memorable words of Marquis Posa: "Gebt uns Gedanken Freiheit, König."[1] I was delighted with Eboli's scene of coquetry, and I shall never forget Levinsky's King Philip. The whole performance struck me as being perfect, even to the smallest parts. It was a masterpiece of stage management, and though in some scenes I should have liked more warmth, more nature, more humanity, yet this first great performance I ever saw made a powerful impression on me, and kept me awake until the small hours in the morning.

The second play I saw was "Schoene Helene" (La Belle Hélène), by Meilhac and Halévy, with Offenbach's music, where Miss Geistinger played the title rôle. What a contrast to "Don Carlos"! I was not quite pleased. I was too young then, perhaps, to appreciate the so-called piquancy of the scene between Paris and Helen, and although I admired highly Miss Geistinger's acting, yet I was almost ashamed to look at the stage, when she took off her peplum, and Paris, with quivering lips, waited for her kiss. I felt humiliated in my high aspirations in art, and displeased

[1] "Give us liberty of thought, O King!"

with this exposition of what I thought ought to be hidden from human eyes. It was, however, not Miss Geistinger's fault that the scene was made objectionable. She was artistic all through. The wretched suggestiveness was all done by Paris. When I saw "Don Carlos" I felt now and then the lack of naturalness in the performance, yet I loved it all. Here I really deplored the brutal realism. This was my first lesson in moderation. I admired already the true realism, and always tried to render my parts as true to nature as possible; but the performance of "La belle Hélène" taught me that I must not go too far in that direction, or I might step out of the circle of art and, instead of painting pictures on the stage, produce mere photographs.

We went to the theatre almost every evening, and I had the opportunity of seeing several good actors and actresses: among them Mademoiselle de Fontlief, my friend from Lemberg, in Dumas's "La Dame aux Camélias." She was dainty, simple, natural, and very impressive, and satisfied all my requirements in modern drama. Her aristocratic figure and face, as well as her intelligence, strongly appealed to me.

I called on her the next afternoon. We fell into each other's arms. I sincerely congratulated her on her remarkable success. She looked beautiful in her soft, gauzy dress, surrounded with objects of art, and a superb dog nestling at her feet. The only discord in this artistic room was a parrot, who insisted on sharing the conversation, and jarred on my nerves by its piercing shrieks. I had not been fifteen minutes with Mademoiselle de Fontlief when her handsome mother came in, and a few minutes later the prince of Thurm und Taxis was announced, a handsome and very young man with melting eyes — at least they seemed to melt when they looked at her. He and "Marguerite Gauthier" [1]

[1] The name of the heroine in Dumas's play.

were engaged at that time, and I saw there before me the man of imperial family who was shortly afterwards to become the husband of the fascinating actress.

To my great regret I missed seeing the greatest German actress of the time, Frau Rettich. Shortly after the announcement of her appearance at the Burg Theatre she fell ill, and the world never saw her act again. Levinsky was the great man, and I saw him in several parts, and took from him a lesson in self-control and in working out details; but I imagined that a woman like Frau Rettich would have had a great influence over my artistic future.

We lost no time in seeing what was worth looking at in Vienna, and we went several times to the Luxembourg galleries, and stayed hours admiring the pictures. All this was new to me. Except the statues, carvings, and pictures of Cracow churches, I had seen nothing until then. The works of art accumulated through ages, combined with what was best in modern work, made me mad with enthusiastic worship of art. I felt small and humble in the presence of the masterpieces of all ages and all nations, and yet, underneath this humility, I felt a glow of superhuman strength, and a hope that one day I might achieve fame, — in a different and smaller way, of course, — for our art was scarcely considered an art at all, but I formed then a strong determination never to rest until I had climbed to the very top of my profession. Again the desire of playing in another language than my own began to make its way into my mind.

I thought of French or English — and Shakespeare — again; but German was the only tongue I spoke passably well, and my people hated Germans with the hatred of a vanquished nation, and I could not think of going on the German stage. However, one attempt more was made by my husband to change my resolve. He formed some friendships among actors and managers of the city, and one day he told me that he had spoken to one of his friends, an influential manager, and he wished me to recite before him some scenes from "Mary Stuart" or "Egmont." I consented, more in hope of hearing his opinion about my ability than of getting the engagement I secretly dreaded.

I do not remember being very nervous when I entered the manager's office; and besides, being encouraged by his compliments as to my external value for the stage, I began to recite the lines of "Mary Stuart" (Eulende Wolken Sägler der Lufte) with all the feeling and pathos I was capable of. I had studied the language so long, with one of the best teachers, the dear Professor Neugebauer, that I finished by loving the sound of the words, the sonority and strength of expression, and I delivered the sentences with delight, and the precise pronunciation of an ardent student.

The manager listened very attentively and patiently, I thought, and when I had finished he said he was pleased; but he also said that my voice, though musical in sound, was neither strong nor deep enough for tragedy. He advised me to play parts like Gretchen in "Faust," or Louise in "Kabale und Liebe," also the girlish parts in comedy, until I grew matured enough for the heavy dramatic parts. I was very thankful for this advice, and I shook hands with him, saying good-by, but he stopped me at the door and said:—

"I forgot to tell you that you must study German at least one year more before you go on our stage, and it would be advisable to stay in Vienna and go to work immediately." I thanked him again, and we left the office. I knew very well that we could not afford to give up the stock company in Czerniowce and stay in a large city without any income, but I wanted to make sure, and asked my husband if we could do so.

"Of course not; it is quite impossible," was his short answer; and I breathed again.

I formed a project of studying for the French stage as soon as I could find a good French teacher, and then again a voice like a distant echo whispered in my ear "Shakespeare," and a vision of myself on the English stage rose before me.

From Vienna we went to Pesth, where we found the whole city in a great excitement on account of the races, and a visit of the Emperor Franz Joseph, then in the prime of youth. We spent the days in the streets and the evenings in the theatres. I have never seen so many beautiful women as in Pesth. It was almost impossible to find an ugly face, except in some ragged old woman, and even among those some possessed such dignity of carriage that it was a pleasure to watch them as they moved along the streets.

There was to be a so-called "Gala" performance at the opera-house. The emperor was to be present, and every one had to appear in national costume. An exception was made for men who could not or chose not to wear the beautiful yet uncomfortable and costly dress, but all women agreed to be attired in Hungarian costumes. We secured seats, and I had to procure a Hungarian headgear. It seemed to be absolutely necessary to do so, in order not to clash with the whole female audience. But I did not object when I saw how becoming was the small bonnet of black lace, heavily embroidered with silver.

At the theatre I was positively dazzled by the aspect of the audience in the boxes. Three tiers of wonderfully handsome women and brilliant uniforms, and every one trying to look their best in honor of the emperor. Never in my life shall I again look at so many beauties and such a display of marvellous jewels, gold and silver embroidered waists, sparkling with diamonds, rubies, and emeralds; misty veils, strings of rare pearls, and aigrettes of gems; and amidst all this scintillating mass the smiling faces of the wonderful specimens of human beauty of both sexes. It seemed to me like a chapter from the "Arabian Nights." My soul was in my eyes. I sat as in a daze, and for the first time in my life I was unconscious of the singers on the stage. When the emperor entered, there was a deafening cheer, "Ellien! Ellien!" And the young monarch, blushing with pleasure, greeted the audience, then sat modestly and directed his attention to the stage, his entrance being the cue for the rising of the curtain.

On our return from Pesth to Vienna we paid a visit to Josephine Galmayer, the celebrated comedienne and the greatest favorite of the Vienna people. She lived then in the country, resting after a long winter season. I shall never forget her eyes. A pair of dark brown, impish, passionate eyes, full of mischief, which in a flash could change to an inexpressible look of kindness and sympathy. We chatted merrily for a long while. Her conversation was full of wit and spontaneity, and though some of her sallies were *risqué*, yet there was so much sincerity and simplicity in all she said that I could not help admiring it all. We parted like old friends, and I do not know what warmth and inspiration came to me from her, but I threw my arms around her neck and kissed her, — a thing I had never done before to a comparative stranger. She was indeed the most magnetic person I met at that time.

CHAPTER XV

When we returned to Czerniowce, the actors pressed me with questions, and I seemed to wear a halo around my head because I had seen things they had not seen. Still, in spite of this distinction, I had not changed my old way of accepting any part, good or bad, long or short, that was given to me. I did not care what I played so long as I could learn something, and try my versatility on the various kinds of characters. Yet my methods had changed. I had gained a great deal in the way of finishing the details and of putting more work on the development of parts. I also remembered the Vienna manager's advice, and avoided as much as I could the tragic parts.

A regular tragedienne was engaged for our company, a tall lady with a deep, big voice and the grace of a grenadier. She charmed the audiences in grewsome parts like "Die Aufrau" (The Ancestor), translated from German, or "Medea," and other heavy characters which she hammered away with her metallic voice, to the great delight of the gallery gods.

In spite of my love for the gentle, sweet parts, I put my mind to improving the quality of my voice by adding some deep tones to it. I worked an hour or more a day reciting, no matter what, and trying to get my voice one shade deeper every time. Sometimes I could not get just the tone I wanted; then I tried again and again, speaking louder and louder, and gaining strength with every effort and expansion of the diaphragm. By instinct I avoided the throat tones, using only my lungs, and with this practice I acquired such stability of voice that when, later on, I played strong dramatic parts I could, on coming home, sing for an hour without feeling any fatigue in the voice. Music I always loved passionately, and having still a little singing voice left, it was my custom, after returning from the theatre, to sit at the piano and play or sing, according to my mood. I never could sleep after the play, and nothing could soothe my nerves better than music.

While keeping the stock company all the year round in Czerniowce, we used to make excursions to the smaller towns in the neighborhood. The artistic direction of these excursions was given to my brother, Joseph Benda, on account of his presence of mind, and his ability to get the best of the situation in any emergency.

We played in all sorts of houses, — sometimes in barns or riding-schools, — but my brother's ingenuity always succeeded in turning these buildings into decent-looking summer theatres, with the help of a few boards, paint, curtains, rugs, green branches, and colored lamps. At least they looked cheerful and cosy, and many times even pretty. I remember one amusing occasion in which my brother's wits were heavily taxed.

It happened in a very small town, which, however, by some chance, possessed quite a decent theatre. We arrived late in the afternoon. The bills announced "The Devil's Mill." My brother, after inspecting the stage and dressing-rooms, came to our hotel with a radiant face, saying that he hoped everything would go smoothly, for there was room enough for the scenery and the actors. The stage was large and the dressing-rooms quite comfortable. When he was still rubbing his hands and smiling with satisfaction, there was a knock at the door, and the property man, covered with dust and perspiration, entered to inform us excitedly that the costumes of the devils were missing.

My brother rushed out of the room, and when he returned two hours later, he looked tired and discouraged. He said he had looked in several inns, hotels, and halls for the trunks, but in vain. There was no telegraph or even railroad in Galitzia in 1864, and therefore it was impossible to make inquiries. I was very anxious to know how my brother would solve the difficulty; the play had to be performed next evening, and there was no time to make new costumes or — what was the most important — to procure black tights for about twenty demons. No such article was to be found in the quiet little town. When I saw my brother the following morning, and asked what he intended to do about it, he answered with a mysterious smile, "Come to the theatre in the afternoon, and you will see something that will amuse you."

When I came at the appointed hour, I found my brother sitting on a high office stool in the centre of the stage. At his feet were lying in a tangle yards of red cotton stuff, and he was telling two sewing women how to cut and stitch the cloth. I understood that they were making trunks.

"What about the tights?" I asked. He smiled, and waving his hand towards a huge can of black paint, he said, "There are the tights, my dear," and then laughed right out.

"You don't mean to paint those poor boys all over?"

"Just what I mean to do, my little sister," and he laughed again.

He followed the property man, who carried the can of paint and a brush in one hand and a bundle of red trunks in the other.

We had not long to wait; in a few minutes my brother opened the door just enough to put his head out, and calling to me: "Attention! Number one is ready!" he pushed on the stage a most frightened boy, painted black all over, with horns on his head, and white circles around the eyes, which made them look like goggles. He had a tail made of a rope, and a tongue of red cloth hanging out of his opened mouth. The red, very scanty, trunks were the only protection to outraged modesty. The effect indeed was monstrous.

I forget the plot of that awful play, but I remember the scene where a man is brought in and sentenced by Lucifer. With a fearful yell the demons fall upon the man to beat him with uncanny-looking weapons, broomsticks, racks, iron bars, etc. The man tries to escape, and hides behind the throne, but the infuriated servants of Hades run after him and strike so hard that he catches one of the devils and throws him over his shoulders, as a shield against the blows. The "supers," all young boys, appreciated the fun, and struck yet harder than before at the exposed part of the devil's body, until the poor imp screamed with pain, and finally exclaimed: "Oh, Lord, Saint Marie, Saint Joseph, stop! For God's sake, don't beat so hard!"

The audience shrieked with laughter and the curtain fell.

One of the most picturesque places I encountered in my travelling tour through Galitzia was a small town placed at the foothills of the Carpathian Mountains, called Zaleszczyki. Another dreadful name to a foreigner, is it not? Well, never mind; we shall call it simply Z. . . .

When I first came to that enchanted spot I was beside myself from the sheer enjoyment of breathing the pure mountain air, filled with the penetrating perfume of firs and pines mingled with the odor of fresh hay, wafted in by the breeze from great green pastures in the valley. I went almost insane over the scenery, — the big mountains and the green slopes of the smaller hills in the foreground, the clear rushing streams, so cool and fresh, and the waterfalls at every turn of the hills.

I shall never forget the sensation when, after a day in the open, I entered my dressing-room. I felt suddenly a horror of the dingy lamplight, and the rouge I put on my face made me laugh at the incongruity of things: nature and art which had to reproduce nature. I just hated myself, and a sense of great humility swept over me when I stood before the looking-glass with all the artifices of my apparel; and when I entered the stage, which was to represent a wood scene, and compared the great effects of nature with our poor scenery, I felt simply crushed. After the first act I went to my dressing-room, and there I sat a long while, forgetful of everything, even of the changing of my costume, and dreaming of the possibility of appearing on some stage of the world where the artists could produce at least a better imitation of nature; and again a great desire to fly away from my narrow circle rose in my heart, and new dreams, one more impossible than the next, took possession of me. "I must! I must!" I repeated loudly, and then began to recite some imaginary poem in some imaginary language. They were merely sounds of some unknown words which I uttered with passionate or tender inflections of the voice. I would have gone on with this recitation forever were it not for a sharp laugh from my sister, who dressed with me in the same room, and her wise words: —

"Helena, you are positively crazy!"

On our return to Czerniowce, I took up my French and music. Mr. Duniecki, the composer of several operettas, who was engaged for our lyric productions, consented to give me lessons. The time passed in studies and work. I played sometimes three or four parts in a space of eight days, and though we only gave four performances a week, yet the rest of the time was employed in memorizing the new parts and in constant rehearsals, keeping every one hard at work.

It may seem strange that I, the wife of the manager, should be obliged to play so many parts, of which some were uninteresting and subordinate, yet the explanation of the question is very simple. I became quite a favorite of the public, and my name drew better houses. There was no selection made of the plays in which I could have what is now called "star parts." The management was obliged to present what was the newest and the most popular in the repertoire without regard to any particular person in the cast.

Life was a dream to me, and it stands before me now as some vision, half sweet and half bitter, too dim to be seen quite distinctly, too distant for detail.

In the spring of 1865 a great sorrow fell upon me, and its blow made the world dark for me. My little daughter Marylka died.

They say that misfortunes never come singly, but are accompanied by other misfortunes, forming a long-linked chain. Blow after blow struck my heart and bruised it to the core. Family considerations do not allow me to give the details of all I suffered at that time; but after fearful struggles with inexorable Fate, I found myself free, but ill and at the point of death. My mother and my brother Felix brought me and my little son Rudolphe to Cracow, and I never saw Mr. Modjeski again.

CHAPTER XVI

In the month of September, 1865, I signed a contract with the Cracow theatrical management. The old endowed theatre of my native city was at that time in the care of Count Adam Skorupka, a cultured gentleman of wit, a great dilettante, and his partner, Stanislas Kozmian, one of the most cultivated men of Cracow.

They started a new era which in the annals of Polish stage history cannot be ignored. The whole personnel of the theatre was changed, new actors and actresses came into view, and only a few of the best old stock were retained.

Count Skorupka, led by the true spirit of a reformer, brought an artistic stage director from Warsaw, Mr. Jasinski, who proved to be the animating spirit of the whole institution, as well as a perfect and accomplished instructor. His gray hair and his bearing inspired respect, and his kindness and knowledge, love and admiration.

I shall never forget my first rehearsal under his direction, which was the first reading rehearsal of the season. He stood on the stage with Mr. Kozmian, as the actors and actresses were coming in. All were summoned to be present. When the last actor entered, Mr. Kozmian introduced Mr. Jasinski to the company and delivered a short speech on his merits, upon which Mr. Jasinski hastened to assure the company of his best efforts towards the needed improvements, and then added:—

"I hope that you will help me, and that we shall work in unison with but one view, — the good of the stage." The company cheered, and then Mr. Kozmian introduced each of us to the director. He shook hands with every one in a most cordial way, and when the ceremony was over, he invited those who had parts in the play we were about to rehearse, to step into the reading-room. There he read the title of the play, and explained in what way it had to be treated, and also described the chief characters to us, then turned to the prompter and gave him the order to be ready. A muffled bell gave sign, and the reading began.

Two days later the stage rehearsal was announced. Though there were only a few characters in the play, the whole company was present; some stayed behind the scenes, and some occupied the boxes and chairs in front, and yet they were so quiet that no sound was heard but the words uttered by the players on the stage or by the director, on whose remarks every ear was hanging with most enthusiastic attention. The occasion seemed almost religiously solemn; every heart was warmed up with the expectation of doing fine, artistic work and the future triumphs of the Cracow stage.

The play was "Solomon," a tragedy in verse by Waclaw Szymanowski, a talented writer and editor of the *Warsaw Courier*, the subject of a mediæval conflict between Jews and Christians, treated in a conciliatory way.

My part of Judith was full of fine sentiments, but too passive to be highly interesting. When I recited my part, Mr. Jasinski said nothing, but he rubbed his forehead several times and looked at me in such a way that I knew he had some remarks to make. Yet he kept silent until the fourth act, when I had a long speech to deliver, during which he showed very distinct signs of impatience; he tapped irritatingly with his foot on the floor, rubbed his forehead more and more excitedly, then, after I finished the sentence, said abruptly:—

"This is a very pretty opera, your voice is beautiful, but your sing-song is entirely out of place." I was so mortified that the tears rose to my eyes, and I scarcely saw when he came to me. He took my hand and told me not to take his remark too much to heart, but to try to change my delivery; then he added:—

"Your gestures, voice, expressions of your face, are good; the only fault lies in the reading of the verses. If you stay here after the rehearsal, I will read the part for you. Alexandrine verses are very difficult to deliver, unless you treat them in a certain measure like prose." I wiped my eyes and thanked him heartily, for it was just the thing I wanted to ask of him.

When the rehearsal was over and every one gone, even the prompter, Mr. Jasinski read the lines, and it was a revelation. It seemed as if a new window opened in my brain and flooded it with light. Until then I had read Alexandrines very carefully, putting the emphasis on the centre and the ending syllable of the verse. He, on the contrary, read the lines naturally and very simply, disregarding their music, and only careful of meaning and expression, still pronouncing every word distinctly and with respect for the rhythm. He did not lose one syllable, and yet the verses sounded like poetic prose rather than rhymed Alexandrines.

I drank in all, returned home, restudied my part, and when I rehearsed next morning I saw Mr. Jasinski's eyes dance with pleasure. After the first act he shook me by the hand, and said he never expected me to get rid so soon of my sing-song.

"Some of the actors," he said, "will keep it forever; they simply cannot get hold of the Alexandrine verses without making tedious drawled-out tirades," and then he added: "You are brave and you show the true spirit, which is to be praised in a person who has already been" . . . here he paused, then added with a most subtle and slightly malicious smile, "a *so-called* 'star,' petted by the audiences and spoiled by the critics. You see I know something about you." I laughed and thanked him again, and on the night of the performance I played well, for I knew that my master was pleased with me.

The Cracow stock company was completed with new forces: Swieszewski, a charming juvenile actor from Warsaw; my brother, Felix Benda; Ladnowski, a dramatic lover; Rapacki, in character parts; Hennig, an excellent comedian; and several others besides six charming or talented actresses in various parts. They were all there except Antonina Hofman, the leading lady, who was taking her vacation, and only arrived on the evening of the performance of "Solomon." I had met Antonina Hofman, the leading lady, at my brother's house, two years before I joined the profession, and we had become friends. She treated me with friendly condescension, and I loved and admired her. She was a handsome woman, with great brown eyes, red lips, and marvellous chestnut hair, very thick, and reaching below her knees. She was highly gifted and much more experienced than I, so it was natural that, when she came behind the scenes after the performance, I should greet her with the joy and respect due to her position and genuine talent. She shook hands with me, but her eyes had a searching, scrutinizing look. It seemed to me that she was not the same person I had loved so much. I had a moment of desperate fear, lest I should lose her friendship because of my success, and without even waiting for a confidential talk I hastened to inform her that I had come to Cracow to learn, that I intended to occupy a secondary position, and had no claim to the tragic heroines, Judith being only one of my débutante parts and not even of my choice.[1]

"You are wise," was her rather cool answer; "you are

[1] It is still the custom in Europe to give to an actor or actress, who is going to be engaged, three good parts for a trial. These parts may be chosen by the actor or by the management.

very wise, because you could not possibly play dramatic heroines." I had no doubt that she spoke those words in kindness and with conviction, but I received them as a sting. They did hurt. I had no word of answer but "Good-night," and returned slowly to my dressing-room. I did not tell her that Mr. Jasinski had offered me several dramatic heroines, that I had refused his offer, saying that they would be safer in the leading lady's hands, and how he received my refusal.

He had said: "I do not understand you. You are adapted to those parts, and it is foolish not to seize the opportunity." I told him that I was afraid to handle them, and it would be better to wait for Madame Hofman, and give her the choice.

"Oh, very well," he said, pettishly, "I will not bother you with good parts any more," and he turned away from me.

As I was taking off my semi-Oriental costume, I thought of my master's words, and of Madame Hofman's cool answer, and when I compared these two opinions a feeling of deep resentment grew in my soul towards the woman I had loved as my friend. When I remembered how I had almost offended Mr. Jasinski for her sake, I felt very uneasy.

Sleep did not come to me that night. I was brooding over it all until the bed became unbearable. I got up and walked up and down, trying to quiet my excited nerves. One of my turns around the room brought me close to a mirror, and looking up I saw suddenly my face bearing such a dramatic expression that I stopped to look closer at the reflection, and then, slapping my forehead with the palm of my hand, I exclaimed:—

"Now I see why Mr. Jasinski wants me to play the emotional and tragic parts. Well, I will play all the heroines he gives me!" With that resolution I went back to bed and fell soundly asleep. Next morning I went to the theatre early, half an hour before the beginning of the rehearsal, knowing that I should find my master at his post, as he always came at least fifteen minutes ahead. I had not long to wait before I saw him enter the stage. When he saw me, he said "Good-morning," and paying no more attention to me, he began to examine some new scenery. I came up to him and said timidly:—

"I wish to speak to you, Mr. Jasinski." He then turned to me and said abruptly, though kindly:—

"What is it, child?" I told him I came to apologize for having rejected the parts he offered me, and having changed my mind, I came to assure him that henceforth I would play whatever he gave me, and that I put myself entirely under his guidance. He smiled, and shaking my hand, said:—

"Since you are in your senses again, I am going to try what you can do. Come to my office to-morrow, and I shall have the parts ready for you."

When I came next morning, the first thing that drew my attention was a pile of manuscripts on the desk.

"You may as well look at them," he said, smiling; "they are the parts you will have to play in the course of the season."

"All these!" I exclaimed with rapture.

"Yes; there are sixty of them, small and big ones."

Sixty parts! What luxury! I picked them up, hugged them, then sat in the chair and began to examine them. The one on top was Princess Eboli in "Don Carlos," by Schiller; the next one, Louise Miller in "Kabale und Liebe," by the same author; then Barbara in a tragedy by Felinski; Ophelia in "Hamlet"; Dona Sol in Victor Hugo's "Ernani"; the wife in "Nos Intimes," by Sardou; "Adrienne Lecouvreur," by Scribe and Legouvé; etc. There were among them sparkling parts of the old and new repertoire, and also some short parts in one-act comedies, sketches, and plays with songs called vaudevilles. I was so much absorbed in looking over my treasures that I did not notice when Mr. Jasinski left the office. I wrapped up the parts and then looked for him, but he was not to be found anywhere. I grabbed my precious package and hastened home, where I gloated over my booty.

I played small parts, and everything seemed to run smoothly between the leading lady and me until the tragedy "Barbara" was called for rehearsal with my name in the title rôle. Mme. Hofman, not aware of my altered decision as to the choice of my parts, was much astonished, and spoke to me about it. It was one of those moments which are not easily forgotten. I answered with great reserve, saying that I had changed my resolution of staying behind all the time, and Mr. Jasinski was kind enough to help me to try my strength in tragedy. She was sarcastic, and being very witty, she had her laugh. Yet we parted good friends. It was only after the performance of "Barbara" that we became rivals, and my line on the stage was defined.

My success in the tragic heroines did not prevent me from playing smaller parts. I also played two or three secondary parts in the plays belonging to the old repertoire in which Mme. Hofman had made a success. It was interesting, because the audience on those nights divided in two camps, one party calling for Hofman and the other for Modjeska.[1]

In "Don Carlos" I made my first complete success. The part of the Princess Eboli fell to my share, while Antonina Hofman played the queen. If she failed in the part, it was her own fault. She could have played the queen beautifully had she cared to pay proper attention to the lines. She was full of spirit during the rehearsals, chaffing and

[1] The European audiences outside of England always call out the name of the actor whom they desire before the curtain. If by chance some one undesired takes the call, they hiss the person off the stage.

joking and making everybody merry with her witty sallies. The result was that on the night of the performance she had to depend too much on the prompter, was often flustered, hesitated, and missed her points. I, on the contrary, having to appear together with my talented rival, took all the pains possible to work out my part: in the first place, I was "dead-letter perfect," and threw all my soul into my acting; in consequence, I did not miss one point, one studied intonation, nor what we call here "stage business." On that evening Antonina's camp was almost silent and mine very noisy. Even Mr. Kozmian, who was her ardent admirer and friend, came behind the scenes and congratulated me on my success.

As far as I can remember, "Don Carlos" was put on the Cracow stage late in January, 1866, a few weeks after Mr. Jasinski returned to Warsaw, where his studies called him. In consequence I had worked my part of Princess Eboli without his help and was rather proud of myself; it gave me confidence in my own talent and made me less timid.

After that memorable evening my name began to creep slowly into the *Warsaw* and also into some of the German papers. During my first season in Cracow I received a great many favors from the people, and my standing was quite assured. Antonina Hofman, however, held her own against me in character and high comedy parts, in which she was indeed excellent.

CHAPTER XVII

It was at that time I came in contact with many of the superior minds and celebrities of Poland.

Mr. Matejko, our celebrated artist, was then the most striking figure in Cracow. He was recognized in Poland and abroad as a painter of great force and expression. The French Academy granted him a gold medal, and many of his historical pictures were exhibited all over Europe.

One day, however, quite unexpectedly, he was introduced to me by Mr. Estreicher in the court of the Jagellon Library, where I used to get historical books, or copy costumes. I was just about to play a part in a play of a remote period, and was hunting for a sketch of a suitable dress for it. I could not find it in the library. It would have been quite proper to ask Mr. Matejko to help me in the matter, but I was so overcome by the presence of the great master that I could not say anything beyond a commonplace expression of my good fortune in meeting him, and then blushed furiously at my own stupidity. Happily Mr. Estreicher was there, and he explained my object in visiting the library. I don't remember what the master said — probably he said nothing, or almost as much. Shortly after this interview one of my fellow-actors, Vincent Rapacki, later a foremost actor of Warsaw, who used to visit the celebrated painter, brought me the desired sketch, which Mr. Matejko had drawn for me. I prize highly the little figure of my heroine, which is still among my treasures.

The next prominent man I met was Joseph Szujski. He was a historian of great knowledge, and a successful playwright, a man of great erudition, of noble soul, and with a heart which melted at every sympathetic touch.

Another playwright, but of totally different nature, because he wrote only comedies in prose, — amusing and characteristic plays of modern life, — was Michal Balucki, who soon became a great favorite with the Cracow audiences, and later grew famous all over the country. He was a child of the people, witty, alert, Bohemian, and an awfully good fellow. His sarcasms were never offensive, because they were never biting or scorching, but irresistibly funny.

There are others of whom I shall speak later, people of great merit and talent. I found myself in the midst of different elements which offered me a great scope for observation. During that first season in Cracow I also became acquainted with the true aristocrats of the country. The Countess Arthur Potocka, though quite advanced in years, was steadily assisting the theatrical performances.

This life among superior minds, artists, men and women of culture, combined with occasional glimpses of the exclusive aristocratic circles, was very beneficial to my artistic development.

One day Countess Arthur Potocka sent Mr. Rembowski, her confidential friend, to me, and that irreproachable gentleman asked me in her name to pay her a visit. I found the countess dressed in black. Her pale, aristocratic face in a frame of silvery hair and black lace, the lace shawl and flounces falling around her form in soft folds, gave her the air of an antique portrait. She was sitting in a large, low, arm-chair. There were other persons in the room, but I saw only her.

After the usual greetings, she introduced me to some of the members of her family and her friends. I was all eyes and ears, anxious to find out what made such a distinction between a high-born lady and an average rich woman of the city. I had not been with these exquisite creatures fifteen minutes before I discovered the secret: those aristocratic ladies were utterly simple, without a grain of snobbishness in their manner. Their grace was like the grace of children, unconscious of their beautiful movements, which, however, were marked with reserve acquired through early training.

They also had beautiful soft voices, which they never raised above a certain diapason, without, however, rendering their speech monotonous. They also had a most distinct and correct pronunciation, giving their words their full value, and paying the due tribute to the grammar. No provincialisms and not the slightest trace of the *argot*,[1] so popular among the "city people," as the nobility called all those who did not belong to their circle. Some of them, alas, knew more of the French language than their own, and sprinkled their talk with French words and phrases. The old countess, however, and the members of her family, spoke the most correct Polish. The countess was simply delightful in all she said. There was wisdom, wit, and manners combined with inexpressible kindness. She was clever, good, charitable, and also versed in matters of art and literature, possessed of that rare gift of conversation which was an art by itself in the past, and which is almost extinct in our modern age.

After some general conversation, she called me to sit near her. That was the sign for the others to retire. In a few minutes I was left alone with the countess, or Madame Arthur, as she was called all through Poland. She then asked me some questions about my brother Felix, who was one of her favorite actors; then she spoke about my parts, criticising some of my acting, and praising what was worth praising. Her judgment was just and most kind. She said she thought I was unsuited to certain parts, but she was much pleased with my romantic personations and also

[1] Slang.

with some of the characters in high comedy. She had seen Rachel and Ristori, and told me I had neither their strong ringing voice nor their tragic, statuesque poses.

"You see," said she, "they were born with those gifts, and God created you differently. You have, instead of those grand qualities, sensitiveness, intuition, grace;" and then she added, laughing, "You are as clever as a snake. You played the other evening the countess in 'The White Camelia' as if you were born among us. Where did you meet countesses?"

I answered that she was the only great lady I had ever laid eyes on.

"You see," said she, "that was *intuition*. Other actresses, when they represent women of nobility, or princesses and queens, walk with a straight, rigid spine, as if they had swallowed a stick. They sometimes in modern comedies resort to a lorgnette, looking snobbishly on people and examining them from head to foot, with a silly, supercilious smile. Thank Heaven, you have none of that insipid nonsense. You are simple, and that is right."

I was so happy to see how much interest she took in me that I did not know what to say. I could only thank her with my eyes. Breaking suddenly a moment of silence, she said, changing her tone of voice, and smiling mischievously:—

"I hear that you snubbed my son Adam." I knew what she meant, but you who will read this do not, so I might as well tell about the incident which the countess described as the snubbing of the Count Adam:—

I was in the greenroom just repeating the lines of the part I had to play that evening, when Mr. Kozmian entered with a tall gentleman and introduced him to me. I was so absorbed in my part that the name sounded distant in my ears, and I had scarcely noticed the visitor's face. I shook hands and excused myself, saying that it was near my entrance, and then hid in the remotest corner behind the scenes, concentrating my mind upon the part and waiting for my cue.

Next afternoon in one of the parks there was a fair for some charity, and I was placed in one of the booths. While I was discussing the merits of a new book with Mr. X., — a writer and a newspaper man, — a very handsome, tall, and distinguished-looking man approached the booth. Taking off his hat and extending his hand to me, he said: —

"How is your health, Madame Modjeska?" I did not recognize him, and without taking his hand, I asked him quite impertinently: —

"To whom have I the honor of speaking?" The count smiled, and said quite politely: —

"I am Adam Potocki. I had the honor of an introduction to you last evening at the theatre." It was like a slap in my face; such manners, such politeness, and the consciousness of the mistake I had made. Yet I did not make much of a case of it. Men in all stations are only men, and women have to be on their guard. I apologized sincerely and we chatted merrily awhile; then purchasing some insignificant object, for which he paid royally, he took leave; and when he was at some distance I was startled by the distressed exclamation of my literary friend: —

"Oh, Madame Modjeska, what have you done? You have snubbed and insulted the King of Cracow.[1] What did you do that for?"

"Oh, nonsense!" I exclaimed. "I did not recognize him, that was all!"

"Not recognize Adam Potocki!" he almost wailed, opening wide his eyes until they grew quite round and white; "why, there is not another man like him in the country!"

"Do not be so distressed," I said, trying to comfort him.

[1] A surname given to the count by the Cracow people.

"I am sure the count understood my mistake, and did not feel offended in the least. On the contrary, he seemed highly amused." But my friend only shrugged his shoulders, and saying dolefully, "Good-by," he left my booth. Evidently he thought I was a most absurd person and an iconoclast.

When I started to repeat my story to the countess, she interrupted me, saying:—

"Oh, pray, do not excuse yourself. I am not angry with you. On the contrary, I am very much pleased." At this moment a tall, handsome woman with a superb crown of brown hair entered the room. "And by the way," added the countess, "I must introduce you to my son's wife." Then, turning to the lady who had just come in, she called, "Katherine! I want you to know Madame Modjeska."

After a few minutes' talk I took my leave, but I met the countess again; and when thirteen years later I was sailing for America, a photograph of her, framed in ebony and ivory, was sent to me in her name, and brought tears to my eyes. All the regret for my young past, for the kind hearts I was leaving behind, rushed to my mind at the sight of that noble face, which I never expected to see again.

At that time I worked very hard. On the mornings which followed the off nights I used to get up at five o'clock, and after the usual cup of coffee for breakfast I went into the open air with my part, sometimes to the Chestnut Alley, but more often to the Botanical Gardens, where I was sure not to meet any one at an early hour. I studied aloud, having for accompaniment the songs of the birds, trees and flowers for inspiration, and, above all, the wonderful gray or blue sky with its fantastic clouds.

My married brother Felix, who was also a member of the company, and in whose house I then lived, was a great help in my studies. We used to rehearse at all hours, without regard for the proper time or place: at the supper-table after the performance, behind the scenes during the rehearsals, and mostly during our walks in the fields or under the chestnut trees of the Grand Alley. At the dinner-table we were often rebuked by my mother or my brother's beautiful wife for these eternal rehearsals. Felix would ask between the courses:—

"Helena, how does that scene begin?" and then we started. Sometimes we would discuss the meaning of the words, and in case we did not agree, we fell into such a heated argument that we had to be called to order. At other times we would find such natural expression for our lines that mother would take it for simple conversation, and then there was my brother's triumphant exclamation:—

"You see, Helena, that was well done. Mother thinks we are having a chat."

We often played those one-act French comedies where only two characters were required. Mr. Kozmian was so pleased with the originality and exactness of our acting that he looked for more of those pieces for us. We liked them because they were holidays after the heavy tragedies and national dramas (Felix used to call them national bombs) we had to perform at the rate of at least once a week. Very often I had to be perfect at the rehearsals, twice a week, in a rhymed tragedy. Happily I had a very good memory, and I loved my work. Strange to say, a little one-act play, though far from taxing physical strength, required often more work than a five-act drama, because it had to be perfect in the minutest details, in order to gain the approval of our rather difficult audience.

But it was not only by hard work that I gained my position on the stage. There was something else; it was by identifying myself with every part I played to such an extent that I really passed through all the emotions of my heroines. I suffered with them, cried real tears, which I often could not stop even after the curtain was down.

Owing to this extreme sensitiveness I was exhausted after each emotional part, and often had to rest motionless after the play until my strength returned. I tried hard to master my emotions, but during my whole career I could not succeed in giving a performance without feeling the agonies of my heroines.

I went through a wonderful training during the three years of my Cracow engagement. There was but little time for amusement. The time free from studies was employed in reading and also in such prosaic occupations as sewing, or ironing of muslins and laces, and often when I had a little time to spare I helped in arranging some finery for my sister-in-law, Veronique Benda, who was also on the stage. I do not recollect going to parties, save to those given twice a year by the manager, Count Skorupka; one dancing party during the Carnival and another at Easter time, and then I danced! Oh, how I danced! with all my soul in it, for I never did anything by halves.

Still I preferred the few receptions at my brother's house, where the artistic and literary element was represented and where many an interesting discussion took place. It was my delight to listen to wise men. Every one of those evenings opened some cells in my brain, and the seed of uttered words fell on a receptive soil, for, once shut in my room, I recalled to my memory every original or clever thought I had heard during the evening; I turned them over and over in my mind, though not without comments on my part or criticisms in case of contradictory opinions. I sometimes wrote down my impressions and kept the notes for future use.

One evening there was a question whether ethics and art ought to go hand in hand. Some young men present positively declared that these two had nothing to do with each other. The wise men, on the contrary, said that art without ethics is not long-lived. It may have some vogue at the moment for its boldness and defiance, but it is sure of dying soon of consumption. A loud protest rose in the opposite camp:—

"Had Terence died? Had the jovial, immoral Rabelais died?"

"No, indeed," sounded the answer; "they live still, but who reads them now? They are stored in the libraries for the students of ancient and mediæval literature, but they do not live with the people, as Shakespeare, Dante, Molière, Schiller, and Goethe."

"Ah, Goethe!" cried one of the opponents; "nice ethics he preaches,—in 'Stella,' for instance."

"True enough," said the wise men, "but we must speak of the work, not of the individuals. Goethe wrote those things, so did others,—even Shakespeare,—but they are never presented on the stage, because of outraged ethics;[1] but the work created during that phase cannot outlive its existence, and must die of its own fever, which, strange to say, is often mistaken for inspiration."

[1] In almost every author's life there is a phase of revolt against moral principles.

CHAPTER XVIII

In the year of 1866 the Count Skorupka sent our company to Posen for the summer months. Mr. Kozmian was then appointed manager of our troupe. His name, which was already celebrated in the Grand Duchy of Posen, his cousin, Mgr. Jan Kozmian, being one of the most remarkable men of the country, added a great deal to his popularity, but the prosperity of the season was mainly due to the excellent training of the company and also to the talented men and women, like my brother, Felix Benda, Rapacki, Ladnowski, Antonina Hofman, and many others. We revived the best plays of our repertoire before the public; which, almost starved on a diet of hackneyed melodramas and old-fashioned plays, received everything we presented with great enthusiasm.

Karol Bozenta Chlapowski in 1866.

My brother became at once the favorite of the city; so did the others, but not in quite so large a measure as he. He jumped, so to say, at once to the hearts of the people, while the others had to creep in by degrees.

During the summer of 1866 I met my present husband, Karol Bozenta Chlapowski. It was at the theatre that I first saw him. I was playing an insignificant part which I understudied for one of the minor actresses who fell ill suddenly on the day of the performance. No one in the company had as good a memory as I, and though the part was small, yet it was written in rhymed verse, and therefore Mr. Kozmian asked me to help him out of the difficulty. The play was one of Count Fredo's classic comedies, and required great care in reading the lines. I rehearsed in the morning and played the part at night. During the play I had a great deal of time to fill up with some action between speeches. The intervals were long, and during one of them, while sitting up stage with my supposed lover, I did a thing I always avoided doing: I looked at the audience. The first face that drew my attention was Mr. Chlapowski's. He sat in the second tier box next to the stage, leaning over the balustrade, his chin on both folded arms, eagerly looking down on the stage.

His mobile face, a slightly sarcastic smile, and the absorbed interest with which he caught the slightest shadings in the actor's words and actions drew my attention. I watched him awhile, then I asked my stage lover, who knew almost every one in town, who that intelligent-looking young man was. When I heard his name I was pleasantly surprised, for I knew already his cousin, Tadeusz Chlapowski, General Chlapowski's younger son, who also sat in the same box in the background.

After the play they both came behind the scenes, and Karol Chlapowski was introduced to me by his cousin. The very next day both of them called on me, and Mr. Karol was re-introduced. During an interesting talk with him I was surprised to find so much learning and such marvellous gifts of conversation in a young man of twenty-five.

He was also charmingly absent-minded, and while he

talked he took a cigarette case out of his pocket and lit a cigarette without asking permission; then suddenly seeing a faint smile on my lips, he put it all burning into his pocket, apologizing humbly for the mistake. I hastened to assure him that I was used to tobacco, having been brought up with four brothers, but I did it chiefly to save his coat from burning inside. After thanking me most effusively for my "kindness," he resumed the conversation. He told me that three years ago he left the University of Louevain in order to join Dictator Langiewicz's corps during the recent Insurrection. He was wounded and sent back to his estate across the border. After having recovered, he was going to rejoin the insurgents, but was arrested by the Prussians and put in prison, in "Moabit" in Berlin, together with many other young Poles, where he remained twenty months. While he was telling us this episode of his life, he noticed the sad expression of the faces around him, and

BOZENTA CHLAPOWSKI (on the left) AND HIS FRIEND SYP. NEIWICZ IN PRISON DURING THE POLISH INSURRECTION.

rising quickly he laughed, and going to the piano, said: —

"Enough of this grewsome past. I will sing you some new Levasseem's songs. But I warn you that my voice, though rather small, is quite unpleasant to the ear." With that he sang with quite a French *entrain* and English accent the famous song of the day, called "Le Cochon de Barbarie." It was just after our midday dinner, and black coffee had been served in the parlor. He wanted his coffee right on the piano, on the place where the candles usually stand. In one moment, while he turned on the piano stool, the cup and coffee were both inside of the instrument. Happily it was only an old rented piano, and no great damage was done. This slight accident put us all in a good humor, and when Mr. Karol left us we had a feeling of knowing him for years. Leaving the room, he turned once more and said: —

"I must tell you that, having nothing better to do at present, I am writing notices about your company." I asked him if he desired to be bribed, upon which he bowed, kissed my hand, and said, "My desire is to write honestly what I think."

And indeed he wrote honestly, for the first thing I came across in the morning paper was a severe dissection of my acting in a one-act French comedy. I liked him for his sincerity all the more, for I knew he was right. This little play was put on in a hurry. It was a revival, but I had never played the part before. I was just studying Juliet, and could not concentrate my mind on anything else. I was so absent-minded that I left the veil over my face during almost half an act, instead of lifting it up at the entrance. I also missed one cue, and did not speak until I was prompted, and all together I was a little constrained in my actions. I had no idea, however, that any one would notice those blunders, but he noticed everything.

Playing only the revivals during our short season in Posen, I had a great deal of time on hand, and was very anxious to study some new parts. I dreamed always of Shakespeare and his plays. We had had nothing but Hamlet in the repertoire until then. I talked about it often to Ladnowski, our romantic lover, who also was a great admirer of Shakespeare. We both were anxious to have one or two of his plays produced during our coming winter season, and to try them on the Posen audience. I spoke to Mr. Kozmian, and he, after a justifiable moment of hesitation, consented to produce Romeo and Juliet. Ladnowski was to be Romeo, and the part of Juliet was sent to me, together with the manuscript.

I had never seen or even read Romeo and Juliet before, and I simply went wild over it. I remember that in my excitement I walked up and down in my room, exclaiming:—

"How great! How beautiful! What a genius! How he, though a man, knew Juliet's feelings and thoughts! There is no other being in the world who can compete with Shakespeare! He is the greatest of the great!" etc. I invoked the spirit of the great man and laid my spirit at his feet. All the time I spent in studying Juliet I walked in a dream, repeating the lines and looking for solitary places in public gardens in order to get the atmosphere of certain scenes. I used to go for long evening walks with my brother, his wife, and Ladnowski, and in some quiet nook among the trees we rehearsed the balcony scene to try our hushed voices in the open. One evening we went to the cemetery, and I repeated the tomb scene, and also my soliloquy in the fourth act. In order to get the atmosphere of the parting scene I spent a sleepless night, and at the first glimpse of light went into the open air. I had been up at dawn many a time before, but the grand awakening of nature had never had so much meaning, it had never given me such a splendid poetic impression as on that morning, when I awaited the rising of the sun with Shakespeare's lines in my very heart and soul.

How I played Juliet then, I cannot tell now. I mean I cannot give the details. When I played it in English I changed some of the scenes, but not the conception of the part. Of that first performance I have only a vague recollection, yet I remember two things distinctly: the way in which Ladnowski and I treated the balcony scene and the effect produced on the audience.

As I said before, Ladnowski and myself studied the balcony scene in the open, and we tried to tune our voices to the surroundings. The scene was spoken in hushed voices all through; every sentence came out with spontaneity, passion, and simplicity. Those two lovers hung on each other's words with almost childish intensity. Juliet's words at times came out broken with quick sighs, indicating the heightened pulse, and accompanied by furtive glances around the place, expressive of fear lest some dreaded kinsman should appear suddenly. The scene was a crescendo, from the softness of the speech to the hurried words they exchanged towards the end:—

Romeo. "So thrive my soul."

Juliet (breaking in hurriedly). "A thousand times good-night;"

then from the return of the lovers until the end the words growing softer and more and more dreamy.

As for so-called stage business, there was almost none. One single rose taken from Juliet's hair, kissed and thrown to Romeo with the words, "I would kill you with much cherishing." That was all. What we looked after was the intensity of the situation, to which we tried to fit our mood and our voices, which remained hushed and yet audible even to the last seat in the gallery.

When the curtain fell, there was a dead silence, which

made me shiver with apprehension of failure, but after a few seconds of stillness, which seemed to me ages, a storm of applause arose and we were recalled ten times before the curtain.

One other detail I remember. In the parting scene I did not use a four-posted bed, as I have seen it done often. I did not think that Juliet slept in a matrimonial couch, but that, on the contrary, her virginal bed was probably narrow, such as the girls use all over Europe. Juliet's single bed was placed in one corner of the stage, overhung with curtains. It was my belief that in that poetic scene Shakespeare had not intended to give an impression of sensuousness. These two children are unconscious of their passion. They meet because they love, because they want to be together, to hear each other's voices, and to look in each other's eyes, and cherish and kiss or die. If they succumb to the natural law and the calling of their southern blood, it is not done with premeditation. There is no necessity, either, to remind the audience what had just happened in Juliet's room by such naturalistic details as a disarranged four-posted bed, or the turning of the key of a locked door at the nurse's entrance, or Romeo's lacing his jerkin, and a dishevelled Juliet in a *crêpe de chine* nightgown. Such details are cheap illustrations and unworthy of a true artist. Shakespeare's plays do not require such commonplace interpretations in order to produce a genuine, vivid, and refining impression upon the audience.

CHAPTER XIX

I MET Mr. Chlapowski quite often while we stayed in Posen, either at our house or in the public gardens, or in society, and we always had most interesting talks about literature, art, or politics. Having been brought up in France, he was more acquainted with French than with his native language. In consequence he often spoke to me in French, and urged me seriously to perfect myself in it. He brought me books and made me acquainted with Alfred de Musset. He also read to me from Chateaubriand and Lamartine, and I read to him in exchange verses of the great Polish poets. He admired my Polish, I admired his French, and while I corrected slight mistakes he made in his native tongue, he took a great deal of pains to correct my bad French.

I occupied then a modest suite of rooms with my brother and his wife. Two of my windows overlooked the street. On the day of the performance I made a rule never to receive callers, and of course this rule extended also to Pan Karol, as his friends called him. But he was ingenious, and found means of seeing me by riding on horseback under my windows. When I heard the horse's hoofs on the pavement, I could not resist looking down, and then I received a sweeping bow and a "good afternoon" which made me stronger for my night's work.

When we were leaving Posen, Mr. Chlapowski and I parted cheerfully, for we were sure to meet sometime in the near future. He promised to come to Cracow during our winter season.

After leaving Posen we went to Krynica, with the intention of playing there until the end of August. Krynica is a health resort in the Carpathian Mountains, charmingly situated among the pines and rocks and with a grand view of the distant hills. There we lived in a large house built in the mountaineer style. Some members of our company, with myself and family, rented this house, in which we lived as in a phalanstery. There were, besides myself, Mr. Rapacki and his wife, Ladnowski's family, my brother and his wife and step-daughter, three young men, a juvenile young lady, and a comedian, all living in the same house. They were all congenial, animated by the same feeling for art, — all young with the exception of two elderly men, — all healthy and full of spirits.

My mother, my little son, my little niece Stasia, and I occupied two rooms on the second floor, and we had a lovely balcony overhung with ivy, shaded by tall pine trees on one side, while the other allowed full view of the mountains. It was a cosy corner where my mother and I in moments of leisure used to sit, read, work, or watch my little son playing.

There was, however, one inconvenience in that house. The walls being made only of plain boards, were so thin and so full of cracks that, although we covered them with rugs and stopped the cracks, placing etchings over the patches, yet we could hear almost every loud word said in the house.

It was a real "charivari" every morning at the awakening of the phalanstery. We had for our neighbors on one side Ladnowski and his friend, and on the other side the comedian, Mikulski. Lying still in my bed, I could hear every word that was said upstairs, and even downstairs, for in the morning all the windows in the house were opened, even on rainy days. It was such a motley of thoughts and comic phrases, interwoven with sentences from parts, which always were studied aloud without regard to time or surroundings. Very often late at night someone repeating a part would wake us up with a tragic exclamation or sentence like this: "Away, villain, or I strangle you!" and then "strangle you" would be repeated a dozen times in different tones and with increased intensity.

Once the shrill laugh of a maniac frightened my poor mother out of her bed and made her say a prayer for distracted souls. When I happened to be up earlier, I would take paper and pencil and write down what I heard. This is what I find among my notes: —

Boleslaw Ladnowski (Romeo) was a great lover of poetry, and he even wrote sometimes very charming verses. He had a habit of reciting aloud the poems of our great masters. Suddenly stopping at the end of some line he would stamp his foot and exclaim: —

"Almighty God! What a genius that man was!" Upon which his friend would say, in sleepy tones of voice: —

"Yes, genius indeed! But look here, — I put on this collar only for an hour last night, and it is already useless! May all the ducks kick it![1] Another three cents gone!" . . . Ladnowski's voice still rang, reciting the celebrated verses of Mickiewicz's "Farys": "Ye forests, ye mountains, peace! peace!"

"Will that crank never stop reciting?" sounded the voice of the comedian.

"Oh, are you up?" spoke Ladnowski's father. "Knight of free thoughts, defender of virtue, how did you sleep?"

"With my eyes shut, dearest patriarch."

"But your mouth was open; you snored all night!"

"Nonsense, youths of sixty, like me, never snore."

"Oh, youth, lend me thy wings!" came from Romeo's room again.

[1] A favorite swearing among actors, invented in order to avoid profanity, yet to supply relief in moments of annoyance.

"Panie Mikulski, Panie Mikulski," called from downstairs Madame Rapacka's sweet voice, "what are you doing there?"

"Cleaning the mushrooms I gathered at sunrise. I thought the ladies might like them for dinner."

"Could you not do it at the creek? The water drips down here and splashes all over the hall."

"Oh, does the water drip down? A thousand pardons, madame, but I cannot manage to make it drip up. However, we will remove ourselves, mushrooms and your obedient servant."

"This way, this way, my pretty maidens," spoke the juvenile man. "The lady who wants to buy your strawberries lives in that room; but will you not sell me some? How much do you say? Yes, I will give you five cents, but I must have a kiss in addition." Upon that a girlish scream was heard, and my mother left the room to stop the enterprising youth's further jokes. Two mountain girls, as pretty and fresh as the berries they carried in earthen pots, entered the room, and while we were relieving them of their burdens, we could hear Ladnowski's voice still repeating:—

"Ye forests, ye mountains, peace! peace!"

We lived in that house as one family. No project was made but that the whole phalanstery took part in it, be it a walk to the woods or a day's excursion to the hills. These excursions were executed mostly on foot, for money was scarce among us; all we could afford was a guide, who carried our luncheon and rugs. Some of us carried parts, for though we only played revivals, yet we were preparing a repertoire for the first months of the winter season in Cracow; and when an hour or two of rest came, sitting on rocks covered with moss we read our parts, having for a background the greenest branches of evergreen, the fantastic sky, and breathing the superb, cool air of the wilderness.

At six o'clock in the evening we had to be back and ready for work.

Mr. Kozmian was not at all pleased with the fact that the best forces of the company lived in one house in friendly harmony. It was soon proved that his displeasure was grounded on good reasons, for one day the phalanstery arranged a strike. I do not remember the real cause of these proceedings, but I know that we all thought at that time that the plays put upon the bills were below our dignity. Most of them were bad melodramas put on in order to attract the rustics in the neighborhood. One day, after rehearsing one of these pitiful concoctions, I was informed that the phalanstery had decided to strike, and that I had to be with them or against them. Without a moment's hesitation I agreed to be with them. After having decided that none of us would appear at the theatre in the evening, a messenger was sent with a paper to Mr. Kozmian, informing him of our resolution. When our envoy came back we all eagerly asked:—

"What was the manager's answer?"

"Oh, he said nothing," said the boy; "he laughed, and then sent the property man to the box-office with the order to close 'the shop.'"

This happened on a rainy day, and we had to face the prospects of spending at least ten or twelve hours shut up in the house. Our spirits, so high in the morning, began to drop to a lower degree. Some men stood on the porch stretching their limbs, yawning, and asking each other how on earth they could spend that dismal day, when my brother suggested a dance. The idea was welcomed with shouts. At once the young men started to decorate the hall with rugs taken from the upstairs rooms, overhanging the walls with them. They also brought for decorations branches of evergreen, which looked greener and fresher after being sprinkled with the rain. One of the men went to hire fiddlers, and the ladies cut slices of bread and meat, and made enough salad to last at least for two days. When everything was ready and the day grew darker, the question rose how to light the hall. There was but one candlestick in each room and a couple of oil lamps. My brother insisted upon an illumination, *a giorno*, and we were provided with enough candles to execute his wish, but no way of getting chandeliers.

"Wait a minute," said my brother; and calling our cooking maiden, asked her how many potatoes she had in the pantry.

"Oh, plenty," was the answer.

"Then to work!" said my brother. "Boys, we must make potatoes stand for candlesticks!" and he went with the maiden, appearing a few minutes later with a specimen of the vegetable in question. He cut out the bottom of it to make a stand, and bored a round hole for the candle on the top. Every one said "Bravo!" and in an hour we had candles on each step leading to the upper floor and around the walls, placed on improvised shelves. The rooms downstairs were also provided with potato candlesticks, which the ladies wrapped up in colored paper or silk ribbons. All the communicating doors of the rooms downstairs were left open, allowing us to dance all over the house, except upstairs, because of the lights on the steps, which prevented all the women from climbing up, lest they should be set on fire.

We invited some friends and a few actors and actresses, who, though they did not belong to the phalanstery, joined us in the strike. We spent a delightful evening, dancing, reciting, and improvising rhymes suited to the occasion. The tone of the entertainment was kept in strictly æsthetic form, and the gods of art and beauty were ever present in the minds of those poor actors who, in spite of their Bohemianism, carried deeply-rooted ideals in their souls.

It would seem by this description that the evening was a solemn affair. It was not so; they were all in excellent humor, and gave themselves up without restraint to the joy of living, only there was not one vicious spirit among them, and their merrymaking was simply an expression of high spirits and happiness. My brother Felix was, as usual, the soul of the party, and enjoyed himself like a schoolboy on a vacation, making fun of himself and giving imitations of some noted people.

Next morning Felix, after a conference with Mr. Rapacki and others, came to my room and told me that they were going to see the manager, Kozmian, and tell him that we were ready for further performances. He said: —

"We have had our fun, and proved that we can be independent, if we choose. Now we are going to see what the manager has to say about it. If he is very nice, well, we shall resume our work; if not, we shall have to look for other engagements." Then he added, laughing, "But I am sure he will be nice."

Mr. Kozmian had been highly amused by the strike, and said that he was glad we had had such a nice entertainment and a little rest from the dismal melodramas which he was compelled to put on the stage just then, but never intended to include permanently in the repertoire. In short, he made us understand that he meant to keep up the standard of our stage, which he did indeed, as long as he was at the head of the Cracow theatre.

Toward the end of our summer season, Mr. Karol Chlapowski arrived in Krynica. He was heartily greeted by the whole phalanstery, for he was a most congenial companion, and an intelligent adviser to the young men who usually crowded around him, showering all sorts of questions on him, or listening to his interesting talk with friendly feeling and real enjoyment. He assimilated himself at once with our improvised family, and took part in our meetings and excursions. His arrival made me particularly happy, for I had missed his companionship and his refined, intelligent conversations, and before all, his personality and the great kindness and forbearance with which he treated all human beings, without regard to their material or even moral value. Under the influence of this truly Christian spirit I learned to moderate my feelings towards my enemies in art, and gained a great deal in modifying my judgments about people in general. During our walks in the fields or woods I had an opportunity of seeing that his theories were not merely a mental attitude but that they came from his heart. His manners towards the poor peasants or workingmen struck me first as being unusual in the son of a nobleman and a prominent landowner, and as such, accustomed to the servility of peasants. When he talked to one of them, he put himself almost on the same level with the man, and made him feel at home at once.

"Blessed be the name of Jesus!" he would say, and the answer came back: —

"Through all the ages, amen."[1] And then they would talk, not as a superior to an inferior, but as man to man. I also noticed that he opened his purse to the poor very often, and when I scolded him in a friendly way for spoiling the people, he excused himself, saying that he had too many silver pieces in his pockets, and they were "so heavy to carry." But I knew well that it was only a pretext, and that he could not see poverty without lending such help as he was able to give.

[1] This is the ancient formula of greeting in Poland. The well-to-do use it to the peasants instead of good morning. That greeting equalizes, so to say, at the moment, the men, and brings them in closer contact. It is used even now, but not so often as in old times.

CHAPTER XX

When we returned to Cracow, in the fall of 1866, Count Skorupka raised my salary to two hundred florins[1] a month, and besides that he granted me six weeks of vacation, which he suggested I ought to spend in Paris in order to see the best French actors.

Before going away I rented an apartment, leaving in it my mother, my little son, and my niece, Stasia, the motherless daughter of my oldest brother.

Paris made a great impression on me. The Champs Elysées, the Arc de Triomphe, and the Bois de Boulogne — these wonders of architecture and landscape combined — made me dream of Olympus and Greece, in spite of the crowds moving along in their modern garments. I shall not attempt to describe the beauties of Paris, so well known to most human beings. To me, who had travelled so little, everything I saw was so new, artistic, amusing, or original, that I lived in constant excitement over the ingenuity of the French people and over the grandeur and éclat of the monuments, speaking so eloquently of the victories and the brilliancy of the past ages. I visited picture galleries and museums. To the Musée de Cluny and to Versailles I returned several times, but of course the Théâtre Français, being mainly the goal of my trip, was most frequented by me. After a week of my visit to Paris, Mr. Chlapowski joined us, and thereafter it was he who directed our excursions to different theatres.

The first play I saw at the Théâtre Français was Alfred de Musset's "Fantasio," with Delaunay, Coquelin, and Madame

[1] An Austrian florin or gulden is worth 40 cents — $80.

Favart. I had never seen before the elegance and finish of a Parisian actor, and I was immensely pleased with the acting of Delaunay. He was as near perfection as a human being can be; besides, in spite of his mature age, he was a most spirited lover. Coquelin *aîné* was a very young man then, but he had already made a mark in his line, and we predicted his future fame. Madame Favart did not appeal to me. She had grand gestures and a beautiful ringing voice, which, however, sometimes turned into a sing-song, which did not please me. The part she played in "Fantasio" would have been better in the hands of a less experienced actress, with less routine and more enthusiasm, and above all, more nature.

Nothing gave me more genuine artistic joy than the Théâtre Français. I saw Madame Madeleine Brohan and M. Bressant, those two great stars of high comedy, and I think I learned a great deal from both. Monsieur Got made me jump up once in my seat and applaud furiously, but I soon noticed that my outburst drew the attention of some people in the audience, who looked at me with astonishment, evidently highly amused by my exhibition, and I tried in future to restrain my countenance and master my enthusiasm.

As I have said, I learned a great deal from these excellent actors, yet I never made any notes. Nor did I try to imitate their tone of voice, their gait, or what we call in America "stage business." It never came into my mind to notice the details. What I attempted to study was the way those actors and actresses treated their parts, the capacity of identifying themselves with the characters of the play, the general movement of the *ensemble*, and the precision of expression and delivery. One thing more I noticed, and that was their careful costuming and "make-up," which was always suited to the characters they represented. How the beautiful dresses were made I could never tell, but if they were out of keeping with the characters, they struck me

most unpleasantly, and I retained them in memory as warnings against bad taste. This, however, never happened at any of the performances at the Théâtre Français at that time.

The chief instructive quality of that theatre was the moderation of gestures and voices of the actors. They never permitted themselves any excess. They never ranted. It was only in later years that some of that unwelcome element crept in. At the time of Bressant, Brohan, Delaunay, and Got the performances made an impression of strictest harmony, which was preserved all through the play, and gave almost an effect of a beautiful symphony, with all the instruments well tuned and a masterly execution. Later on many things changed, and I have had the sorrow of seeing a talented young man on this stage, once famous for its excellency, tearing passion to tatters for the sake of the applause.

At the "Gymnase" we saw Madame Pasca, the direct pupil of Delsarte, but oh, how different she was from those who are proud of being pupils of the so-called "Delsarte system"! Strange to say, that man, so much spoken of in America, never left anything that could be called a "system." He left several pupils, mostly opera-singers, but he never inflicted on them anything as dreadful as a "system." One of his intimate friends, and a great admirer of his admirable art, made minute notes of his acting, describing the gestures, expression, and the quality of his voice in the pieces he recited or the songs he sang with inborn delicacy and inspiration. Yet he himself never pointed out to his pupils any of those attributes which his imitators tried to present as a part of the "system." These qualities were born with Delsarte and belonged to him only; to imitate them would be quite impossible — as ineffective as to wear an imitation Roman nose, or to speak with a falsetto voice, and try to render it sweet. The effect would be comical if not disastrous.

Madame Pasca in the "Demi Monde" was a living example of what good training, combined with talent, can produce. She was most moderate in her actions, and I did not notice any of the ridiculous flourishing waves of the hands, so well known in some of the pupils of the "system," nor any contortions of the facial muscles, nor any of the absurd motions of the body. She was as correct and as natural as an actress could be who went on the stage after thirty. She was very effective at given moments, and maintained the character from beginning to end. Hers was a fine performance.

A most pleasant though different impression was made on me by Madame Delaporte. She was all spontaneity and emotion. She played her part of *ingénue* with great delicacy and such truth of gestures and voice that she made the audience share her slightest change of mood. She was simply captivating. So natural, so vivid, was her acting that one could forget the stage, the audience, and the footlights, and only see the dear little pure girl thrown among the corrupt people, who, by her simplicity and truth, put to shame those who endeavored to wipe the bloom off that fresh flower and bring it down to their level. I was delighted with her. She was not pretty, but real talent is more desirable than mere beauty.

Madame Pierson made a mark in her characteristic part of Madame de Santis. She was subtle, and her beautiful face was full of expression. The part she played was rather difficult and risqué, and she deserved much credit for the delicacy with which she treated it. Her little sigh at the exit was delightful.

I will refrain from further descriptions of the theatre and actors. We visited the Odéon, Gymnase, Palais Royal, and we returned often to the Théâtre Français and to the "Vaudeville."[1] Every time I saw something new

[1] The name of Vaudeville has nothing in common with the American vaudeville theatres. The Théâtre du Vaudeville, where the best modern

and original which made me happy. At the Grand Opera we admired Madame Sachs and M. Faure, that most distinguished baritone of his time. My stay in Paris was one series of the most delightful emotions, and I do not remember anything which made me so happy and so completely satisfied in every way as those few weeks spent in that world-metropolis. It was an artistic feast as well as a sort of epicurean enjoyment. There is no place in the world, I think, where one can feel "le bien être" as completely as in that wonderful city.

The return to Cracow was marked by an ovation on my first appearance before the public. My friends were also pleased to see me back among them. Men were anxious to hear all about the new movement in art; the gentle sex crowded around me to see the new modes, and eager to hear about the curtailed dresses the Empress Eugénie had just brought into fashion. They were not pretty: over a small hoop fell a round, gored petticoat, almost without folds, and very short in order to show the laced boot, called Hungarian, with tassels at the top. The women looked from the waist down like bells. That sort of dress made them look short, and the flat, square hat in the style of Roman peasant women intensified the tendency toward diminishing their height.

I resumed my work in Cracow with renewed strength and energy and played many parts, some of them in Shakespeare's plays, to my great delight, for I loved the great dramatist so much that I preferred a small part in any of his works to a melodramatic one, no matter how important or effective it might have been in other plays. I played Lady Anne in "Richard the Third," Titania in "A Midsummer Night's Dream," Juliet, and Desdemona.

We also had Victor Hugo in our repertoire, and I per-

plays were performed had a fine reputation for the excellence of the acting.

sonated Blanche in "Le Roi s'Amuse." A quantity of French plays were produced at that time, mostly those of Dumas *fils*, Feuillet, Augier, and Sardou.

Most frequently, however, our Polish dramas and comedies were presented, — the ones by Count Alexander Fredro, Slowacki, Szujski Felinski, as well as modern plays by Balucki Narzymski, Checinski and others. The French plays were most appreciated by the fashionable audiences, while the Polish ones were favorites with all classes.

During the two following years of my Cracow engagement I took up history and made a quantity of historical notes. I also worked at my French and music, for though I had stopped playing singing parts, yet I needed a certain amount of cultivation in music and voice for such parts as required this accomplishment. I never liked to let slip any opportunity when I had a chance of perfecting myself in anything the stage required. And if I had to do a thing, I wanted to do it well.

I remember making quite a hit in Sardou's "Les Vieux Garçons" in the part of an *ingénue*, where I had to sing snatches from "Rigoletto," accompanying myself on the piano. I sang and played, but it was not my voice which was applauded, or the execution, but the spirit of it. I used to come home from the opera almost crazy over the music and the singers. The only relief in this state of enthusiasm was to sit at the piano and repeat snatches of airs and ritournelles before some human being, and this time it was an old bachelor who was the victim and the sharer of the girl's impressions. One difficulty lay in rendering the airs in such a spontaneous manner as to give the audience the impression of a thoroughly musical person, who finds no difficulty in execution, and plays and sings by ear. Another difficulty was in the treatment of the scene. There were the interruptions of musical themes, by gasps, ejaculations, and rapid speech. There were numerous subtle details to observe, which, without drawing any particular attention to the music or the voice, brought out the one effect, that of an innocent, spirited girl under the spell of Verdi's genius. My brother liked my interpretation so much that every time we played the piece he stood behind the scenes and applauded. I thought more of that than all the compliments of the critics or the repeated applause of the audience, for Felix Benda did not usually lavish praises on me. His attitude was that of a loving but by no means blind judge.

I studied so much during the season of 1866–1867 that one morning I experienced the horror of a temporary loss of memory. It was the most dreadful experience.

During the stage rehearsal of "Kabale und Liebe" I could not recollect one word of the part of Louise, which I had played often before, and even rehearsed on the previous day. I seemed to have forgotten it all, even the cues. When the prompter gave me the first words of my part, I did not recognize them, and had to be reminded that it was my turn to speak. I repeated one or two lines mechanically, but not being used to follow a prompter so closely, I stopped short. The prompter also stopped, and looked at me with questioning eyes. My head began to swim, and there was such a terrible blank in my mind that I believed I was on the verge of insanity. The despair and terror must have been clearly painted on my face, for my brother led me to my dressing-room and sent for a cab to take me home. When alone in my room, I burst into violent sobbing, which after a while brought a slight relief. A doctor was summoned, and he ordered a complete rest and country air. I was not allowed to read or write. Music, however, was granted to me in small doses; also sewing and embroidery. I could not go to the country on account of bad weather, but took drives between rains, and shut my doors to visitors.

After two weeks of this quiet family life, I came back to work, and the dreadful thing never repeated itself.

CHAPTER XXI

On the 12th of September, 1868, I was married to my present husband, Charles Bozenta Chlapowski. On the next day we both left Cracow for Warsaw, where I had been offered an engagement of twelve performances during October. This was a great honor but a dangerous one. The Warsaw Imperial Theatre is entirely run as a stock company, the star system being unknown there. It is an enormous and unwieldy machine, controlled as well as subsidized by the Russian government, and is composed of an opera company, a comic opera, a ballet, a drama, and a comedy company. Three orchestras, two choruses, a ballet school, a dramatic school, and a large number of officials, high and low, workmen of all kinds, belong to the organization. The salary list includes from seven to eight hundred people. The theatre owns a main building, the area of which is equal to a large square block in New York, containing two theatre auditoriums, besides concert halls and ball-rooms. Another small theatre in town, called "Maly Teatr," also belongs to the organization. Three daily performances are given in the various auditoriums.

At the head of this establishment is a high official called the president, usually some general, whose authority is absolute. Being somehow under the control of the viceroy of Poland, in certain cases he has the right of appeal to the emperor himself. The organization is entirely of a bureaucratic character, all its employees are exempt from military

The Warsaw Theatre.

obligation, and after a lapse of so many years of service they are entitled to a pension for life.

Its artistic force was recruited mostly from its dramatic schools, and if any outsider was admitted to the ranks, is was usually to the lowest ones. It therefore came to pass, that the rule of seniority, customary in the military and civil services, was often applied in the theatre to the distribution of parts and to the question of emoluments.

A new president, Count Sergius Mouchanoff, had been appointed in the early half of 1868. This gentleman, of very high intellectual attainments, had been aide-de-camp to the Grand Duke Constantin, viceroy of Poland in 1863 and 1864. His high social position, his education, his personal character, his influence in court, and his marriage with Madame Marie Calergi, daughter of the celebrated Chancellor Nesselrode, made him one of the marked personalities, not only in Warsaw but in the highest circles of Russian society. The name of Madame Marie Calergi was a very popular one in Europe. She was personally a queen of beauty, but more than this, her intellectual superiority, her charm of manner, and her artistic accomplishments made her one of those *grandes dames*, in the noblest sense of the word, who played such an important part in the social life of Europe; a friend of Alfred de Musset, of Chopin, of Liszt and Wagner, she was herself one of the foremost pianists of her day. The memory of her is one of the precious recollections of my past, and I shall always cherish and revere it, for she exercised a strong and refining influence upon my future artistic development.

Count S. Mouchanoff held in his hands the reins of the Warsaw Theatre; he desired to infuse new life into its veins. The old bureaucratic institution, though possessing several artists of the highest rank, able to compete with the foremost actors of the world, was going at a very slow pace.

Count Mouchanoff decided to leave the beaten track, and

to look outside the charmed circle in order to find some new talent. Mr. Hencinski,[1] the same gentleman who had seen my first appearance a few years before in Bochnia, happened to speak to him of me in favorable terms. His judgment was confirmed by those who had seen me on the Cracow stage, as well as by the opinion of the Galitzian press. A correspondence followed which terminated in my engagement for twelve performances on terms similar to those of a regular American star engagement.

This innovation was not favorably received by the majority of the members of the Warsaw Theatre. It was against all rules, a break in the old time-honored system, and looked like a revolutionary attempt. A resolution was formed that "coûte que coûte" the innovation must be discredited, and the newcomer must fail. On the day of my arrival in Warsaw there appeared in the leading paper of the city, whose chief editor was the husband of the leading tragedienne of the theatre, a scathing article upon the arrogance of some incipient provincial actors or actresses who dared to enter into open rivalry with the favorites of the metropolitan stage. The management was accused, though in covered words, of introducing a new policy, which might destroy the high standing of the theatre, etc. This article was answered as a premature and unjustified attack by other papers. Its effect upon the public was not a bad one, as it only increased interest in my appearance, but I confess that personally it affected me deeply, and might have dampened my courage had I not brought with me a great supply of it.

My first appearance in Warsaw I regard as the decisive turning-point in my career. I did not dream then of playing ever in foreign countries. Though speaking some French and German, I did not know these languages well enough to be able to perform in either of them; and our own lan-

[1] Checinski in Polish.

guage, which I think is one of the richest and most beautiful in the world, is too little known to be used on the stage outside of our own country. Therefore all my dramatic ambition was concentrated on our national stage, and as the Warsaw Theatre was the highest representative of dramatic art in Poland, a success behind the Warsaw footlights was my highest dream, and I was determined to realize it.

The welcome I was accorded by Mr. and Madame Mouchanhoff strengthened my energies. Finding people that expressed the same notions upon dramatic art which I treasured myself, I felt more at home.

When I came to my first rehearsal, I was received by my professional brothers and sisters with great courtesy (Warsaw people are celebrated all over Poland for their exquisite politeness), but in a ceremonious and somewhat cold manner. The atmosphere was entirely different from the warm, congenial one of the Cracow theatre, where we all were like members of one family. The play was "Les Idées de Madame Aubray," by A. Dumas, *fils*, very popular at that time and, according to my judgment, one of the best he had ever written. I was to play Jeanine, a part sympathetic, simple, not exacting any display of great dramatic power, though having very affecting moments. I felt safe in it, as much as one can be safe in anything.

When we began to rehearse, I acted as though I were before the public. I was excited by the importance of the occasion, and it seemed to me that several of the actors and actresses present were pleased with my acting, and even moved at moments to tears. I felt very happy after the first rehearsal; two or three of the actors congratulated me, and assured me that if I played in the evening as I had at the rehearsal I would win my cause.

The other members, however, after the rehearsal was over, gathered aside and held a prolonged conference, at the end of which the stage manager told me that it would be impossible to produce the play for my first night, as Mr. X., who was to take part in it, felt unwell, and would be obliged to stop playing for some time. Mr. X. had been present at the rehearsal, and looked the picture of health. I was distressed. Some of the members present — those who had congratulated me — exclaimed, "This is a shame," but they were not listened to. The stage manager then asked me what part I would select instead of Jeanine for my first appearance.

"Why will you not play "Adrienne Lecouvreur"? The company is ready in it, and there will be no difficulty in the production."

Now "Adrienne Lecouvreur" was then considered to be one of the most difficult parts in the range of any actress. It had been played years before in Warsaw by Rachel, and many of the old actors; many among the public remembered her magnificent performance. Several of the leading tragic actresses of the Warsaw Theatre had attempted to play it afterwards, but success did not crown their efforts. "Adrienne Lecouvreur" was included in the repertoire I had chosen for the engagement, but I had put it at the last, desiring first to gain the favor of the public in easier parts, and being afraid of appearing too presumptuous in playing it at the start. The members of the Warsaw Theatre had only smiled contemptuously when they learned of my ambition to play Adrienne, and they felt that I could not succeed where only Rachel had succeeded and every one else had failed. I hesitated when the proposal was made so abruptly to me. I saw the snare, but, determined to brave it, I answered, "Yes."

I went straight from the theatre to Mr. Jasinski, my old friend, to seek advice and consolation. When I told him the story, he asked me who was present at the rehearsal. When I gave him the names, he said:—

"How could you be so foolish as to act before them? But you must have done it well, if they decided not to let you appear in Jeanine. These same people look upon you as an intruder, and have decided that you are to fail. Now when you rehearse next time, be careful, and do not show how you will perform at night."

I followed his advice. At the rehearsal of Adrienne I repeated my words in a commonplace manner, and indicated very superficially my stage business. The actors belonging to the cast of the piece were not so hostile to me as those who were to play in "Madame Aubray." Some of them thought I had been unfairly treated, but, nevertheless, they all were in an expectant mood.

A few days before my first performance, what was my astonishment when I saw that the bill of the theatre was "Adrienne Lecouvreur," with one of the leading actresses, Madame Palinska, the wife of the hostile editor, in the title rôle. The president had been obliged to leave Warsaw for a week, and the cabal had profited by his absence to prepare this scheme. Adrienne had not been played there for three or four years. But the lady above named was the wife of the editor who had written that anticipatory condemnation of me, the object of which was to take off the prestige of the comparative novelty of the play. Besides, my informal rehearsal had led them to believe that the comparison would crush me in the most effective manner.

I went with my husband to the performance. Hardly had the lady in question entered and uttered a few words, when my husband turned to me and said:—

"Well, you are not afraid any more, are you?"

"I am encouraged," I said; and so I was.

At last the great night came. The house had been sold out. They were anxious to see how this young actress, yet unknown to fame, would accomplish her task. The premature polemic in the papers had excited public curiosity. Besides this, it was the first stroke of the theatrical policy of the new president. What would be its outcome? The viceroy, Count Berg, — an old, conservative, mummified dignitary, — was not particularly favorable to Mouchanoff, and would have liked to see him make a failure, and official Russian society, of course, followed his lead. Polish society was equally interested, but from different motives. Marriages of actresses into aristocratic families were rare events in Poland, where there still exist a great many old prejudices and notions. Moreover, whenever this had happened before, the actress had always left the stage. Why was it otherwise now? The husband of this new actress belonged to a very exclusive and strictly religious family. Why did he pursue a different course from others, by allowing his wife to remain on the stage? Was he justified in doing so, as some claimed, by her exceptional talents, or did he act in defiance of the accepted ideas, and so on? Well, they all came there in numbers, to see and to judge.

I received a very pleasant greeting from the courteous audience, though it was immediately hushed into silence. And what a deep silence it was! Such listening is never known in America. Polish audiences go to the theatre really to enjoy a performance and therefore they listen and look in an almost reverent manner, so as not to lose one intonation, one delicate shading of the voice, nor one slight gesture, one passing expression of the face. After the first line I lost my fear; after a few of them, I was in my part! Meantime, the silence continued until I came to the fable of the two pigeons. At its close there burst in the theatre such a storm of applause as I had never heard before, and have seldom heard since. A few moments later, at my first exit, the applause was repeated in the same manner. The first success gave me courage and inspiration. I played as one can only play for life or death. The public, once well disposed, showered upon me the favors of its encouragement. And then came the last act, which was one of my best-loved scenes. When the curtain fell on poor dead Adrienne, the public did not want to leave the theatre. They called and called, and the curtain was raised time and again. But my greatest, or at least the most high-priced, triumph was reached when the actors who had played the parts of the prince and of Michonnet, our great Zolkowski, the most perfect comedian I have ever seen, and Richter, second only to him, came and embraced me with tears in their eyes, greeting me as a sister in art.

JAN RICHTER OF THE WARSAW THEATRE.

I shall always remember how kind Richter was at the time of my first appearance in Warsaw. I had been so frightened when waiting for my entrance behind the scenes, that, though I heard my cue, I dared not go on. He was on the stage then, and, seeing my hesitation, he came very near my entrance, and, while he improvised to fill the gap, he succeeded in whispering to me: "Come on! Do not be afraid! You will win the battle!" Then he turned to the people on the stage, "She is coming!" he exclaimed triumphantly, "and here she is!" His look and the tone of his voice were so encouraging that I stepped bravely on the stage, and, once there, I recovered my wits immediately.

When the curtain fell on the second act and the audience

called me before the curtain several times, he came to me, and, shaking both my hands, he said radiantly: —

"You see! The battle is won! I congratulate you!"

"Oh, but I am afraid of the fourth act!" I said, shivering.

"Nonsense!" he answered. "Don't you see that the audience is with you? Go! Change your dress and think only of your part! Forget the audience!"

When the fourth act was over, I sank on my knees behind the scenes, whispering: "I thank Thee, my Lord! It is over!" and I hid my face in my hands. He came to me and, lifting me from the floor, said: —

"What are you thinking of? The public is applauding furiously and you start now on your evening prayers? Come, take your call quickly!" And he dragged me on the stage, a shivering, tear-stained creature, glad and thankful to him and to that dear public who waved handkerchiefs and threw flowers at me out of sheer kindness. For I knew well I was bad in that act, — written for Rachel's tragic powers and Rachel's deep, strong, almost terrible voice, if one is to believe tradition. My voice had a merely nervous power, and it was never very strong. I could not render the recitation from "Phèdre" to my own satisfaction, yet these dear people applauded and called me six times before the curtain. I had a feeling of receiving alms and was rather more ashamed than happy. Yet I had one consolation. I knew I could honestly win my applause in the fifth act.

Richter seemed to be as pleased with the reception as he wanted me to be.

All the members of the company appeared in my dressing-room, those who had been friendly and those who had been hostile, and congratulated me in the most affectionate way.

Next day the president asked me to prolong my present appearances to twice their number, and offered me an engagement for life in the Imperial Theatre. The press, not excluding the Warsaw *Gazette*, which had previously attacked me, praised me much above my deserts, and as to society, — well, during the following two or three days it left at my door about two thousand visiting cards (which I have kept for curiosity's sake), and I do not know how many invitations to receptions, dinners, balls, and the rest. The battle was won.

I told the president that I was willing to remain in Warsaw forever, but I could not do so at once, because I was still under contract with the Cracow management, which expired only next summer. He agreed to this postponement of my reappearance in Warsaw, but expressed the wish that I should sign the contract before my return to Cracow. I had no objection to that, and then the question of salary arose.

"What sum do you require as compensation for your services?" asked the president.

"Twenty-five thousand a year," I answered timidly. Upon that he looked a little perplexed, and saying he would beg a few days for consideration and for necessary consultation with authorities, he left me. I was rather puzzled by his change of manner, and thought that perhaps I had asked too much.

When I was thus brooding over this difficulty, Mr. Hencinski came in. He was visibly anxious to know the result of my conversation with the president, and when I told him that Mr. Mouchanoff was willing to engage me for life, but seemed to hesitate when I named the figure of the salary, Mr. Hencinski looked puzzled. Then he said abruptly: —

"Pardon my indiscretion, madame, but could you tell me what was the salary you demanded? It is not simple curiosity on my part, believe me. I want to help in clearing up an obscure point."

When I told him what my sum was, he looked at me just as the president did before; then suddenly his countenance changed, and he asked: —

"Twenty-five thousand?" Then, after a short pause, he added, "Of what, roubles or florins?"[1]

"Of florins, of course," I said, almost vexed. Then I added: "And I think it is not too much. It is only what Mr. Zolkowski gets. I may not be yet as great as he, but I know I am a strong attraction." Upon that Mr. Hencinski laughed, and said:—

"That, of course, is not too much, but the president thought you asked for twenty-five thousand roubles; and you know there is no such high salary in this country, unless it is a Cabinet minister's."

Then I understood the president's cool manner, and we both laughed heartily over it.

"I will go this minute to him," said Mr. H., "and comfort him. I knew there must have been some misunderstanding." And with these words he took leave and departed.

The very next day, early in December of 1868, I signed a contract for life, beginning in the autumn of 1869. Mr. Mouchanoff was so pleased with the moderate salary I required that he granted me a benefit performance every year, and also added eight hundred roubles yearly for my theatrical modern wardrobe, — the costumes of past ages being furnished by the government. On my part I begged his permission to insert two conditions of my own in the contract. Knowing the unwillingness of the management to make innovations and to introduce new plays, I demanded that I should be permitted to produce six new plays of my choice every year, and to include them in the repertoire, and also that I should not be forced to play more than three times a week. These conditions were accepted and the contract signed.

A few days after the signing of my contract a friend told me that he was just calling on the viceroy, General Berg, when Mr. Mouchanoff came and told him that it was

[1] $6\frac{2}{3}$ florins = 1 rouble.

doubtful whether he could secure Modjeska for the Warsaw Theatre because she demanded such an unheard-of salary. "Nothing less than twenty-five thousand roubles will satisfy her!" he stated. The governor whistled softly, and then turning his face towards the president, said, smiling, "Well, I suppose you will have to give it to her."

OPEN-AIR THEATRE IN THE PUBLIC PARK, WARSAW.

This little story flattered me, but did not incite any greedy regrets on my part. I was well pleased with my arrangement, especially with the security of staying permanently in such a charming city as Warsaw.

Our departure from Warsaw was touching. All our friends and a great many strangers came to the station. Students appeared in a large body. We were actually smothered with flowers which friends and the public threw into our compartment. We departed amidst cheers, good wishes, waving of handkerchiefs, and exclamations: "God be with you!" and "Come back to us!" and "Long live art!" and many other cheers which escape my memory.

Warsaw is called the heart of Poland, and no name could better fit that city, throbbing with never extinguished love of the country and mutual love of people because of the chains, wounds, and constant terror which link that sensitive, warm-hearted, imaginative mass of human beings so closely together that they seem like one body, which, in spite of mortal injuries, lives, and is all ready to face new trials. "Heart of Poland," indeed, for the blow aimed at it disabled the whole body.

I took leave of my new friends with tears in my eyes, and I felt such a strong bond of sympathy for those I was leaving behind that my heart seemed to leap toward them; and to ease that overflow of feeling I had a strong desire to take them all, strangers and friends, in one embrace and tell them how much I loved them.

CHAPTER XXII

We went to visit my husband's relatives in the Grand Duchy of Posen. Almost all the members of his family were landowners, living on their large estates in Prussian Poland.

One of the Residences of the Chlapowski Family, near Posen.

We payed the first visit to my sister-in-law, who married her cousin, Mrs. Casimir Chlapowski. She came with her husband to Breslau to meet us. We went together to their home, in Kopaszewo, a large colonial mansion with a beautiful park, a superb drive, and an abundance of flowers and

rose-bushes. We were warmly welcomed, and I lived a few days there, in an atmosphere of tenderness, peace, and refinement not easily equalled. The cordial way in which I was included in their circle made me feel at home at once, and when we departed I left a large part of my heart with them. We returned to Kopaszewo many times, almost every summer, and it was always the same delight to be there, to drive, to walk together in the park, to chat and read aloud, etc.

There is in the park of Kopaszewo a certain old tree under which, as tradition tells us, our great poet Mickiewicz wrote his celebrated poem, "Pan Tadeusz." I paid daily visits to that venerable tree, and addressed many questions about our great bard to its widespread branches.

We visited also my husband's grandmother, Madame Morawska, almost ninety years old. There was so much warmth in her greeting that when I kissed her hand and she embraced me, I could not restrain my tears. She was one of the most intellectual women of her time, a writer,[1] and a wise and clever adviser of the younger generation. I had a long talk with her, in which I expressed my happiness at being included in the family, and I asked her if she had any objection to my remaining on the stage. She answered: —

"By no means, Helena. On the contrary, we all want you to perfect yourself in your art, and who knows if one day, when you appear abroad, — I hope it will be on the French stage, — you will not make a Polish name famous in all the world."

After leaving her, we went to Turvia, to the beautiful home of General Chlapowski.

General Desire Chlapowski was one of the most prominent

[1] She wrote Polish history in rhymes for the young generation, and every child in the family and schools of the province knew passages of it by heart.

men in Poland in the first half of the nineteenth century. As a young man he served under the great Napoleon, and was personally attached to him: first, as a page of the Empress Josephine; later, as an officier d'ordonnance of the emperor; last, as commanding a regiment of the celebrated Polish Lancers. He left the French service when Napoleon sacrificed the Polish cause.

The General was of middle size, with a beautiful face and a figure of perfect proportions. As a young boy, at the court of the great emperor, he was called, according to the contemporary memoirs, the little Cherubino. He also had been known as the best horseman of his time. In 1830–1831 he joined the Polish revolution. Though by marriage he was the brother-in-law of Grand Duke Constantin, viceroy of Poland, he was one of the bravest and most brilliant of Polish soldiers. After the Napoleonic wars, General Chlapowski studied the latest methods of agriculture in England and introduced them into Poland. His home became the training-school of scientific agriculture. When, in 1848, the Prussian government established the emancipation of peasants, for the Polish provinces it was on the plans elaborated by both General Chlapowski and Mr. Joseph Morawski.[1] The measure was so perfect that it contented both the landowners and the peasants.

I shall never forget my first impression of the visit to his house. We arrived about nine o'clock in the evening, and were received by the General's unmarried son, Thadeus Chlapowski, the same I had met two years before in Posen, and who introduced my husband to me. The dinner was over, and we were told that the General and his brother-in-law, Count Gutakowski, were both in the chapel, where the family gathered every evening for prayers. We were

[1] Mr. Joseph Morawski was my husband's grandfather on his mother's side. He held a prominent position during the Grand Duchy of Warsaw, where he introduced the code of Napoleon; he also was one of the eminent logicians and philosophers of our country.

ushered into the choir, in order to avoid making a commotion and disturbing the devotions by our entrance into the chapel. As we knelt next to the organ, I beheld a picture which even now is vivid in my memory:—

On the altar steps were kneeling two gentlemen past eighty years of age, the General and his brother-in-law, both deeply engaged in prayers. We could not see their faces, only their silver heads bent forward in fervent devotion. In the benches sat some relatives; some so-called residents,[1] and also the servants, knelt, scattered about the chapel. All the women wore veils over their heads. A perfect silence reigned in the chapel, broken only by a soft rattle of rosaries and a sigh of whispered prayers. After a long while of this general concentration, some one started a Litany; we all repeated, "Have mercy on us!" and when I looked down on those aged men prostrated before the altar, another picture rose before my soul's eyes. I saw the field of battle covered with the blood of our youths, flames, smoke, gallows, and all the horrors of our last insurrection, the cruelties of the Cossacks, and the perfidies of the Prussians,—all the wrongs practised for more than a century over the people who had borne the Christian standard high above their heads fighting for faith and civilization; and when my thoughts returned to the present time, and I saw no ray of hope, no sunshine, nothing but disappointment, bitterness, hatred, and oppression, then tears flooded my face, and I repeated, sobbing, "Have mercy on us!"

We spent three most delightful days in Turwia in the company of the General, this veteran, admired, respected, and loved by all who knew him. His talk was that of the past, most quaint and interesting. He seldom frequented

[1] It was a custom of the Polish nobility to maintain several poor gentlefolk in their castles, most of them widows, orphans, old soldiers, and other unfortunates.

theatres, he said, and confessed frankly that I was the first "person of the theatre" he had met since Talma.

On the evening before our leaving Turwia, the General took his leave of us, saying that he had to be on horseback at dawn, and might not come back until noon, while our train was leaving at ten A.M.[1]

We returned to Cracow, and I began my work of old. My position, however, had undergone a slight change. Before my Warsaw experiences the actors and the public regarded me as a talented, struggling young actress, while at my return from our metropolis, where I had made a decided success, I was raised in their opinion to the dignity of a true artist.

All the critics, especially those who had predicted my advancement, were glad to acknowledge my success, and the public greeted me with flowers and even poems. Some of these were printed in the periodical papers.

It is such a satisfactory feeling to be a discoverer of a new planet, a gold-mine, or a talent, even of a failure. It is always pleasant to be able to say, "I told you so." And one of the critics who had stood by me from the beginning of my engagement in Cracow wrote a long article on the subject of my so-called "Victorious Débuts" in Warsaw. I beg the reader not to accuse me of presumption, if I quote this criticism, or rather eulogy. I do it simply to state the fact.

CZAS. No. 234

DEC. 19, 1868.

"When the name of this genuine artist, to-day acclaimed all over the country, occupied yet a modest position in the cast of our theatre, we had first the opportunity of drawing public attention to the hopeful resources of her uncommon talent. We paid a just tribute to her, often in opposition to the opinions of several local so-called connoisseurs, who did not suspect that a child of the

[1] At eighty-nine he still rode his favorite horse. Men like him are very rare at the present time.

manor born, a native of Cracow, could harbor a higher flight of mind which would raise her above the common level, and carry her into the sphere of the elite of art. We were accused of spoiling her by our praise, which our opponent said would only benumb and blunt an undeniable talent. The effect was just reversed. Instead of acting as a narcotic, the praise acted as a stimulant. The young actress was in love with her art, as well as full of noble ambition. And after each favorable criticism she grew in power, and surpassed herself. Each performance was better than the preceding one, and the slight defects which occasionally appeared soon vanished, thanks to continual studies, in which she was guided both by Nature and a remarkable artistic instinct. In consequence her name grew more and more popular, and her talent received more and more recognition. To-day all opposition is gone. The verdict of Warsaw, where artistic feeling has been developed by so many exquisite models, surrounds Modjeska's head with a nimbus, — our young Cracovian artist has become, contrary to the common saying, a prophet in her own country. In one word, she has achieved an unparalleled triumph.

"Cannot we claim a pale reflex of that triumph for having discovered and supported her genius, struggling in its behalf against local coteries and prejudices, and are we not entitled to-day to ask boldly, 'Who was right'?"

CHAPTER XXIII

Soon after our return to Cracow, my husband became the editor of a new daily paper called *Kraj* (The Country). This periodical was to be the organ of a new national party, including representatives of all three parts of Poland under Russian, Prussian, and Austrian governments. Its character was therefore more national than merely local. Without being radical, it was of a decidedly progressive type. Mr. Chlapowski was elected as editor-in-chief at a general meeting of the new party.

Among the owners of the paper the chief ones were Prince Adam Sapieha and Mr. Sammelson, a Polish Jew. Both of them were natives of Austrian Poland. Among the contributors to the paper there were some eminent Polish publicists and literary men.

Our house became the centre of the artistic and literary world, and we spent many delightful evenings receiving remarkable and congenial men, each of them having strong individualities and characteristics. Of the women of our circle I can say only that they were most charming, and some of them very clever and witty.

The soul of these gatherings was "Sever," Ignacy Maciejewski, of Russian Poland, a great patriot, who had taken an active part in the last insurrection, was seriously wounded in 1863, and when the uprising of our country was crushed, he went to London, whence he wrote interesting letters to Polish papers. The subject of those letters varied according to the mood or surroundings of the author. Some of them were political, some purely literary. It was he who first made known to us Ruskin, Morris, Millais, and Henry Irving. He wrote most flattering criticisms of the great English actor, under whose spell he remained to the end of his life. After five years of sojourn in London, during which time he wrote a play called "The Duel of Generosity," based on English themes, he returned to the country and settled down in Cracow, entrance into Russian Poland being denied to him.

He was original, witty, and entertaining. His very entrance in the house used to stir the company. He pretended contempt for the present form of greeting between people, and used to come in with his head slightly bent down, and with a subdued voice pronounced the popular peasant salutation, "Blessed be Jesus Christ." These words were in utter contrast to the roguish expression of his face, and always called forth laughter from his friends. The strangers, when there were any, looked puzzled until a witty word or some sober, rational sentence of his enlightened them.[1]

El***y Adam Asnyk, our young poet who, during the Insurrection, had occupied one of the most responsible positions in the national government, though born in Russian Poland, came also to live in Cracow. His poems were exquisite, and I recited many of them in private and in public. He soon became one of our guests and one of our best friends also. His manners and conversation were of the choicest, and his eyes, of the bluest blue, shone under his blond, bushy eyebrows like two magnetic stars, intense and almost fanatic in their expression. He had one peculiarity: though he was very modest concerning his poems, he was very proud of his culinary talents, and would rather stand a severe criticism of his verses than the slightest depreciation of his cooking. He liked to invite friends to his dinners

[1] He wrote many novels of the life of peasants and middle-class city people.

when the favorite dishes cooked by himself were served, and woe to him who had not eaten them with relish.

Lucian Sieminski was also one of our guests. Author of many historical books, he made an excellent translation of Homer's "Odyssey," but above all he was a prominent critic in literature and art. He and Maciejewski were often engaged in a friendly combat of words, from which the latter came out very often victorious, through his sheer humor and presence of mind.

Ludwik Kubala was a highly gifted, studious, quiet young man who belonged to the ultra "red" republican party. He was equally intense in his love for the country as in his hatred of the three foreign governments now ruling in Poland. His friends called him "Robespierre." Endowed with a poetic nature and imagination, he spoke little, but all he said was so original and so beautifully expressed that I often wrote down his words. Later on he became professor at the Lemberg University, and wrote several historical plays presented on the Cracow stage, but his most valued works were historical sketches. One of them, called "Chmielnicki," inspired Sienkiewicz to write "By Fire and Sword."

He had a friend, Alfred L. Szczepanowski, a genuine tribune of the people of a very radical type. He was the very contrast of Kubala. While the first was dark, with bristling hair and black eyes, the second was blond, with soft blue eyes; while the one's voice was loud and of a quality of a basso profundo, the other's, on the contrary, was soft and mellow. They differed in everything except in their political aims and opinions. They carried great plans for the restoration of Poland's independence in their young heads; they were always seen together, and for that reason were called Castor and Pollux.

Our old national bard, Vincent Pol, also honored our house with his presence. He was almost blind when I first met him, but the absence of his eyesight did not prevent him from being one of the most picturesque and interesting men. When he came in, the voices were hushed, and every one was waiting for the first word from his lips, but his congeniality put them soon at their ease, and the conversation became livelier than ever.

Prince Adam Sapieha, the so-called "Red Prince," lived in his ancestral palace in Lwów (Lemberg), but paid frequent visits to Cracow on his way to Vienna and Pesth, where his various duties called him. He was a strikingly handsome man about forty years of age, with regular features and eagle eyes, — slender, tall, erect, full of life and vigor. Though leader of the liberal party, he was an aristocrat to his finger-tips. Most affable with men and courteous with women, he knew how to freeze with a look any unwonted forwardness or dishonesty, until the object of his contempt would writhe under the mocking or cruel expression of those eyes which gazed so kindly in the face of misery or injustice, and knew how to melt, oh, so sweetly, in the presence of a pretty woman. The prince was considered the most brilliant orator and debater, both in the Polish legislature of Galitzia, and in the house of peers in Vienna. He was very fond of my husband, and remained our faithful friend to the end of his life.

Count Stanislaw Tarnowski belongs to one of the most ancient aristocratic families in Poland. He distinguished himself as a statesman, a writer, and a scientist. Professor at the University of Cracow, he had been several times its rector. At present he is President of the Academy of Science and Letters, an office which he has occupied for quite a number of years. A very prolific author, he has published a great number of essays and articles. Although his pen was devoted often to historical, political, and social subjects, his most valuable work has been done in the field of literary criticism.

He is equally distinguished as an orator. His eloquence

is brilliant, though somewhat ponderous, his language rich, his style exquisite. He is one of the leaders of the so-called Cracow party, a conservative organization, though progressive in social questions. He deserves great credit for being one of the first among the aristocracy of Poland who has devoted his life to literary and scientific pursuits. His example has been largely followed, so that to-day we have a great many representatives of the first families among the professors, physicians, and scientists of our country. In 1864, on account of his activity during the Polish Insurrection of 1863, he was imprisoned for several months in the Austrian jail. Later on he served several times as a member of the legislature of Galitzia, and also as a member of the Parliament in Vienna.

Anczyc, Balucki, Narzymski, and Sabowski were all prominent dramatic authors; the last two were deeply engaged in the revolutionary movement of 1863.

Count Adam Skorupka, the manager of the Cracow endowed theatre, and his partner, Stanislaw Kozmian, belonged to the ultra-conservative party, so-called "whites," yet they used to join our receptions as well as some other men of their party. Count Skorupka and his brother Leon were known as the greatest wits in the country.

To this circle of friends belonged also many young men of talent who later on became quite prominent, as the two brothers Count Badeni, Count Alexander Fredo, Jr., August Gorajski, Chlendoski, and Kazimierz Skrzynski, one of our most faithful friends. Our home soon became the neutral ground where people of different creeds and opinions met each other face to face.

CHAPTER XXIV

It was during this time that I, by a mere chance, became a reporter.

During the winter of 1869 our prominent philosopher and scientist, Charles Liebelt, came to Cracow to deliver a lecture on "Spectrum Analysis." My husband's duty as the editor of *Kraj* was to print an article upon the lecture. He came from his office in the afternoon, very much annoyed, saying that no stenographer was to be found anywhere, and much of the account of the conference might be missed. He appointed Mr. Sluzewski, one of the staff, to write the article.

I did not say anything, but I conceived a desire to be of help in this emergency and to write down the words of the celebrated man. I had not the slightest idea of the subject, which I had never studied, and I was in total darkness concerning "Spectral Analysis." But I was determined to remember as much as possible of the lecture; and sitting in a quiet corner of the hall, I listened with all intensity of mind. When some technical expression occurred, or names I never had heard before, I spelled them and repeated them three times mentally, and then went on listening. I could have written them down, but that would have drawn people's attention, which I wished to avoid. I had a remarkable memory then, which, moreover, was trained by rapid learning of my parts, and I knew I could remember the lecture. The only difficulty was to retain these technical words, some of them in Latin, and I was much afraid of forgetting them. Yet when I returned home I sat down and wrote the résumé of the lecture rapidly, with my brain on fire, though perfectly lucid. The whole of it, with all its strange terms and foreign words, came to me as vividly as if it had been written for me in the air. Mr. S.'s report and mine were compared, and mine was used with Mr. S.'s introduction.

When Mr. Liebelt came next evening to our house and told Mr. Chlapowski that he had read the article, I had a moment of very uncomfortable feeling, and trembled lest my name should be mentioned, and spoil my evening. Happily my husband and Mr. S. kept the secret, and the rest of the evening was a great treat with the remarkable man in our circle.

On the 28th of April, 1869, my work at the Cracow theatre was done with, and we left for Warsaw. During the three seasons I had spent in my native city I had studied one hundred and thirteen entirely new parts. The first season I played fifty-six parts, of which sixteen were in one-act plays and three in comic operas. The next season, during which many revivals were produced, I studied but twenty-six parts, of which only three were in one-act plays. During the season of 1868–1869 I studied thirty-one new parts, of which eight were short ones — all the rest being four- or five-act tragedies, dramas, and comedies.

Before we left for Warsaw I had a pleasant surprise sent to me from Paris — the French magazine edited by Arsène Houssaye, entitled *L'Artiste*, which contained an article on my performance of Jeanine in "Les Idées de Madame Aubray," followed by a general criticism of my acting. My portrait and a sonnet were placed on the front page of the magazine.

CHAPTER XXV

WARSAW in spring is beautiful! Streets, public squares, and parks swarm with people; young men with bright faces, latest fashions, and that nonchalance which can be seen only in large cities; beautiful women trotting on their small, perfectly shod feet, and shading their eyes with parasols often used as shields against the bold gazes of men; sweet-faced and white-haired matrons escorting their daughters; children; men and women of all stations; rich and poor; and among them, here and there, the brilliant uniforms of Russian gendarmes. But on a glorious spring afternoon who cares if even a million protecting official eyes are watching around? Gay and light-hearted are the Warsovians; at least they appear so in public. The great storm which only six years before had shaken the whole nation down to its very foundations had apparently left no traces on its vitality. "Life" seems to be written on every face, to vibrate in every countenance; the whole city is sparkling with it, and there is such a tremendous current of sympathy in the air that strangers meet each other with a smile upon their lips, ready to call each other friend. To be in a crowd is usually a rather unpleasant experience, but it is a real pleasure to move among the spirited throngs of that "oppressed" people.

We are carried by the current as far as Jerusalem Avenue; there we take a cab and drive to Lazienki (Baths), a beautiful park with a summer residence built by the last Polish king, Stanislaw August Poniatowski. The palace, with its lake, statues, and orange trees, resembles some Italian villa, and its interior reveals the very exquisite artistic and luxurious home of an artist-monarch, one who possessed almost all the qualities of a successful ruler: tact, beauty, taste, suavity and persuasion of speech, grace, generosity, great kindness of heart, — all, except the energy and art of ruling. In the park are many charming diminutive villas where the king's guests used to live; most of them were occupied by the exquisite creatures who adorned the royal bachelor's court.

The king was very fond of the theatre. He built in the park, on the shore of a lake, an open-air auditorium after the model of one of the ancient Roman amphitheatres. The stage, which represents the ruins of a temple built of marble, is on a small island, and the audience, in seats forming a semicircle, is separated from the stage by water. On the night of the performance the actors are brought to the stage in front of the public in boats and landed upon the stage on both sides of the temple. At the time of Stanislaw August, all sorts of plays, even tragedies, were presented there; but at the present time the management arranges only one or two performances of ballet or light opera every summer, and these only on special occasions, such as the arrival of the emperor and his court, a visit of foreign powers, or an inauguration of a new governor. The poor wounded Syren[1] is still smiling, still captivating, and more and more alluring in her languor of pain!

The palace of Lazienki, as well as all the other imperial residences, was under the supervision of Count de Mouchanoff, the president of the theatres. His wife, Madame de Mouchanoff, of whom I have spoken already, was known in the artistic circles of Europe under the name of her first husband, Calergi. Tall, blonde, with exquisite figure and fine, sensitive features, Madame Mouchanoff at fifty was still very attractive. Her grand yet perfectly simple man-

[1] Warsaw wears a Syren in its coat-of-arms.

MADAME MODJESKA (1869).

ner served as a model to many a young woman who came in contact with that exquisite woman.

Madame Mouchanoff's rôle in life seemed to be that of a good fairy, and she proved to be such also to me. She encouraged and protected me in many cases, especially in my wrestling with the censorship. It was she who many a time persuaded the censor that the forbidden plays were unjustly and unreasonably condemned. When I selected "Hamlet" for one of my yearly benefits, the censor-in-chief peremptorily forbade the performance because of the murder of a king which occurs in the play.

"Such things must not be put before the audience, because they may suggest disloyal ideas," was his arbitrary reason.

I went to Madame Mouchanoff and told her of my disappointment, and also of the reason given me by the censor. She invited the gentleman in question to her house, and in a few words persuaded him that the murder was a family affair only, and therefore perfectly harmless. "Hamlet" was performed, and remained in the repertoire. The public was almost frantic over the performance of Mr. Krolikowski (Hamlet), and next day, in the park which I had to cross going to the theatre, the students were quoting passages from the play; some of them walking right behind me recited my lines or sang softly the mad Ophelia's songs. It was a genuine success.

Another play that Madame Mouchanoff rescued from the censor was "Mazeppa," by Slowacki. By the way, this tragedy has nothing in common with the spectacular exhibition performed in the past on the European and the American stage, the feature of which was a well-built girl (Mazeppa) in pink tights, fastened to a horse. Slowacki's tragedy is a beautiful and interesting play in which Mazeppa appears as a young and handsome page, innocently involved in the domestic tragedy of the proud and cruel

Voivode (Palatin), who, at the close of the fifth act, gives the order to tie the boy to a wild horse of the steppes, and thus sends him to his death. The censor would not pass the play because there was a Polish king in it. He said to me:—

"A Polish king? Who ever heard of such an absurd thing! Polish kings never existed. There are only Russian emperors of Poles and of all the Russias;[1] you understand, Madame?"

When I tried to persuade him of his error, he cut me short with the words:—

"Do not think of it. It will never do, never!"

I was not discouraged. I went again to Madame Mouchanoff. She had a talk with Monsieur Censor, and this time concessions had to be made on both sides. Mr. Censor had a lady friend in the ballet. It seems that this ambitious beauty desired to become a dramatic actress. Now, Monsieur Censor said that if Madame Mouchanoff would obtain a "little" place in the dramatic company for his "little friend," he would pass the play. He put another condition, and that was the substitution of the title of "prince" in the play for that of "king." The play was performed, made an enormous hit, and no one was taken in by the transfiguration of the Polish king. The ballerina became an actress — of small parts, and Mazeppa is even now in the repertoire of the Warsaw Theatre, being one of those plays which can be called "classic" for its perfection of language and its construction.

Monsieur and Madame Mouchanoff's house was one of the most hospitable in Europe, and we were often invited to their dinners and five o'clock teas. We met there the élite of society as well as all that was notable in art, — our

[1] The actual title of the Czar is king of Poland and emperor of all the Russias. There are several provinces called "Russia," as White Russia Red Russia, Little Russia, Great Russia, etc.

local celebrities and foreign stars. All great musicians who had engagements in St. Petersburg usually stopped in Warsaw to give one or two concerts, and we met them all at Monsieur and Madame Mouchanoff's house. We met there Anton Rubinstein, Hans von Bülow, Joachim, Henry Wieniawski, Laube, and many other celebrities. At one of the dinners I was presented to Princess Bariatynski, of the imperial family, who urged me to study Russian, kindly assuring me that I could obtain a brilliant engagement in St. Petersburg should I comply with her suggestion. I thanked her most heartily for her great kindness and appreciation, but could not promise to follow her counsel. At the same time Madame de Mouchanoff advised me to study in German three Shakespearian parts,—Juliet, Ophelia, and Desdemona,—in order to perform them at the great dramatic festival in Weimar, where she would introduce me to the German stage and also to the greatest German of the time, Wagner. It was also suggested that I should appear in Italian with Tomaso Salvini in America.

But all these tempting projects and invitations paled in the face of the important work I had to do on the Warsaw stage. Through my contract I was entitled to put on the stage six new plays of my own choice every year, and in fact the greatest part of the progress of the Polish stage was in my hands. I felt very proud of my position and responsibility and could not think of giving it up. I was perfectly happy. My only wish was to serve loyally my own country, and I gave up the old dreams of shining in foreign lands.

Besides, I loved our artistic, literary, and social circles. Every Tuesday evening we received our friends. Many questions were discussed and left unsolved, many newly written poems read, and the best music played during those memorable evenings.

During the carnival there were dancing parties and

balls given by almost all our friends, and I loved dancing. To move lightly on the waxed floor to the rhythm of a Strauss waltz, a Levandowski mazurka, intoxicated me as much as would poetry, mountain air, or a beautiful landscape. It often happened that after a night spent in the ball-room I went to rehearsal next morning without feeling at all fatigued. One evening I played Juliet, and after the performance we went to a party, where my two nieces had preceded me, accompanied by my husband, who left them there, then came to the theatre to bring me to the ball. We had that night three invitations to three different houses. We left one house at one o'clock A.M. and went to the next, where we stayed two hours, then finished our evening, or rather morning, in the third house, where we stayed until daybreak.

By the way, I feel obliged to inform my readers that the Polish dancing parties and balls are unlike any other country's terpsichorean entertainments. It is a custom in our country to dance all night, and the feature of those balls is not a cotillon, which usually is danced at midnight, but the so-called "White Mazur," performed by *daylight*, if you please. The ladies whose complexions cannot stand too much inspection usually retire before the dawn; but those who do not use the "bloom of youth," or rouge, wash their faces, put on a fresh pair of satin shoes if necessary (they often carry an extra pair with them), arrange their hair, repair the torn flounces, and return to the ball-room fresh and ready for the "White Mazur." At eight o'clock in the morning a breakfast is served: bouillon, "barszcz,"[1] eggs, coffee, rolls, cold meat; and that closes the ball.

We remained with my two nieces until the very end of the above-mentioned party. Then, with cloaks and hoods hiding our ball attire, we stopped at the church to hear the

[1] A clear soup made of beets.

Mass. We drove home in the bright light of the sunny morning. It was glorious. The snow glistened like myriads of gems, and there was a delightful tingling snap in the air. I opened the windows of the carriage and chaffed my sleepy nieces. Poor things, — they were really tired, and I am afraid I was not a very considerate chaperone. As soon as we got home I took a shower bath, dressed in a great hurry, and went to the rehearsal, leaving my family plunged in deep slumber.

Speaking of "Romeo and Juliet," I remember I had some difficulty in producing it. During the time the play was in rehearsal our president and Madame Mouchanoff were in Weimar. In the president's place Mr. B. was substituted, — a man of great administrative ability, a staunch, honest official, but of little education except in his own business. He opposed "Romeo and Juliet" very strongly.

"Why," he asked, "Madame Modjeska, do you want to put on the Warsaw stage such a poor play?"

"What do you mean, Mr. B.?" I asked.

"I mean that it is not worthy of your talent to act in a play taken from an opera. We had Gounod's "Romeo and Juliet" recently, and did not think the plot very remarkable. It succeeded because of the beautiful music, but what are you going to do without it? It will surely be a failure, and I sincerely advise you to stop the rehearsals."

"But, Mr. B., it is Shakespeare's play!" I exclaimed, highly amused.

"I never heard of him. All I know is that it will be an imitation of the opera!"

Seeing that I could not restrain my sarcastic smile, he grew a little angry, and said: —

"You do what you please, Madame. Your contract gives you the right of choosing your plays, and I cannot prevent your doing so; but I warn you that you shall have neither new costumes nor new scenery. You may use what there is, but it would be folly on my part as an imperial officer to spend money on a failure."

I saw that there was no use arguing, and I left the office, but we produced the play in spite of Mr. B.; and, in spite of his predictions, we made a hit. Shakespeare was always appreciated and greeted most heartily by the Warsaw audiences, though he had been but recently introduced to them. Only one of his plays, "Hamlet," had been produced years before, and it was given in a heavy translation in Alexandrine verses. Needless to say, it was not in the repertoire when I joined the Warsaw stage. But — *revenons à nos moutons.* The scenery was very decent, and we used the same costumes that had been worn in the opera, after taking off the profusion of gold trimmings with which they were adorned. I had a new costume, though, made by the theatrical costumer. Mr. B. was kind enough to grant me that favor, though he grumbled a little while signing the order for it.

When the president and Madame Mouchanoff returned from Weimar, we had a good laugh over Mr. B.'s appreciation of Shakespeare. Madame admired the great dramatist intensely. She used to say of him that he created as many characters as God himself, and she was a stanch ally in my endeavors to introduce his plays and also other poetic works of high rank upon the stage of Warsaw.

The censorship, however, continued to slash the plays to pieces. Madame Mouchanoff was not always in Warsaw. She travelled a great deal, and in her absence there was no one to protect them, and I had great difficulty in introducing such plays as I liked. All the modern French repertoire was allowed, however. Even when the plays were not highly moral, they were kindly dealt with; but our censor always objected to the poetic drama. He seemed to have a special pleasure in cutting my speeches in such a way that it was quite impossible to get any sense out of them. It was very annoying and sometimes quite ridiculous, and our actors had a great deal of fun every time a play came from the censor's office. Every noble sentiment was forbidden. Even some words were found disloyal, among others the word "slave." In one of the melodramas it was cut out and replaced by the word "negro," and the sentence, which ran as follows: "He was a slave to his passion," was changed to "He was a negro to his passion"! On another occasion a Catholic priest had to say "I love my country and my people, and I shall never leave them." The words "country and people" were replaced by "wife and children"! In another play the words "He walked arm in arm with the emperor and whispered in his ear," were changed to, "He walked three steps behind the emperor and whispered in his ear"! These and like blunders were so amusing that the censorship became a standing joke among actors, who used to enlarge and invent some of the comical mistakes. I do not quote more of them for fear they may not be all authentic, but the above may give an idea of the censorship at the time of my engagement at the government theatre in Warsaw. It is never right to be more Catholic than the Pope. I am sure that our censor was overzealous in his services to the government, and too ignorant of the language to see his absurd mistakes.

CHAPTER XXVI

The Warsaw Theatre is the first theatre in Poland, and occupies the same place in that country as the Théâtre Français in France, or the Burg Theatre of Vienna in Germany. Being endowed by the government, and therefore not forced to produce only such plays as "pay the best," and having, besides, a very large company, the Warsaw Theatre is able to give performances that are perfect in every detail. At my time, our stage was hardly second to either of the two abovementioned theatres, and belonged to the first rank in Europe.

Zolkowski, of the Warsaw Theatre.

Among the actors were some who had no equals on any other stage. Such was our great comedian, Alois Zolkowski. In elegance of manner he could be compared to M. Got of Le Théâtre Français, yet in his genuine comic effects he surpassed the latter. His acting was simple and without any visible effort on his part to produce effects; they seemed to come spontaneously with the development of the part. And yet he worked out every detail, polishing and perfecting it at each rehearsal. Very often he interrupted the rehearsal, and turning to the company, asked: —

"Don't you think it is better now? Don't you like it?" And we all applauded, exclaiming: "It is perfect! Grand!" etc., which pleased him immensely.

His genius, combined with the gift of observation and studies from nature, made him a unique actor of his type. His physical advantages completed his histrionic greatness: tall, handsome, with a fine figure, large, most eloquent eyes, and extraordinarily mobile expression of feature, he was a striking figure on the stage. As soon as he entered, all eyes were upon him. He became the centre of attraction at once.

I never shall forget any of his performances. Once he presented a *nouveau riche* Jew, who, through his large fortune and influence, tries to become a member of high society. His manners are correct, his house is splendid, and his servants perfectly trained. He uses the most correct language, speaking slowly and choosing carefully his expressions, hesitating here and there in order to find the most fitting word. Yet in everything he does there is a visible effort to appear strictly correct. All this was done with wonderful discretion and subtlety, and yet produced a highly comical effect. But the crown of the performance was the last act, in which the hero loses his temper and falls into a fit of rage. Immediately all the elegance of manner and speech disappears, and he abuses his opponents in the most graphic language of the Polish Ghetto, wagging his right hand with the palm turned outward in the face of the chief offender. The effect was irresistible, and entirely his own. There was no suggestion of it in the author's directions.

I had no chance to play much with him, for his best parts

were in plays in which there was no suitable place for me. He played with me Polonius in "Hamlet," the prince in "Adrienne Lecouvreur," and the father in "Frou-Frou." But I went often to see him act, and he always made me laugh or cry at his will.

In private, Mr. Zolkowski was of a rather melancholy turn of mind. He spoke very little, and his favorite promenade was the cemetery, where he used to walk from one grave to another, reading the epitaphs and imagining, as he said once to me, how those dead people looked and acted while they were alive. He was not what we would call highly educated, but, well posted in our Polish literature, he expressed himself exquisitely, and his pronunciation served as a model to the younger generation, but he knew little of foreign literature or history.

The great actor at the time of my leaving Warsaw in 1875 was failing in health. He was past sixty then, and troubled with rheumatism. A few years later he died, leaving behind him a sort of diary which consisted in enumerating all the plays given at the three government theatres during his long career, and also in recording the parts he played, together with the number of calls he received from the audience. He wrote this diary in copybooks such as are used by schoolgirls on their examination day, bound in white, glossy paper, with gorgeous ornaments in red and gold. Some of them were tiny little books used for poems or orations on birthdays.

Here are some of the translated notes of the great actor. The titles of the plays in which he took part are written in red ink and in large, elaborate type; the rest is in small handwriting and black ink. The letters S. T. stand for Summer Theatre, G. T. for Grand Theatre, and V. T. indicates the Variety Theatre.[1]

[1] The names should be just the reverse, for on the variety stage they play nothing but high comedy and drama, while at the Grand Theatre, —

The list of plays performed at the Grand, Variety, and Summer Theatres in 1871:—

ALOIZY GONZAGA SARON ZOLKOWSKI

1	Saturday	G. T. Third time tragedy "HAMLET"	It went well. Glory to God!
	V. T.	Enterprise. Wedding in Ojcow	
2	Sunday	G. T. Flick and Flock	Excellent!
	V. T.	I, or "EGOTISTS"	Glory to God! 6 Calls.
3	Monday	G. T. Faust (Italian Opera)	
	V. T.	Fire in the Convent. Poirier's son-in-law.	
4	Tuesday	G. T. Faust	
	V. T.	Mademoiselle de Belle-Isle	
5	Wednesday	G.T. (for hospitals) "EGOTISTS"	Splendid! Glory to God! 7 Calls.
	S. T.	Joan's Wedding. Insect's Revenge Ballet.	
6	Thursday	G. T. Bluebeard.	
	V. T.	Everybody's Uncle.	
7	Friday	S. T. GAVAUT MINARD & CO.	Laughs and numerous applause. Glory to God!
8	Saturday	G. T. Faust.	
9	Sunday	Theatre on the island at Lazienki[1] Wedding by lanterns. Ill guarded Daughter (Ballet).	

operas, comedies, comic operas, tragedies, farces, concerts, and ballets are performed. I have seen even prestidigitators and acrobats on it.

[1] The out-of-door theatre in King August's park.

Though this diary may seem amusing, yet this almost religious respect paid by him to the appreciation of the audience shows how ardently he desired it, and how earnestly he worked in order to gain this appreciation. There is also much simplicity and lack of presumption in the exclamation "Glory to God!" It suggests the anxiety and then the thankfulness for the accomplished and well-rewarded work.

Jan Krolikowski was our great tragedian. He played also characters and the parts called, in French, *raisoneurs* in modern drama and comedy. His power was unquestionable, and though he did not seem to be as spontaneous as Zolkowski, yet the finish of his parts was so fine that they bore the stamp of greatness upon them. He was gentle by nature, kind-hearted, and sensitive; yet, when he played Iago or Franz Moore in Schiller's "Brigands," he seemed the personification of evil, so much so that sometimes the impressionable public hissed him during the performance; but when the curtain fell on the last act, they realized the greatness of the actor, and then there was a storm of applause and endless calls before the curtain.

The recollection of that outwardly quiet, but highly strung nature, that fine actor and excellent husband and father, brings to my mind sweet memories of the moments spent in his family circle, over which reigned his most charming wife and daughter. And when I think of what trials the man went through, I go back to those past days with my soul full of pity, compassion, and greatest admiration. His two sons were both born deaf and mute. This was the grievous sorrow of his life, and he bore it bravely to the end.

I had an opportunity to be often in the same bill with Jan Krolikowski. He was an excellent Carnioli in Feuillet's "Dalila," and his Tolosan in Sardou's "Nos Intimes" was considered one of his best performances. His Hamlet was very fine, and there were parts like the Voivode in "Mazeppa," and others, on which he left such a strong stamp that after his death they could hardly be replaced by younger actors.

Jan Krolikowski, though usually seen with an expression of melancholy in his eyes, was not altogether made of sadness and patience. No one could tell a better theatrical anecdote than he. He had a large repertoire of stories, and told them with art, never missing a point. I first met him in 1860, a few months before I became an actress, at my brother's house, and remember how one of his narratives made us all shriek with laughter.

My editor tells me that the American public likes anecdotes; therefore I have written it down as well as I could, though it would be impossible to describe the expression of Mr. K.'s face while he told the story, and his incomparable, subtle smile, which rendered even the risques passages acceptable and highly amusing. Here is the story:—

There was an actor in Mr. Krolikowski's young days who was not much liked by his brothers in art on account of his great stinginess, a fault almost unpardonable among the actors of those days. Being, also, only a mediocre performer, he could not possibly claim much respect or consideration, and became soon an object of fun and mischief to the actors, who were always on the lookout for a practical joke. One evening he had to impersonate a Roman senator, and his entrance had to be very dignified as well as original. He had to be brought upon the stage in a chariot drawn by two lions, represented by two supernumerary men dressed in lions' skins. Each of these skins was divided in two; one part represented the head, the chest, and the fore paws; the other represented the lower part of the body, with the hind legs and the tail. These two parts were put together after the man was inside, by means of a seam around the middle of the body which joined them to each other. As it was in July, the evenings were very warm, and the men hated to be put in the lion's skin with their clothes on. They stripped themselves, and then allowed the stage costumer to transfigure them into kings of the desert. When the senator climbed upon the chariot, he looked the picture of stateliness. Clad in a crimson toga, with the stylus in his right hand and a laurel wreath on his high forehead, he had the air of the emperor himself. He was so engrossed by this magnificent attire that he did not deign to glance at the people gathered behind the scenes, nor did he respond to the "Good evening" offered by a young actor standing near the entrance.

In the meantime, while waiting for the august appearance of the proud Roman dignitary, a young, mischievous boy nailed the tails of the lions to the wooden posts used in those days to support the wings of the scenery, and between which the lions had been placed, ready for entrance. When the cue was heard, the senator whispered to the lions, "Now go!" The lions made a start, but could not advance because their tails were fastened to the posts. "Go on!" repeated the senator, — another start of the poor animals, and then another stop. Here the senator gave way to his anger. Using his stylus, he prodded both lions with such violence that the poor brutes used a supreme effort, and breaking loose, galloped on the stage, but, alas! — leaving the hind parts of the skins behind them. The temporary seam could not stand the effort, and broke off. Tableau!

The third great actor — for it seems there must be a trinity in all associations — was Jan Richter. He was unsurpassed in the part of Michonnet in "Adrienne Lecouvreur," in the title rôle in Molière's "Miser," in Fredro's comedies, in the part of the father in "Kabale und Liebe," and in many others. I did not know him quite so well as I knew the former two, because soon after my Warsaw engagement he left Russian Poland and went on a starring tour through the Grand Duchy of Posen and through

Galitzia; but while he stayed in Warsaw he was a kind friend to me.

He surely deserved applause, for he was an excellent Michonnet. I thanked him over and over for his great kindness, of which he gave me numerous proofs during my first season, and I was very sorry when he left Warsaw. Our stage lost one of its pillars which could not be replaced for years.

At the time of my début the leading tragedienne was Madame Palinska. She had parts in all classic plays and also in some modern dramas. She made a great hit in Sardou's "Miss Moulton." When I first met her, she was a pale, handsome brunette, past thirty. She died shortly after my entering the Warsaw Theatre, to the great regret of the public.

Madame Rakiewicz, née Ladnowska, was an exceedingly beautiful and talented woman, but, alas, she was stopped on her road to fame by the too rapid increase of her progeny. There was a newcomer almost every year, and it even happened that in one year there were three children born, one in January, and twins in December. Though she became a great favorite of the audience from the very start, yet the prolonged intervals between her appearances on the stage cooled considerably the original enthusiasm; and the imagination of the people dressed her in a maternal glory which by degrees killed the romance usually floating around young and handsome actresses. Her complexion was a marvel, and she was tall and slender. Ah! if she could only have remained so always.

Her great part, so I heard, was Schiller's Mary Stuart. Warsaw was wild over her. This, however, happened some years before my arrival. She did some fine work afterwards in foreign and Polish drama, and her ringing, warm voice and the simplicity of her art made a deep impression on me. We played together in Lindau's "Mary Magdalen," and

also in some other plays. After my third tour in America, she played with me Elizabeth in "Mary Stuart," but her face was even then too beautiful for the part.

Madame Bakalowicz was the finest product of the Warsaw dramatic school. Her line was the *ingénue*. She was exquisitely finished in all her parts. The precision of her language harmonized with her well-polished nails and her dainty shoes. Of rather small stature, she was *bien tournée*, as the French say, and, without being strictly beautiful, she had captivating ways in the turning of her head, and a bewitching smile. In her art there was no attempt at concealing art. The work was obvious, but it was of such fine quality that it could not fail to gain admiration. Her sudden death produced a great sensation, the more so as it happened shortly after Madame Palinska's departure from this world. Both deaths were ascribed to the unsanitary condition of the two theatres. I saw the president on that occasion, and told him about these conditions, of which he was not aware, and which were then, indeed, in a most deplorable state. Some improvements were made immediately, but the complete remodelling of the building took place after my departure for America.

After Madame Bakalowicz's death, Romana Popiel inherited her repertoire, though the plays in which these two *ingénue* actresses had acted together never saw the footlights again. Such was a little one-act play called "Grandmamma's Little Sins," of which these two actresses made a real gem by their perfect acting. In their Louis XV costumes they looked like two exquisite porcelaine figurines, and every one of their gestures could have served as a sculptor's model. One of her best parts was Philiberte in Augier's play. She was also very charming as the princess in "l'Etrangère," by Dumas, *fils*, and in the *ingénue* part in "Dalila," by Feuillet. Her repertoire was very extensive and she was the best *ingénue* I ever saw on any stage.

Romana Popiel is described truly and flatteringly by Brandes in his book entitled "Poland." She left the stage when quite young, to marry Mr. Swiencki. She is still a charming and beloved woman, the lovely mother of two beautiful girls.

Jan Hencinski (the man who discovered me) was not a great actor, though very conscientious and correct. But he was a splendid stage manager and a fine poet and playwright. Many of his plays are even now in the repertoire of all Polish theatres in the country and also in Bohemia. Most of them are written in rhymed verse. "Nobility of Soul" is one of the most popular of his works.

What I admired immensely, besides his literary achievements, was his capacity for work. He never had a moment of idleness, and all he undertook was done on time and done well. A more conscientious stage manager I have rarely ever met, or a more competent. On the spur of the moment he could change an obscure or insipid phrase of the play into a clear and sensible one, mend all the gaps made by the censor's scissors, correct the language of a commonplace translation, make judicious cuts, or coach young actors and actresses. Very often the success of the performance was due to his stage management rather than to the company.

The poor man died, I believe, from overwork, due to his pecuniary difficulties. If author's rights had existed in Poland, he could have had a good income from his plays, but there was nothing of the kind then, and even to-day the authors are robbed with impunity.

Tatarkiewicz was the leading man, or rather became one, during my engagement. He was a young enthusiast, sensitive, ambitious, nervous, romantic, and always in the clouds. His pale, handsome face and tall, slender figure made him adapted to the parts of lovers; and he gradually became a lover par excellence, though often unrestrained in his acting. But there is an old saying of actors, "It is better for a young aspirant to give too much than too little, for it is easier to curb a fiery steed than to urge a lazy one." Romeo, Laertes, Mortimer in "Mary Stuart," and Roswein in Feuillet's "Dalila," were his best parts. Being an untiring worker, he was cast in almost all the modern and romantic plays produced in the Warsaw theatres. Playing almost exclusively poetic and sympathetic parts, he soon became the public's favorite and the schoolgirls' idol. After the death of Hencinski, he became the stage manager, and, like the latter, he died before he grew old.

Boleslaw Leszczynski is a superb man. Nature lavished on him all the gifts a human creature could desire. He has also enough genius to spare, and if he but possessed a capacity for work equal to his talent, he would be the greatest actor in the world. But I am afraid he is indolent. As every part seems easy to him, he takes them all easily, yet in some exceptional cases he suddenly proves to the audience that he can be great when he chooses to be so. Taking him all in all, he is a grand actor. There is nothing small about him. In stature, face, voice, gesture, he is a man to satisfy all the æsthetic requirements of an audience, and his acting, though at times he is not quite perfect in his lines, is electrifying to the audience, from the gallery to the boxes, by the power and truth of his accents. Boleslaw Leszczynski was engaged at the Warsaw Theatre a few years after I went there, and I played Desdemona to his Othello. I shall never forget the first performance of the play. Leszczynski was so real in the last act that when he approached me, with murder written all over his face, I became so frightened that I shrieked and jumped out of the bed. He started on a chase after me, caught me in his arms, carried me back to the couch, and accomplished the dreadful deed, half hidden by the curtain, which he succeeded in pulling over one-half of the bed while he threw me down. The public was hushed by the horror of the situation, but I trembled lest the audience might criticise, severely, this departure from tradition, but to my great amazement Mr. L. and myself were recalled several times before the curtain after the play. And, what was still more gratifying, some prominent opera-singers who witnessed the performance came behind the scenes, with Signora Mariani at their head, clapping their hands, and calling, "Brava! Brava!" They were wildly enthusiastic over Othello, and loaded him with most extravagant compliments. And yet, these were people whose God was Salvini. As to me, they went so far in their enthusiasm as to lift me in their arms and carry me all over the stage, exclaiming, "Oh, bellissima Desdemona, cara, cara!" I believe they would have carried Othello in triumph, also, had he not been over six feet tall and too heavy to lift. Leszczynski is still a member of the Warsaw Theatre, playing various parts, for he is extremely versatile, and as amusing in comedy as he is dignified and intense in tragedy. I believe that all the parts of Zolkowski, and some of the tragic parts of Krolikowski, fell to his share.

RAPACKI IN A FAVORITE RÔLE.

During my stay in Warsaw some of the Cracow actors made their débuts and were engaged by our management. Among them, the two best were Boleslaw Ladnowski and Wincenty Rapacki. They are still living there, and occupying prominent positions.

Wincenty Rapacki, besides being an excellent character

actor, is a fine writer. His play, "Wit Stwoss," a poetic and semi-historical drama, has been for a long time in the repertoire. He was, I believe, the first actor to introduce a perfect make-up. He could make himself look stout or thin at wish; and could paint his face in such a skilful way that no one, even standing near him, could detect the artifice. He could never be recognized in a new part until he spoke, for he could be identified only by his voice, which was of such a peculiar quality as to be unlike any other voice I ever heard. His articulation, also, was his own, and unmistakable. His best parts during my time were Iago, King Philip in "Don Carlos," and Shylock, as well as character parts in Polish and French plays. He made many hits after I left Warsaw, but I was not there to see his new achievements.

Boleslaw Ladnowski — my former Romeo — came to the Warsaw theatre after my departure for America. He made a hit in Hamlet and other parts, and was engaged to take the position of a romantic lover. His best parts were Hamlet, Romeo, Roswein in Feuillet's "Dalila," and all the parts in Alfred de Musset's repertoire. He also made a strong impression in several Polish plays by Fredro and Slowacki. At present he occupies the post of stage manager, to which he is entitled by his knowledge of ancient and modern literature, as well as by his talent for writing. A stage manager in Europe differs from the American stage manager. Education is essential for the position, and whenever, by necessity, or some managerial whim, a manager without deep knowledge of literature is chosen, sooner or later his ignorance is felt in the productions.

One of the popular figures of the Grand Theatre was the cashier, Zalewski. He knew almost every one in Warsaw, and every one knew him. Sitting in his box-office, he acquired a great knowledge of human nature by being in contact with so many different individuals. He possessed the almost supernatural gift of divining what persons would come to see certain plays, and always kept seats reserved for them. For this courtesy he was rewarded by some additional sum of money, which was scrupulously added to his steadily increasing capital. He rarely made a mistake in choosing his favorite customers or in his calculations as to their taste and generosity. He was highly appreciated by the public for his politeness, wit, and courtesy to women. Many of them lavished their most bewitching smiles on him in order to get good seats. He rarely refused to satisfy them, and sometimes even disappointed men on their account, though he knew well that all they would offer him as extra compensation would be a smile.

After the second act of a play, when all his accounts were made, he would come to see the performance; and so accurate was his well-trained instinct, that he knew at once if the play was to be "a go" or a failure. In his moments of grim humor he amused himself by placing the worst enemies next to each other, or a jealous wife next to the acknowledged sweetheart of her husband, even a divorced woman beside her former lord. Those accidents, however, happened very rarely. His chief amusement was to place the bald-headed men in one row, or to form two rows of bald heads, one line in the middle of the stalls running parallel with the stage, and the other beginning in the middle of the first row and running backwards to the end of the seats, so that the two lines formed a perfect cross. Then he would sit in the second gallery and chuckle over his scheme. The students, always quick in noticing and appreciating fun, laughed and applauded; but the poor bald heads never knew the cause of this commotion. Only the author of the joke smiled to himself, enjoying in full the effect produced by his impish design.

It would be impossible to speak of Warsaw and not mention one of the most popular men of that time, Dr. Titus Halubinski. As a medical man he occupied an exceptional position, equal to that of Dr. Da Costa in America.

Of a very striking personality, tall, handsome, with magnetic eyes, charming manners, wit, and wisdom, he was a fascinating man, and ever welcome guest in the most exclusive houses in Warsaw and Petersburg. He was a man of great courage and great heart as well as a man of high culture and a lover of art and nature. During the years of the Polish Insurrection he occupied a conciliatory political position, and was a personal friend of the Marquis Wielopolski, the so-called "Political Sphinx."

During my engagement in Warsaw we often in summer visited the Carpathian Mountains. There we lived in the clean mountaineers' huts, making excursions to the different points. The village of Zakopane was particularly fascinating to us, and is still the place of our predilection. It is situated in a valley and surrounded by the majestic peaks of Tatry. We spoke to Dr. Halubinski about the village and its quaint, intelligent inhabitants. He went there, and fell so much in love with the place and the people that he built a villa on the outskirts of the village, and became the patron of the mountaineers. They simply worshipped him. He discovered that these unlearned, uncultivated people had more inborn manner, more real artistic feeling, than any of the average city-bred. He founded for them a wood-carving school, where even now the young boys learn that art, so unique among them. Encouraged by his example, I, at the same time, started a school for lace-making which is still in existence.

The celebrated doctor died long ago, but his memory lives among the people, and his friends will always remember him with keen regret. When I was in Poland four years ago, I saw in Zakopane the monument which the grateful mountaineers and friends erected in his memory.

Besides the link of personal friendship which binds me to the memory of Dr. Halubinski, there is yet another: it was in his house and through him that I first met Ignace Paderewski. Of that meeting I shall speak in due time.

CHAPTER XXVII

During the Franco-Prussian war there was a break in my activity. I was ill with typhoid fever, which I brought upon myself by my own recklessness. Every summer I used to take three months' vacation, which I usually spent in star engagements. A few weeks before my illness we went to the Carpathian Mountains to spend the rest of my vacation in Zakopane. We loved that place for its quaintness, its magnificent views, and the splendid, invigorating air. There was no hotel in the village at that time, but it seemed quite delightful to live in a clean mountaineer's hut, with a green lawn in front and a rushing brook behind the house. I felt unusually restless, nervous, and fatigued that summer, and I could not join the excursions in which my husband and my little son Rudolphe took part. I stayed in the village with my mother, and to strengthen my overstrung nerves I bathed in the ice-cold brook and walked barefoot on the dew-sprinkled lawn. Unfortunately, the weather was merciless that summer, yet, in spite of the cold and rain, and my mother's warnings, I would not give up any of my baths or my barefoot exercises.

Deprived of the excursions and walks, I had to spend most of the time in my fir-scented, cushioned, and carpeted room, reading and writing letters. Here is one that I wrote to a friend in Warsaw. This letter never reached its destination, for I found it unfinished between the leaves of a discarded part, where it was probably put in a hurry and forgotten:—

"What frightful weather we are having here, my dear! It rains almost continually. You could not imagine, were you here, that you were in the mountains, for there are no mountains. From my window I usually can see Gevont, Gerlach, Lomnica, those kings of the valley, but now I vainly strain my eyes; I can see nothing but fog and drizzling rain. In spite of it all, I bathe in the creek every morning and walk barefoot on the lawn. This heroic treatment, according to the verdict of some German celebrity, is bound to strengthen my shattered nerves and establish a blissful equilibrium through my whole system.

"Charles and Dolcio[1] are on an excursion. I could not join them because I do not feel quite strong enough to sleep in tents or sheds. I read and do fancy work. Mother stays with me, so I am not quite alone. I am just reading 'As You Like it,' of Shakespeare. The translation is bad, but the play is a most beautiful idyl, and I hope that some day I shall play it, though I doubt very much if my Warsaw intimate friends would like to see me in boy's costume, and Rosalind wears a page's dress. You would not, I am sure. I know your prejudices, and yet,—and yet,—this dramatic poem is so beautiful that some day I may break the bonds of modesty and bring it into life. You will bristle up, of course, because you and some of my friends see in me more or less a nice woman, the wife of a nobleman. The artist is a secondary consideration, an accomplishment worthy to adorn Madame Chlapowska, whom you would not for the world see before the footlights dressed in tights. And yet, I assure you, I look quite modest in male attire. I played such parts before. To my mind, I, as a society woman, am only at my post because of my husband's title, but I consider my artistic standing above the social position I occupy. My husband is of my opinion, otherwise he would not let me remain on the stage. But I will not torment you any longer. Let us change the subject.

"Two days ago, I felt quite melancholy. The weather was desperate, almost suggesting suicide, and I had a feeling of some great misfortune hanging in the air. I imagined my husband fallen over a precipice, my boy crushed by a falling pine tree, and other pleasant accidents; when, suddenly, I heard a knock at the door. In my riotous imagination, I took it for the knock of Mother Death. When I said 'Come in,' I trembled, and then I fairly shrieked with joy, for, instead of some grewsome messenger, the angelic face of Dr. Karwowski appeared against the misty background. That dear, lovely man travelled from Warsaw to

[1] A pet name for Rudolphe.

pay us a visit, and to see how we lived here. Our mountaineer girl was just serving the afternoon tea, and I kept him until supper-time. We chatted and chatted, and he told me so much about Warsaw and the theatre that he made me quite anxious to return at once to my work.

"Next day he called again. It was still raining. When all subjects of conversation were exhausted what do you suppose we did to kill time? We killed flies! But we did it in quite an original way. I found among Dolcio's toys two tiny little bows. The arrows were simply made of matches, with a needle at the end. We aimed at the drowsy, sprawling, sleepy flies which ornamented the wooden walls of the room, and one by one our victims fell at our feet. What do you think of that kind of occupation for Juliet or Mary Stuart? This is not all. I assure you that both the doctor and myself were as serious about it as though we were hunting wild animals.

"Charles and Dolcio are coming back. A village boy saw them from the hill, and came on horseback to bring me the news. I will write more . . ."

When we returned to Warsaw I was ill, but I insisted on performing my parts, though I suffered from frightful headaches and fever. The dear Dr. Karwowski told me to keep away from the stage, but no persuasions could induce me to do so. I was determined to fight the disease. When my mother and husband in their turn tried to make me give up acting and take care of myself, I went into an uncontrollable fit of weeping, and they did not insist any more. I realized the seriousness of my state only when, after the fall of Amelia in "Die Räuber," I could not lift myself, and had to be carried in my husband's arms to the carriage and then up the two flights of stairs to our apartment. There I fainted, and the rest was oblivion.

The first faces I saw when I opened my eyes were those of the two doctors, Dr. Halubinski and Dr. Karwowski. Behind them stood my dear mother, watching me anxiously, and I felt my husband's cool hand on my forehead. Of that period I have but slight recollection. Most of the time

MODJESKA WITH HER BROTHER, FELIX BENDA, TAKEN AFTER HER ILLNESS IN WARSAW.

I was unconscious, and all I can remember now was the agony of heart I felt when, dreaming of war, I imagined the French nation crushed by Prussians. I dreamt of battles, of regiments following each other, and always, always, the black and white standard was floating in the air over killed and wounded men. I also had strange dreams about my own country.

When Dr. Halubinski pulled me through my illness and I was recovering, one morning my little son came to my room and, standing at my bed, told me that he had learned a poem which he wanted to recite. It was one of the patriotic poems of Pol. All my feverish dreams came back to me, and I was seized with a cramp of the heart, which ended with a flood of tears and a hemorrhage from one of my injured lungs. This incident put me back for some time.

The first day I left my bed was marked by the erroneous news of my death. A woman of the name Modrzejowska died, and the fact was announced in the papers; hence the mistake. Though the initials of her first name were different, yet the false news of my death spread like lightning over the country. My poor husband had a great deal of trouble answering letters of condolence and dismissing, not very gently, I fear, the hair-dressers who came to buy my hair, or the undertakers who insisted on taking the measure for my coffin. The only compensation for his pains was a beautiful poem written by El***y (Adam Asnyk), who, hearing of my journey to the other world, composed, on the spur of the moment, one of his best poems. What a great satisfaction it was to read those lines! It was such an original way of learning the degree of his esteem and the place I had occupied in that friend's heart. Great as was my joy in reading the beautiful poem, it was slightly marred by the idea that I might have caused a sort of disappointment to the poet by being still alive, and nothing was more welcome than Asnyk's letter, flooded with unmistakable joy over my resurrection.

After my illness I lost my hair, and it had to be cropped close to the scalp. In order to avoid people's attention I wore a wig, and this concealment of my capillary deficiency brought a calamity upon me. One morning, when I was rehearsing "Frou-Frou," an Italian opera-singer stood in the wings watching the rehearsal. When, in the fourth act, the indignant husband in the play has cast from him the poor flippant wife, and she falls upon the ground, the wig, which was not well fastened, slipped from my head. When I extended my hand to reach it, I perceived the puzzled, disappointed, frightened face of the Italian tenor. The expression of that face was so amusing in its perplexity that, looking at him, I forgot to put on my wig; and when I saw him crossing himself, I sat on the floor and burst into a loud fit of laughter, which visibly frightened the man, for he ran away as fast as he could.

That incident made me put away the wig and replace it with a cap made of white gauze and lace. It was not very becoming, but less disappointing, and much lighter and neater than a mass of false hair. On the stage I wore wigs, of course, but they were carefully secured, and never again was I exposed to the humiliation of parting with that important ornament. Spring and youth combined helped me to a speedy recovery, and with the returning strength my hair grew fast. In a few months I was able to cast away both wigs and caps.

When I was still wearing caps, my half-brother, Felix Benda, was invited to give several star performances in Warsaw. He made a great hit, and an engagement on good terms was offered him, but the Cracow management under Mr. Kozmian asked him to stay a few years longer in Cracow. My brother had great appreciation and friendship for Mr. Kozmian, and he refused the Warsaw engagement, though it was a more lucrative one, besides being also more comfortable. In Cracow he was burdened with the stage management, which, together with studying and acting, led to great exertions on his part. He worked too hard, and, at one time, having a bad cold, he would not take any rest, but attended the rehearsals in spite of his failing health. Two years after his début in Warsaw, he died of pneumonia, at the age of forty-two, leaving a widow and a little daughter.

The news of his death reached me without any preparation. During the performance of Rapacki's drama, "Wit Stoss," I received a telegram: "Felix died last night." How I ever went through that performance I do not know. Next morning my husband and I went to Cracow to render my beloved brother our last service.

Felix Benda's death was a great loss to the Cracow theatre. His place has never been filled by any one. There have been some substitutes and imitators without soul. Later on several excellent — even great — actors occupied important places on that stage, but none with that magnetism, spontaneity, humor, that irresistible charm, that made my brother not only admired but beloved by every one who saw him on the stage, and especially by those who came in closer contact with him. He was regretted by all, as was proved by his funeral. It seemed as though the whole city, from the highest aristocrats of birth and brains down to the working class of people, accompanied him to his eternal rest.

CHAPTER XXVIII

In order to recover entirely from the effects of my illness, we spent a few weeks in Krynica, another summer resort in the Carpathian Mountains, and there we met the De Reszke family,—the father, Jan, Eduard, and their sisters. Jan de Reszke was then a beautiful young boy about nineteen; his sister was eighteen; Eduard, sixteen; and the younger sister, Josephine, no more than fifteen. Those four children sang quartets, duets, and solos most beautifully, and on one occasion, when I was arranging a concert for some local charity, I asked them to take part in it. They consented readily, and it was one of the finest concerts ever given in that part of the country. I have kept in memory the pleasant recollection of that evening. The De Reszkes had never sung in public, and it fell to my share to introduce Jan de Reszke to the audience on his first public appearance. It was easy to foresee, even then, a brilliant career for these four wonderful children. Only three of them, however, went on the stage. The elder sister married soon after her visit to Krynica, and retired with her husband to their handsome estate near Warsaw. That delightful family was a bright and brilliant feature of our season. They were so happy, so handsome, and such artists! They made friends wherever they turned their steps. Success was written on their sunny countenances. Loved and admired in their early youth, they passed to fame without the struggle and effort that are often the share of the world's celebrities.

* * * * * * *

Once back in Warsaw, we resumed our Tuesday evening receptions, and I have the dearest recollection of those

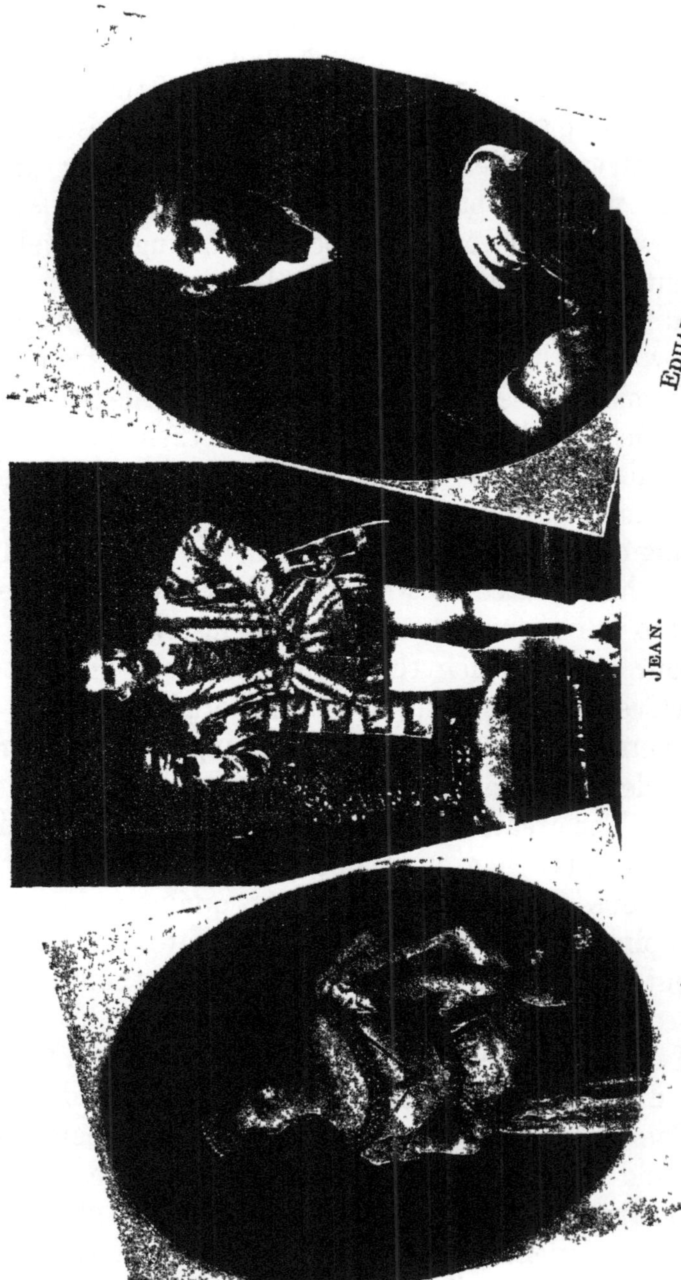

JANA. JEAN. EDUARD.

THE DE RESZKE FAMILY.

moments spent in the company of many distinguished men and women. The receptions had a literary and artistic character, but there were also persons of the so-called "best world" who were pleased to be among our guests and come in contact with celebrities. For young, aspiring artists, our house was the place where they could discuss art and life with people of high social standing as well as with scientific and literary men. This association served to modify somewhat their ultra-radical views. They lived for a few brief hours in different surroundings from their own Bohemian circles. It was beneficial to them in one sense, though it had nothing to do with their art. This they carried in themselves wherever they went, filling the place with an atmosphere of their own. My husband loved those young celebrities "in spe," and they loved him. His young spirit harmonized so well with their own that they rarely missed our evenings, and made themselves entirely at home in our house, which they rendered more brilliant and attractive by their natural wit and originality.

There were three inseparable young artists who regularly attended our evenings, — the most extraordinary trio ever seen. The greatest of them was Joseph Chelmonski,[1] whose pictures, just then on exhibition, were admired by all who saw them. His way of dressing, his quaint, unique language, his opinions, were all original and picturesque. He had the talent of saying in three words what another person could not express in a long talk, so clear was his perception and so keen his sense of observation. He was a tall, reddish blond man, with a most interesting and handsome face.

The other two members of the trio were Adam Chmielowski and Stanislaw Witkiewicz. These three usually came to our receptions very early, ahead of other guests, in order to have a friendly chat. Several times we knew before we heard the door-bell that they had come, because Joseph

[1] Read Helmonski.

Chelmonski announced himself and his friends by a plaintive air skilfully executed on a sort of reed called "fujarka," the primitive instrument of shepherds. When the footman opened the door, he did not stop playing, but walked right into the living-room. There he stood in a "burka,"[1] with the hood over his head, the picture of a handsome anchorite playing for his sheep and birds. We might have been the one or the other, for he never paid any attention to us until he finished his air; then, throwing back his hood, he would ask how we liked it. He had quite a repertoire of those airs. Some of them he played from hearing, and some were his own compositions.

He loved to see a good play, and if I happened to perform a part of which he approved, he paid me a compliment in his own original way. Instead of saying (as any other person would), "You were splendid, so charming," etc., he would look at me for a while, then sigh, and, rubbing his profuse hair in all directions, would say: "Yes, yes, dear lady, Poland is a wonderful country. Mickiewicz lived here, and Chopin, and now you!"

Shortly before we left for America, he went to Paris, where he received a golden medal; and many of his pictures were sold at a high price by the picture dealer, Goupil, to different private and public galleries in Europe and America. I saw one of them in New York in the Stewart Gallery. After several years of success, in which he learned to speak French with a Parisian accent, this purely Polish painter of nature grew tired of the over civilization of the European metropolis. He wanted to paint snow, but there was scarcely any snow in Paris. He liked rustic scenes, but there were no models for Polish peasants or animals. It was a well-known story among his friends that once he transported from Poland, as models for one of his pictures, two peasant horses, with their quaint harness, and a couple

[1] A cloak with a hood.

of pigs. These animals he kept in his immense studio in a faubourg of Paris until his picture was finished. Then the pigs were sold, and the horses sent back to Poland. Even when he found models for people and animals, he missed the native sky, the pine woods, and the meadows. Finally he was seized by such overpowering homesickness, and such dread of deteriorating in his art, that he suddenly returned to Poland, bought a farm-house in the country, and settled down in the very heart of nature, where he could breathe the fragrant air of the fields and feast his eyes on ever changing clouds, sunsets, and the ruddy cheeks of our pretty peasant girls.

The second one of the trio was Adam Chmielowski.[1] He was, and still is, a living spirit of all Christian virtues and true patriotism, — a soul more than a body, breathing poetry, art, and charity; a pure, unselfish nature, whose motto, if he had any, would be: "Happiness to all men, glory to God and art!" During our last insurrection he joined the ranks, and came out of the skirmish with the loss of one of his legs.

In the art of painting he occupied the place of a fine colorist, and one day he expressed the desire to paint my portrait. As our rooms had not the proper light, having a southern exposure, he asked if I could not pose in "their" (the trio's) studio; "provided," he added, "you can climb the stairs."

"Of course we can climb," my husband answered, and the very next morning we started on a visit to the studio. When we came to the house described by Adam Chmielowski, and asked the porter where the trio's studio was, that individual grinned all over, and then said, "On the seventh floor." My husband and I looked at each other in dismay.

"Seventh floor!" we both repeated.

"Well," said my husband, "we promised to come; but

[1] Read Hmieloski.

if you think you cannot climb so high, we can leave a note with the porter and return home."

"It will be such a disappointment to Mr Chmielowski," I answered, "and I think I can climb." We started on our way upward, but when we came to the end of our journey I was quite exhausted. I leaned against the wall to rest before entering the studio, lest the artist might see my fatigue. But as soon as we stopped the door opened. The three heads of the trio appeared against the light, and a flood of warm welcome greeted us. When we entered Adam Chmielowski noticed my fatigue, and called himself a brute for letting me climb so many stairs.

The studio was a large room, bare and cold, but with a soft northern light most favorable to artists. Against one of the walls was an immense piece of canvas spread over a frame, and on it the figure of a woman at least nine feet tall, done in charcoal.

"What is this?" I asked innocently.

"This is your portrait," the young artist answered. "I sketched your figure from memory, just for the dimensions."

"But the figure is too tall!" said my husband. "It is immense!"

"Just so," the artist said gravely. "Your wife is immense. She must be painted differently from any one else. Besides, this portrait is going to be hung up high over the entrance to the National Museum which is bound to be built some day."

I did not like to contradict him, and though I could not relish the idea of being so magnified, I consented to give him a sitting. He began to sketch my head on a separate piece of canvas while my husband was chatting with the other two artists. In the intervals, while I was resting, I noticed how bare the room was. In one corner there was something like bedding piled up and carefully covered with a rug and a bear's skin. This, with a table, two chairs, and a trunk, was all the furniture; and had it not been for numerous sketches pinned on the walls, the aspect of that vast, cold room would have been simply unbearable. My observation led me to the unmistakable conviction that these young men were extremely poor; and yet here was one of them painting a portrait with the idea of offering it to an imaginary museum instead of doing some more lucrative work. Oh, the dear, fantastic dreamer! The portrait, however, was never finished, for the artist would not invite me again to climb seven stories to the studio. He said he would have to put it off until the time when he could rent one on the first floor. That time never came, and after we left Warsaw he gave himself up to the religious life.

When, years later, after my tours in America and Europe, I met him in Cracow, he was called "Brother Albert," and wore the picturesque gray cowl of a monk. It was his desire to bring back to life the so-called "Third Order of St. Francis," which had fallen into desuetude and become simply a pious fraternity. He succeeded in his endeavors, and restored the original meaning of the order, making of it a regular congregation devoted to the care of the lowest and most destitute classes of society. The work of this congregation can be compared to that of the Salvation Army, without the drums and songs. Although wrapped up in his piety and charitable work, he did not give up his art. He still paints portraits, for which he selects his models from the various types of the slums, for whose physical and spiritual welfare he is toiling. While painting, he preaches to his models, pointing out to them in his jocular way the ugly lines brought to their faces by their brutal life; and telling them how handsome and dear to God they might become if they had but the strength of will to control their wicked instincts. These unfortunates worship him for his unbounded patience, the quaintness of his speech, his simplicity, and his good humor.

The third and youngest member of the trio was Stanislaw Witkiewicz, called "Stach" by his friends. When he was a little boy, his father, being involved in the insurrection of the Poles in 1863, was sent by a decree of the Russian government to Siberia. His wife accompanied him, taking the children with her. After her husband's death she returned with the children to St. Petersburg, where, at the age of fourteen, "Stach" tried to make his own living and suffered many hardships. Finally he and his family moved to Warsaw, where they settled down.

At the time we met him he was a blushing boy of twenty, with great blue eyes, black hair, and heavy black eyebrows. Even then his pencil and charcoal sketches were highly appreciated and admired, but we were not aware of the literary talent which he developed later. After we left Warsaw, he went to Munich, where he remained some time, studying art. When he returned, he married, and then, attracted by the beauty of the Tatra Mountains, he settled down among them in the village of Zakopane, where he still remains, and probably will remain until the end of his life. At present he is not only a painter, but an art critic and a writer. His work entitled "Art and Criticism" established his literary reputation and won for him the name of a Polish Ruskin. His language is very rich and original. He has actually augmented the Polish vocabulary by many new words. His style is crisp and picturesque, and his descriptions of the mountains unique and very valuable to artists. He also introduced the original mountaineer designs into the decorative art of Poland, their native architecture and ornamentation into modern buildings, and their quaint mediæval language into literature. He is one of the most popular, striking, and picturesque personalities in that part of the country.

Besides this interesting trio there was the caricaturist, Kostrzowski, a man of great wit and irrepressible spirit.

His caricatures and his pictures of popular scenes were highly appreciated on account of their striking types. He was a welcome guest everywhere, and the aristocratic circles made a great deal of him. Another guest was Gerson, an artist of great merit; the name of Gierymski also was mentioned wherever there was any discussion about art. That young artist was living in Munich at that time, and I never met him. Years later, however, his younger brother, A. Gierymski, came into prominence, and his pictures made quite a sensation in Warsaw. He was a frequent guest in our house. Mr. Chlapowski and myself took a great interest in his artistic career.

The literary element of our circle was represented first by Count Przezdziecki, an archæologist and historian, and one of the richest men in Poland. I had met him occasionally during my engagement in Cracow, and several times he helped me in my studies by providing me with necessary information and books.

Next came the poet, Felician Falenski, and his wife, both of strong personality, and intimate friends of ours; then W. Szymanowski, also a poet, and the editor of the *Warsaw Courier;* Edward Lubowski, a playwright; Boguslawski, a dramatic critic of importance, and author of the "History of the Polish Theatre"; Swietochowski, known for his picturesque style and noble ideas, a most interesting and talented man; and last but not least, Henryk Sienkiewicz, whom I am bound to mention often in my memoirs.

One of the prominent and popular men of my time in Warsaw was Edward Leo, a lawyer and editor of the *Gazeta Polska.*[1] He and his charming wife were our faithful "Tuesdayers" and very best friends. He was a brilliant man, and his wit was known in our country and abroad as well. He was simply bubbling over with it. His friends used to say that often, in the middle of the

[1] The *Polish Gazette.*

night, he would wake up his wife to tell her of some joke that he had dreamt of. Besides this irrepressible wit, he possessed a high and well-grounded wisdom, and it was worth watching him discussing serious matters with a face which in an instant changed from an expression of the god "Pan" to that of a stern philosopher. Many were the kind deeds of Dr. Leo; and great was his knowledge of human nature, his taste, and his judgment in matters of music, art, and literature. He published in his paper one of the first novels of Sienkiewicz, "Hania." He took the young writer under his wing from the start, and pulled him through the first trials of an unknown author. He recognized at once the extraordinary resources of the author of "Quo Vadis," and predicted his future fame. Dr. Leo and his wife were intimate friends of ours,—friends in a true meaning of that word,—and they remained such to the very end of their lives.

HENRYK SIENKIEWICZ, IN 1876.

It was on a visit to their country home that we met Henryk Sienkiewicz, and that glorious young man came almost regularly to our receptions. I can see him even now, sitting in a cosy corner of the room, his handsome, expressive face leaning against his hand, silent, for he rarely spoke, but his brilliant, half-veiled eyes saw everything and his ears drank in every word. The whole room, with its contents,—men, women, and objects, was unconsciously yielding food for his acute observation. He sometimes outstayed the company, and when only a few of our intimate friends remained he took an active part in the conversation, to our great delight, for his many-sided intellect and slightly sarcastic humor acted like a stimulant upon others, calling forth most clever and interesting replies. I was usually a mute listener to the intercourse, which sometimes became so fascinating that our guests did not notice when the candles were burnt out and replaced by fresh ones, while the dim white light peeped across the window-blinds. This, however, happened rarely, but one or two o'clock in the morning was the usual hour for our guests to say good night.

These prolonged and regular receptions attracted the attention of the police, and every Tuesday evening detectives and one or two gendarmes were posted at our door, observing and writing down the names of every visitor. They even went so far as to ask those who came from abroad where they lived, and their names and business. A detective followed my husband wherever he went, and I noticed a vigilant spirit hovering even over my person whenever I happened to be out.

One day the gendarmes were quite alarmed on our account. We were driving back from the races, when we perceived the youngest of the "trio," S. Witkiewicz, sitting on a fence and deeply engaged in sketching horses. He wore a blue linen workman's blouse, partly because it was a cool garment, and partly because it matched his blue eyes, I thought. We stopped the carriage to speak to him, and, as we did so, two gendarmes on horseback approached us, and some individual with a repulsive face came very near us to listen to our talk. When, after exchanging a few words with Witkiewicz, we took leave of him, one of the gendarmes escorted us to the very door of our house. The other guardian angel stayed to watch the artist, who had to undergo a regular investigation.

All this was amusing at first, and in some ways comfortable. We could go into the biggest crowd without being afraid of pickpockets, against whom we were protected by our official guardians. But it became annoying with time. Moreover, it was perfectly unnecessary on the part of the police, for we were not holding conspiracy meetings. Our sole object was to bring together as many talented and brilliant people as we could gather. I do not wish to say that we were contented and placid in our slavery. We strongly resented and always shall resent the government's unfair or cruel proceedings. But we saw the uselessness of an active protest, and tried to keep quiet on account of the young people around us, who were very incendiary in their nature. Even a tiny spark thrown in their midst might have set them on fire, which would have endangered their lives and brought more oppression upon the country.

CHAPTER XXIX

OUR musical friends were represented first by Moniuszko, our foremost composer. Though his genius was appreciated everywhere, and particularly in Italy, he remained a simple, modest man. His opera "Halka" and a kind of oratorio written to the words of Mickiewicz's "Dziady," made Moniuszko's reputation. Poland is still ringing with his exquisite songs. During my engagement in Warsaw, when we were rehearsing "Hamlet," I was fortunate enough to obtain from him the music for Ophelia's songs, which he composed expressly for me, and which I sang even when I played with Edwin Booth, adapting the melody to the English text.

Zelenski, next only to Moniuszko, was then a rising man of considerable popularity. Whenever he appeared, he was greeted with acclamation, being one of the best and most entertaining of companions. Endowed with a healthy sense of humor, he could give a splendid parody of any musical composition. Even Chopin did not escape his comic interpretation. But he was just as merciless to his own works, and made us many times hold our sides with laughter over his irresistible improvisations. He composed symphonies and several operas on Polish themes which were highly appreciated. He still lives, and is always admired as a thorough artist and one of the best of men.

Zarzycki, the director of the Conservatory of Music (a public institution), was then a young, ambitious pianist, and a great friend of ours. He often played his latest compositions at our house. One of them, called "Song of

Love," is equal to Rubinstein's piano pieces, and entirely original. Zarzycki was as well versed in literature as in music, and his talk was always interesting. He was one of those friends we missed when he failed to appear at our Tuesday evenings.

The musical house *par excellence* in Warsaw was that of Ludwig Grossman. Besides having one of the largest piano concerns in Poland and Russia, he was an excellent musician and the composer of several comic operas. One of them, called "The Ghost of the Voivode," was for a long time in the Polish and German repertoires. In his house — where the guests were greeted most cordially by the host, and fed most copiously by the little, dainty, blonde Mrs. Grossman — all that was known in the musical and artistic world of Europe met. They not only met, but they sang, played, and recited in that hospitable and congenial home. We heard there Joachin and Henry Wieniawski, those two violin kings, Anton and Nicolas Rubinstein, Hans von Bülow, Madame Artot, the sisters Marchisio, Madame Mariani, Carlotta Patti, the violinist, Wilhelmij, that most picturesque and handsome man, and Laub, Madame Essipoff, Leschetizky, and many others. The atmosphere of those receptions was so favorable to artists that they did not wait to be asked,

LUDWIG GROSSMAN.

but offered to perform, knowing that there was no one present who was not worthy of their efforts.

At several musical evenings at Grossman's house I had the opportunity of meeting Hans von Bülow. When first

ANTON RUBINSTEIN.

he was introduced to me by Madame Mouchanoff, I almost avoided him on account of the many stories of his irascibility, his erratic disposition, his offhand treatment of the public, his brutality towards musicians, and many other crimes of this sort. On closer acquaintance with the great pianist I experienced great astonishment to find him quite different from the picture I had drawn of him. I saw before me a man of strong mind yet gentle nature, enthusiastic, well-bred, artistic to the finger-tips, and of an exceedingly nervous temperament. Irascible he might have been at times, but I am sure that the moments of ungovernable anger were always provoked by people's stupidity or some unpardonable mistake in musical execution. His nerves simply could not endure any musical jar or an idiotic word or action.

The picture I give of our social life in Warsaw would be quite incomplete if I did not mention an entirely different set with whom we were in close contact. It consisted of my husband's relations in the Polish capital, and was exceedingly numerous. The Lubienski family played not long ago quite an important part both in Polish society and Polish history. Exceedingly prolific, it was connected by marriage with almost all the foremost aristocracy of the country. The last Minister of Justice of Poland, Count Felix Lubienski, reached the age of ninety-nine, and of his ten children eight lived to be over ninety. One of them was my husband's grandmother, Madame Morawska, the charming old lady of whom I have spoken before; and most of the others were yet living in Warsaw, where we knew and visited them. Almost all had played a prominent part in the first half of the nineteenth century, and all were exceedingly interesting figures of the past.

Besides Madame Stephanie, Dr. Leo's wife, I had at that time two intimate friends, — Mademoiselle Emilia Sierzputowska and Madame Falenska, the poet's wife. I used to call the first my inspiration and the second my conscience.

Mademoiselle Emilia was made up of spontaneity, impulse, and enthusiasm. Tall, rather robust in build, with aristocratic bearing, shapely hands and feet, expressive eyes, and a charming smile, without being beautiful she made the impression of a handsome woman. Also she carried with her a healthy, breezy atmosphere, and people fell easily under her charm. A warm heart and charitable mind always attract our fellow-beings; and she had many admirers of both sexes. Highly cultivated, she was, moreover, a staunch patroness of art. Like Madame Mouchanoff, she also had a cult for Wagner, and paid frequent visits to Weimar, where she met the great man and his wife, Madame Gosima, with whom she was in correspondence until the end of her life. "Panna Emilia," as she was called by friends, belonged partly to the Polish and partly to the Russian society. Her father and her brother were both generals in the Russian army. Her mother was of the Polish nobility. She had relations among Poles, and friends among Russians, and could have been a happy link between the two sets had it not been for the strong prejudice on the one side and the suspiciousness on the other.

Madame Falenska formed a contrast with "Panna Emilia" in many ways. In fact, they agreed firmly on but one point, and that was their warm friendship for my husband and myself. Madame Falenska was more of a scientific and ethical, than artistic, turn of mind. A great patriot, she shrank from Russian society. Her mind and her whole heart were filled with many bitter recollections of past wrongs, and she bristled at the mere approach of a uniform or a Russian dignitary. A faithful and devoted wife, she always found time to lend a helping hand to different charities, as well as to guide young people's minds and lead them into the right paths of life. I called her my "conscience," for she never flattered, but spoke openly what she thought of me and my art; and, though her opinions had sometimes the effect of a bucket of cold water poured upon my head, yet they were so just that I could not but agree with her. She also advised me as to whom I might receive and whom I should avoid, and in this she never was guided by prejudice but by real friendship. The daughter of Polish noble parents, she married rather late in life Felician Falenski, the well-known poet and the translator of Petrarch and Juvenal. They both were frequent guests in our house, and Madame Falenska brought me in contact with a serious set of people, among whom was Alexander Jablonowski, the historian and archæologist, and Odyniec.

Odyniec was our romantic old poet, author of many beautiful ballads and poems. Friend and companion of Adam Mickiewicz, he travelled with him, and they both visited Goethe in 1829 at his home. It was a delight to hear Odyniec when he referred to that meeting with the greatest of German poets. Goethe was then over eighty years old, and Adam Mickiewicz and his friend were young men, full of enthusiasm, faith, and patriotism. They were introduced to the German bard by Madame Szymanowska, the Polish court pianist of St. Petersburg, over whom Goethe was in rapture, calling her the most exquisite person in the world. Odyniec, in turn, was very enthusiastic over Madame Otilia, Goethe's daughter-in-law, and Madame Vogel, both of whom he met at the poet's house. He called the latter "Paradies Vogel."[1] During the talk of the young Poles with the great German poet, the ardor of my young countrymen was considerably cooled by the pure philosophical principles of Goethe. Odyniec also resented the title of "Excellency," which he had to use with every phrase he uttered to Goethe. "Excellency" suggested to him a government official; there was something very stiff and formal in it.

The great Scandinavian critic, George Brandes, in his remarkable book called "Poland," speaks also of the meet-

[1] Bird of Paradise.

ing of the two great poets. He describes it according to Odyniec's narrative, with all the skill of an experienced writer of great talent.

Next to Odyniec was Jadwiga Luszczewska, our great woman poet, whose "nom de plume" is Deotyma. Deotyma was, as a child, a wonderful being. She could write verses and improvise by the hour. At sixteen she held men of letters spellbound by her philosophical turn of mind and her marvellous facility for expressing her thoughts in beautiful verse. All that was remarkable in science, poetry, and art flocked to hear the wonderful young muse.

When I met her, she was already past thirty years of age and in the full swing of her fame. Not very tall, with rather a handsome face, she was a type of the blondest blonde. Her complexion was matchless, her eyelashes and brows pale yellow, and her eyes very blue. She carried her slight *embonpoint* with dignity, and her dresses were never made to suit the fashion. One time she would wear an Elizabethan high collar, and again she would appear in ancient Greek draperies, or a costume of the Borgias.

She wrote a great many poems, but her dramatic poem "Wanda" and the epic poem "Sobieski" are considered the best among her works.

CHAPTER XXX

SHORTLY before the plans for our departure for America were made, we visited Vienna, where I had the opportunity of seeing Madame Wolter, the greatest German actress of that time. She played "Adrienne Lecouvreur." A beautiful, statuesque person, with fine voice and expressive face, she was more adapted to classic tragedy than to modern French drama. Though Adrienne belonged even then to the so-called "old school," yet the exquisite "facture" of Scribe and Legouvé required more brightness and naturalness than the Burg Theatre actors could offer. In the second act, when Adrienne recites La Fontaine's poem of the two doves to her lover, instead of being near him and speaking to him, Madame Wolter stood before the footlights, speaking to the audience, while Maurice stood a few steps behind her in a pose of admiration.

Several of these mistakes were noticeable, and made me think that though there is a saying that art has no nationality, yet the French plays are always best rendered by the French actors, while Shakespeare or plays from the German are almost impossible with them. I heard that "Hamlet" was produced in Paris, but I am sure that I would not travel far to see a French "Hamlet." Germans can play Shakespeare because the spirit of the language is similar. Moreover, they possess the necessary weight and repose, and their translations of Shakespeare and other English plays are excellent. Schlegel's Shakespearian translations are most faithful, and his language perfect.

I would have enjoyed seeing Madame Wolter in Goethe's

Charlotte Wolter.

or in Schiller's plays, and I was sure she would have been an admirable Lady Macbeth or a Katherine of Aragon, but we had to leave Vienna before seeing her in another play. Years later I heard that she made an enormous hit in Wilbrandt's "Messaline," and I can imagine with what effect this great actress employed the resources with which she was so richly endowed, and what a vivid, fascinating, passionate Messaline she presented.

From Vienna we went to Berlin on purpose to meet Madame Ristori and to see her act. She gave at that time several star performances. Among the plays of her repertoire were "Mary Stuart," "Judith," and Giaccometti's "Elizabeth." This last part made an everlasting impression on me. It was the perfection of actor's art. The changes in Elizabeth's appearance and manner as she grows older from act to act, until she appears an aged, decrepit woman, haunted by ghosts and visions at the hour of death, were rendered in a masterly manner.

In "Judith" she used too much pantomime, and the red wool representing blood on her garments was not artistic. But her voice reciting the verses was like music, and the murder scene very realistic, except for the red blood. In "Mary Stuart" she was classic with her really queenly bearing. In the third act the meeting of the two queens was wonderful. Yet I missed the womanly element in that character, the most intensely feminine in history. But it is almost impossible to possess great tragic power together with the sweetness which belongs to the weaker sex. The play was arranged especially for the star part, and the second act was cut out.

I was in raptures over Madame Ristori, and came to the conclusion that Italians are the best actors in the world. They can impersonate characters from all the plays in the world. The French are at their best in French plays, but Italians are universal. There is something significant in

Photograph by Sarony.

MADAME RISTORI.

their ancient Roman culture. They are not made but *born* artists.

We called on Madame Ristori during our stay in Berlin. After a few minutes of waiting in the hotel drawing-room, we heard quick steps outside, and Madame rushed in, —all vigor, spontaneity, and hospitality. Though she was past fifty then, she radiated youthful ardor, and the clasp of her hand was warm and cordial. She seemed glad to hear about the Warsaw Theatre, where she had been given a most cordial reception some years before. "And how is Zolkowski, that admirable artist?" she asked. When I told her that he was still in good health and a great favorite with the public, she said, sighing: "Ah, men are happier than women! They may be seventy years old and the people will still admire them, while in a woman of fifty they see nothing but wrinkles." Upon which my husband quoted a passage from Cleopatra, alluding to her. She smiled, visibly pleased. When we rose to go, she asked if we would not stay to see her play "Elizabeth." "Of course" was our simultaneous answer, and we parted.

After seeing her last performance, we returned to Warsaw, where we were surprised by the announcement of six performances of Shakespeare by an American actor, Maurice Neville. Of course the name was a stage name, for the actor was born in Hungaria, but educated in America. His real name was Grossman. Maurice Neville played "Hamlet" according to Booth's conception of the part, and made quite a pleasant impression. His "Othello" and "Merchant of Venice" were equally well received. There was no greatness in his acting, but he had a good deal of talent, a fine voice, and very distinct delivery. Moreover, he made our Polish actors acquainted with the traditions of the English performers of Shakespeare. He played in English with a Polish support.

It was he who first encouraged me to study English and

come to America, but his words did not take root in my mind at once. Other motives stronger than ambition and wealth compelled me to leave Warsaw. I shall soon come to this sad chapter of my reminiscences, which, however, resulted in glorious freedom in art and life.

Soon after the departure of Maurice Neville for America, we met Cyprian Godebski, the sculptor. He was then a widower, and being a handsome, fascinating fellow he soon became very popular and a favorite with the fair sex. He lived in Paris and had come to Warsaw to execute some statues. He found the city so pleasant that he stayed there the whole winter season. A staunch patron of young artists, he was greatly beloved by them; they found in him a congenial, charming friend as well as a consummate artist and adviser. He came often to our house, and there he met his fate in the person of a charming widow and our intimate friend, Madame Mathilde Natanson. They became engaged at our house at dinner. I had placed them side by side, though without any previous design. Some one remarked that the charming widow and the handsome widower made such a delightful pair that they should be married. This remark was repeated at the end of the dinner, and their friends escorted them to the drawing-room with great attentions, calling Madame Natanson bride and Monsieur Godebski bridegroom. They both laughed, and treated this indiscretion as a huge joke. But "there is much worth in jest." A few weeks later this fascinating pair were married. They went to Paris in the spring, where they remained. Madame Godebska shared her husband's friendship for young, struggling artists and opened her house to them. They used to pour their troubles into her compassionate ear, and she always found words of consolation. They were not mere words, however, for she took all possible pains to change them into action, — selling their pictures or inviting critics to meet them at her house.

Many unknown young men of talent would have remained in obscurity for years to come had it not been for these two warm-hearted people. We spent many happy hours in the hospitable home of the Godebskis, and always met there some talented men and women.

Cyprian Godebski created the monument of Théophile Gautier, of Count Goluchowski, the viceroy of Galitzia, and that of our great poet Mickiewicz in Warsaw, besides many others.

CHAPTER XXXI

ABOUT that time Madame Mouchanoff died, after a long and painful illness. Her death was a great blow to her husband and her friends, and I cannot even now speak of this sad event without tears in my eyes. I lost in her the great warm-hearted woman who had proved to be my friend; I lost the artistic support that she had always been ready to offer me; and above all I lost that irresistible charm which emanated from her. Every one who came in contact with her felt subjected to that refining influence which may be called "the emanation of divinity." Even apparently commonplace people became interesting in her presence. Such was the power of her mental and artistic attitude that she could force people to give what was best in them.

The death of Madame Mouchanoff occurred in 1875, the year in which I lost my brother Felix. I felt then instinctively that the work I had most at heart, the elevation of the artistic and ethical standard of our theatre, was endangered and made almost impossible by her loss. Deprived of her protection, I lost a great deal of my buoyancy, and, as a natural consequence, things began to look less bright than hitherto. I felt less elated at the good points in my situation, and more despondent at the dark spots appearing on my horizon. In one word, I grew discouraged, pessimistic; and this disposition, increased by the nervousness produced by overwork, made me oversensitive to the drawbacks and shadows.

In every artistic career and especially when one has attained a high position, one is bound to meet with jeal-

Madame Mouchanoff, Daughter of Count Nesselrode.

ousy. Our poor country is not exempt from this. Its sad political condition, where government persecution penetrates into the most intimate recesses of private life, causing a continual nervous tension, cannot exist without demoralizing effects. One of those is a special form of meanness which our great Polish writer, Henryk Sienkiewicz, has called "Platonic envy." Anywhere else people are inclined to become jealous of those who have succeeded in their own profession or in their own line of business; but in the case of "Platonic envy" they become jealous of any one who attains a high position in any rank of life. Thus, the singer is envious of the success of a literary man, the shoemaker of a poet, the laundress of an actress, and the artist of a society man.

Of course, having achieved success, I was subjected to many attacks. People seemed to find fault with the popular actress who was also a society woman. They objected both in the press and in private circles to the alleged influence exerted by our so-called literary and artistic "salon." They found fault with our gatherings, where people of society were met by young talent, the promising authors, painters, and musicians. A play in which my husband and myself were caricatured under fictitious names and where our Tuesday receptions were represented in a most unfriendly manner, was produced during the president's absence. In fact, the tide turned, and while I was always acclaimed on the stage, I felt that the pedestal on which I had been placed was shaking, and the number of my adversaries grew in force and hostility.

But my chief grievance was the increasing severity of the censorship. There was no longer Madame Mouchanoff to moderate it, to help me through her influence and her tact. Yet I could have stood this annoyance had I felt any support in the struggle. Unfortunately this was missing. No such comfort came to my share. Compelled to appear in plays which were not of my own choice, while those I selected were ostentatiously rejected, I was maliciously blamed for it by my "Platonic foes." The more they blamed me, the more severe the censorship grew, and I usually came out of the struggle, between the critics' opinions and the censorship's insane despotism, broken and discouraged. My health began to fail. I was at times exceedingly nervous; then, again, a sort of torpidity came over me and made me indifferent to my parts and my surroundings.

My husband suggested a total rest and my retirement from the stage. His position in the insurance company, together with his inherited modest fortune, were quite sufficient to yield a comfortable income, and we seriously thought of retiring into some secluded part of the country and leading a domestic, everyday life. We began by closing our doors to all except our best friends.

It happened on one winter evening in 1875. I always consider that evening as a stroke of fate which, in spite of our plans for a peaceful life, was to push us into a mightier whirl than we had been in hitherto. Our circle was quite large that night. Among others there was Sarnecki, who had just returned from a journey. There was also Victor Baranski, who had come to take leave of us before his departure for Paris. He was one of those friends who could come at any hour of the day and be always welcome. Several of my women friends, my two nieces, together with a few more men, formed an entertaining circle.

They were all so congenial on that memorable evening, and so jolly, that even I woke up from my torpid state of mind and took part in the conversation. Someone brought news of the coming Centennial Exposition in America. Sienkiewicz, with his vivid imagination, described the unknown country in the most attractive terms. Maps were brought out and California discussed. It was worth while to hear the young men's various opinions about the Golden West: —

"You cannot die of hunger there, that is quite sure!" said one. "Rabbits, hares, and partridges are unguarded! You have only to go out and shoot them!"

"Yes," said another, "and fruits, too, are plenty! Blackberries and the fruit of the cactus grow wild, and they say the latter is simply delicious!"

"I have heard," said another, "that the fruit of California is at least three times larger than in any other country!"

"Yes, everything is extraordinary!" sounded the reply. "Fancy, coffee grows wild there! All you have to do is to pick it; also pepper and the castor-oil bean, and ever so many useful plants! One could make an industry of it!"

"Besides gold!" said a wise voice. "Gold! They say you can dig it out almost anywhere!"

"There are also rattlesnakes," added Baranski, in a cynical tone of voice.

"Yes! But who cares! You can kill them with a stick!"

"Oh, how brave you are,—sitting in this cosy room!" said our sceptical friend.

"Rattlesnakes are bad, of course, but think of a grizzly bear and a puma, the California jaguar!"

"What a glorious hunt one could have!" exclaimed Sienkiewicz, and then added, "I should like to go and see that country of sunshine and primitive nature!"

Everyone had to say something about the promised land, and Witkiewicz took a pencil and drew fantastic pictures of my nieces sitting on two huge mushrooms, while an enormous rattlesnake was nestling at their feet. The cherries that hung on branches over their heads were as large as apples. Dr. Karwowski entered just when we were most interested in Sienkiewicz's description of an imaginary storm on the ocean, and said to me jokingly: —

"You need a change of air, Madame. Why not make a trip to America?"

"That is a good idea," my husband answered. "Why not?" and he looked at me.

I repeated, smiling, "Why not?"

Chmielowski laughed and exclaimed: "Let us all go. We will kill pumas, build huts, make our own garments out of skins, and live as our forefathers lived!"

"Just so!" added Baranski. "And Pani Helena[1] will cook and wash dishes, and instead of violets and heliotrope, her perfume will be the flavor of dishwater. How enticing!" We all laughed, and the subject was dismissed as an impossibility.

During the intermissions of the rehearsals, I used to write some thoughts and impressions on the vacant pages of my parts. Here is one that expresses my mood at that time: —

(Warsaw, 1875. Written on the acting copy of Phèdre.)

"Peace! Almighty Father, put an end to my tortures. Is my life to be an eternal expiation for sins, mine and not mine? If I could fly from here, far, far away, with my dearest ones, and begin a new life, a life of work and peace! Oh, the people here! that jealous, cruel crowd! They make sport of my tears! they mock my heart's agonies! If I knew how to hate, perhaps hatred would bring me relief. But I am weak. I cannot brave adversity. My heart is only filled with tears and love, while I ought to have a brazen brow and a heart of stone. But what true artist, what actress, possesses such attributes? Only one who feels can produce feeling, only one who loves can inspire love. How can she wear a steel armor over her heart? Her only weapon is contempt. But is this enough? Will she suffer less when she appears cold and haughty? No, no, a public life is not fit for a

[1] Polish for "Mrs. Helena." All my friends called me so.

woman! Some one said, 'The happiest woman is the one of whom nothing good and nothing bad can be said.'

"Who knows how much truth is in these words, and whether any woman should seek happiness outside of her home, which seems to be the proper place for her. There she reigns. Her life is inaccessible to human curiosity. To the mysteries of her life only the chosen ones have the key. And so it is with all quiet and happy wives and mothers. But a woman who has dared to raise her head above the others, who has extended her eager hand for laurels, who has not hesitated to expose and throw to the crowds all that her soul possessed of love, despair, and passion, — that woman has given the right to the curious multitude to interfere in her private affairs, to rummage in the most secret recesses of her life, to count her very heart's pulsations. There is nothing as amusing to the public as some overheard snatches of an actress's talk, or the rumor of some misunderstanding in her home, or outside of it. They censure her sadness, they make commentaries almost invariably false. Yet all these paltry annoyances would not count if they touched us only. But when they touch those who are dear to us, when cruelty and malice combine to tear with their claws our dear ones, then, oh, then, an invincible horror fills our soul towards that pillory called the "Stage," and a great doubt rises in our mind. Was it worth while to give all that we had of the best of ourselves to the world, in order to obtain as a reward a momentary applause followed by a cup of bitterness?"

Another scrap is shorter but equally pessimistic: —

(Warsaw, 2/12, 1875. On the part of Portia.)

"In the old Roman times they used to throw prisoners to the lions. I threw all that was best of me to the hungry crowds, but they still ask for more, and I am so poor, so poor, that there is not enough of feeling left in me to give me comfort in everyday life."

Then one morning during the Christmas holidays my son Rudolphe, whom I had sent to Cracow with my mother in order to place him in a Polish school, came to Warsaw to spend his short vacation with us. He was even then determined to become a civil engineer. The first thing he spoke of was the coming exposition in America; and the lad, looking at the maps, declared that some day he would build the Panama Canal. He said it would be so nice if we could go to America now, see the great fair, and then cross Panama to California. He looked so happy planning this journey that both my husband and myself began to look upon the crossing of the ocean as a possibility. "Why not?" we repeated again, and my son put his arms around our necks and, kissing us in turn, said, "Oh, let us go there soon!"

"How soon?" my husband asked, smiling.

"Not before my school is over, at any rate," he answered eagerly.

"Good boy! Well, we will think of it, and please you if we can." And fresh embraces followed my husband's words.

To a fourteen-year-old lad such a journey must have seemed a realization of all his dreams. Rudolphe adored travelling, as all boys do, but little he knew, when he expressed his wish and we half consented to it, what an enormous stride we were undertaking, and what effect this little intimate talk was to produce on our lives, on his career and mine. He is now one of the successful civil engineers and bridge-builders in America. Even then, in his boyhood, I was proud of him, and I had so much confidence in his cleverness that everything he desired seemed to me reasonable.

I wrote at that time the following lines about him to my brother, Simon Benda:—

". . . he takes at present piano lessons from Mr. Hofmann,[1] and in seven lessons he learned four of Kohler's études by heart and almost the entire sixth sonata of Mozart. Besides this, he studies shorthand writing, languages, takes gymnastic exercises and horseback riding. With all these extra instructions he is always the first in his class and wonderfully strong in mathematics. My darling boy! What could I ask more of life, when God has

[1] The father of Josef Hofmann.

given me such a son! But this is not all; Stasia writes me, 'He is modest and good.' It frightens me sometimes to think that he possesses so many qualities. I wish he were sometimes a little bad, and would show it, too, that I might correct him while he is still a boy. I tremble lest the badness may come out too late, etc."

I quote these lines only to prove that it was almost impossible to refuse anything to the boy, my only and beloved son. Yet I could not have taken such a resolution as crossing the ocean for his sake only, had not my husband also looked at the possibility of that journey favorably.

Once the idea entered our heads, we communicated it to a few intimate friends, who treated the project as an insane one. No one but our young artists, Henryk Sienkiewicz and my husband's friend and Moabit prison companion, Mr. Sypniewski, took our extravagant enterprise seriously. My husband, having only my health in view, proposed a six months' vacation and the trip to America with the idea of visiting the most interesting places. We were to return at the end of the term, and then I should continue my work on the stage if I felt strong and well. If not, I should retire into private life. My desire was to get away from Warsaw and the unfriendly spirits as soon as possible.

As soon as we decided to leave, my impressions on the vacant pages of my parts changed their tenor and became more and more optimistic. The following one begins with a quotation from El***y's poem, written after my supposed death: —

"'Poor victims![1] They are not allowed to stop their flight.' No, indeed, they are not allowed. Their destiny is to fly higher and higher. Woe to those who rest, for the night will surprise them and they will lose their way. In vain will they look for it with the coming day. Therefore do not pity those who fly, but rather deplore those who lose their strength, or, discouraged, give up the flight. Movement means life! Toil is life! Pain is life! It is a hundred times better to suffer and live than to sleep."

[1] An allusion to actors.

(Warsaw, February 2d, 1876. On the part of Princess George.)

"'Why think?' you say. 'Why torment yourself with these continual mental struggles?'

"Is not *thought* a part of the divine in us? When the body is weak, the spirit can save it. Our soul is high above things of this world. I can lift myself in thought so high that no human being can reach me, and the struggles are indispensable. When I struggle I know I live.

"Great despair leads sometimes to suicide. The weak run away from the pain of life. Only in one case is suicide a courageous deed, and may even be a virtue: when we sacrifice our life for an idea, for our country, or for those we love. Hamlet's 'To be, or not to be' found an echo all over the world. I say: 'To be, to be, to be! To gather all the strength of our soul and go ahead farther and always higher!'"

(Warsaw, February 15, 1876. On the part of Marion Delorme.)

"I do not feel as happy when receiving homage as when I myself can adore. Every noble thought, every beautiful work of art, every brave deed, gives me moments of real happiness. Have I not given in a small measure a little of the same happiness to others? And yet I must go! My heart is sore, my wings are drooping. I need more strength, more vigor. When I return, I shall be a different woman. They say travel widens the view of life. Once on the ocean, how small everything else will look to me! '*Vogue la galère.*' I am ready to face the elements."

As I mentioned before, my husband's only desire was to take me away from my surroundings and give me perfect rest from my work. He thought, and the doctors agreed with him, that a long sea voyage might restore my health and strengthen my nerves. This project was, however, changed in the course of time. Our friends used to talk about the new country, the new life, new scenery, and the possibility of settling down somewhere in the land of freedom, away from the daily vexations to which every Pole was exposed in Russian or Prussian Poland. Henryk Sienkiewicz was the first to advocate emigration. Little by little others followed him, and soon five of them expressed the desire to seek adventures in the jungles of the virgin land.

My husband, seeing the eagerness of the young men, conceived the idea of forming a colony in California on the model of Brook Farm. The project was received with acclamation. Regular meetings were arranged, and the different points of the enterprise discussed. They planned the journey; they wrote statutes, with the firm decision of obeying blindly the points of law they composed. All together they treated the project as a most serious matter.

Stanislaw Witkiewicz, Painter and Author.

What wild dreams we dreamt! What visions of freedom, peace, and happiness flitted across our brains! I was to give up the stage and live in the midst of nature, perhaps in a tent! I pictured to myself a life of toil under the blue skies of California, among the hills, riding on horseback with a gun over my shoulder. I imagined all sorts of things except what really was in store for me.

Those who were willing to share our voluntary exile were Henryk Sienkiewicz; our married friend, Jules Sypniewski, who was anxious to bring up his two children under the influence of nature and the advanced educational system of America; Lucian Paprocki, an amateur caricaturist and my husband's relative; and Stanislaw Witkiewicz and his friend, Adam Chmielowski. The latter a few weeks later gave up the project of joining our excursion, but still belonged to the intimate circle of our emigrants, and came regularly to our meetings. It was he who suggested the study of English. My husband engaged a Miss d'Albitte to teach us. She was the daughter of an Englishwoman and a Frenchman, and her accent was a little affected by this combination of the two nationalities. But she had a great advantage in being thoroughly acquainted with the French language, which rendered our study more intelligible and more pleasant, too, for very often we reduced our lesson to a pleasant talk in French.

One evening when we were dining at the Kronenbergs' palace, with that delightful family, our host asked me if it were true that we intended to emigrate to America. I told him that such was our desire. "What folly!" he exclaimed. Then, looking at me for a while he added, "Unless you will study English and play on the American stage!"

These words touched a string that had been asleep in my soul for a long time. It awakened again the wild hope of playing Shakespeare in his own language. I returned home, dreaming impossible dreams. But the next day I was taken down from my heaven by our friends' plans. They looked to me as to a sort of providence of the colony, to look after the moral and material welfare of the hard-working farmers they were to be, — in a word, to be a guardian angel and a *cordon bleu* ordinarily known by the name of cook.

"Oh, but to cook under the sapphire-blue sky in the land of freedom! What joy!" I thought. "To bleach linen at the brook like the maidens of Homer's 'Iliad'! After the day of toil, to play the guitar and sing by moonlight, to recite poems, or to listen to the mocking-bird! And listening to our songs would be charming Indian maidens, our neighbors, making wreaths of luxuriant wild flowers for us! And in exchange we should give them trinkets for their handsome brown necks and wrists! And oh, we should be so far away from every-day gossip and malice, nearer to God, and better." Yes, the prospect of a simple life, so mocked at to-day, had for us the charm of a revivifying novelty. It seemed like being born again.

I obtained a leave of absence from the president for one year. After that time, I was bound either to return or to pay the forfeit of 6000 roubles for breaking the contract. President Mouchanoff had not the slightest doubt but that we would be back even before the expiration of my leave of absence. He treated our expedition in a most cheerful manner. So did the rest of our friends for that matter; none of them even suspected our resolution of staying in America any longer than it would require to visit the Exposition, Niagara Falls, and the principal cities.

In the early spring Henryk Sienkiewicz and Julian Sypniewski sailed for the New World. The rest of us were to follow them in July. Sypniewski returned with glowing accounts of the beauties of California. According to his opinion, paradise was nowhere to be compared to that land of green meadows, blue hills, and orange-blossoms. Of course it must not be forgotten that our friend was there in spring, after heavy rains, and the country really looked green.

The letters of Sienkiewicz were also most convincing, and we began to make preparations for the journey. Many, many articles were bought,—heavy rugs, telescopes, brass knuckles, guns, etc.; among other things two huge medicine boxes and a large array of surgical instruments, above all, — six revolvers! Even I was presented with one of the latter, a very dainty one set with mother-of-pearl. Our furniture was put on sale, but our books, pictures, and our entire wardrobe were all carefully packed for the journey, to go with us into the wilderness as the most indispensable companions of a "simple life."

There was no custom of having a farewell performance in our country, but my last appearance of the season was announced in the papers, and the house was packed. Next morning the following notice in the *Warsaw Courier* greeted me at the breakfast-table: —

(*Kurjer Warszawski* (*Warsaw Courier*). June 22, 1876.)

"'Is it true that she leaves the country to-morrow?'

"'Where to?'

"'To America, I hear. Can this be true?'

"'They say the passage is already reserved on the steamer.'

"'And will she stay there six months?'

"'Possibly a year.'

"'She is going to Philadelphia.'

"'Not at all — to Chicago.'

"'Is she going to act there?'

"'In what language, Polish or English?'

"'What will our stage do without her for such a long time?'

"'A great artist! Yes, a genuine great artist!'

"These rumors and sayings were passing last night from mouth to mouth. The fact is that last night in the Summer Theatre Madame Modrzejewska gave her last performance before her departure on a leave of absence which begins to-day. She selected for this occasion two scenes of Shakespeare, the balcony scene of 'Romeo and Juliet' and Ophelia's mad scene in 'Hamlet'; the last act of 'Adrienne Lecouvreur,' and the whole of Fredo's comedy, 'The Maiden's Vows.' There is no need to repeat here the praises that have been so often showered on our great artist for these remarkable creations; we only want to say that her last appearance, combining as it did in one single night so many distinct impressions of the highest kind, will long remain in the memory of the fortunate ones who succeeded, after a vigorous struggle at the box-office, in getting tickets. It allowed them to admire a cycle of parts so different from each other, and executed with a perfection that could hardly be equalled save on one or two of the first European stages. The enthusiasm of the audience was aroused to the highest pitch. Applause followed applause and the calls before the curtain seemed to never cease.

"The greeting extended to the artist implied the hope that she will soon return to us and shine on our stage for a long, long time.

We do not doubt but that this will be so, and we base our hope on what follows :—

"After the performance," the *Warsaw Courier* said, "the whole audience, *en masse*, formed into a double rank extending from the back door of the theatre through the whole length of the park, up to its main gate. Everybody remained waiting for the appearance of the artist. As soon as she came out, she was received by acclamations and cries of admiration, intermingled with expressions of most cordial good wishes. 'Come back to us!' they cried, 'Come back as soon as possible, for you leave behind you a void impossible to fill.'

"And, indeed, there will be a great void on our stage without one whom we have been used to look upon as the first and main support of our drama and comedy. It will indeed be sad for the lovers of art without this artist, who during her stay in Warsaw has introduced to our stage the masterpieces of the great writers of the world, which acquired a double value by the force of her genius.

"Moved to tears by this extraordinary expression of sympathy, Modrzejewska promised the assembled art-lovers that she would soon be back, with strength and vigor renewed by a needed vacation.

"We, too, add our voice to the general public in expressing on this occasion our best wishes for a happy journey, the complete restoration of health, and a speedy return."

During the eight years of my Warsaw engagement I made almost every year excursions to Cracow, Lemberg, and Posen, where I produced the plays of the old and new repertoire. These star engagements were delightful. In every city I was welcomed as an old friend, and the people did all they could to entertain my husband and myself. Invitations followed invitations, and they were often so numerous that I had a good excuse for not accepting any of them.

In 1876 my time was limited. We were to sail in July, and there was scarcely four weeks left until then, in which to visit Galitzia and Prussian Poland. I accepted, however, some short engagements urged upon me. Both my husband and myself wanted to say good-by to our numerous friends and relations, and to inform them of our decision of settling down in California.

It was during our visit to Lemberg that I met our poet, Kornel Ujejski. Besides being a lyric poet, he wrote a great many poems of a purely national nature. He was the author of the famous National Hymn, sung in every part of the country by men, women, and children. That hymn was written in 1846 during the outrages of the peasants against the nobility,[1] and was taken up by the people in 1861-1863. The spirit of this hymn is one desperate, passionate cry to God for justice: "Punish not, O God, the sword, but the hand!" All through, it is a sublime protest against the perfidious government. Priests used to teach that hymn to boys, and it was sung in churches and public squares wherever there was a cross or a statue of the Holy Virgin. They would kneel at its feet and sing that ardent appeal to God until the whole square would be black with kneeling men, women, and children. Printed copies of the hymn were distributed among the people by some patriotic hands, and soon the great majority of the population in all parts of Poland knew the words of Ujejski's poem by heart.

At the time we met Ujejski, he was a man in the full vigor of maturity, — tall, with plain, manly features, rather dignified, and yet simple in manner. There was a great deal of vigor and youthful enthusiasm in his speech, and he had by no means given up the hope of seeing Poland one day restored to its former magnitude and power.

The impressive music to the National Hymn was composed by Josef Nikorowicz, whom we met in Lemberg and who soon became our friend. As a sort of tribute to dramatic art he also composed music to four of my parts:

1. The massacre of nobility by peasants, instigated by Metternich.

Juliet, Mary Stuart, Dona Diana,[1] and Aniela, an *ingénue* part in "The Maiden's Vows," by Count Fredo.

I shall never forget the last few days we spent in Lemberg. It is a picturesque city surrounded by hills and full of trees. One evening after the performance, accompanied by some friends, we went to the park called "Jesuits' Gardens." It was a bright night, and the place was resounding with songs of nightingales. We walked along, breathing in the warm and fragrant air of night and exchanging thoughts, — free thoughts of wisdom and of inspiration, art, poetry, prophecies for the future of our poor country, things of the past and of the future, — all spoken to the magnificent accompaniment of the nightingales' concert. The recollection of that night makes me, even now, long for those dear moments of enchantment, for the dreams I dreamt so long ago among my own people.

One evening we were rowing on the lake. Some one recited verses. The name of Undine was mentioned, — Undine, the favorite story of my youth. Then new verses were recited, verses with living words. Each of them touched a new chord in my soul, now plaintive, now joyful, until my whole being resounded with passionate rapture. The moon was bright and warm. I put my hand in the water. It was tepid. Its emanations intoxicated me, attracted me. I held my husband's hand in dread of sharing the fate of Undine, which at that moment I both feared and desired. In the mood of poetic madness I felt myself enveloped at that hour of parting. I wanted to sink into the depths of the lake and perish with the memory of that evening, which I was sure would never repeat itself.

Next morning we left for Cracow to say farewell to my mother, my sister, and friends, and also to get my son, who, judging by his letters, was impatiently awaiting our

[1] Moretto's play of the sixteenth century.

departure for America. The majority of the Cracow people had left the city on account of the heat, so many of our friends were absent when we returned to say "good-by" to them. I left my two nieces in my mother's care, with full instructions concerning their education; and, having shed mutually many tears, we departed for Prussian Poland, where my husband's family lived. Here more tears were shed, and armed with good wishes and benedictions, we proceeded to Bremen, accompanied by my husband's two brothers, Franciszek and Josef, who wanted to have a last glimpse of us.

Sypniewski, his wife and two children, were already waiting in Bremen, and also Lucian Paprocki. Witkiewicz did not come. He sent a letter, in which he informed us that, although he had a great desire and firm resolution to join our colony, yet he was forced by circumstances to give up the journey. When we were on the point of departure, my husband's third brother, Michal Chlapowski, appeared in Bremen. After taking most affectionate leave of those three dear, brave young men with whom we had long chats about our future prospects, — after having written numerous letters to our families and friends, — on a bright summer morning, full of good hopes and cheerful spirit, we sailed into the great Unknown.

PART III

THE NEW WORLD

CHAPTER XXXII

On a bright July morning, in the year 1876, we stood on the deck of the German steamer *Donau*, waving our handkerchiefs to the three Chlapowski brothers, who stood in a small boat looking sadly towards us, exchanging signs of farewell, and while our ship was sliding farther and farther from them, we heard their faint voices calling: "Do widzenia"[1] and "Come back soon!" That echo of loving hearts made me shiver with regret, and I had a feeling as of some irreparable loss.

Soon, however, the shrill, loud gong dispelled the sadness, and we all proceeded to the dining room, where luncheon was waiting for us.

Our colonial party consisted of eight big and small human beings: Mr. Sypniewski, his wife and their two little children, Mr. L. Paprocki, Mr. Chlapowski, myself, my boy Rudolphe, and a sixteen-year-old girl, whom I had engaged to take care of the children, with an ultimate view of training her for housemaid on our future property, farm, or ranch, whatever it was to be. This rosy, pretty maiden, by the name of "Anusia," who had been brought up in a convent, and never had seen even a steam-engine before she started on that journey, suddenly found herself going to America on "a house on water," as she called it, bewildered, stunned, but not seasick.

As soon as we established ourselves on the boat, unpacked

[1] Until we meet again.

our grips, arranged and marked our chairs on deck, each of us assumed an independent line of occupation.

We spent the first evening together, watching the phosphorescence of the waves, but the next morning found us all scattered. My husband and Mr. Sypniewski made various acquaintances, and tried to pick up English words and expressions from obliging fellow-passengers. Mrs. Sypniewska nursed her baby girl, Paprocki was drawing caricatures, for which he found numerous and splendid models on board, my son was trying the piano, and I was walking up and down the deck, stopping from time to time to look at the ocean. In my first round I found Anusia sitting with the little boy in her lap, looking at the sky and then at the water, and muttering something to herself, while her young face wore an almost tragic expression. When I came nearer, and asked her how she liked the trip, she said, evidently following her thoughts and without looking at me, "O Holy Mother, nothing but wind and water!"

On one stormy day, when the sea was high and the ship rolling considerably, she became totally numb and quiescent. With each stronger roll of the steamer, instead of holding to the bench, she let herself and the baby roll down to the very edge, and there waited until some passer-by picked her up, or until the opposite motion of the ship rolled her and the baby back to her bench. After a time she seemed to rather enjoy the sport, for I saw her repeating the exercise, with a broad grin on her face.

Our journey across the Atlantic was also a novelty to me. I was fascinated by the spell of the sea. It evidently had a soothing effect on me, judging by some notes which I then scribbled down in my nautical enthusiasm.

Note 1st.

"We are in full ocean; the weather is fine. Our ship moves majestically, cutting the azure depths, which retreat with a hiss and throw milliards of bubbles on both sides, leaving behind her a long wake of pale green and white. The sky is clear, here and there spotted with tiny white clouds. The surface of the water is quiet, though wrinkled by the breeze with small, sharp waves, almost pointed; their summits catch the sun, forming thus millions of dancing, scintillating lights. There is such fulness of peace in me! My riotous thoughts, calmed by the influence of the immensity of nature, do not disturb me any more, but carry me to some mysterious land, filled with inexpressible charm. I like to be thus thrown upon the mercy of the Ocean, who, like a monstrous giant, carries me on his back. This shell in which we are travelling might at any moment become his prey, but he is to-day in a good mood, and bears swiftly the burden on his wrinkled back, murmuring some sad and solemn hymn.

"The screw of the steamer works hard, lending to the boat the semblance of a living being, in whose bosom a monotonous motion repeats itself like the beatings of the heart."

NOTE 2d.

"Heavens! What color! What a maze of emeralds, sapphires, and topazes! The sea is one immense treasury of gems! And the air! the air! What a delicious, cool, fresh breath! I feel so light that I imagine, lifting myself on my toes, I might start upwards and fly!

"Is there no regret for my country left in me? Or is it that the ocean, with its immortal beauty, has filled my soul to the very brim, leaving no room for anything else? I do not care to analyze the present state of my mind; I only know it is made of happiness and peace. My soul, lulled by that strange nurse, is dreaming. What are these dreams? Ah, there are no words in human language to express them. The thoughts are as unseizable as birds in their flight, like clouds which scarcely take a shape, ere they change into mist and melt away. This is bliss! A sharp and fragrant air strokes my brow. I take it in with full lungs — I nearly faint away under its caressing breath, drawing from it strength and health."

NOTE 3d.

"The breeze has stopped. The ocean, smooth and peaceful, has lost its color, and looks like a chasm filled with melted lead. The sky is gray, and only at its farthest edge shines a narrow blue strip, and above it spreads a long and wide stain of sulphur-yellow, closed by a dark hem of clouds. Stillness! The sun, peeping here and there through the dense mist, is scorching hot. Does it mean the approach of a storm?"

NOTE 4th.

"To-day is Sunday. Next Wednesday we shall be in New York, if the weather continues to be fine. The young men on our deck are playing leap-frog. There are sixteen of these frogs jumping around. Our European young men would be ashamed to play this game in public; they would rather imitate older men and sit by the women, talking nonsense or flirting. How much more wholesome the leap-frog seems to me!"

NOTE 5th.

"I looked into the sapphire depths of the ocean. The mystery and danger of its abysses attract me. The thought of drowning does not frighten me. On the contrary, I would rather die that death than any other."

NOTE 6th.

"My senses are wrapped up in the sea, but my soul wanders back to Poland. I send continually my thoughts to those I left behind. If a thought has power, it will reach them, it will be felt and welcomed. Illusion? Well, let it be! Is happiness anything but illusion? Life can never give us complete satisfaction, but we can create a world of peace in our souls, a world we can carry with us wherever we go. What a wonderful toy is such a little world?"

NOTE 7th.

"The day after tomorrow we shall be in New York!

"The ocean is blue again. Every one is on deck. The first-class passengers are looking down at those of the third class. There is a regular beehive there, but the people seem miserable. A band of barefooted, dirty children, young women with tangled hair, unwashed and untidy. Boys with starved or brazen faces, mothers knitting and fathers smoking. Some sleep on the bare deck, with faces to the floor. Our fellow-passengers of the first class amuse themselves by throwing amidst that pitiful crowd small coins and oranges, which produce a great commotion among the young ones. They fight, push, and nearly strangle each other, in their endeavors to catch a coin. Oranges passing from hand to hand, mashed, torn, and squeezed nearly dry, are grabbed by the victors, while the poor children retreat, crying, and extending in vain their tiny, dirty hands, in hope of getting their share of the booty.

"This exhibition was painful to me, for there was no charity in it, but a mere heartless sport. So I crossed to the other side of the boat, where I could see the aristocracy of the steerage amusing themselves with dancing. Several sailors also danced with them. Some men moved with most ridiculous motions of feet and body, but with the solemnity of undertakers. One girl was so pretty, and danced with such grace, that everybody admired her. She had blond hair and sad, sky-blue eyes. What will become of that child, I wonder; has she anybody to protect her? I feel so sorry for her, not knowing why. The musician who played on a harmonica had the face of a Richard Wagner, and must have been a German. He looked to the upper deck, tracing on our faces the effect of his music. We applauded, of course.

"Encouraged by the example of the steerage, the first-class people began to plan a dancing party for tomorrow, a full-dress affair.

"Late in the afternoon we had a beautiful sight. The sun was setting simultaneously with the rising of the moon. On the right the bright red light, dancing on the water like a laugh, on the left the solemn and soft face of the moon floating among the rainbow shades of the skies, throwing in its wake a long stream of silver light. It was curious to watch these two astral potentates looking at each other freely, with nothing between them but the gigantic pane of the ocean, and almost touching each other by the long rays of light which the water carried there and back."

I have but an indistinct recollection of our landing in New York, but what I remember is the first picture of the city on our approach through the bay, a picture most enchanting, almost magic in its ethereal beauty. There were no shadows in it, no perspective,—all was flooded with sunlight. The delicate, dim coloring gave to the whole a soft, lovely, unreal, and altogether most wonderful effect. Alas, as we came nearer, the beauty gradually vanished, and when we reached the docks the charm was totally dispelled.

When all our bags were brought on deck, and while we were waiting for our turn to descend the narrow bridge leading to the pier, I took a glimpse at the members of our colony, and they all looked happy, they all smiled, except Mrs. Sypniewska, who was pale and drooping like a water-lily.

Paprocki's eyes twinkled with mischievous merriment, and when they met mine he laughed outright. I asked the cause of this extraordinary symptom, and he answered with a broad grin: "Ah, Madame, when I think at last I am coming to a country where there are no Jews, I cannot restrain my joy. I must confess that one of the reasons why I left Poland was their great number there, so when I read in a paper that America was free from the Hebrew invasion, I said to myself, 'Let us go to that happy land!'"

Paprocki was one of those who consider Jews as enemies to civilization and a most dangerous element. Like many Europeans, he had a profound contempt for the whole race, and was most unreasonable on the subject. What was his amazement and disgust when the first person who addressed him in the "happy land" was a Polish Jew, selling matches and Russian cigarettes. Paprocki grew pale with rage, and shouted "Go away!" to the poor inoffensive Hebrew, who stepped back, very much astonished that any one should treat him so rudely in the free country. I apologized to him in Polish, saying that my friend was not well, upon which the jolly pedler said, touching his forehead with the forefinger: "Mishuga,[1] I understand," and laughing, proceeded on his way. Paprocki did not hear the Jew's remark, for he stood aside, deeply engaged in his tragic-comic reflections upon this unwelcome encounter. We all laughed at the incident, but our friend became gloomy for the next few days. His only consolation was the hope of going to California, where he was sure not to meet Jews of any description, "not in the country, at least"; of that he seemed to be quite certain. We knew better, but did not like to dispel his illusions.

[1] "A madman" in Yiddish.

There were some reasons for his moods and his hatred of Jews. During the Insurrection of 1863 he had enlisted, with other young men, under the Polish standards. The detachment in which he served was defeated by the imperial troops, the insurgents were routed, and while Paprocki, with another young man, Count Z. Lubienski, a cousin of my husband, were beating the country in trying to reach their homes, they were captured by Russians, put in prison, and sentenced to death. It seems that the spy who informed the police of their whereabouts was a Jew, — hence this horror at the sight of a Semitic face.

Imprisonment and even instant death would not have been so horrible as the suspense under which those two young men lived for several months. Every time the prison doors opened they were sure they were to be led to their death. They experienced the preliminary agony almost every hour of their confinement.

Finally, through Paprocki's father and some powerful friends' influence, they were both liberated.

Still the dark moments Paprocki spent in jail left on his impressionable mind a lasting mark, and often made him subject to gloomy moods.

The following extracts from a letter to S. Witkiewicz gives some idea of my first impressions on land: —

"NEW YORK, July 13, 1876.

"DEAR MR. STANISLAW: —

"It is Sunday to-day, and so quiet! The whole city seems plunged into a deep slumber.

"We shall stay here a few weeks on account of the Centennial Exhibition, then we intend to start for California on the steamer *Colon*, across Panama, and we probably shall settle in California. There are yet many miles before us, and much anxiety as to our future prospects. Sad thoughts assail me — this morning I heard singing in the neighboring church. The songs were pleasant, though different from ours. I cried, not knowing why, and I knelt down to my prayers. I opened the prayer-book at haphazard, and the first words I read were: 'Give yourself up to God, and fear nothing. He will fill your heart which the world lures, intoxicates, tortures, and disturbs without filling it.' I found consolation and calm in these words. Peace entered my soul. I wonder for how long!

"New York is a monstrous, untidy bazaar. The buildings are large, but without style. Brick or chocolate houses (the latter called here brownstone), with green window-shades, look simply awful. The whole city is as ugly as can be. But what makes the streets look still more unattractive are the soles of men's boots in the windows. Imagine that men have here the singular custom of sitting in rocking-chairs and putting their feet on the window-sills. You can see and admire the size of their shoes in the hotel lobbies, the barber shops, the clubs, and even in some private residences. Wherever you turn, these soles stare at you.

"A few days ago we went to Central Park, with the desire to take a walk and breathe some cooler, fresher air, but, oh! what a disappointment! Most of the trees are too young yet to give any shade, and the roads and paths are asphalted. The asphalt melts under the scorching sun and poisons the air. We returned as soon as we found a conveyance. There is, however, one thing that I like quite well. In the evening we go to watch the ferries. They are large boats on the two rivers that encircle New York on both sides, and carry passengers to and from the different suburban towns. When all these boats are lit inside, they make a pretty sight. The colored lights placed in front of each ferry, reflected in the water, increase the effect, and as there are many, many of those moving small palaces, going back and forth, the whole river looks as though it were on fire. Of course we went to Philadelphia several times to see the Exposition, and Rudolphe was happy, for he takes great interest in all sorts of engines, which are most magnificently represented there. I saw what I could see, but aside from gigantic cucumbers and pears from California, I did not notice anything superior to what I had seen before in Paris, Vienna, or Warsaw. But we walked around, admiring the order and cleanliness which were noticeable in every part of the exhibition grounds. We tried to do as others did; we even tasted peanuts and pop-corn, wondering why people ate those tasteless dainties. Paprocki predicts that in a few years our palates will so change under the influence of American air and food that he will have the satisfaction of seeing me carrying peanuts in my pocket and pop-corn in a bonbonière. We visited the art department. How poor that art looks here! The first thing we saw was a portrait of Rapacki in 'Hamlet,' by Miller; you may imagine how amused I was. There were some good paintings sent by France, and their

From a photograph, copyright by Aimé Dupont.

AGNES BOOTH SCHOEFFEL.

section was, to my mind, the best represented. I saw here also the celebrated 'Mother of the Maccabees,' by Beher, but br, br, br, — seven hanging corpses, a regular morgue!

"In the Austrian section, outside of Makart's 'Cornarina,' very few paintings of any interest. In the Belgian room are two pieces of sculpture by Godebski: an intoxicated peasant and a Russian peasant woman. Among the Russians two statues of Cengler. . . .

"Dear Mr. Stanislaw, you must go to Paris and stay and work there. You will dwindle to nothingness if you remain in Warsaw. The different cliques are too strong there, and you are not the man to cringe and bow. It is not in vain that our poet called Warsaw 'Madame Mediocrity.' Do we not know a number of these mediocrities that would not be noticed in any other place, but who prosper and grow in wealth and flesh in Warsaw?

"I wish you would paint a convoy to Siberia, just as you saw them yourself, and described them to me. That mother who had to leave her frozen child and proceed on her forced trip to Siberia is more tragic than the 'Mother of the Maccabees.'

"We are awaiting to-day the president of the Polish Dramatic Society in New York, Dr. Zolnowski. We had a long chat about the theatre when we first met him. It seems that I may be able to play in English, but first we must go to California, according to our original plan. 'Litwos'[1] is there in a place called Anaheim Landing, on the seashore, writing more of his 'Charcoal Sketches,' and his letters tell wonders about the climate, scenery, and vegetation of that promised land, so that we are all crazy to go. Perhaps after we get established in this new paradise I may pick up enough English to play there, and when I get more mastery over the new language, I may come here; for, however unattractive New York seems to me, it is the metropolis of America, and it will give me pleasure to conquer it. Ah! these are only vague projects, yet when I think of the possibility of their realization, and of making a name for myself here and in England, and also a great deal of money, I yearn to return afterwards to the old country and to do some good to my people, for I have not done anything yet, save acting. Pray for my success, for, indeed, I wish it not only for myself, but also for others.

"Good-by for the present. Charles and the rest of us send greetings to you.

"Yours ever the same, etc."

During our stay in New York we went to different theatres. At some of them farces were played, or melodramas, but at Booth's Theatre we saw "Sardanapalus," with Mr. Bangs

[1] The *nom de guerre* of Sienkiewicz in his young days.

and Mrs. Booth[1] in the chief parts. The production was magnificent, and Mr. Bangs imposing and very impressive in his character. Mrs. Booth, however, did not seem to like

Photograph by Sarony.

F. C. BANGS.

the heroine. Her part and herself were so far apart that they never met for an instant. I saw Mrs. Booth several years later in a small comedy entitled "Old Love Letters," in which she was perfect. We also saw Mr. and Mrs.

[1] Mrs. Agnes Booth, later Mrs. Shoeffel, sister-in-law of Edwin Booth.

Florence at Wallack's Theatre in the "Mighty Dollar." His "P. I. G." and Mrs. Florence's "Libby dear" sounded a long time in our ears. As for the rest, we could not re-

Photograph by Sarony.

MRS. FLORENCE.

member much, for we were too deficient in English to follow the dialogue. As far as I could judge by the facial expression and gestures, I thought Mr. Florence an exceptionally good comedian and his wife naturally amusing.

At Gilmore's Garden we heard a soprano famous at that time, — Madame Pappenheim; she had a great voice, and gave us a few moments of real pleasure. The place did not please us, however. There was nothing attractive about it. It seemed to be put up in a hurry, without taking time to give finishing touches to details. You could see bare boards here and there, and the main adornments consisted of stands with pop-corn and cheap candy, a few plants, and a platform, or rather an improvised stage, painted in garish colors, — the whole lit up with glaring gaslight.

As I looked at the promenading audience, I noticed that women still wore hoops, while that ugly fashion had been given up a year ago or more in Europe. I had seen them before in the streets, but I thought they were only worn by the poorer class, which could not afford too many changes in fashion. But here the public was made up mostly of the well-to-do people, and yet hoops reigned supreme. I realized only on that evening why passers-by were staring at Mrs. Sypniewska and myself. They not only stared, but went so far as to point at us and giggle. They evidently imagined something was wrong with our slim skirts, though the latter were made according to the latest French fashion. While they were laughing at our garments, we were amazed at the size of their hoops and their heavy black or dark skirts, which were worn that summer in New York with white calico or muslin jackets, such as we used to slip on in the morning in the old country before dressing for the street and in family circles only. Times have changed indeed, since, in New York.

CHAPTER XXXIII

We started for California on the steamer *Colon* in good spirits, for the weather was glorious. Our Polish friends from New York came on board with flowers and good wishes. We took leave cheerfully, hoping to meet soon again. The journey promised to be very fine, and we were in ecstasies over it, but we were scarcely three days on the ocean when the bursting of the main steampipe disabled our ship. It happened on Sunday morning. All the passengers were in the dining room, where a religious service was being held. Our party had joined the rest, prompted by a combined motive of devotion and curiosity. The captain officiated, reading prayers, and some young people were singing hymns.

Suddenly we heard a fearful crash, like a thousand china plates falling on the floor. The boat gave two big lurches, and then a violent hiss of steam followed.

The captain dropped the Bible and rushed up to the deck, while the entire congregation was turned into stone. All were so frightened that there was no sound, not a word uttered. Slowly, almost creeping, we mounted the stairs, and arriving on deck we learned of the calamity that had befallen us. My first thought was for my boy, for whom I looked in vain. Terror seized me. Knowing how fond he was of machinery, and how often he tried to get into the engine-room, I imagined all sorts of terrible things. When at last my husband found him and brought him to me, my joy was so acute that I fell in a dead faint.

When I recovered my senses, Mr. Chlapowski was trying to fasten on me a life-preserver, but somehow he could not succeed, putting it wrong side on. He had learned that the lifeboats were being placed in readiness, and thought it would be better to have our life-preservers on, if we had to get into them. As soon as the news about the boats was spread people began to gather objects they desired to take with them. It was quite amusing to watch those preparations. A young German dude took nothing but his comb and hand-mirror. Some old people were taking a package of sandwiches and a coffee-pot; a young girl wrapped up in a parcel her best dress, a boy carried his flute, and a sensible Irishman took a large bottle of whiskey. When they were all ready to start, one of the officers came to announce to us that, owing to the fine weather and perfectly smooth sea, the crew had succeeded in fastening the broken parts of the engine and machinery. There was no immediate peril for us, and we were not obliged to take to the boats.

This announcement was received with cheers. In a few moments more every face looked sad, for we learned that two people in the engine-room were dead, actually cooked in the steam. The burial was to take place next morning. In the afternoon two mysterious forms, wrapped up in white cloth, were placed on a bench at the stern, and the solemnity of Death spread its wings over the ship. The people grew silent, thoughtful, and strangely softened. In the evening, though everybody was on deck, you could hardly hear a sound. The two white, human forms rose and fell with the slight roll of the ship, and the ocean whispered strange things to them. I do not know anything so depressing as a burial in the midst of the sea. The coming up of the body to the surface after it has been thrown down seems like a sport, and it is simply appalling. The funeral service also, without the presence of a priest and the usual accessories, lacks the solemnity to which we are accustomed on such occasions. Possibly it might be better to have such burials at night, instead of their being made a spectacle and sometimes a sport for passengers. There were two men who made bets on the number of times the bodies would "pop up," as they called it. Horror!

Next morning, when I came on deck, I was told that we were tied to the stern of an English steamer, the *Etna*, and soon afterwards I became conscious, by the motion of our ship, that we were on our way back. We progressed very slowly, and it took us more than a week to return to the Hoboken docks. This week was spent by the passengers in dancing, singing, card-playing, and various sports and games. I avoided these entertainments, especially the social games, the forfeits of which consisted mainly of kisses. It amused me, however, to look at them, and I noticed that the men blundered on purpose to obtain their share of the punishment, while some unattractive ladies took a special care in being awkward, if the "executioner" was young and good-looking.

On our return to New York we learned that in a few days another steamer, the *Crescent City*, would take us to Panama, and in the meantime the poor disabled *Colon* extended to us its hospitality. This latter was emphasized by a champagne dinner every day while we remained in dock.

(A letter to my mother. On board *Crescent City*.)

"To-morrow we shall be in Panama, or rather in Aspinwall, three hours by rail from Panama. But we have before us yet three weeks of sea voyage on the Pacific Ocean before we reach San Francisco.

"Our life on board is rather pleasant. Charles has a great many acquaintances,—some young, and some not very young, women try to captivate him by coquettish smiles and graceful hand-shakes, but I am a watchful sentinel. Paprocki is also a great favorite on account of his drawings and caricatures. As to Dolcio,[1] he has gained the reputation of a marvellous boy pianist, while I am taken for an opera-singer, because I sing sometimes snatches from some light operettas. The people on board are not musical

[1] A pet name for my son.

a bit, hence our success; but they like to sing, although their voices are harsh and nasal.

"Charles is studying English and Spanish at the same time, and Dolcio is busy almost all day with his Ollendorf. He learns by heart long English sentences. As for me, I shall not begin to study the language until I get a good teacher in California; in the meantime I enjoy my *dolce far niente* and let myself live free from work and worry.

"It is rather warm here, and some of the men sleep on deck in their bathing-suits, in the expectation of a shower-bath when they awake, for every morning, about half-past four, the sailors begin to wash the ship, and with long hose sprinkle every corner on the deck. They are easily induced to use their hose on the passengers desirous of a morning bath. There is plenty of fun, especially if by chance or on purpose a current of water strikes some enthusiast not well prepared for the shock. Yesterday a certain stout lady, who suffers constantly from heat, got up on deck about five in the morning and asked for a sprinkling bath. It was a great amusement for the sailors when, after a copious shower, they began, pretending a good-natured solicitude, to wring out the duster which was her outer garment, and in doing so to lift it on every side higher and higher, until the poor lady shrieked with anguish, for she had but scant attire underneath, a very thin piece of lingerie. Of course this courageous woman became the subject of conversation for the whole day.

"There are three very charming young girls on board, one American and two Spanish, all three very young, beautiful, and modest. As to the rest of the women, or at least most of them, they are almost constantly attended by men, with whom they whisper and exchange 'white' glances. That is what is called 'flirtation.' One young lady, whom we call 'bluebird,' as she is always dressed in blue, carries this proceeding on with a high hand. Her husband lost his eye while attending her in her illness on a previous voyage. Some poisonous drug got on his fingers, and he carelessly touched his eye. Instead of staying with him, consoling, or cheering him in his misfortune, she promenades the whole day with a young man, the purser, and 'flirts' by moonlight, while the poor husband remains alone with his sad thoughts, pale and emaciated by his pain. I am told by a very polite elderly German lady, who has lived years in America, that it happens here not infrequently, that when a husband becomes a cripple, loses his good looks, or the means of support, he will be left by his wife, who gets a divorce from him. And indeed no one seems to pay any attention to this flirtation of the wife. Divorce, it seems, is easily obtained in the United States, and the thrifty little 'bluebird' is trying to capture a new husband. 'Business! that's the chief object of human existence,' said a middle-aged man with whiskers and no mustache, when the 'bluebird' and the purser walked by. This sentence was translated to me by the German lady, who speaks English fluently. She also explained that the word 'business' is very expressive and has a very extensive meaning. It really means money, affairs, speculation, but it is applied almost to everything. When I know more about it, I shall tell you.

"Good-night, dearest Mamusia;[1] I shall write again to-morrow."

ASPINWALL, Sept. 9th.

"We arrived here very early this morning, and as we came near the pier, a crowd of dark creatures began to pull the ship by means of a long cable rolled around a wheel, and while they were turning the latter, they sang in chorus most beautifully. Under the spell of this music we slowly came nearer and nearer to the landing-place, until we could distinguish the black, brown, yellow, or ghastly pale faces of the singers. Panama fever, that terrible curse of these regions, stared from their eyes.

"Charles and Paprocki were the first on shore. As soon as they touched the ground they were surrounded by a group of black beauties who stroked their faces, patted them, endeavored to attract them by their charms. The poor men had lots of trouble in trying to disengage themselves from the clutches of those forward and enterprising enchantresses. Fortunately they had but little money about them, or it would have most probably disappeared under the skilful hands of the dark nymphs. They say there is no place on earth where they steal better than in that small town.

"Aspinwall is a funny little place. It has only one street, or rather one long row of houses, mostly occupied by stores. Little shanties and other buildings are scattered here and there.

"In front of the stores negresses, Indian girls, mulatto and metis women are promenading up and down. Numerous vultures are also enjoying a walk along the road, and seem to be quite at home. They evidently are aware that men cannot do them

[1] Little Mother.

any harm, — for the law forbids the shooting of the scavenger birds under a heavy penalty, — so they stroll or flop about with great dignity, and they are justly entitled to their pride, for the people have a great respect for them. They help to keep the town clean by eating up all the dead rats, dead cats, as well as all the refuse thrown in the streets by the indolent and *sans gêne* population.

"The beautiful sex of Aspinwall is remarkable for its original and ludicrous attire. Some of their dresses remind me of our peasant costumes, only of more garish colors, and they loop up their skirts in their own way, over one side, showing the leg up to the knee. One woman made me stop and take a good look at her. She wore an old-fashioned but pretentious bonnet, trimmed with flowers and feathers, while her brown bosom was scantily covered with a red bandana, leaving her shoulder-blades and arms bare. The skirt was loosely tied with a string around the hips, far below the waist line in front. The prettiest in their general appearance are the Indian girls, in their white draperies.

"But the most amusing sight of all is the soldiers. Imagine very small fellows of boys' size dressed in full uniform and barefooted! One of them had no trousers on, only short trunks. With his gaudy uniform, his long gun, and a broad-brimmed Panama hat, he looked like a comic character in a burlesque. There is a very beautiful statue of Columbus here, but it is not quite completed. The pedestal is missing.

"I feel very homesick for you, and for our country. Do write, please. Our address will be: 'Anaheim, California, poste restante.' Charles and Dolcio join me in kissing your hands and feet most reverently and lovingly.

"HELENA."

The crossing of the Isthmus of Panama was a two-hours enchantment, — a panorama in which we saw most beautiful scenery flitting before our eyes. Forests with all kinds of unknown vegetation, rivers where alligators dwell, hills covered with orange, lemon, and cocoanut trees, avenues of palms, arbors formed of wild grapevines, negroes' huts with thatched roofs, brown women with skin shiny and firm like bronze, in their white draperies looking more like statues than living creatures, — unconscious of their scanty attire and chaste in their nudity; negro women in red and yellow, children swinging in hammocks, looking like monkeys, flowers of wonderfully brilliant colors, large blue butterflies, parrots of gorgeous plumage, various birds never seen before, wild turkeys flying over our heads, and the opaline sky for background.

This short trip across the first tropical country that we had ever seen was like a dream, and we were all sorry when it was over.

When we reached Panama, we learned, to our regret, that on account of the delay caused by our accident, we would not stop at any of the usual stations in Central America and Mexico, where the regular steamers make short stays, but go straight to San Francisco. Our boat, the *Constitution*, not prepared for such a long trip, had to be supplied with provisions from Panama, which fact caused a delay of a few hours. It was quite late when we got on board. The night was warm, and we climbed the steps to the upper deck. There we saw Paprocki leaning over the railing. Being dark, we could not see what he was doing, but fearing a vertigo or some whim, my husband approached and touched him on the shoulder. What was our relief when we saw Paprocki's face brimming all over with merriment. Turning to me, he said, "Is it not a great satisfaction to be able to say, 'On the ninth of September, 1876, I spat in two oceans'?"

The *Constitution* was a very old side-wheeler, three hundred and sixty-five feet long and sixty feet wide. Being built all of wood, she cracked and squeaked most dismally, waking us up several times during the first night. Twice we were on the point of dressing and rushing on deck, in fear that our old veteran boat must be going to pieces. Next morning we got up fagged and sleepy. When I was going to breakfast, I met Anusia, looking very much perplexed and pale. On my inquiry what happened to her, she answered, with tears in her eyes: "I do not want to sleep in the same room with that black woman (the stewardess). It is not only her face which is black, she is black all over; I saw it when she undressed, — and the sun cannot burn her skin under her clothes. Why, she may seize me in my sleep and carry me down to Lucifer!" And the poor thing burst out in sobs. I tried my best to calm her, explaining that the stewardess was a human being like herself, only belonging to another race. It was all in vain; she still repeated: "Black all over, she is no woman; she is something else." Finally I had to promise to get a separate room for her. I now knew some English words, such as "my maid, negro, room, sleep," etc., and I thought that I might explain my request to the captain. I met him on the deck, and directly put before him my plea for a separate room for my silly, superstitious maiden. My husband, who had better command of the language, succeeded in explaining the matter, and the polite captain, after a hearty laugh, consented to supply Anusia with another berth. Captain Dearborn was a very charming gentleman, and at the same time a very strict and dutiful officer. Nothing was overlooked by him, and while continually on the lookout for anything on sea or in the sky, he paid strict attention to the ship herself. He visited every corner, inspected personally the passengers' rooms, to see if everything was clean and tidy. He was everywhere, and the sailors had to be constantly on their guard lest the watchful eye of their chief surprise them in fault. With all this, he was much loved by them, because he was just and kind and knew when to punish or reward. He invited us to his cabin, where, among photographs, knicknacks, and souvenirs, he kept a tame squirrel in a cage. The little animal, he said, was an interesting companion in his moments of leisure. Then he took us to the other end of the ship, and there was something we never expected to see on board, — live cattle, pigs, sheep, hundreds of chickens, and also some ducks with their little ones. I went into raptures over these tiny "dukes," as, with my foreign pronunciation, I called them, to the great delight of the captain. The more we knew of him the more we liked him, he was so kind and wise. He explained to us the convenience of keeping live stock on board on such a long trip, and said he did not believe in preserved meat, adding that one of the reasons why he stayed on that old ship was that there was plenty of room for the animals. "It was in this way passenger ships were provided in the old times," he observed, "and the *Constitution* is one of the few survivors of that system, and like many other old and good things, she will soon go to rest."

There was a company of minstrels on board, and one evening they gave a performance in the steerage, to which everybody went. It seems that, through a mistake of the cook or his assistants, tea had been served to the steerage passengers made with salt water. This was a splendid opportunity for the minstrels, who composed many songs on the incident, directing their sallies straight at the captain, who sat in the first row of seats. I understood but little of these jokes, but I saw the captain laughing heartily, and after the performance he sent them a basket of wine.

I made but few acquaintances on the *Constitution.* The person I liked best was a Mrs. Jones, who had with her two little sons. The boys, like many American children, were almost too clever for their age, but somewhat loud and naughty. Their mother, however, was sweet and patient as an angel, and altogether very sympathetic. I spent most of the time with her, and though we could not well understand each other, yet we succeeded in communicating mutually our impressions by the aid of looks and signs. I learned from her several most useful sentences, and we exchanged points on embroidery and needlework. Of the other fellow-passengers of our journey to San Francisco I do not remember much, though I have a dim recollection of a lady with golden teeth, and a young woman with such a huge mouth that, when I first saw her, she gave me a nightmare. I dreamed that she was lying on the floor right close to my berth. Her mouth was wide open, and it seemed to grow larger and larger, until it became as large as the opening of a good-sized trunk. As I was rolling up and down in my bed, I imagined that with the downward motion I must lose my balance and fall into her mouth. I woke up with a shriek and found myself lying on the floor.

The three weeks on the *Constitution* passed rapidly. The sameness of the ocean, the ever blue sky, the same slow motion of the ship and her constant creaking, to which we had grown quite accustomed, — even hymns and songs such as "Darling, I am growing old," or "In the Sweet Bye and Bye," sung every evening in unison by the passengers, — all this was soothing in its monotony. I let myself be lulled by the warm salt air, gaining health and equipoise in body and soul. The farther north we advanced, the cooler became the temperature, and one day, not far from San Francisco, a dense fog covered the surface of the sea, and enveloped us in its cold and damp mantle. For two days the steamer was prevented from landing because of the thickness of the fog. I remember standing on deck, wrapped up in a blanket, for the cold was quite penetrating, and straining my eyes in the direction of the Golden City. But there was nothing to be seen but the milky mist, and even when the fog became less thick, and at last we had entered the bay, we could distinguish only lights piercing through the veil of mist, and some nondescript forms that might be rocks or palaces, vague and mysterious.

It was quite dark when we reached the port, much disappointed not to have seen the famous Golden Gate. We were, however, rewarded by a pleasant surprise awaiting us at our entrance to California. Several Polish gentlemen, residents of San Francisco, had heard of our arrival, and had come to greet us. At the head of the group was Captain Korwin Piotrowski, the prototype of Sienkiewicz's "Zagloba," and with him were Captain Bielawski, Dr. Pawlicki, General Kryzanowski, Horain, Bednawski, and Captain Lessen. I mention all these gentlemen because they were more or less connected with my début on the American stage. Our joy at meeting these countrymen was great, and the greetings exchanged quite demonstrative. There surely exists a sort of freemasonry between people of the same class or education, especially as in the present case, when they all belong to the same nation and meet abroad. All of these gentlemen belonged to the same station in life as ourselves, some among them being members of Polish noble families. It took but a short time to cement between us and them a friendship which lasted many years. At the time I am writing these lines, after thirty-two years, there remains only one survivor of these seven men, our dear Dr. Pawlicki.

CHAPTER XXXIV

THE very next day after our arrival in San Francisco I learned that a celebrated American actor, called Edwin Booth, was in the city giving a series of performances.

Our first intention had been to go at once to Southern California, to Anaheim, which we, or rather Mr. Sypniewski, had selected for our new home, because of the German families he had met there during his previous voyage to America. He thought it would be easier to commence our ranch life among people with whom we might be able to talk. All of us spoke a little German, while some were not able as yet to grasp English at all.

When Mr. Sypniewski consulted me about our trip south, I told him that we desired to stay at least a few days in San Francisco, because I was anxious to see Edwin Booth, of whose wonderful acting I had heard from our Polish friends. My husband persuaded Sypniewski to go ahead of us with his family, Paprocki, my son, and poor bewildered Anusia.

The very evening after their departure we went to the California Theatre to see Booth's Shylock, and a few days later we saw him in Marc Antony. This is what I wrote about him to one of my friends in Poland: —

"His first entrance denoted a great actor. He was magnificent in his simplicity, complete and artistic all through. His Shylock was a revelation to me. The scene with Tubal was the most perfect piece of acting. He was a genuine Jew, spiteful and mean, and yet so human that I could not but sympathize with the bloodthirsty wretch, feel for his wrongs, and deplore the injustice to the righteous people. In Marc Antony he was eloquent, eager, passionate, and full of youthful vigor, and with all that so subtle.

Photograph by Cummins, Baltimore.

EDWIN BOOTH.

His whole countenance expressed the task of the Tribune, his voice was well modulated, growing from soft and easy tones into a stormy outburst, and all the time a wonderful facial expression, and such marvellous changes and flashes of the eyes as I had never seen in any actor on the stage."

These were my first impressions of Booth. Farther down I wrote: —

"Imagine how indignant I grew when I heard men in the gallery whistling when he came before the curtain to take his call. I thought the people must be crazy, and turning to Captain Lessen, who sat next to me, I exclaimed: 'What an outrage! To whistle at such an artist! I am sure I shall never play before such a stupid audience.' Upon which my friend explained to me that whistling in this country did not mean an insult, as it does in Europe, where such a thing is worse than hissing; on the contrary, young men here whistle when they are pleased, to emphasize their approval. 'They simply imitate birds,' he added."

My Polish friends in San Francisco were anxious to see me on the stage, and General Krzyzanowski thought that I might play Ophelia in Polish to Booth's Hamlet. I found that project rather extravagant and not very desirable, but the General and the others insisted so much that I finally yielded to their persuasions. He introduced to me Mr. McCullough, then manager of the California Theatre, and the plan was discussed seriously. It was then laid before Mr. Booth, who, however, feeling too tired for extra rehearsals, and probably not having confidence in the abilities of a foreign actress, of whom he had never heard, would not risk the performance, and declined the offer. I thought him a very wise man, and felt really glad that this polyglot performance did not take place. Other projects were forming in my brain.

On our arrival at Anaheim (a small town in Southern California, inhabited mostly by German colonists and Spaniards), all our party came to the station to welcome us.

Sienkiewicz, who had just returned from Anaheim Landing, also came with the others. He looked sunburned, strong, and healthy. "You must have taken a good rest," said my husband, "you look so strong." "Swimming in the ocean, and the sea air have done that," answered the novelist, "for I have not been altogether lazy; I wrote two more 'Charcoal Sketches,' which I am going to read to you before sending them to the publisher." This promise was received with joy by all except Paprocki, who looked pathetic and sad, and from whom, on my asking him for the reason of his crestfallen countenance, I did not get a reply, but a deep sigh. We learned from Sienkiewicz that our eccentric friend had met a Polish Jew on the first day of his arrival at Anaheim, and had been in a melancholy mood ever since.

"I met this same Jew some time before," said the author of the 'Charcoal Sketches,' "when I first came here, and the encounter was rather amusing. It seems that our countryman of the Mosaic persuasion (a favorite appellation of Polish Israelites, who dislike the name of Jews) had a touch of homesickness, for when he learned that I was from Warsaw he shouted with joy, 'Welcome, welcome! you come from Poland!'

"Yes."

"Let me shake hands with you!"

"All right."

"Tell me, do you know my cousin Pistolet?"

"No."

"You do not? and yet you say you come from Poland?"

"Yes."

"How can it be? you come from Poland, and you do not know my cousin Pistolet?"

"'I never heard of him,' I said, laughing, and tried to go away. But it was not easy; he stepped right in front of me, and asked more questions about some other relatives living 'behind the Iron Gate' (a Jewish quarter of Warsaw), and he enumerated them all, repeating always the same refrain: 'You say you come from Poland, and you do not know them,—that is very, very strange,' until, half amused and half annoyed by his insistence, I succeeded in breaking away from him." You may imagine how mad Paprocki grew when he met this individual and the latter began to pester him with the same questions.

MADAME MODJESKA'S FIRST HOME IN CALIFORNIA, THE FARM AT ANAHEIM.

We found the rented house rather small: two bedrooms, a dining room, a so-called parlor, with a square piano and a sofa. The commonplaceness of it all was painfully discouraging, and the front yard, with its cypresses, shaggy grass, and flowers scattered at random, looked like a poorly kept small graveyard. The only redeeming point was the view of the mountains of the Sierra Madre to the north, and of the Santa Ana Range in the east.

But my disappointment was great, and I was on the point of exclaiming, "Oh, why do we not live in tents!" but feared to wound the feelings of Mr. Sypniewski, who had chosen for us the farm and cottage, which he thought cosy and pretty. He, with his wife, occupied the larger bedroom on account of the children. We took the smaller front bedroom, my son slept on the parlor "sofa," and Anusia had a little nook near the kitchen.

SHANTY IN SANTIAGO CAÑON

About a hundred feet from the house stood a barn, part of which was changed into a sort of camping-room ornamented with rugs, mattings, guns, harnesses, etc. This improvised and picturesque abode was occupied by Sienkiewicz and Paprocki.

My housekeeping days began. At seven next morning, attired in one of my pretty aprons which I had brought from Europe, I went to the kitchen. Breakfast was rather a complicated affair. Everybody wanted something different. Tea, coffee, milk, chocolate, and wine-soup had to be served every morning, besides other things. Our simple life did not include privations of that sort. The other daily meals, however, did not require any special effort. Quantity was often more appreciated than quality, especially after a day spent in the fields. Though Anusia and I tried our best, yet it happened sometimes that the chops were too dry, the steak too well cooked, but our men were good-natured and never grumbled. Hunger was a helpmate of mine, and I fear, sometimes, my accomplice.

The first time our gentlemen started on the cultivation of the orange orchard, they looked eager, full of energy and enthusiasm, anticipating great joy from the touch with Mother Earth. My son, though only a lad of fifteen, went also to work with them. When they returned at noon for an early dinner, they were still full of spirits, chaffing each other, discussing different ways of farming, and nursing brilliant hopes of making fortunes out of the fertile ground of California.

In the evening they came back tired but hopeful. My boy went to the piano to play one of Chopin's waltzes, — he wanted to see if his fingers did not get stiff from the hoe, — and after supper Sienkiewicz, in spite of fatigue, read us one of his "Charcoal Sketches." It was a beautiful evening, and even the commonplace furniture and a smoking lamp did not interfere this time with our enjoyment.

Next morning some of the party were late for breakfast; the third day some one complained of a lame back; and a week later there were only two who insisted still on working, my husband and my son. Sienkiewicz had to write an urgent correspondence to Warsaw; Paprocki, unable to walk from rheumatism, passed his time in making fine drawings; and Sypniewski was obliged to stay at home and attend to his wife, who was indisposed.

My husband returned that day very tired and discouraged, yet he would not blame any one, for each of them had a good reason for remaining at home. In the afternoon he and my boy went back to their task. I tried to keep them away from that work, which neither of them, nor any of our companions, were used to. It seemed to me absurd that they should waste their strength in such a way, while each of them could choose a more fitting and more lucrative occupation. My husband asked me to be patient; and the work went on as well as might be expected from these amateur farmers, who were full of good-will and fine theories, but sadly lacked experience. Sypniewski was the only one with any agricultural knowledge, but he could not apply it well to the new conditions of soil and climate. Besides that, there was no system among our idealists; they worked or not, they discussed a great deal, they sometimes even quarrelled and then made up and hugged each other; in one word, they lived under a nervous tension which could not last long.

For recreation they used to ride on horseback, in which exercise my husband, my boy, and myself often joined them. We had several saddle-horses, which we named after some well-known characters in Poland. Paprocki gave his vicious and ungainly pony the name of a Warsaw Jew famous for his absurdity. Except the buggy team, each of the horses had some peculiarities, not very pleasant. They all were broncos, they bucked and kicked,—sometimes bit,—but we did not mind it, and galloped all over the plains among the sagebrush, cactuses, and sumach, frightening away the squirrels, quail, and rabbits. Hunting and shooting expeditions were also one of the chief pastimes of the colonists, and my larder was well supplied with quail, hares, rabbits,—occasionally wild ducks or geese. Anusia dressed the birds, and she used the wings of the quail as ornaments for her hat. I counted seventeen wings pinned to it in all kinds of positions. She was very proud of them, and scorned mockery. One day she was dressing hares, and suddenly she screamed fearfully; I was standing by, picking flowers from the climber near the kitchen window and talking to my husband. We turned to her, afraid that she had cut herself, but she stood dumb and erect, with an expression of horror on her face, pointing with her finger at the half-skinned hare. On examining the animal, we understood why the ancient Jews were forbidden by the Mosaic law to eat hare, for the one on which Anusia was operating had two protuberances on its interior skin con-

taining worms. This happens very often with the hares (jackass-rabbits) in California, and is caused probably by the pricking of the cactus thorns. Cactuses, or rather cacti, as the botanists call them, are, I hear, as plentiful in Palestine as on the Pacific coast, and evidently affect the hares in the same way, which would account for the tabooing of their meat. After this we became quite cautious with hares.

Several weeks elapsed since our establishment in Anaheim. I noticed that my husband grew despondent and unusually nervous, and I also began to feel restless, and at moments felt a sort of pang around my heart. Madame Sypniewska looked like the globe of a lamp, pale and transparent, and her large eyes grew larger and larger, and were often fixed on some distant object, looking but not seeing; her husband had sometimes a gloomy expression on his face and walked with his head down, grumbling and slapping his little boy for relief. Sienkiewicz was seen on the porch, with his elbows on his knees, eyes turned to the ground, and his jaws twitching with nervous ticks, as though he were chewing some unpleasant thoughts; and one evening we came across Paprocki leaning against a tree and crying. We realized that we were all homesick.

One afternoon, when I sat at the window, sad, unnerved, brooding over our fate, I saw two people approaching the house: a man about forty years old, with sharp, clear-cut, regular features, blond hair and beard, — a perfect American type, — and a woman, forming a strong contrast, with her olive complexion and black hair. She looked Spanish, but her high cheek-bones and the shape of her nose betrayed the addition of Indian blood.

They came to the window, and an introduction took place. The name of the man was Mr. J. E. Pleasants, and his wife was called by her Christian name, Donna Refugio. The couple seemed very sympathetic. I called my husband, who invited them to the house, and had quite a long talk in two languages, — broken English and broken Spanish. I understood that they expressed a wish of our visiting them in their homestead in the Santa Ana Mountains, where live oaks grow and clear brooks wind around the rocks. We had not the faintest idea then how closely this visit was connected with our final settlement in California.

The talk with these two strangers inspired us with the desire of taking a few days' vacation from farming toil and housekeeping drudgery, and visiting some neighboring places. Every one agreed to the change, and we commenced our excursions by going to Anaheim Landing. All the colony went on this trip, even Anusia and the children, the weaker sex and the babies in a buggy, and all the men, including Rudolphe, on horseback. We must have presented a curious picture, for when we passed through the town, there was not one person in the streets that did not stop to take a look at our convoy. We met many interesting figures of Spaniards and cow-boys, among others the "Señora Coyote," driving her half-starved horse. This unkind nickname was given to the old lady by Indians working in her vineyard. She had come originally from northern Europe years ago, and was one of the first settlers of the place. She enjoyed a reputation of extreme economy, and hated nothing so much as to waste anything. It happened once that a coyote was killed and brought to her. She did not thank the fellow who killed it, only scolded; but when he was gone, she skinned the animal and cooked the meat for the dinner of the Indian workmen. A little boy saw her doing this abomination and betrayed her. Hence the name of "Señora Coyote."

Halfway to Anaheim Landing we saw for the first time a fantastic, beautiful, but deceiving picture, — a mirage.

When we arrived at the Landing, Sienkiewicz showed us the interesting spots, his favorite walks, and the shanty where he had lived for some time and where he wrote his stories.[1]

I listened and looked at everything, but I grew quite sad when I turned my eyes to the ocean. The blue waters of the great Pacific reminded me of our first sea-voyage when we left our country. The recollections of the happy past, spent among beloved people, — Cracow, with its churches and monuments, the kind friends waiting for our return, the stage, and the dear public I left behind, — all came back to my mind, and I felt a great acute pang of home-sickness. I stepped away from the rest of the company, threw myself on the sand, and sobbed and sobbed, mingling my moans with those of the ocean, until, exhausted, I had not one drop of tears left in my eyes. A sort of torpor took the place of despair, and the world became a vast emptiness, sad and without any charm. In that state of mind I returned home, and for some time remained indifferent to the surroundings, until one day we made a new excursion to the Santiago Cañon in the Santa Ana Mountains, where our new friends, the Pleasants, lived. On our way we stopped at a charming spot, called the "Picnic Grounds" (at present the Orange County Park). With its magnificent old live oaks overhung with wild grapevines, its green meadows and clear, limpid brook, the place was so beautiful that it excited our greatest admiration. Towards the evening we reached the upper part of the cañon, in the heart of the mountain, and the sun was quite low when we arrived at the home of the Pleasants. The couple were away on some errand, but the spot they selected for their residence was so enchanting that we were fully rewarded for our long trip.

On an acre or so of level ground stood a tiny shanty, the dwelling-house; a few steps farther was an arbor covered

[1] Altogether Anaheim Landing was a desolate place, and at the present time it is even more so.

with dead branches, vines, and climbing roses. Inside of the arbor a rustic sofa, table, and chairs, an outdoor dining room and living room in one. Next, a kitchen consisting of an iron stove under the shelter of widely-spread oak branches, with pantry shelves built in the cavity of the same tree. Some rose-bushes, a few flowers, a small palm, and an olive tree were the only improvements on nature. This primitive miniature house holdwas the centre of a crescent formed by a sloping mesa, thickly covered with bushes of wild lilac, wild honeysuckle, etc., and oaks. In front the grounds were closed by a swift creek, and a precipitous mountain, called the "Flores Peak." All around, like a living dark green frame, oaks and oaks, some of stupendous dimensions. In the distance, mossy rocks and mountains. The whole picture looked more like fantastic stage scenery than a real thing, and looking at it, my imagination carried me far, far beyond the hills, back to the footlights again.

A few years later we bought this place, and I called it "Arden," because, like the "Forest of Arden" in "As You Like It," everything that Shakespeare speaks of was on the spot, — oak trees, running brooks, palms, snakes, and even lions, — of course California lions, — really pumas.

It was quite dark when we left the Pleasants' homestead. An old Indian who, in their absence, took care of the place, advised us to go to Mr. Shrewsbury's, a neighbor living about a mile off, who had a larger house, and could therefore provide us with more comfortable hospitality. Old "Tio Ramon" lit a lantern, and we followed him. It was very dark, and we were among the trees. We heard strange noises in the woods, which put every one in an expectant mood. All were looking for some strange occurrence, when suddenly a hushed, trembling voice whispered, "Look, look, a mountain lion!" and indeed we saw above us two shining yellow eyes. "Get your gun ready; we'll shoot him." "Can you see?" "There! Shoot now!" "Wait!" While these brief commands were being uttered, the Indian asked us what was the matter. He did not understand our words, but the scared tone of our voices had attracted his attention. After a brief talk in Spanish, my husband translated to us that the ominous fiery eyes did not belong to any wild beast of prey, but to a peaceful owl. Our semi-heroic mood gave way to a fit of wild merriment, and we were still laughing when our buggy and the horsemen stopped before a white wooden house.

Two brothers lived there, two squatters by the name of Shrewsbury, who very politely offered to put the whole house at our disposal. They were the kindest of hosts, and after serving us with tea and placing before us everything that was left in the pantry, they said "Good night!" and went to sleep in the barn. Before going to bed, our attention was attracted by some book-shelves in the room. We were amazed by the titles of the books: there were geological, scientific, and philosophical works of the best and most modern authors, and with them Shakespeare, Emerson, Tennyson, Longfellow, and others of more recent date. We certainly did not expect to find so much good literature in a squatter's home, and we were glad to know that there were other people with culture besides ourselves who had forsaken the so-called civilized world to seek in the wilderness close contact with nature. When we met our hosts next morning, we greeted them with cordiality and respect.

They gave us an excellent breakfast of "flapjacks," eggs and bacon, and coffee, and accompanied us on horseback for a while in order to show us the best road.

CHAPTER XXXV

On our return to Anaheim we found a letter from Captain Piotrowski, announcing his intention of visiting us. Before our departure from San Francisco the captain had expressed a wish to visit us, whereupon my husband invited him to our new home, to stay a week or so with us. In his letter he announced his arrival. We made suitable preparations for our guest: removed the sofa from the parlor and replaced it by a bed, while my son joined the party in the barn. The most important question was the *menu*. The captain was a *gourmet*, and as he was so very tall and so very stout, his huge body required a vast amount of food to satisfy his almost colossal appetite. For the first dinner we decided upon a roast turkey, and Sypniewski, as the most competent judge in those practical matters, went to town and bought a huge and fat bird. And then the question arose, Who shall kill the turkey? Our idealists looked at each other and one by one dispersed in different directions; while they were going away, I heard their voices muttering: "Not I." "Nor I." "I never killed a turkey." "It is the business of the cook," etc. "Anusia!" I called, "can you kill this turkey?" "O, Holy Virgin!" she exclaimed, laughing, "that big thing? I could not hold him; he is stronger than I; and then I never killed anything, not even a chicken; you know the gentlemen shoot them for us when we want them for dinner." Seeing that it was impossible to coax this innocent to commit murder, I went to my husband and told him that if some one did not kill the bird, there would be no dinner for the captain.

After a while, watching from the window, I saw him returning with Sienkiewicz and Paprocki. They held a short consultation, and then Sienkiewicz went to the barn and soon returned with a "ciupaga," a kind of hatchet used by the Carpathian mountaineers as a weapon, several of which had been brought by our men from the Tatra. He sharpened his tool on the grindstone and put it against the stump used for wood-chopping. Then the chase for the turkey took place, and after having secured the victim, the three men stretched it, with great ceremony, upon the stump. My husband held the legs, Paprocki the head, and Sienkiewicz, with the stern expression of an executioner, picked up the hatchet and decapitated the innocent culprit.

The captain arrived next morning, and with his entrance gloom changed into merriment. Every one smiled and talked, and all at once became witty and entertaining. Piotrowski was a curious type. He seemed suited rather to the sixteenth or seventeenth century than to our modern era. His humor reminded me sometimes of Sir Toby Belch or Falstaff. Even his language was unusual. It was quaint, much more correct and crisp than our diluted and distorted gabble of the twentieth century.

Before dinner my husband asked our guest what wine he liked best. "I only drink milk," he answered with a malicious twinkle in his eye, "but I like to prepare it a little." Then, making himself at once at home, he opened the kitchen door, and seeing Anusia, the maid, exclaimed, "Halloo, pretty maiden!" Then turning to us, he said, with a wink, "Where did you pick up this dainty?" When we told him that we brought her with us from Poland, he laughed. "Oh! if she is a Pole, I must give her a Polish greeting!" With these words he entered the kitchen, and almost at the same time we heard a shriek, a slap, and Anusia was running away into the yard, while the captain was standing at the kitchen door, holding his sides and laughing.

When he was able to catch his breath, he called, "Come back, little shrew, and give me some milk, or I'll perish. Don't you see how thin and wan I am? If you don't get that milk, I shall die, and you will have to weep on my grave."

But poor Anusia was too frightened to return. My son brought the milk and handed it to the captain, who retired with it to another room. When he returned, he poured out the white liquid into glasses and passed them around. Scarcely had my husband lifted the glass to his lips when he put it down, coughing and holding his throat. "What is this frightful stuff?" he asked; "is it one of your jokes?" Upon that Piotrowski raised his eyes to the ceiling, and said, "O God, thou hearest and dost not thunder! If my wet-nurse, whose name was Krasicka,[1] had fed me with such milk I would not have been weaned even until to-day!" This delightful compound proved to be made up of one part milk and three parts brandy. It seems that his physician had prescribed for him a month of milk-cure, and that was the way in which he followed the doctor's instructions.

Born of a noble Polish family, the captain came to America in the early forties. His prolonged stay in different parts of this country, together with his faithfulness to old Polish traditions, made of him a strange combination of old-fashioned culture and modern American notions of politics and business. In his devotion to his adopted country he often would use Polish phraseology for American things, and amongst others would call the prominent men of the United States "Nobles" and "Magnates." In his native idiom he used the language of the sixteenth century (the golden era of Polish literature); he also spoke French fluently, and his knowledge of English was perfect, all except his pronunciation, which was exceedingly ludicrous. He would say "vyter" for waiter, "anoog" for enough, and "hoorh" for church, — the latter, I suppose, because the sound "ch"

[1] A very aristocratic name in Poland.

in Polish is pronounced like "loch" in Scotch, as a strong aspiration. When my husband remarked that his words sounded differently from what we heard around us, he replied: "I tell you these Anglo-Saxons do not know how to pronounce their own language. It should be pronounced as it is written; but no; they twist every word, they push their tongues forward against their teeth to say a simple 'th,' and that is the reason why so many old maids have such long, protruding teeth, which they cannot keep behind their lips. It is all nonsense; every one understands me in San Francisco, and I am not going to cripple my tongue or disfigure my mouth in trying to imitate the deficiencies of that absurd and intolerable pronunciation."

When we met him, he was a widower, but he had lived separated from his wife long before she died. He spoke often about his married life, and we learned from him that his wife was born in the south of France.

"Perhaps you are not aware," he said once, "that the people of southern France are fond of garlic. Yes, they are; but how could I have known that the pretty, delicate girl whom I took for my wife would share that horrid taste? When I courted her there was only a perfume of verveine floating about her; but when, on our wedding-tour, I entered one day our private dining room in the hotel, O Saints Peter and Paul! the smell of garlic struck my nostrils with a club! It was the soup *à l'ail*, so popular in Marseilles. I did not say anything for the moment, but refused the soup. I suffered agonies when I saw that pretty, refined wife of mine smacking her lips after each spoonful, for I knew I had to avoid contact with her for at least twenty-four hours. I could not kiss her 'good night,' and that was the first misunderstanding between us. Then came another; I was very fond of cheese, and she detested it. Every time she ordered garlic, I ordered some strong, delicious cheese. When the soup came on the table, I opened doors and windows and waited outside until the abominable stuff was taken away. When the cheese appeared on the table, she rose from her seat with the air of an offended queen and walked off, leaving me chuckling over my dessert. We managed, however, to live a few years together, in a sort of compromise, but when the Almighty blessed our union with a little daughter, my wife's affections concentrated entirely upon the child, and the garlic appeared daily in all forms on the table. It was an open war, and I, who had stood bravely in the ranks against the Russian army in 1830, succumbed in this domestic battle and, like a miserable coward, ran away, and stopped only on the shores of this blessed land of liberty. And yet, when a few years afterwards I heard of my wife's death, I shed real tears, and went to France to make provisions for the future of my daughter."

Notwithstanding his age, the old gentleman had a young heart, and liked to dwell on the remembrances of his love-affairs, none of which ended happily; "for, you see," he said, "I am still a widower."

The captain's visit to our farm did not pass without incidents: the very first night the bed broke under his colossal frame. We did not hear the noise, because, having sat up very late that night, we slept very soundly, but the captain told us his tale of woe in the morning.

"When the cardboard bed fell to pieces under me, I thought I might find shelter and a bale of hay in the barn, with the boys. I took my pillow and blankets and went into the yard. But I lost my way in the dark and entered the stable instead. The horses, frightened probably at my bundle of bedding, began to kick and neigh; one bronco tore himself off and rushed out into the open, passing so close to me that we nearly smashed each other against the wall, and when at last I reached the barn and opened the door, I saw by the dim light of a candle our young men sitting on their couches with guns pointed at me, and shouting, 'Stop, or you are dead.' They said it in good English, too. 'You Tartars, you barbarians,' I screamed, 'you bloodthirsty heathens, put down your guns.' They obeyed quickly, and came to me. 'We took you for a burglar or a horse thief,' said Sienkiewicz, laughing, and directly they built a bed of hay for me, for I refused to lie down on any of their filigree couches. I slept well, I thank you, but feel a little tired. Anusia! you paradise apple, bring me some milk, and don't fear; I shall not kiss you this time; there are too many people in the room. I will catch you when no one is by." Anusia brought the milk, dropped a courtesy, and said, "You never shall catch me, Captain, for I can run quicker than you." "Do you see this saucy damsel?" he shouted merrily; "the chicken has scarcely cut through the shell of its egg, and already it opens its beak from ear to ear." The girl left the room, scarlet with indignation, which increased the captain's hilarity.

One afternoon we all took a stroll to the vineyard for grapes. After having filled our baskets, we noticed that the captain was not with us. On our return, and when we were quite near the house, we heard his voice shouting, "Go and call some one to help me out of this." "Something must have happened to him," said Sienkiewicz, hurriedly, and ran to his rescue. The others followed, and I also started on a run home. Seeing Anusia in the yard, I asked her what had happened. "Oh, nothing," she replied, grinning; "the captain took a bath, that is all." "A bath—where?" But Anusia did not answer, for the baby began to cry. "I must see to the baby, Madame," and she left me, but I saw that she knew more about it than she would say. At the same time I perceived the poor captain, led by our young men, with his clothes soaking wet, his face purple, walking with difficulty, groaning and limping. "He fell into the irrigation ditch," some one whispered; "quick, some hot brandy!" They took him to his room, took off his wet clothes, and put him into bed, which by this time was a new, strong one. When he had rested awhile, I went to inquire how he felt, and then he told us the whole adventure in his quaint, untranslatable language.

"I was very thirsty when we came to the vineyard, and not wishing to disturb the company, I left unnoticed, in search of a glass of water, or — hm — never mind what. I thought I might get to the cottage by a shorter road and took a bee-line. When I was at a short distance, I saw Anusia in the yard, hanging up the linen, and I called jokingly to her, 'Now, my little bird, I will catch you and kiss you!' To my astonishment, the girl did not run away, but called back, 'Come, come, Captain, kiss me!' The imp knew of the ditch separating us, but I had only my foolish fun in the head, and the girl looked quite pretty. Besides, I could not see the ditch, as it was all overgrown with weeds. I clapped my hands and started on a run, when suddenly — O Maria, Joseph! shall I ever forget the sensation? I sank plump into the cold water up to my hips. I tried to get out of the ditch, but this confounded soil of Anaheim is genuine quicksand; the more vigorous were my efforts, the deeper I sank. I called to that little demon of a girl to help me or to call some one, but that incarnation of imbecility only laughed more and more, while I was sinking lower and lower. When the water reached to my armpits, I gave up the struggle. Perish will I, and my fleas with me! I thought, and then I asked the Holy Virgin if she was not ashamed to let me die this miserable death. The cruelty of my fate brought tears to my eyes, and I hung my head upon my breast, when suddenly I heard this angel's voice," pointing to Sienkiewicz. "I raised my eyes, and my hopes revived, for he was extending his hands to lift me up, which, however, considering my weight and his slender form, was almost impossible.

Then you all came and saved me from that ignominious death. And now, my good Samaritans, don't you think I am entitled to a drink of my milk? That water sucked all the juice out of me, and nature calls for compensation."

Such was the man who may have given to Sienkiewicz the suggestion of Zagloba in his historical trilogy of "Fire and Sword," "Deluge," and "Pan Michal." Having known personally the captain, and having read the works of my great countryman, I could not help feeling the sincerest admiration for the genius and the fertile admiration of the writer who, taking a few features of that character, filled them in, extended them, adapted them to most numerous and various situations with a sense of artistic proportions, and thus created a type the equal of which might be looked for only in Shakespeare or Cervantes.

CHAPTER XXXVI

It was late in November when the captain left us, after a visit of one or two weeks. The weather became cloudy and windy and threw everybody into a gloomy mood. The desert wind coming from the northeast, and locally misnamed the Santa Ana wind (because it passes through the Santa Ana Cañon), is a kind of sirocco. Hot and dry in summer, its breath dries up the plants, gives headaches to people, and prostrates them. Furious in winter, it uproots trees, tears off roofs, and devastates fields.

On one of these cloudy days we were all seated on the porch, exchanging notes upon our anticipations of ideal life awaiting us in sunny California and the realities of the present day. We all came to the conclusion that our farming was not a success. Everything seemed to be a sad failure. We had several cows, but there was no one to milk them, and we had to buy milk, butter, and cream from the neighbors. We had chickens, but our fine dogs made regular meals of the eggs. We had a vineyard, which yielded beautiful muscat grapes, but there was nobody to buy them, and often people would come and fill their wagons with them without more ado; they said that such was the custom of the country. We were too courteous to contradict them, and smilingly consented to be robbed, respecting the practice. The hares continued to be diseased, and our winter crop of barley was fast disappearing in the mouths of the neighboring cattle, although I tried myself to shoot at the latter with my revolver. My shooting did not even scare them; they did not seem to mind it at all, except one little calf, which got frightened, and with a treble in A minor, trotted away, seeking a refuge between its mother's legs. Some of these mishaps might have occurred even to experienced farmers, but the most alarming feature of this bucolic fancy was the rapid disappearance of cash and the absolute absence of even a shadow of income. This latter crude reality gave the final blow to our cherished bubble. My husband had already spent $15,000, yet he was ready to sacrifice the last penny of his small remaining capital to keep up the colony. I could not allow that, and disclosed my plan of going to San Francisco in order to study English, and try to get on the stage.

This project was received with acclamation, for they all believed that I would succeed, and besides, all of them wanted a change, except Sypniewski, who saw the difficulty of moving with his wife and children. We agreed, however, that for the present he and his family might live on a farm which my husband had bought in the summer, and if we should sell that farm, or, later, if my dramatic venture turned out a success, we would give him the means to go back to Europe.

In the first days of January, 1877, I went with my husband to San Francisco. We were met at the station by Captain Piotrowski and several of our Polish friends, amongst them good old Captain Bielawski, who came with his wife to offer us the hospitality of his house until we should find some suitable lodgings.

Next morning my husband returned to Anaheim in order to sell the farm, if possible, and provide for the return home of the Sypniewskis. He would soon be back in San Francisco, and bring my son with him. We parted in good spirits, for he left me in care of kind people, our good friends.

Captain Bielawski was a lovely old gentleman with a handsome face, clear complexion, and snow-white hair and beard. In his youth he had served in the Austrian army, where he had attained the position of Captain of Engineers,

Paprocki. Madame Modjeska. Charles Bozenta Chłapowski.

THE RETURN FROM AMERICA. CARICATURE MADE BY PAPROCKI SOON AFTER MODJESKA'S FIRST APPEARANCE IN AMERICA, IN 1876.

and had done valuable work in building fortifications. But the terrible massacre of landowners in 1846, in Austrian Poland, instigated by Metternich, excited such indignation in his heart that at the first opportunity he left the military service and emigrated to America. He reached California in the early fifties and, thanks to his knowledge of engineering, easily found occupation as draughtsman in the United States Land Office. He retained the latter for forty-five years, and was generally considered as a pillar of that department in San Francisco. He personally surveyed most of the old Spanish grants in California, and with his splendid memory was the best authority to be consulted in regard to land titles. His experience and knowledge in those matters was rendered the more valuable on account of his perfect honesty. It would have been easy for him to accumulate a very large fortune, but he was exceedingly scrupulous, and never availed himself of the opportunities offered by his official position for his private aggrandizement. I dwell on these features of my old friend because they were not common at that time. In his political opinions he was rather a radical, a Republican both in the American and in the European sense, enemy of all the monarchs, and, I am sorry to say, equally so of the Church, quoting Voltaire and Ingersoll and shunning priests,—with all this, kind-hearted, generous to a fault, very stubborn in his ideas, and very devoted to his friends. He was generally respected and inspired confidence in all who knew him. It was an original and curious relation that bound him to his friends, Captain Piotrowski and Dr. Pawlicki. The former had aristocratic leanings and prejudices, and the latter, the doctor, was a staunch Catholic. The whole time they were of different opinions and were very hot in their discussions, but when it came to action, they all went hand in hand. They all three were the soul of honor and all great Polish patriots.

Mrs. Bielawska was an Englishwoman by birth, small, alert, nervous, neat to perfection, and always active. She possessed a very tender heart, and was fond of rendering many kind services, even to strangers. Both the captain and his wife were very hospitable, and I was not the only guest in their house. The son of some friends, Johnny, a boy of nineteen, occupied permanently a room on the third floor. I learned later that he had been invited to stay in the house till the end of his studies. I actually took my first lessons in English from that boy. At every meal I asked him for the names of different objects, and he always gave me the required information patiently and with good humor.

On the evenings when there was no company Johnny became the central figure of our small circle, for he knew a number of funny stories and many jolly songs, to which I had to play the piano accompaniment. I also was asked sometimes to sing, but I knew only songs with Polish, French, or German words, which were well received by our host, familiar with those languages, but not much relished by his wife, who spoke and understood only English, and not being musical, cared more for the meaning of the words than for the tune. Realizing my failure in that direction, I determined to learn some American songs, and I began with the "Suwanee River." One evening, when Mrs. Bielawska had gone out, I learned a duet with Johnny, as a surprise for our kind hostess. The surprise was greatly enjoyed, and so I studied some more of the trashy but amusing songs of the day to please the dear woman. One of them was her great favorite, and began with the words, "In her hair she wore a white camellia." Johnny corrected my English pronunciation, and I made a hit.

In the meantime I advertised for an English teacher, and soon afterwards I answered the bell to a tall young lady who consented to give me every afternoon one hour of her "valuable time." For about two weeks I was taking lessons from her, learning a great many words, as well as sentences, when one day my hostess, wishing to talk to me, entered my room. The lesson being over, the teacher was ready to go. I introduced her to Mrs. Bielawska, and the two ladies had a bit of conversation between them. As soon as the tall young person of "the valuable time" disappeared behind the door, my young hostess said to me, in an alarming tone of voice: "My dear! your teacher is a German, and has an awful accent. Send her away, for you are already beginning to catch her horrible pronunciation."

I was glad to be able to understand this time all she said to me, and following her advice, I wrote my first English letter (revised and corrected by Mrs. B.) to my teacher, informing her that I should not require her tuition further.

Captain Piotrowski came quite often to see how I was getting along with my English, and when I told him of the teacher, he said: "My dear Madame Helena, you don't need any professor. Do as I do: pronounce the words just as they are written, as you would pronounce them in Polish. That's the only reasonable way to speak English. Don't you spoil the shape of your mouth or harden your voice trying to get impossible and harsh sounds. And above all, do not try to pronounce the "th," as they do, for you'll never get it. Plain "t" or "d" are far more pleasant to the ear than their lisping "th," and, besides, let me tell you this, — the worse they'll think your accent, the better they will like you. Believe your true, experienced friend, and remember my words." These words, however, instead of encouraging me, made me despondent. I did not know what to make of them, and I began to doubt my success. If I followed the captain's advice, I would become a sort of freak, to be laughed at, and applauded on account of the ridicule. What would become, then, of my artistic ideals?

He said I could never get a correct pronunciation. This verdict cooled a great deal of my enthusiasm, for I believed in his sincerity and in the truth of his statements. While I was brooding over it in my room, sad and gloomy, Mrs. Bielawska entered with a package of delayed letters, addressed to Anaheim and forwarded to me. They were New Year's greetings from Poland, — dear letters from my family and friends, filled with heartfelt wishes and the desire of seeing us back in our old home again. Besides, there were also letters from society people, literary men, artists, and one of them from our eminent patriot and poet, Kornel Ujejski.

While reading all these friendly messages the tears rolled down my cheeks, and I had to use all my will power not to collapse under this renewed fit of homesickness. The dinner bell compelled me to wash the tears away, and the enforced cheerfulness with which I greeted my dear host established a sort of equipoise in my soul. To complete the victory, I sang in the evening all the new, funny songs I had learned in San Francisco. Next day, coming out of the church, I met the companion of our sea voyage, the sweet Mrs. Jones, who told me that I had made quite a progress in English, and that my accent was not "so very bad." This was but little comfort, but I felt strong again and ready for further struggles.

I had also many letters from my husband during the few weeks of our separation. In one of them he informed me that he, Paprocki, and my son had left Anaheim and gone to the Santiago Cañon, where they took a claim one mile above the Pleasants' home and lived in a shanty amidst oak trees and rocks. "We cook our own meals," he wrote, "and I have learned how to make 'flapjacks.' Paprocki is quite an expert in roasting quails, and Dolcio bakes fine tortillas. He is also a very good shot, and we have game every day.

"We sleep all three in the only room of our shanty. Last night the Santa Ana wind tore off the roof of our palace. We had to get up and put it on again, and then passed a rope over it, and winding the two ends around our wrists we succeeded in holding it in place until daylight, when the wind subsided. We go every day to see Pleasants and his wife, whom I am teaching French. She is very nice and refined by nature, etc."

Later on he wrote: "I am coming soon with Dolcio,[1] whom I will leave with you, for I shall have to go back to Anaheim, or at least stay somewhere in the neighborhood, on account of the farm, which must be sold, and also because Sypniewski may feel quite deserted since Litwos (Sienkiewicz) also left for the north, where he will live with Piotrowski's friend. It is awfully hot here now. Yesterday we spent the noon hours sitting in the cool creek and frightening the water-snakes. Rattlers also are very numerous at present, and we have to be very careful. We kill them with stones or guns. Notwithstanding these inconveniences, this cañon is the most beautiful spot on earth." "We have a neighbor," he wrote another day, "a burly Russian with a shaggy beard all over his face; a tall, muscular fellow, who changed his name for some reason or other, and who calls himself Williams. He lives in the upper cañon, about half a mile above us, where he built a log cabin with his own hands. He came to see us, and we returned his call. He showed us the tracks of a grizzly bear, for which he has been patiently waiting ever since he came to this wilderness. He has also a magnificent skin of a mountain lion he killed near his house, and a great many skins of wildcats, etc."

In one of his letters my husband at last announced his and my son's arrival, to my great joy and relief, for I trembled lest some accident happen in this wilderness.

[1] Polish diminutive for Rudolphe.

I left the hospitable roof of the dear people with whom I had been living more than a month, and moved to a small but neat apartment on O'Farrell Street, where I welcomed my two squatters, who looked very healthy, but brown as Indians. We spent the six weeks of my husband's stay in San Francisco in getting acquainted with the different Polish families residing there. All those good people had been wandering across the whole width of the American continent until they came to the Golden City, where they remained, because they could not go farther. Had they not been stopped by the Pacific Ocean, they would have been still going on farther west, far away from despotism, and in quest of freedom, peace, and happiness. The finest and best element of Polish emigration in America was represented by these few families. Next to Captain Bielawski there was old Mr. Bednawski, of the same age or older even than the former, an old soldier of the Polish Insurrection of 1830–1831. For some time after that he was exiled to the Caucasian Mountains, and later on went to France, where he served in the army. He was a pensioner of the French government for his military services. In spite of his advanced years, he was polished and poetic, and a great admirer of pretty women. Though he could not see them well, on account of his weak eyes, he pretended the contrary, and went into ecstasies over every well-dressed woman he met in the street. Beauty in every shape appealed to him, and when he spoke of nature or of women, his face became so radiant, and the language he used to describe their charms was so expressive, that it was a real pleasure to listen to him. He had a little weakness; he did not like to acknowledge that he was getting pretty well advanced in years. He never confessed in what year he was born, and we could only judge of his age by the episodes which he related to us, of which he was a contemporary. Anyhow, among his acquaintances he passed for being ninety-nine. All together he was a fine old gentleman, and proved a true friend to me during the trying months of my preparation for the American stage.

To finish with the oldest generation, there was yet another veteran of 1830, old Captain Wojciechowski, called usually Captain Francis, an old companion of Piotrowski. It was at his place that Sienkiewicz took up his abode when he left Anaheim. I did not know him so well, but he was spoken of very highly, and they say that Sienkiewicz reproduced some of the features of his personality in another great character in his "Fire and Sword," the wonderful and heroic "Podbipienta," for like him he was more than commonly tall, very thin, and reserved by disposition. I heard Sienkiewicz say that when once he walked between Captain Piotrowski and his friend, he was much amused by their respective shadows on the white, sandy road. The contrast of his own medium figure next to those of his giant companions was so striking that he thought he would make a description of himself with his huge friends in a letter to his Polish newspaper. He changed his mind, however, but a few years later memory brought them back to him. He utilized their outward characteristics as well as his own, and created three incomparable types, "Zagloba," "Podbipienta," and "Pan Michal."

About ten years younger, but closely connected with the former gentlemen by friendship, was Dr. Pawlicki. He was not a relic of the past, like the others mentioned before, and although older than my husband and I, he was more familiar with modern Poland and its troubles, which we had witnessed ourselves. A staunch patriot of the finest type, an ardent and practical Catholic, he took a very lively interest in everything which happened in our country. In former years he had been a surgeon in the Russian navy, but had left the service during the insurrection of 1863, the same in which my husband had taken an active part, and had come to San Francisco, where he married and remained ever since.

There were several others, most of them interesting. In order not to make my picture-gallery too long, I will mention only Mr. Julian de Horain, General Kryzanowski, and Captain Lessen. The latter had fought in 1848 under Kossuth, in the Hungarian revolution, while the General had gained his military title in the American Civil War, where he had rendered distinguished services according to Carl Schurz, who mentions him very favorably in his Memoirs and under whom he served. The General took a more lively interest than any other of my Polish friends in my future dramatic career in this country — at least he was better acquainted with theatrical people and things, and together with his friend, Governor Salomon, was later very active in my behalf. As to Mr. Horain, he had come to California only a short time before us, and it was in part due to his letters, published in Polish newspapers, that we were first tempted to come to California. He was one of our better humorists, of a rather sarcastic turn of mind, but full of spirit and of fun. He was called, among our American friends, "Mr. I lofe you," because these were the only English words he knew, and he used to tease young girls by greeting them with a low bow and the words "I love you," but which he pronounced, "I lofe you," chuckling over the embarrassment of the girls. He had a French wife, delicate, modest, retiring, who gave him five children.

CHAPTER XXXVII

Ever since I dismissed my German teacher of English I had looked for the real article, but without success. At last I found a girl who was a genuine godsend to me.

One day, despondent and almost giving up all hope of learning English properly, I was leaning out of the window, when I saw a graceful, girlish figure coming out of the door of our house. As she passed under my window, she raised her head, looked straight in my face, and smiled. Her pretty face, of Oriental type, her dark, splendid eyes and dazzling teeth, won me at once and I smiled back. She went on, and I watched her quick steps and her elegant, diminutive form until she disappeared in a house on the same side of the street. "We are neighbors," I thought, and when we went downstairs to our lunch, I asked Mrs. H., the landlady, who that pretty person was who had visited the house in the morning. "Oh, that was our dear Jo," answered Mrs. H. "Jo? a funny name for a young lady," remarked my husband. "Her name is Joanna or Josephine, I do not exactly know which, but we all call her Jo; her other name is Tuholsky." "That sounds Polish," we both exclaimed. "Well, I think her father came from Poland, and, by the way, she is very anxious to meet you." We arranged a meeting for the very next day.

The moment she entered the room I knew that I had found a friend. We chatted merrily in three languages, — French, German and English, — for, though she was born in Poland, she was only four years old when her parents brought her to America, and consequently she did not speak a word of Polish. She showed me so much sympathy that

I did not hesitate to tell her of my great difficulty in finding a good English teacher, and even asked her if she knew of some one she could recommend to me. What was my amazement and joy when she told me that she was willing to teach me.

"I speak good English, and I know I can help you, but it will be a work of love, for, not being a professional teacher, I cannot take money for my instruction." I tried to persuade her that she ought to be remunerated for her pains, because she would have hard work to teach me, but she absolutely refused, and put all money matters out of question. "I could not do it for money," she repeated, and there was nothing left to me but either to lose this excellent opportunity or to accept her friendly offer.

I was a little afraid that my amateur teacher might be irregular in her lessons, but I wronged her. She came every morning at the same hour, and when my husband returned to Anaheim she positively stayed with me from eight in the morning until the evening, taking only a little time for meals. Very often she even remained during the evenings, and we took walks or went to the theatres together, and all that time she compelled me to speak English by not answering my German or French questions until I translated them into English.

My husband had remained six weeks with me this time, but he was obliged to return south. He left with me my son, Rudolphe, who became at once my fellow-student. He then changed, with our approval, his name to that of Ralph, because, he said, Americans do not like long foreign names. Besides, we thought the names were really one. My boy also was a diligent pupil, and we both began to learn English with an energy verging on frenzy. There was not an hour of time lost; every minute was turned to profit. Of course he, being so much younger, learned much more quickly than I and could talk fluently long before I was able to put a few sentences together. He made such rapid progress that in March he wrote a farce in English, which was performed at Governor Salomon's house by the latter's sons and himself. We had met the governor during our first stay in San Francisco, and he took a great interest in my prospective début.

My American friends were very encouraging, and called me a wonder as soon as I managed to say a few simple things correctly and succeeded in getting the right sound of "th," which feat, on the other part, excited the derision of Captain Piotrowski, who scorned supremely my capacity for imitating that particular sound, saying that parrots could do the same, but he would prefer me to remain original: "I would not object so much if it were pretty, but that lisping sound is simply awful!" Yet I got the lisping sound, which he predicted I never could, and I got many other sounds besides, and it was all due to my dear Jo and her constant watching over my enunciation. At the very first lesson I insisted upon reading "Adrienne Lecouvreur." We took every day a page or two. After getting a more or less right pronunciation of the words, I memorized the whole part, and recited it over and over before my patient teacher, who corrected every wrong pronunciation and accentuation. In the same manner I learned also Juliet and Cleopatra. I also memorized every day about a hundred new words and wrote pages of exercises.

It was not only that Jo watched over my accent, she also inspired me with hope and encouraged me sincerely, predicting success. Every now and then I would have my moments of doubt, but she was there, never allowing my head to droop or letting me be lost in sad contemplation of the future. "You must succeed, and you will!" she repeated constantly, and as these words were the echo of my wishes, they cheered me up for a while; yet there always remained the despondent query, buried in some recess of my brain: "If I do not succeed, what then?" I often liked to go with Ralph and Jo to Oakland for the sake of the ferry trip. That fatal "What then?" came to my mind every time I leaned over the railing of the boat, looking down at the water, and it seemed to me that the answer to that question was only to be found in the green depths of the bay. But Jo was there, diverting my mind with her original remarks, and my gloom took flight before her witty sayings and her radiant countenance.

While I studied Juliet, I became more hopeful. I believe that the mere repeating of the part in Shakespeare's beautiful language made me happy, and happiness spread over me a glow of hope. I could not well analyze my feelings, but I was aware that neither fear nor apprehension tortured me any more, and that my mind was gradually returning to its normal state.

Among the many letters I had received from Poland there was one, much delayed, from a friend of mine in Warsaw, Madame Leo, the wife of Edward Leo, the managing editor of *Gazeta Polska,* the paper of which Sienkiewicz was a correspondent, and in which were published his "Charcoal Sketches." Madame Leo's letter was simply an urgent appeal to us to return to Poland, combined with a sound scolding for remaining buried in the wilderness, or what was worse, in an obscure village. (She thought I was still in Anaheim.) I had not answered immediately, because the uncertainty of my projects was too great at the time, but now, about this time, as my hopes were reënforced by successful study, I wrote my old friend Madame Leo the following letter, which was returned to me at my request, when I first conceived the idea of writing my reminiscences:—

San Francisco, March 15, 1877.

"Dear Madame Stephanie: —

"How shall I thank you for your remembrance and your scolding? Well, I will not thank at all, because written words often look conventional, and I do not want to be conventional with you. I broke the wafer [1] with only the nearest ones to my heart, because your letter did not find me in Anaheim, but in this city, where I have been for two months together with Charles and Dolcio. The rest of our colony remained in the south, except Litwos, whom, I believe, you will soon see again, as he does not intend to remain here longer.

. . . . "You must not think that we left the farm because I was tired of Nature, which I still love and admire ardently. She is the only rival of Art in my mind. When, as it happened not long ago, I am on the ocean, Art disappears somewhere behind a veil of mist, and my soul, free from fetters, sinks into the infinite and floating above earth has no other desire but to remain thus forever and ever. These are delights you cannot realize, accustomed as you are to pavements resounding with the noise of horses' hoofs and rolling carriages, and therefore I was not surprised when I read in your letter that you did not believe in my enthusiasm. You also wrote me that such a life is no life at all, that our idyl may be amusing only for a short while. You might have been right if the idyl had been only amusement, but I assure you that my occupations were not all of the diverting sort and might have become insufferable had I not been able to breathe this glorious air of California, or look at the blue mountains and send them my greeting every morning and evening. When I wrote to you about these charms of nature, I did not go into raptures over our cheese and butter, I did not glorify the noble occupations of a cook, I simply made 'bonne mine à mauvais jeu,' and laughed at myself to prevent others from laughing at me.

"At present I do not perform any domestic duty, but I am hard at work, studying. That was my secret plan, at the very beginning of our venture. Country life was simply to restore my health and strength, which it did so effectively that people give me twenty-four or twenty-six years of age, not more; and yet I wrote to the management of the Warsaw Theatre, asking for a prolongation of my leave of absence, on the plea of poor health. Do not betray me, pray, but listen: I study, but what? You surely guess! Next autumn I want to ask the president [2] what he prefers, either 6000 roubles for breaking my contract, or my return

[1] There is an ancient Polish custom of breaking bread, in shape of wafers, on Xmas eve. People send such wafers to absent friends by mail.

[2] Mr. Serge de Mouchanoff, president of the Imperial Theatre, in Warsaw.

in two years with fame. The truth is, that if I wanted to return now I could not do so. All the money my husband brought from Europe was swallowed up by the costs of our travels and of our ranching and the purchase of a farm, which is now managed by Sypniewski. I do not wish Charles to make further sacrifices, and I believe I can in a short time square up everything by making money enough to send the colony back to the country, for they are all homesick. Of course Litwos is independent, for he writes, and is well paid for his work, — your husband takes good care of that, — and Paprocki might secure a position as a cartoonist, that is, if he spoke English; but in the meantime both he and the Sypniewskis have no other resources but farming, which cannot and does not bring any income.

"Besides these material reasons, there is another, of more importance to me than anything else. Call it vanity, if you like; I prefer to call it pride or ambition. Some people in Poland know of my intention of appearing on the English-speaking stage, and I hear they already predict my failure. If I returned now, without even one small leaf of laurels gathered here or in England, they certainly would look upon me as a bird with broken wings, and treat me accordingly. They would condole with me and patronize me. Horror! Can you imagine anything more awful than that? No, dear friend, I must try to rise. If I fail, you will never see me any more; but if I succeed, nothing will prevent me from flying back to Warsaw, and then I will stop at the Green Square,[1] climb up the two flights, open the door, and cry: 'Good morning, my friends, how do you do?' Am I right, or am I wrong? In my present situation I am guided simply by instinct. And then something whispers to me, that my staying away for some time will not hurt my standing with the critics and the public of Warsaw. They were beginning to get tired of me. Had I remained, they soon would have called me old and passée, but when I return, and return with new success, they will receive me with open arms! Everybody will find me younger and more attractive, because I shall bring with me fame from abroad to exalt my position. Somebody said, 'Une duchesse a toujours dix-huit ans pour un bourgeois.'[2] I left Poland as the leading lady of the Warsaw Theatre; I will return as an acknowledged star of foreign stages.

"There is only one thing which troubles me. Will my proceeding with the Warsaw management be strictly honest? For,

[1] The place of residence of Mr. and Mrs. Edward Leo in Warsaw.
[2] "A duchess is always young in the eyes of a commoner."

though I intend to pay the forfeit, and though I do not take a penny of salary during my absence, yet I am afraid that what I am doing is not quite fair. Pray tell me what you and Mr. Edward think of it, and please be candid, sincere. Give me your opinion without

Photograph by Sarony.

MRS. JOHN DREW.

reserve, without any regard for my sensitiveness; but above all, do not tell any one of my hopes, for I want to surprise my little world.

"Just imagine how happy we shall be together, after our return, sitting in your library before the fireplace, in the circle of a few select spirits. How I long sometimes for a glimpse of Warsaw, and yet I would not return now for the world! Time will come when nothing will keep us here, but at present my soul is smarting yet, though my body has recovered its normal health. I need

Photograph by Echerson, Hamilton, Ont.

E. A. SOTHERN.

more strength of mind, and that strength I will find in my present struggles.

"Pray forgive this selfish letter, but you wished to know all about me, and so you get this long scribble filled with nothing but wretched 'Me.' Do write soon, and in turn do tell me everything about you and yours. Charles sends greetings to both of you and kisses the pretty hands of Madame Stephanie. How are the children? Do write soon; I embrace you, sending a thousand good wishes for yourself and your dear husband.

"HELENA."

I went several times to the theatre during that time. I saw and admired Mrs. Drew in "School for Scandal" and Mr. Sothern in "Lord Dundreary"; also Charles Coghlan and Adelaide Neilson, each of the latter in three different parts. I thought Coghlan a most exquisite actor. His parts in the "Lady of Lyons" and "Money" were played with a finish rarely seen on any but the French stage, while his Iago in "Othello" was surely the best I ever have seen before or since. To begin with, he looked what Othello calls him, the "honest Iago": in his bluff, soldierly appearance there was no trace of the stage villain, no cringing poses, nothing that might betray him to Othello, whom Shakespeare certainly does not make an idiot, and who would not have been deceived by a man with a Judas-like appearance. His honest countenance makes his villainy the worse. In Coghlan's personation the coarse, vulgar nature, combined with the cunning of an Italian peasant, was made visible to the audience by his cynical smile, behind Othello's back, the twinkle of his eye, and numerous other subtle touches

Photograph by Sarony.

CHARLES COGHLAN.

of his inner base nature, which were always concealed before the Moor. The general appearance gave the impression of a strong, brutal soldier, who would drink and sing and treat the villainous plot against his master more as a cruel joke than as a crime. With all the inborn envy and hatred of a low nature towards his superior, he chuckled over his tricks, and it was not done with grimness, but rather with the enjoyment of a callous temperament over the tortures of a man whom, in spite of Othello's distinction, he despised for his race and color, and considered as belonging to a lower grade of mankind. The dagger is, or at least was, so generally used in Italy that its use does not necessarily suggest refined villainy, but rather brutality and rage.

Adelaide Neilson was beautiful and perfect in the "Hunchback." She was emotional, sincere, and her beauty was radiant. I always remember the incomparable pathos of her voice in her appeal to her lover: "I call you Clifford, and you call me Madame!" There was such a true ring in this short sentence that it thrilled me through and through. I did not like the play, but I was fascinated by Neilson's acting. The effect of the balcony scene in her Juliet was spoiled to some degree by a coarse interruption of the gallery boys, who sent her loud kisses, which seemed to annoy her greatly; but I think the boys could not help themselves, when they saw that beautiful vision, flooded with moonlight, brought nearer to their view by the elevation of the balcony. On account of these interruptions, I could not well judge of her acting in that scene, but her impulse of throwing flowers at Romeo at the end was spontaneous, and brought the house down.

I have only one criticism to make of this performance. I did not like, in the first act, her kissing her hand on the same spot where Romeo kissed it before, because this particular stage business was unnecessarily borrowed from a modern French play, where it was in its proper place.

Photograph by Sarony.

ADELAIDE NEILSON.

I would not have mentioned this slight deviation from the true poetic spirit with which her part was impregnated all through, were it not that I saw later some younger actresses imitating from hearsay just this action, while they entirely failed to follow Neilson's footsteps in her great qualities,—her intensity and her identification with the characters personified. She did not seem to act her parts, but to live them on the stage. She was really a born actress, and there are but few of whom one may say this.

Every time I went to the theatre I sniffed the air like a battle horse before a skirmish, and a great longing for the footlights expanded my chest, finding no relief but in a deep, almost painful, sigh. For consolation I turned to my studies, and spent delightful moments in reciting my parts aloud, while Ralph was playing on the piano the delightful nocturnes of Chopin. He practised a great deal, and I was glad of it, not only for his sake, but also for mine, because the music helped me wonderfully to bring out the poetic value of Shakespeare's lines. I would not have it on the stage, because I always disliked the melodramatic effect of incidental music, but I liked to study certain passages to the harmonious sounds of my favorite tunes.

In June I thought it time to take steps towards securing my début at the California Theatre, which was the only one then having a good supporting stock company. Then it was that I passed the most trying moments of my stage life. Materially, I had to recur for help to some of our old silverware and jewellery, which I managed to dispose of with the assistance of my dear Jo, and its sale supplied me with enough money to keep Ralph and me alive for a few more months; but morally, no rescue came to relieve my sad apprehensions when, after seeing Mr. Barton Hill, the stage manager of the California Theatre and the representative of Mr. John McCullough (the lessee and head of the concern), I received the answer that there was no opening for me, all the dates having been filled until the following winter. My Polish friends, on hearing the news, became at once discouraged. Some advised me to return to Warsaw, some tried to induce me to go to New York or London, and I could see plainly in the expression of their faces that scarcely one believed in my success on the English-speaking stage.

Jo, however, was not discouraged, and asked Mr. Hill to let me rehearse before him an act of Adrienne, Juliet, or Cleopatra. He promised to do so, but when we came to his office at the appointed time, he was very polite, called me repeatedly Madame la Comtesse, insisted on speaking French to me, but absolutely refused to give me a rehearsal, saying that it was quite impossible, as the stage was occupied every morning and afternoon. From what he said further, in the form of good advice to give up my "fancy," I understood that he had doubts as to my being an actress at all, and supposing he had before him only an amateur stage-struck society woman, he tried to get out of this difficult situation as smoothly as possible. Unfortunately, I had not one scrap of paper to convince him of his mistake, as I never kept a scrap-book, seldom read criticisms, and never thought of preserving what was written about me. It was only many years afterwards, when I first thought of writing my recollections, that I began to gather the more interesting articles written about me, and then I had old notices copied from newspaper files. At that moment I had nothing at hand to present to Mr. Hill as a proof of my standing in my profession.

I considered my situation a desperate one, and when, after leaving the manager's office, I proposed to Jo to take a ferry-boat to Oakland or Alameda, she refused to comply with my request, knowing the temptation to me of the blue waves of the bay, and said, laughing: "No, no, my dear lady, we shall not go for a bath until you know how to swim." Her cheerful face and her words dispelled somewhat my morbid fancy; I returned home, and Jo began to make new plans of campaign. She suggested that I see Governor Salomon and ask him to intervene with Mr. Hill. I did so, and he promised to take up my cause. I also told General Krzyzanowski of my unhappy attempts to secure Mr. Hill's attention to my request. He sincerely sympathized with me, and promised to enlighten the unbelieving stage manager as to my artistic value in the old country. He added: "It is unfortunate that John McCullough is not in town at present, for I am sure he would give you an opening at once. Mr. Barton Hill cannot act entirely on his own responsibility in this matter, as he has to consult his superior, and it might be wiser to wait until Mr. McCullough's return."

"Wait, wait, and wait!" when I was burning all over with feverish longing for the thrill of expression! when I knew my parts and was almost sure of success! Jo and I went once more to the theatre, but this time we were humiliated by a word sent to us at the door that Mr. Hill was too busy to see anyone. "I never experienced anything of that kind yet," I said to Jo. "What a shame! I feel like a beggar to whom alms were refused!" I really felt the ground slip from under my feet. It would be difficult to describe the bitterness of my comparisons between the abject situation into which I was thrown and the past, full of honors and love. I forgot the persecution, the enmities, the petty cavillings of my life in Warsaw; I only recalled the dear public, our numerous friends, our artistic circle, and yearned, oh! so ardently, to be again with them. Were it not for my strong determination I would have returned home at once. Yet a glimpse of hope was left to me still. I wanted to see Mr. McCullough before planning any desperate stroke. I waited. The month of June was nearly gone, and there was no star on my horizon. Still Jo, the General, and Governor Salomon believed in my success, and spoke in the most encouraging terms of my future prospects. There was another who shared their confidence — the dear old poetic Bednawski. When he heard of my difficulties, he grew quite indignant, and in his enthusiasm delivered an imaginary address to the theatrical managers and to the whole population of the United States, extolling my merits and proclaiming my superiority over all existing and non-existing actresses. The dear fellow made me laugh, and I was thankful for this diversion. As a finishing touch to his endeavors to cheer me up, he proposed an excursion to the Cliffs next morning, to look at the sea-lions and take a lunch under the rocks. He also invited Jo and Ralph, who was overjoyed with the prospect of fishing. The next morning I woke up cheerful and full of hope. Why? Because of a strange dream I had that night. Please, gentle reader, do not imagine that I attach undue importance to dreams, although it is a fact that I have had some curious ones, almost prophetic, in my life. I usually did not think much of them at the time, but their veracity, proved by future events, made me reflect. This dream, however, which I dreamed on the eve of our excursion to the Cliffs, was so strange and so vivid that, I confess, it made a great impression on me, though I realized well that my nerves being unhinged by unusual tension, my brains were bound to work in sympathy and create fanciful pictures, which concentrated in the following vision: —

I was walking through many streets, led by the hand of a little boy, who had the face of my friend Jo. When, tired by the long walk, I stopped to rest, the boy looked up to me, saying, "You have to go a little farther!" and we went on again, until suddenly we stopped before a dark opening, very low and narrow. "Come along," my companion whispered. I thought, "I shall never pass through," but the child pulled me by the hand. I bent down and crouched through that pitch-dark passage, until I saw a dim light and, going in that direction, I reached some steps which, always led by the boy, I began to ascend. The higher I mounted, the brighter shone the light and the broader became the steps. In the middle of the staircase the boy sat down and said, "Now, you will find your way alone." I reached the highest step and stood in a large arched and ornamented door; before me was a magnificent hall, supported by Grecian pillars. The hall was full of people and, to my amazement, I saw those who were still living, and those who were dead long ago gathered together, talking and moving about. They were all noted people of the world, — writers, poets, composers, artists, sculptors, and actors. While, filled with awe and reverence, I was looking at the various groups of celebrities, one man detached himself from them, and, coming down to me, took me by the hand and said, "Come in!" His face was radiant, and I recognized in him Poland's greatest poet, Mickiewicz. The shock of rapture was so great that it woke me up, but nothing could shake off the impression of that dream, which, unreasonably no doubt, filled my heart with wild hopes and joy.

When we came to the Cliffs I was in high spirits, and I volunteered to reward Mr. Bednawski for his unswerving friendship and faith in me by reciting for him some Polish poems. Poor man, he had not heard for long, long years the music of the Polish verse, the poetry of his beloved country. I remember delivering Ujejski's "Hagar in the Desert," with the rocks in the background and the hot sand under my feet, which was consistent with the poem It is true the accompaniment of the surge of the ocean, beating against the rocks, did not altogether fit the drought of the desert, but the sun made up for it, as it was almost fierce on that June day.

As we were coming home we met Governor Salomon, who told me that Mr. Barton Hill had promised to arrange a rehearsal for me. I hated to approach that busy man after his refusal to see me, but Jo remarked that unless we try again we never would be able to succeed. Mr. Salomon also assured me that this time Mr. Hill would receive me. I agreed to face my fate once more.

CHAPTER XXXVIII

GOVERNOR SALOMON soon afterward secured another appointment for me with Mr. Hill. When we knocked at the door of the theatrical office, we were asked to be seated, and Mr. Hill complimented "Madame la Comtesse" upon her looks, and nearly killed her with politeness, and told her about Mr. McCullough's return to 'Frisco, where he was to play Othello and Hamlet, and about the great actress, Miss Rose Eytinge, coming to play in a grand production of Cleopatra. Then we learned that new, gorgeous scenery was going to be painted for the queen of Egypt, and that soon the Midgets would also be here, and so forth, and so forth.

I never uttered a word, but Jo, after listening awhile, fired out her point-blank question: "And when will you give Madame Modjeska a hearing, as you promised Governor Salomon?" This time Mr. Hill looked at me attentively, and, after a pause said, "Let me see; will next Tuesday do?" "Yes, it will do! Good-by!" "Au revoir, Madame la Comtesse!" "Until next Tuesday," said Jo, and repeated, "Next Tuesday, don't forget!" "By no means, Miss Tuholsky!"

Next Tuesday we returned. Mr. Hill was in despair because the stage was occupied by a scenery rehearsal, but he suggested the lecture hall in the same building, which had a platform about fifteen feet wide. It was a rather trying proposition to rehearse in this bare hall, with dusty windows and dusty platform, without any furniture except a shaky table and rickety chair, but I was ready for any emergency, and took off my hat and gloves. While I was looking for a clean place where I might put them, Mr. Hill, who seated himself in the first row of stalls, opposite the platform, called out, "Madame la Comtesse, I must warn you that I shall be candid and sincere in my criticism." "Yes, of course," I answered; "I expect you to be sincere and severe, but please do not interrupt me until I am through." Mr. Hill bowed, and the rehearsal began.

All these proceedings, my repeated visits to the office, the repeated refusals, my friend's pleadings, had produced the most stirring feelings in my soul. I was glad that all this had happened far from my country, and that my husband was not the witness of it all. My revolt against these petty annoyances, my anxiety for triumph and for the rebuke of the sceptical attitude of my judge, were so great that I was burning with the desire to crush the Philistine.

Poor, dear Mr. Hill, who was only doing his duty as a cautious manager, did not suspect those antagonistic feelings, which put me on my mettle from the start and made me deliver my very first speeches with so much intensity and realism that I myself was startled at my new intonations. I was sure of victory from the very beginning of the rehearsal. I had chosen the last act of Adrienne, and Jo gave me the cues. Gradually I forgot all except my part, in which I lost myself entirely. During the casket-scene, however, I saw vaguely Mr. Hill's handkerchief; the whiteness of it and the motion of the hand attracted my attention for a second; and when, after the final death-scene, I was sitting, tired and panting still with emotion, Mr. Hill came to me with tears in his eyes. He shook hands with me, and I asked directly if he thought he could give me one evening for my début at the California Theatre. "One evening!" he exclaimed; "you shall have the whole week, and more, if possible!" And then he complimented me upon my acting.

This time I did not want to take a ferry-boat to Oakland,

but I invited Jo, Mr. Bednawski, and Ralph to a French dinner. A few days later John McCullough returned to San Francisco, and a note came from Mr. Hill that, if convenient to me, he should like me to rehearse the same act before Mr. McCullough. "This looks like the examination of a young beginner," I said to Joe; "cannot Mr. McCullough take his stage manager's word?" and I rebelled against the idea of going through the same ordeal in that horrible hall, and declared I never could do it. But the wise Jo made me do it, and this time the surroundings were more favorable, for I rehearsed on the stage, and before several judges instead of one, for some other persons were present in the auditorium. Among them was Mr. Richard Hinton, the chief editor of the *Evening Post*, who, by the way, smoothed considerably my way to success and has remained my faithful friend ever since.

Photography by Roehn, Chicago.

JOHN MCCULLOUGH.

After the rehearsal Mr. John McCullough came to speak to me. He was visibly touched and said many flattering things to me, and at once set the date of my début for August 13. Before leaving, he asked me how I spelled my name. I wrote it in full, just as it is spelled in Polish, "Helena Modrzejewska," and handed it to him. He looked at it, smiled, and rubbing his head, said: "Who on earth could read that, I wonder? I fear you will be compelled to change your name, Madam!" I told him I did not like to do so, but I might, by the omission of a few letters, make out a name which would sound pretty much like my own, and yet not frighten people away, and I wrote down "Modgeska." He smiled again, saying it might remind one of "Madagascar." I soon perceived the point, and changed the "g" into a "j". He spelled aloud "Modjeska." "Now," he said, "it is quite easy to read, and sounds pretty, I think." We parted good friends, and I began to make preparations for the performance of "Adrienne Lecouvreur."

Mr. McCullough was then playing his classic repertoire, and I went with Jo to his performances. I had already seen him, during Booth's engagement in "Julius Cæsar," and had admired greatly his truly Roman appearance and his fine delivery of Brutus's lines. This time I witnessed his personations in Othello and Virginius, and was very much impressed by his acting in the latter part.

A few days before "the great day" I was advised by my friends to move to the Palace Hotel, and there I received from my husband the sorrowful message that on account of an accident, a bad fall, he was unable to come for my first performance, but he would hasten to San Francisco as soon as his "scratches" would allow, for they were not dangerous, though painful. This was a great disappointment to me, yet I consoled myself with the thought that perhaps it was better as it was, for his nervous temperament might have been contagious and thrown me off my balance, when

I needed all the calm I was mistress of to go through my task.

Well, there is little more to say about my American début. I played, and succeeded, and sent a dispatch to my husband consisting of one word: "Victory." A curious feature of this, my first performance in English, was that I was not in the least nervous. The happiness of being again behind the footlights killed the stage-fright, and I walked serenely on, never forgot a line or became confused when I did not get the right cue, which, I am sorry to say, happened several times that evening. Even when my veil caught fire from the footlights, I had enough presence of mind to put it out immediately. Tom Keene was a manly Maurice de Saxe. The charming Miss Wilton played the princess, and Harry Edwards was Minchonnet, and a very excellent one. After the play, the Polish colony, which had turned out in full and had applauded furiously, as well as Governor Salomon and some other new friends, came to my dressing-room, elated with the result, to offer hearty congratulations.

Gentlemen of the press, among them Mr. R. Hinton, H. St. Maur, and Jessup, came also, and we had as much of a chat as my defective knowledge of conversational English would allow. I remember that I finished my sentences, when short of some word, with gesticulation, which must have been expressive, as I received right answers from my very much amused guests. The critics wrote next day fine notices about my Adrienne, while Sienkiewicz, who had come for this occasion to San Francisco, sent a long letter to his Warsaw paper.

Next morning at eight o'clock a card was brought to me. This early visitor was Harry Sargent, a theatrical agent. I sent him word to return in the afternoon. Several other agents called soon after, but I selected the one who rose the earliest.

Mr. Sargent returned in the afternoon, with his wife, a delicate, pretty woman, who had been an actress before her marriage, and who came back to the stage in later years. He proposed to me a starring tour in the East, beginning in New York. I accepted the proposition, on his terms, and he went immediately to work in order to obtain dates for me in New York, Boston, and Philadelphia. The very next day he informed me that the earliest open time he could get in New York was from the middle of December until the end of January, 1878, and we agreed that I should go East late in November.

In the meantime Mr. McCullough asked me to play another week, with change of plays. He said there was quite a rush at the box-office to see the new Polish actress, and though next week belonged by right to Miss Rose Eytinge, the latter kindly consented to postpone her engagement for a week. Her scenery was not quite ready, and so she preferred to wait, though she might easily have filled that week with other plays of her repertoire. I called on her and thanked her heartily for this concession. Mr. McCullough wanted me to play Juliet, alternating it with Adrienne, and he also asked me if I could play Ophelia to his Hamlet during one night of that following week, which he had selected for his benefit. I told him that I did not think I could learn the mad scene in English so as to be quite easy in it, at such short notice, but if he thought that the public would stand my rendering of this scene in Polish I might be ready to play the rest of the part in English. He consented, and rehearsals were called. John McCullough at that time was occasionally showing signs of the nervous disturbance which led him to that disastrous disease of which he died. While I was rehearsing with him the scenes of Hamlet, I noticed that several times he wiped tears from his eyes. When I inquired what affected him this way, he answered, "It is your voice, Madame!" "Is, then, my voice so dreadfully lachrymose," thought I, "that it breaks up that seemingly strong man?" Jo, who was present at every rehearsal, also found it strange, but she added: "Your voice also has the same effect upon me sometimes; but then, I think it ought not to affect such an experienced actor. It does so, however, and this is a great compliment to you." Alas, several years later I fully understood the reason of the effect produced upon that unstrung instrument, which already was going slowly but surely to its utter destruction.

The second week proved quite a financial success, which was doubly welcome, both as an omen of the future and as a relief for our material difficulties. I began to breathe freely. During those two weeks I lived in a whirlwind of excitement. People would flock to my dressing-room every evening, with tears in their eyes, shaking my hand, embracing me, and saying the most lovely things. I alone had dry eyes, and alone could not weep, though tears would have relieved the tension of my nerves. It was only when one of my friends took me to an orphan asylum that the floodgates opened and I had a good cry.

Soon after, my husband came to town, healed from his bruises, and we had some delightful parties with our Polish friends, and also were invited to receptions in the "upper ten" circle, which stood there for the "four hundred" of New York. Evidently Adrienne and Juliet had made me fashionable.

z

CHAPTER XXXIX

THERE was at that time in San Francisco an Irish comedian by the name of James Ward. He proposed to arrange and manage for me a short tour in the small towns of California and Nevada. He also could be my leading man, he said. I thought that it would be excellent practice. My husband and Jo agreed with me that nothing could be better, in order to get my parts "trippingly on the tongue," than repeating them for a few weeks to less imposing audiences, before my New York engagement.

Previously I had met a young newspaper man and well-known humorist, Mr. Sam Davis, who also advised me to "rough it" for a while. He jokingly alluded to my Irish comedian and leading man, warning me that I must watch him, or else he might make funny faces during my death-scenes. Mr. Davis promised to go to Virginia City, where I was to begin my "Wild West" tour, ahead of us, because, he said, he was bound to see me through my first trial there, not knowing what effect my European manners and foreign accent would produce upon the miners. "I know them, you see," he said, "because Nevada has been my home for some time. If you could begin your plays with your death-scenes, you would make a hit at once, because these miners are thoroughly soft-hearted, although rough, but I do not know how your talky scenes will affect them. I am afraid I shall have to be there with a club in my hands in case of some unruly demonstrations." We laughed a great deal over these anticipated dangers, and I did not believe he would go to Nevada, but he was as good as his word, and he packed up his satchel and said "Good-by" with the assurance that we would soon meet in Virginia City.

My husband returned to Anaheim. The farm he had bought so easily was very difficult to sell. He hoped, however, to get rid of it, though with loss, but as long as his duties towards the colony were not fulfilled, he had to stay with them. "I brought them here; I have to send them back home," he argued, and I did not oppose his sense of justice.

As an addition to my repertoire, I studied "Camille," which I had refused to play in Poland on account of its doubtful influence upon young people. I was told that it was quite popular in America, — my friends' advice overcame my scruples, — and so for my opening night in Virginia City I chose this spontaneous work of youthful genius, this love-story full of emotion, but not free from morbidness.

Contrary to the apprehensions of Mr. Davis, the performance went through without disturbance, and though my comedy Armand was always out of the picture, and several times I had to bite my lips at the expression of his face and his funny gestures, yet the public did not take notice of these details. They sincerely applauded the heroine, and shed copious tears over her fate. During the supper-scene of the first act I took a look at the audience, expecting to see a very rough crowd, but I was most pleasantly surprised at the manly appearance and excellent behavior of the miners, who, together with cow-boys, constituted the vast majority of that picturesque and interesting assembly. To be in Virginia City and not to see some of the celebrated Comstock silver mines, then in the full flush of their prosperity, would have been the same as being in Rome and not seeing the Pope.

Ralph, who accompanied me on this tour, was most anxious to go underground, and spoke of his desire to Sam Davis, who immediately procured for us permission to visit one of the largest and richest local mines. Next morning we all three started on our way to the subterranean world. After being provided with a cap, a pair of breeches, and a cloak, I was shown to an adjoining room, where I accomplished my disguise. When I returned to the office, I faced a very tall, handsome, and statuesque man in buckskins and silver buckles, who bowed to me. "This gentleman," said Davis, "will show us the mine." The gentleman in buckskins looked sharply and haughtily, I thought, at Sam Davis, and then, turning to me, said, "Yes, Madame, come along, and excuse my going ahead!" While we were following him, Ralph preceding me and Mr. Davis behind me, I asked the latter in a whisper who that stunning man was. "Oh, he is only one of the miners," answered the humorist, with a mischievous twinkle in his eye. "I wonder if all the miners dress with such elegance," I whispered further. Davis laughed, and added: "By no means; but this one is a very vain man, and spends all his salary on dress and in courting women. He is quite a dangerous chap." "I believe he is," I whispered back, "to women!" At this moment the superb man paused at the opening of the shaft, turning his buckled front to us, thus putting a stop to our mezzo-voce conversation. We were asked politely to step into the cage. When Ralph and I were entering this awe-inspiring lift, I heard a subdued conversation between Sam Davis and the buckskinned gentleman, but I could not distinguish the words, except the last short sentence of our friend: "No, not now."

Whoever visited mines can easily imagine my sensations when, going down on a square plank lower and lower by the dim light of a lamp, hearing only the splash of the water dripping along the walls of the shaft, feeling the air growing more and more oppressive, and thinking this descent will never stop until we reach some place near the very centre of the earth. To say that I was not nervous would be a blank untruth. I was downright afraid, and clung to Ralph with both arms, so that, in case anything should happen, we might both perish in the abyss together. Yet I tried my best to appear calm and answer the remarks of Ralph or Mr. Davis. Our guide did not speak, but from time to time he stretched his arm to protect me from contact with the edge of the shaft, when our cage, with its swinging motion, made us sway from one side to the other. At last we stopped, and began to walk through long, narrow tunnels, lower and lower still. "We are nineteen hundred feet under the ground," explained Mr. Davis. The air became very hot, and our conductor turned to me and asked if I would permit him to take off his coat. "Of course," I said, and he pulled off his buckskins, exposing an immaculate silk shirt, which made Mr. Davis wink at me, as if to say, "Did I not tell you how vain the man is?" He and Ralph also took off their coats, and I envied them, for all I could have taken off was my coat, with which, however, I hated to part, for my breeches were rather close-fitting. We arrived at a place where, on account of extreme heat, the men were working stripped to the waist, and it was a fine exhibition of human muscles in action. All those miners were young men, and most of them, in spite of hard work, looked cheerful. When I made a remark about it to Mr. Davis, he said: "The wages are high, and in a few hours they will be free to roam about with their sweethearts, or gamble away every penny they have toiled for. Youth and strength seem to them inexhaustible, and while they last who cares for the rest? They also rely upon a stroke of luck, for some of them have become quite rich." When we were leaving this *inferno*, a cannon was discharged, and, had I not been warned before of this flattering salute in my honor, I surely would have collapsed at the tremendous shock and noise, which made the ground tremble under our feet and the narrow tunnels howl with its echo. When it was over, Davis thanked the silk-sleeved gentleman for the "gentle attention," and we all laughed and proceeded on our way back.

After returning to the office and changing our clothes, I asked Mr. Davis how I was to thank the magnificent man who showed us such courtesy. He hesitated awhile, and answered, "Oh, give him something; his courtesy was nothing else but obedience to higher orders." "Surely this demigod will not accept money?" I exclaimed. "Won't he? You don't know that kind of men! They always take what they can get." "But he is so gorgeous I would not dare offer him less than twenty-five dollars, and I have only a miserable five-dollar gold-piece about me," I said piteously. 'Twenty-five dollars! The idea! One dollar is quite enough." "Oh, Mr. Davis!" "You have an exaggerated idea about the fellow; he is fond of money and will take anything you give him."

The man in question returned to the office, and I went to him and said: "Thank you very much for your kindness, and please, . . . I was not prepared and have not—" I stammered out, "more," extending my hand with the small gold-piece to him. Seeing my purpose, the demigod stepped back, drew himself up, and grew almost black with anger. He gave Mr. Davis a look which made me shiver, and I imagined that, were these two alone in the room, it might have been very dangerous for my humorous friend to meet the flash of the other's eye. This, however, lasted only a moment. The strong man composed himself and answered politely, "You are welcome, Madame!" and added something which I did not understand, except the last word, "pleasure." I timidly retired, and when we were sitting in a cab, on our way to the hotel, I told Mr. Davis: "You see I offended the man, and you made me do so!" Davis only laughed: "He will get over it; don't worry." I was then so preoccupied with my parts and my English studies that this uncomfortable subject did not dwell long in my mind, and I soon forgot all about it. We left Virginia City in a week, and Mr. Sam Davis returned to San Francisco, while I went with the company to other towns.

Twenty years later, in Santa Barbara, at a convention of California newspaper men, to which my husband and I were honored with an invitation, our jocular friend, Mr. Sam Davis, related in a bright manner the foregoing incident, which I have tried to describe. Then he publicly confessed that the handsome and polite man in buckskins was nobody else but the famous Mr. X., the owner of the mine, one of the multi-millionnaires of the West and a political potentate. As soon as Davis came back from the platform, I addressed him excitedly: "Oh, for shame, Mr. Davis; why did you not introduce him to me?" "Oh, because, first, I had a grudge against him; and besides, the chap was such a lady-killer and visibly on a mash! It tickled me to death when you offered him the coin and he drew himself up, because it was the first money he ever refused, I assure you."

Besides "Camille," I played "Romeo and Juliet" and "Adrienne Lecouvreur" on the tour. Mr. Ward gave up the parts of Romeo and Maurice de Saxe to Mr. Maeder, a safe and experienced actor, who was the son of that very well-known actress, Mrs. Clara Fisher Mæder. The latter had been a star in her childhood, and had in the past played with Macready. She had the most extensive Shakespearian repertoire ever known, because it included both the female and the male leading parts. In later times she was a member of my company, and it was a pleasure for me to watch her acting and her matchless delivery of the lines.

I did not make a great hit in these smaller towns, in Nevada, or in California, my fame having evidently travelled at a very slow pace. I remember having played in San José to about thirty people in the house. The play was "Adrienne Lecouvreur." The few victims that came to the theatre that evening must have wondered at the shortness of the performance and the chill which ran through it. My dressing-room was awfully cold, and I was advised not to change my costume between the acts, and so it happened that Adrienne lived and died in her Turkish costume of Roxane. The stage manager hurried up the play, and it was presented with but one intermission during the five acts, and consequently it was finished at a quarter-past nine.

This unsuccessful experience was rather amusing to me, but not so to my manager, who had hoped, after my success in San Francisco, to obtain handsome results from the tour. When we closed our engagement, Mr. Ward came to my room, looking quite distressed. He owed me a couple of hundred dollars, but I knew he could not pay them. Yet he was an honest man and was willing to fulfil the terms of the contract. I shall never forget how I laughed when he took out his watch and ring, and placing them before me, said: "This gold watch and this diamond ring constitute my whole wealth; will you accept them instead of the money I owe you?" I refused, of course, and assured him he owed me no money, since I did not make any for him. In fact, I was very well pleased with the practice I had obtained during that time as well as with my experiences in the "Wild West." The poor man was much more disappointed than I, and when I told him of my acquitting him of any obligations, his face at once brightened up, and he thanked me with effusion, calling me "a brick," a word I did not understand in this application, but which must have meant something nice, of course, so I shook hands with him, and we parted good friends.

On returning to San Francisco I learned from Mr. Barton Hill that two weeks were left for me in October, and would I take them and play Camille, alternating with Juliet and Adrienne? This was a godsend for me, and I accepted with enthusiasm. I added to the above-mentioned plays Feuillet's "Dalila," but that drama, so full of subtlety and refinement, was not very well presented by the stock company, and was dismissed from my American repertoire after a few fruitless attempts. Camille, on the other hand, was quite a hit, and my two weeks proved a success.

CHAPTER XL

During the month of December, as I was driving on Broadway, I perceived a monstrous, absurd bill representing me in the costume of Juliet, with two plaits of hair, one in front and one down my back, an open parasol in one hand, while the other was gracefully lifting the dress in the act of mounting some steps that led to a temple-like building. Beneath that incongruous picture was an inscription as follows: "The famous Polish actress, Helena Modjeska, Countess Bozenta."[1] "Oh, what barbarians!" I thought; "it was not enough to put up that horrid cheap picture; they also must make a show of the 'Countess' to attract the mob, always curious about titled persons." I had already realized that in this free and republican country many people were crazy for titles, but I deplored the cheapness of that kind of advertising, and spoke of it to Mr. Sargent, who withdrew the horrid posters after a while replacing them with others containing only my stage name in huge types. "Why such big letters?" I asked him. "Because people are too busy here to stop and read a small bill," he answered. "Unless they can see your name across the street, they will pay no attention to it." I had no choice but to submit.

When I arrived in New York, Mary Anderson was playing

[1] Chlapowski, the family name of my husband, being too difficult to pronounce by English-speaking people, he used only his middle name, Bozenta, and so it came that he was known by that last name to the general public in America.

her repertoire at the Fifth Avenue Theatre, where I was to follow her. I saw her in "Ingomar" and in "Fasio," and was amazed to see such tragic power in such a young person. Her beauty also struck me as being unusual; there was not only a beautiful face, but the harmonious perfection of the whole body. Very tall, and with long, beautiful arms, she made, without effort or without study, gestures which were the natural motions of her classic figure, and consequently were always graceful. Her voice was deep and mellow, and I admired her without reserve, and predicted a glorious future for that most talented actress. She was most picturesque in "Ingomar," and in the part of the jealous wife in "Fasio" full of tragic power and expression.

Photograph by Sarony.

William Winter.

The Fifth Avenue Theatre was then under the management of Mr. Stephen Fiske, and his wife, Mrs. Fiske, a bright, intelligent lady, was in the box with me at Mary Anderson's performance. Between the acts she pointed out the foremost critic of New York, Mr. William Winter. When I looked at him, he made me think of the romantic period of America; I connected him with some of Nathaniel Hawthorne's types, with Edgar Poe, and at the same time he reminded me of a portrait of Hamilton that I had recently seen. No

Photograph by Van der Weyde, London.

MARY ANDERSON.

one had told me that the critic was also a poet, but to me he looked like one, and I was glad to find out that my first impression was right. The appearance of William Winter was certainly romantic. He was introduced to me that evening, but I felt that I did not make a favorable impression, as I was unable to express myself in English, except with a few ready-made sentences, and must have appeared awkward, and what is worse, commonplace. I felt at once that he could not help being very reserved in his first criticism of me.

The memorable moments I spent before my opening night in New York were the rehearsals. Dion Boucicault, at the request of his protègé, Mr. Sargent, had consented to direct the rehearsals of Adrienne. It was an act of great kindness and a great concession on his part, and I owe him a debt of gratitude never to be repaid. He corrected here and there the text of the translation, which he said was bad, and introduced some changes in the scenic effects, making clear the too intricate situations and passages, so as to make them better understood by American audiences not acquainted with the manner of the French authors, Scribe and Legouvé. He also selected the cast for the play. It was a study to watch Mr. Boucicault at the rehearsals. In my country I had been used to actors creating their own parts, without the help of the stage manager. What stage business was introduced was done by a mutual understanding among those in the scene, and during rehearsals was sanctioned or rejected by the artistic director. Here, on the contrary, most of the parts were conceived by Mr. Boucicault, who actually taught some of the actors how to speak their lines. All the stage business was given them, thus relieving them from any extra brain work, reducing it to the memorizing of their parts. When I rehearsed my first scenes, one of the actors asked me, "What do you want me to do now?" "What you please," I answered, rather

Photograph by Mora, New York.

DION BOUCICAULT AS "CONN" IN "THE SAUGHRAUN."

astonished. Here I heard Mr. Boucicault laugh. Taking me aside, he said: "They are not used to such independence. Stars usually direct the actors about stage business." I told him as well as I could in my broken English that it was difficult for me to identify myself with my part and to instruct others at the same time. He told me he understood I was not used as yet to the star system, which consists in making the company behave so as to bring out in relief all the points of the star. I was on the point of replying that I did not think much of this system, having most of the time played with good actors, and often with excellent ones, and that the applause they received only helped the emulation and resulted in a better *ensemble*, but suddenly I remembered how in San Francisco the company was allowed to do as they pleased, how they sometimes failed to give me the right cues, and how they refused to let me have the fireplace in the right place, which would have obliged me to change all my positions and stage business in the last act, had it not been for the vigorous remonstrances of Jo, who succeeded in making them yield to my demands.

When I compared the strict order of our rehearsals at the Fifth Avenue Theatre with the laxity of those in the California Theatre, I acknowledged Mr. Boucicault's superior judgment, and held my peace. He took infinite pains, teaching most of the people not only how to say their lines, but what to do, how to bow, how to enter or exit, even how to hold a snuff-box and how to brush off with a graceful gesture the snuff from their ruffled frill. The low bows and curtseys were the hardest to teach. As I watched Mr. Boucicault I sincerely admired him for his authority and skill in managing each individual and his imagination in the scenic arrangements. When I tried to express my gratitude for the pains he took in directing the play, he only said he was glad to do so, because I was a stranger and he knew from experience that even the foremost actors in

Europe do not trouble themselves about the stage management. He thought he might help me out of the difficulty by looking to all those things, or else the play might prove a failure, in spite of my personal efforts. His remarks taught me a lesson by which I meant to profit in the future.

During the winter it was my good fortune to see Mr. Boucicault in the title part of his own play, "Shaughraun," and I did not know what to admire most, the wonderful originality, wit, and clever construction of the author, the perfect production of the stage manager, or the finish and truth of his exquisite acting. He looked eighteen on the stage, and was simply irresistible.

To return to Adrienne, I remember that we had our first rehearsal without Maurice de Saxe. My manager had the greatest difficulty in finding a leading man on account of the lateness of the season, and, after many fruitless attempts, Mr. Burroughs was engaged "to support Modjeska," as I read in a paper. I could not make out why any one had to "support" me, until some kind person explained to me that this was the usual way of indicating the position of the leading man. When I first looked at handsome Mr. Burroughs, I thought it would be I who would have to "support" him in the exciting scene of the last act to prevent him from breaking in two, he was so delicate and thin. During the rehearsal I found out, to my satisfaction, that he was a good, safe actor, but I was distressed about his diaphanous appearance in the part of the Count de Saxe, that robust soldier and brave adventurer, as well known for his physical strength as for his *bonnes fortunes* and his military exploits.

Some time in December, 1877 (I forget the exact date), I played Adrienne in New York for the first time, and I do not remember anything of that evening except that I was so absorbed in my part that I carried in my hand a shoe-horn instead of a fan, and never noticed it until I wanted to fan

Photograph by Sarony

myself, and also that after the end I was handed by Mr. Sargent a telegram from my husband, with his good wishes, which, according to the rules, he had kept the whole day in his pocket, lest its contents might disturb my acting. When, after the last act, I returned to my dressing-room, I was met by a number of lovely people who came to compliment the new star; and next morning my parlor at the Clarendon Hotel was gay with flowers, sent by my new friends. The criticisms of the press were flattering, though naturally reserved. Mr. Winter gave me a very fine notice. Some of the writers spoke of my age: "Adrienne, the mother of a young man!" (Ralph was sixteen then.) One of them, in his anxiety to appear well informed, added even five years to my age. This was neither truthful nor gallant, and ruffled very much the temper of my impresario, Mr. Sargent, who, fearing that this disclosure of my antiquity might keep the public away from the Fifth Avenue Theatre, devised a scheme of passing me for my son's sister. It afforded a great deal of amusement to Ralph. Almost every day he was accosted by many questioners about me. Some people, led by the manager's fiction to believe that he was my brother, asked him how his sister was. He always answered, "Thank you, she is quite well." Others, who knew that he was my son, asked how his mother was, and received the same answer. It happened once that the two opposite versions were brought in contact, when one person asked him about his sister and another about his mother at the same time, and he was obliged to confess the truth; whereupon the believer in the sister theory grew quite indignant, exclaiming: "Nonsense! she does not look more than twenty-six!" "That is so," answered the boy, "I am just ten years younger than my mother."

It was only a few days after my first performance that I realized how well my company was selected. Mr. Burroughs was a well-padded Maurice, and made a much better appearance than I had anticipated. Mr. Couldock was great as Michonnet, Mr. Whiffen light and charming in the Abbé, and the Princess de Bouillon was excellent in every

Photograph by Sarony.

S. W. COULDOCK.

detail. The other members of the company were careful in their costuming and perfect in their lines.

However, we did not draw crowds to the Fifth Avenue Theatre with Adrienne, partly because the French title of the play was not attractive to the New York audiences of 1878, and partly because the approach of the Christmas holidays kept the people busy shopping. For a change I played the balcony scene of "Romeo and Juliet" as an addition to Adrienne. I was rather reluctant to appear in Shake-

Photograph by Sarony.

THOMAS WHIFFEN.

speare before the critical public of the metropolis, but I was kindly dealt with by the critics and the audiences. The *Tribune* and the *New York Evening Post* were especially good to me.

Adrienne remained three weeks on the bills. Then, in January, 1878, it was changed for "Camille." The latter made a decided hit and established my success. During the rehearsals Mr. and Mrs. Stephen Fiske predicted this happy result. There had been many Camilles in America before me, and I heard a great deal about the wonderful performances of Clara Morris and Matilda Heron. But the managers seemed to like my entirely different conception of the character and the changes I introduced. Being sure of success in advance, I threw myself into my part with all my heart and soul, and this time the press was unanimous in my praise, without any reserve. Of course some critics preferred to see on the stage a common, fallen woman, such as one may meet in the streets after dark, but I had read Arsène Houssaye's story of "Marie Duplessis," who was the model of "La Dame aux Camélias," and who, it seems, looked so refined and cultured and spoke of art with such good judgment that Franz Liszt, meeting her in the foyer of the theatre, took her for a princess. Dumas, *fils*, makes her resemble the duke's daughter, thus indicating the delicate style of her personality. I liked this picture, and I followed Houssaye's description, making my heroine more refined than the usual type. It pleased my imagination to present Camille as reserved, gentle, intense in her love, and most sensitive,—in one word, an exception to her kind. This conception found favor with the public, and Camille's sensitiveness proved contagious, for everybody wept over the poor pirl. In the third act of the first performance even the prompter threw away the prompt-book and retired to a dark corner, behind the scenes, where he indulged in a good cry. Jeannette Gilder came to my dressing-room with her face flooded with tears, and we fell into each other's arms, laughing heartily, she over her previous crying fit, and I because a laugh was such a great relief after the emotions of the third act. Richard Watson Gilder, the poet, and his beautiful madonna-like wife also came to shake hands with me, and I was happy. These dear and distinguished people were the first friends I found in New York, and both my husband and myself spent many pleasant hours with them in the "Studio," and also on Eighteenth Street, where old Mrs. Gilder lived with her three daughters and her youngest son, Joseph.

An amusing incident during that first evening nearly ruined my scene with Armand's father. In order to make a strong contrast between Camille's former luxurious surroundings and the quiet country life to which she had retired, and to emphasize the sudden conversion of that rather gay person into an angelic creature, full of love, of simplicity, and of nature, the stage manager had hung up a cage with a live canary as a realistic touch of restful, rustic existence. The pretty bird, dazzled at the start by the light, behaved quietly through the first scenes of the act, but by the time Mr. Duval was introduced, it felt quite at home, and finally started on a long, elaborate song, so shrill and loud that I, fearing that this vocal exhibition might interfere with the play, took down the cage and put it out of the stage window. I saw some one standing there, and naturally thought that the cage would be taken from me and carried back to the property-room. But the person, for some unknown reason, stepped back, and the cage fell to the floor with a loud thump. Next morning I received a large envelope containing a letter from the Society for the Prevention of Cruelty to Animals, in which I was accused of having deliberately murdered an innocent bird, for which crime I must, according to the statutes of the society, be fined, etc. I had to prove that the poor little bird was not injured before I was left in peace. As I was then becoming quite popular, the papers wrote a great deal about this incident.

A few days after the first performance of "Camille," my manager told me that there was not one seat left for the remainder of the week, and there was a demand for the next week. Indeed the houses were so crowded that the orchestra was taken out from its place and the latter filled with chairs for the public. Many persons had to be accommodated with seats behind the scenes. The success was complete, and Mr. Fiske urged me to stay in New York two or three months more, but Mr. Sargent, having already planned my tour, refused to accept the proposition.

It was about that time that Sienkiewicz passed through New York, on his way to Europe, and came to take leave of me. He looked so happy that I sincerely congratulated him on his return from his voluntary exile, where "the orange grows," back to the land of the snow-storms and the sleigh-rides.

I do not remember the order of the different cities I visited during this first tour. It will be sufficient to mention a few. I played one week in Philadelphia, in Mrs. Drew's Theatre, with her stock company, and the next thing that comes to my memory is the trip by boat to Boston. The weather was frightful, and we had a bad storm, which delayed our arrival in Boston for ten hours. I was a little nervous about my appearance in that critical city, but the New York press criticisms, and several private, friendly messages made the field smooth for me. Mr. George W. Childs, whom I had met in Philadelphia, and who, with his well-known kindness, had shown me great courtesies, wrote on my behalf to Mr. George Bancroft, and Mrs. Gilder had also sent several letters to her Boston friends, the most important one being to Henry W. Longfellow.

I opened my two weeks' engagement at the Boston Museum with "Adrienne Lecouvreur," and played with the stock company, celebrated for its excellency, for there were Mr. Warren, Miss Clarke, and other fine artists in the personnel. Apparently I was doomed to meet on my first nights with some mishap or accident. As I related before, in San Francisco my veil took fire; in New York, on the first

Photograph by Sarony.

WILLIAM WARREN.

night of "Adrienne," I carried on a shoe-horn instead of my fan; and on the first performance of "Camille" there was the canary-bird episode; but here it was something still worse. There was a wooden bar running along the back drop, joining the two sides of the door, which I had not seen at the rehearsal, because the stage was not fully set then. So it happened that when I was leaving Michonnet in the fourth act, with his hands full of the money for the delivery of Maurice de Saxe from the hands of his debtors, I was in such haste to get to my dressing-room to change my costume that I started on a run, and holding my head up to express defiance and pride, I tripped over that unfortunate bar and fell headlong through the door. An audible and distressing laugh struck my ear most unpleasantly, but when I returned, a few minutes later, the audience applauded my entrance. I bowed, covering my face with the fan up to my eyes, my whole attitude expressing how much I was ashamed of my awkwardness. This seemed to establish a bond of sympathy between the house and myself, and the rest of the performance went on undisturbed.

One of the most important events of my stay in Boston was my meeting with Henry W. Longfellow. Mrs. Gilder wrote that the great man would call on me at my hotel. Although I was forewarned of his visit, yet I was quite overcome with emotion when one afternoon his card was brought to my room. One look of his kind, deep-set eyes and a warm hand-shake soon restored my mental equilibrium and put me at my ease. The presence of this true, great poet, this man endowed with the finest qualities a man can possess, was a spiritual feast for me.

He spoke to me of Boston and its celebrities, and made me acquainted with the names of Oliver Wendell Holmes, Aldrich, James T. Fields, Celia Thaxter, etc., then chaffed me about going up Bunker Hill Monument, and asked me how I compared the California weather with the beautiful climate of Massachusetts. He went on speaking in that manner, that of a perfect man of the world, and simply charmed me. Then my son Ralph came in, and we were

Copyright, 1882, by J. H. Lamson.

LONGFELLOW.

both invited to lunch at the poet's house in Cambridge. Longfellow's great charm was just that perfect simplicity, so rare in celebrated men. There was not a shade of the patronizing air so frequently assumed by people of superior standing, not a particle of the pomposity I had observed more than once among much less-known writers. A celebrity without conceit is rare, but there was none in the author of "Evangeline" and "Hiawatha." He did not seem to care much for compliments. When I attempted to speak about his poems, he interrupted me, and pointing to a handsome arm-chair standing in his studio, drew my attention to it, remarking jokingly that the children liked his verses, because he had received that present from a school on the—here he paused, and added, with a laugh, "centennial anniversary of my literary activity." Then, as if regretting that he had spoken lightly of the gift, he grew suddenly serious, and stroking the back of the chair with his hand, he said, almost tenderly, "I prize it highly." I made another attempt, and said I would gladly study some passages from his poems and recite them to him, and I mentioned "Hiawatha," but he stopped me with the words: "You do not want to waste your time in memorizing those things, and don't you speak of "Hiawatha," or I will call you Mudjikiewis, which, by the way, sounds somewhat like your name."

After lunch Ralph played one of Chopin's nocturnes, while our host recited Campbell's poem about Poland, and made me cry. Needless to say, I left his house quite fascinated.

My husband arrived in Boston during the second week of my engagement, happy, and looking better than when I left him. From his letters I already knew that he had sold the farm and sent the Sypniewski family back to Poland. Lucian Paprocki, however, had remained in America, looking for work as a cartoonist for a newspaper or magazine.

While in Boston we received many invitations from prominent people, but I was prevented from taking part in social entertainments because, owing to the success made by "Camille," I was induced by Mr. Sargent to play three extra matinées, which made ten performances during six days. The seats were sold at auction. After the Saturday matinée, when I was returning with my husband to the hotel, people crowded the street so thickly that the carriage could scarcely move. Strangers mounted the steps to shake hands and shower all kinds of compliments and blessings. Girls with moistened eyes threw flowers in my lap, and a young mother lifted her child to be kissed by me. The enthusiasm of the Boston public on that occasion reminded me of my performance in Warsaw on the eve of my departure. I was as much dumfounded as gratified by such tokens of approval and appreciation in a city supposed to be cold-blooded and renowned for its culture and its critical spirit.

My impressions of my first visit to Washington were equally delightful, only there the success was rather more of a social character. I really was spoiled by people's attentions, which were shown in calls, invitations, receptions, dinner-parties, etc. We met there many men prominent in public life, amongst whom I prized most the acquaintance of Carl Schurz, General Sherman, Governor Boutwell, Eugene Hale, then a promising young Congressman, and Senator Roscoe Conkling. I deplored my insufficient knowledge of English, which made me shy and diffident in conversation, but I listened attentively to all that these great men said. One evening, however, at a dinner at Mr. E. Hale's house, I ventured to speak about the condition of my country, at Mr. Conkling's request. On that subject I never lacked eloquence, even in English.

It was our good fortune to meet subsequently all these eminent men, and I remember with gratitude the kindness they showed to me. The one I knew best in later years was Mr. Conkling. It was to him I owed the privilege of making the acquaintance of General Grant, after his terms of Presidency. His exquisite manners might have served for a model to the most refined European men of the world, and women were fascinated by his mere presence in the room. When this unusually tall and handsome man entered, he became at once the centre of attraction.

It was with regret that I left Washington, having visited many places and monuments, but leaving unseen many others of equal interest.

We went to Baltimore, where we saw again Dion Boucicault, and where, at a jolly terrapin supper, we met Mr. Sothern (the father), one of the most congenial gentlemen I ever encountered. He had a charming way of talking to people he saw for the first time as though he had known them for years, and when he left the room with a warm hand-shake and that peculiar, quizzical, but kind expression in his eyes, every person present was sure of having won a friend for life.

The next city which comes to my memory is Louisville, and there I first knew Mr. Henry Watterson. The great journalist made a vivid impression on me. It was easy to recognize in him a man of genius, highly cultivated, strong-minded, full of vitality and energy; when I knew him better, I found that these brilliant qualities were combined with inborn kindness and tenderness of heart. Our first meeting was the commencement of a friendship which still lasts. We spent many a happy hour in Mr. Watterson's hospitable and truly Southern home, with its charming *chatelaine*, Mrs. Watterson, in their family circle. All through my American career this faithful friend gave me numerous proofs of his kindness.

It was during my Louisville engagement that my manager conceived the "glorious" idea of providing me with a fat little pug-dog, in order to give me more style, because, as he said, "all prominent stars had pet dogs," and though I never cared for that small canine specimen, being fond of large dogs, I had to yield to the appealing eyes of the pug, and promise to keep him as a living proof of my "artistic greatness"! But this was not the only token of the "eminent" position I had reached, or rather of the ingenious mind of my impresario. I was reported as having lost my stage jewels (advertised as real diamonds), because "every great star always loses hers at least once a year." That scheme of being reckless about valuables was considered a splendid advertisement. Poor art!

I was told that this mode of exciting the public interest originated with Mr. Barnum, especially when he introduced Jenny Lind in America. Yet there was something grand in Barnum's manner of humbugging people, as, for instance, his offering of the first night's concert to charity in the name of the celebrated singer, and paying her share out of his own pocket. That was fine, but his would-be imitators cheapened his style considerably in the time I am speaking of, and I had to submit to a great deal of ridiculous *réclame,* until I grew independent and stopped all that nonsense.

Chicago in the first months of 1878 was not one of the great cities of the world, as it is to-day, and I had no curiosity to go out and visit any of the parks, then in their infancy. I stayed in the hotel, studying, and unhappy over the dismal weather. I went out only once to a reception, tendered to me by a society of young enthusiasts, the "Owl Club." But the other days I did not leave my rooms until it was time to go to the theatre. There everything appeared brighter. The profusion of good scenery, an excellent supporting company, and a house packed brimful with nice-looking people, were things good to behold after my solitary confinement in the gloomy hotel room. I was at my best on the first night, and the success of my two weeks' engagement was secured. But the lack of exercise and of fresh air brought me into trouble. One morning I woke up with a sore throat and an unpleasant hoarseness in my voice. A physician had to be summoned, and he cleared my throat in the style of chimney-sweeps, brushing it up and down with a small brush on a long wire, until I was nearly choked. I would not recommend that energetic process of clearing the vocal chords to Madame Sembrich or to Calvé, but it did help me at the time. I went on with my engagement without interruption, though I had to live on milk and sweet oil for a while.

In St. Louis I saw Mr. Eugene Field, another of the dear friends I gained in America. I admired him for his genuine poetic talent, his originality and almost childlike simplicity, as much as for his great heart. He had indeed a many-sided and rich nature,—most domestic in his family relations, a delightful host by his own fireside, and yet a perfect Bohemian in artistic circles. The author of exquisitely dainty poems, and withal a brilliant and witty humorist, he was equally lovable in all these various characters. He was full of original ideas which often gave a quaint touch to his receptions. In later years, when he lived in Chicago, I remember a dinner *en forme*, which he called a "reversed one," beginning with black coffee and ice-cream, and ending with soup and oysters. After the first course he delivered a most amusing toast. We were laughing so much that tears stood in our eyes. He looked compassionately around the table, and saying, "I see that you are sad and depressed; let us have some fun," he went to a mechanical piano and gave us a few bars of a funeral march. After each dish he returned to the instrument and treated us to some doleful tune. On a later occasion he sent us a formal invitation to a party at his house, "to meet a friend from abroad." But when we came, there was no such friend, and as the evening went on, the foreigner did not make his appearance. When we were on the point of leaving, we heard a strange sound at the window. "At last," exclaimed our host, and opening the window, called out some name which I cannot remember. After a few seconds we saw the head of a donkey, and a most frightful braying filled the room. Eugene

Field stroked caressingly the long, soft ears, until the soothing effect of his hands stopped the musical entertainment, and the introduction took place. "This is my belated friend! He is, indeed, a great donkey!" remarked our host, quite seriously. After taking leave, I overheard some of the guests saying, "That was indeed a bitter satire, but I should like to know who was really that friend from abroad, personified by the donkey." Thus are commentaries written, looking for some deep, hidden meaning in a simple joke.

In the summer of 1878 we took a steamer from New York and first went to Ireland, where we spent a week or so visiting the places of interest, not omitting Blarney Castle. We had there the pleasure of witnessing a young American girl, held by the heels, attempting to kiss the famous stone.

After a last look at the Killarney Lakes, the beauty of which still lingers in my memory, and a short visit to Dublin, we crossed to England and spent a few days in London. There for the first time I saw Henry Irving, in "Van der Decken." The performance was of a sort entirely new to me, but certainly picturesque and full of beauty. It brought back to my mind the enchanting fairy-stories which had delighted my childhood. Irving himself appeared to me weird and unreal, like the story, and this lack of realism, together with the actor's artistic appearance, appealed to me strongly. When he stepped out of the picture-frame, the illusion was perfect, and he truly gave one the impression of a supernatural being.

From London we went to Poland to see our family and friends. Every one seemed overjoyed at our return, as well as at my success in America. My good mother looked at me with an expression of pride and assurance, saying, "Well, it is as it should be!" Dear, conceited mother, I had to kiss her good-by again and leave for Paris, where we were going to see the Exposition, and also to get new gowns for Camille, Frou-Frou, and Juliet. Besides our excursions to the Exposition, the theatres, etc., we also spent a great deal of time in the studio of Carclus Duran, to whom I was posing for a life-sized portrait. The picture had been ordered by an American friend of ours, Mr. Paris Haldeman, with the object of presenting it to the Philadelphia Art Gallery. It is there still, I hear, but I am sorry to say that, though the painting is very fine, there is no likeness in the face, nor in the proportions of the whole figure. It was amusing to sit, or rather to stand, for Carolus Duran and see how very Spanish he tried to look in order to suit his name. He had a guitar in the studio, and played on it, humming some Spanish songs, with a very French accent, every time we took a few moments of rest.

One morning a tall, attractive young man came in and was introduced by Monsieur Duran as "Mr. John Sa*rrr*gent, from Ame*rrr*ica." The young artist had brought with him a small canvas, and while Carolus was painting the chinchilla of my dress, he painted Duran's head. In an hour or so he made a sketch which looked to me like a finished portrait in its wonderful likeness. When he left the room, Carolus said, "Il a du talent, ce garçon-là!" It was a sort of offhand praise, at least we thought so. We wished very much to meet again *ce garçon-là*, but he did not return to the studio, at least while we were there.

Many of our Polish friends came to Paris for the Exposition, and of course they also were greatly excited over my success. The result consisted in many delightful dinners, drives, and all kinds of pleasure parties. We found our old friends, Cyprian Godebski and his wife, settled in Paris, and spent again some purely artistic evenings in their house, which, as in Warsaw, was the meeting-point not only of Polish painters, but also of most prominent lights of art of other countries. Among others there was our old acquaintance, Nicolas Rubinstein. One afternoon he brought

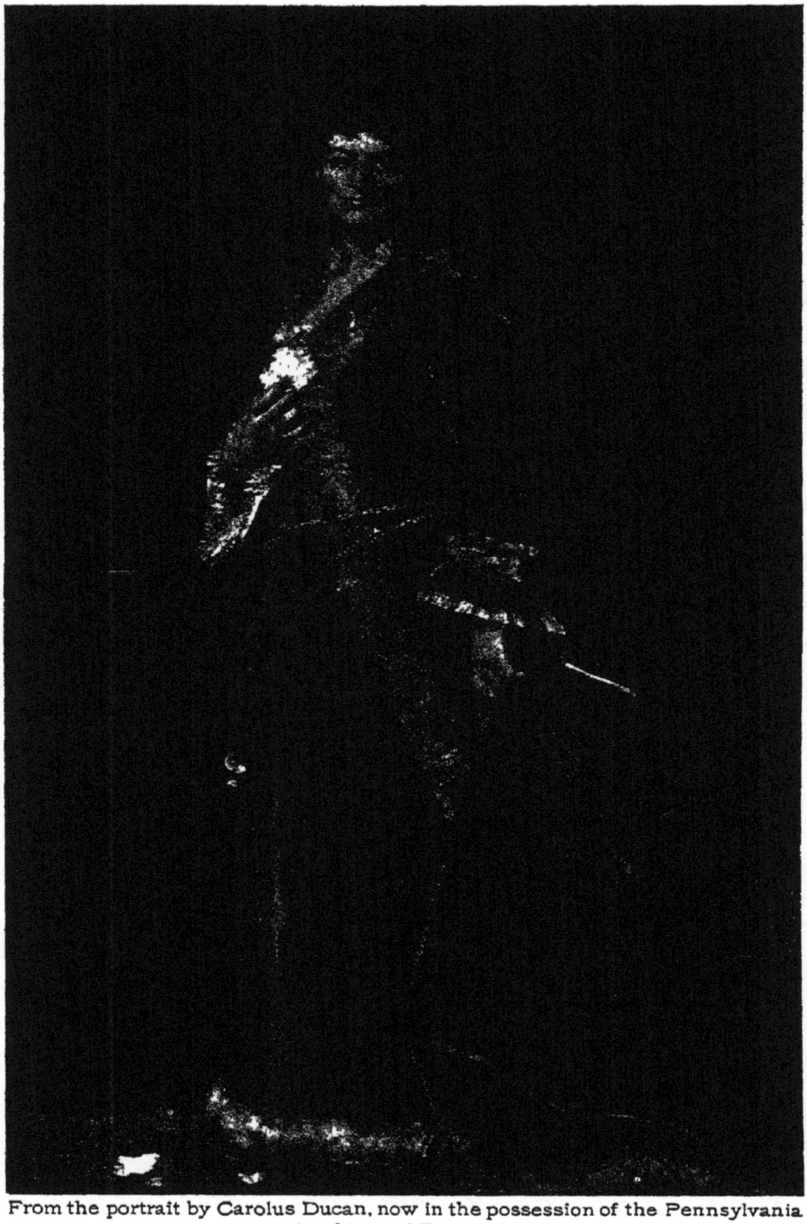

From the portrait by Carolus Ducan, now in the possession of the Pennsylvania Academy of Fine Arts

to our hotel Liszt and Tourgenief, the exquisite Russian writer, but the luck was against me, for I was out and the only souvenirs I had of these two great celebrities were their visiting-cards. They left for Italy next morning, and I never met them afterwards.

"Ernani," the tragedy of Victor Hugo, was then being played at the Théâtre Français for several weeks, and I saw the wonderful Sarah Bernhardt for the first time, in the part of Donna Sol. I was carried away by her passionate and desperate scene in the last act, and quite realized the enthusiasm of the public for the rare artist. She conquered me as she did many others, and I have still a most vivid admiration for her continued and successful work. I was sorry there was no change of bill during my stay in Paris, for I wished to see her again in some other part.

Having made with Mr. H. Sargent a contract for another season, a long one this time, lasting thirty or more weeks, we had to return to America. I left my son in the care of my Polish friends [1] who lived in Paris. He was determined to become a civil engineer, and wished to prepare himself for L'École des Ponts et Chaussées (School of Bridges and Roads). In the month of September Ralph and our friends accompanied us to Cherbourg, and I parted from my boy with a heavy heart, but full of hope for his future.

[1] Miss Anna Wolska and her father, Mr. Calixte Wolski.

CHAPTER XLI

On our return trip to America we met on the steamer Miss Mollie Elliott Seawell, the well-known author. She was then a very young girl, with a refined mind and delightful Southern manners, and attracted me by her lively conversation and her ingenuous and candid remarks. Her enthusiasm for nature was another link between us. This started an exceedingly pleasant acquaintanceship, which we cultivated for years, both by correspondence and several visits to her home in Washington, where I had the occasion of increasing my knowledge of Washington society.

I was happy to be back in New York again, — the city of constant improvements, always yearning for perfection, so difficult to obtain on a long, narrow strip of land. Still, even after two years, New York seemed different to me from the city we landed in on our first arrival from Europe. Many handsome new buildings had been erected, and Central Park was greener and more varied. We were glad to see the improvements, but above all glad to see the dear friends we had left there.

We met first Jeannette Gilder. She was then a young newspaper woman and wore semi-masculine dress, —a melon hat, a high collar, a cravat, and a tailor-made coat, but under those manly garments was hidden an essentially womanly nature and a heart full of sympathy and kindness. She always seemed to me a wonderful combination of talent, work, enthusiasm, abnegation, and serenity. She possessed a wonderful recuperative power; after toiling almost to exhaustion, she would enjoy, in her moments of leisure, all the fun and pleasure of life with the buoyancy of a little girl. We met often in the seventies, and then we drifted away from each other, but neither space nor time count with her, for no matter how many years might have elapsed

WALT WHITMAN.

since our last meeting, she always remains the same, *Sempre la stessa.* By the way, this Italian motto I had adopted in former years for myself, but since Count Fredro, Jr., wrote once at the foot of a letter addressed to me,

"Always the same, only a little older," I ceased to use it personally, and preferred to apply this epithet to my friends, especially those who, like Jeannette Gilder, are unchangeable, both in appearance and character. We were also welcomed by her brother, Richard W. Gilder. We spent many delightful hours in his house on Fifteenth Street, called "The Studio," because the living-room was arranged as an artist's *atelier* for his charming and gifted wife, Madame Helena de Kay Gilder, who painted there her portraits and sketches from life. I shall always remember the glorious evening spent in that artistic abode, where all that could be found best in art gathered around the madonna's tea-table. In that house Clara Louise Kellogg sang, Salvini recited, Joe Jefferson was a frequent guest on his visits to New York. Poets, artists, sculptors, as well as people of highest social position, found respite from the daily humdrum in that atmosphere of refinement. Amongst others, we met Clara Louise Kellogg, John La Farge, Augustus Saint Gaudens, and also Walt Whitman. I shall not easily forget the impression the latter made on me. His whole appearance was unusual. The expressive, rather large-featured face would have fitted King Lear to perfection. His hair and beard were white, and his deep eyes were both eager and sad. I read in them wisdom and concentration, but also a great deal of pessimism in the twinkle of the lids. He was sparing of speech, but when he spoke it was like his poems, deep and concise. When, taking leave, he put his large-brimmed hat on, he looked like one of those traditional, picturesque squatters of old times, rarely seen at the present day.

I opened the season of 1878–1879 in New York at the Fifth Avenue Theatre, with "Frou-Frou." The title part of Frou-Frou was more difficult for me to learn than any other I had played before, because of the rapid speeches. In the third act, especially, my scene with Louise called for so much speed that my tongue, not being quite used to the foreign language, in addition to my nervousness, made me make such a havoc of my words on the first night that I could scarcely understand myself, not to speak of the audience. To my great amazement, a young critic, Mr. Steinberg, of the *New York Herald*, said quite seriously in his notice about "Frou-Frou" that my rapid speeches were like Wagner's music to him, — the less he understood, the better he liked them. He added, further, that this rushing cataract of sounds was most impressive.

Though the whole notice was most enthusiastic, and though I was thankful for so much indulgence, yet I considered it more as a youthful outburst of admiration than a truthful account. Had it not been so sincere, it would have sounded like satire. I laughed while reading it, but blushed also, and went directly to work over my speeches, repeating them first slowly and then more and more rapidly, until I succeeded in making them more distinct. I was told that my second performance was quite an improvement. Yet one who has never played in a foreign language has no idea how difficult it is to render all the necessary lights and shades, when one is hampered by the lack of familiarity both with the foreign words and the pronunciation. No lessons, no exercise, can take the place of the language we have been born to. Actors, however, have the advantage of illustrating their words by action and facial expression. Were it not for that, every attempt to play in a foreign tongue would be fruitless. That was the reason I never liked to give English recitations on a platform, because I had nothing to help out the deficiencies of my pronunciation.

I had my own company this time: Frank Clement, from England, was my leading man, and Louise Muldener the leading lady. That excellent actress was a German, and spoke English with a slight accent. I heard Mr. Stephen Fiske, the manager of the theatre, say that it was a mistake

to have engaged her, because one star with a foreign accent might be excused, but two in the cast, one speaking with a Polish, and the other with a German, accent would only supply food for criticism and for malicious remarks to the quick, mischievous American newspaper men, and indeed many jokes were made on the subject. Some one wrote: "No wonder these ladies quarrelled and that Madame Modjeska was teeming with rage in the third act, when she, in her sweet accent, addressed Miss Muldener as 'seester,' and was called in return 'Oh! Oh! Schvisterrr!' Who could stand that insult?" There was a great deal of exaggeration in that, because Miss Muldener's accent was not unpleasant, but the fear of ridicule made my manager exchange her for another young lady, far less competent.

I played Juliet during this season. It was on that occasion that *Scribner's Monthly* published a long article about me, — written by Charles De Kay, — inserting several of my photographs and my portrait by Carolus Duran. The article helped to spread my reputation a great deal, for *Scribner's Monthly* seldom gave space to theatrical matters. Besides, being considered one of the best, if not the best, magazine of the times, it was read all over America and abroad.

During my engagement in Philadelphia I was advised by my friends to add "Peg Woffington" to my repertoire. It was not a good choice, for I could neither catch the Irish brogue nor dance the jig in the last scene. Lotta, who came to see me in the part, had a good laugh over my dance, and when I met that little lady, she invited me to an extra matinée to show me how she danced the jig. As soon as that tiny, nervous creature entered, I knew that I had before me a woman of great talent and originality. The style of her plays was not, of course, elevated. The one we saw was a popular, amusing comedy, not even well written, with commonplace characters, but her individuality covered all

Photograph by Sarony.

LOTTA (CHARLOTTE CRABTREE).

the sins of construction. She infused life in the part she played, and her realism was simply wonderful. She was an ideal type of the mining-camps, and very pretty, too. Several actresses imitated her, even in the slightest gestures, and one of them, having seen Lotta, repeatedly copied all her stage business, and appropriating her plays, went to London and produced them. She made a hit, but when Lotta, who really originated the types, came after her to London, she was considered a second edition of her imitator. Such proceedings as stealing somebody's artistic creation are unpardonable, yet they happen often, and the people are not any the wiser for it. Happily there are many recording angels among the audience and in the press. The shallow imitators usually disappear from the surface, as it happened in this case, for I forget even the name of Lotta's facsimile, while her own name will never be forgotten by any one who saw her on the stage.

Before I went on a regular tour, I asked Mr. Sargent to show me the route he planned for me. There were several one-night towns on the list, and I anxiously inquired if I should be obliged to wake up to catch trains early in the morning. He answered that, sometimes, it was inevitable, of course. Upon that I declared that I could not possibly consent to it, because I must have at least eight hours of uninterrupted sleep, or I could not act at all. Usually I could not go to sleep immediately after the play, being too excited. When we had no guests, I would read or play the piano before going to bed; then I would sleep soundly until nine in the morning. I was simply unable to sleep in the daytime. I advised Mr. Sargent to cut out the one-night towns. He looked rather amused, and said he could hardly do so, having much higher percentage in those towns than in the large ones, and tried to persuade me that, in my own interest, I should accept the route as it was. I stood firm in my decision, and Mr. Sargent went away discontented.

Next morning, however, he came in, smiling, and said he had found a way to give me as many hours of sleep as I desired by renting a private car.

It was an ordinary Wagner's sleeper, without drawing-room, but it was a great comfort not only for me but for the actors, who were so thankful for this consideration that, at the end of the season, they gave Mr. Sargent a present for his "glorious" idea. Thus it happened that I had the first theatrical private car on the road. All the "stars" soon followed the example, and now it has become a necessity to travel in this manner.

When I returned from England, after my London début, in 1882, I used the private cars, in their improved state, every season. While my husband had the management of my tours, which he had for several years, we had the whole company located in the private car, but later on, under the *régime* of the Theatrical Trust, he gave up his connection with the business, and my seasons were conducted by regular impresarios. Under their rule the private cars were reserved for the star and her party, and, of course, for the manager or his agent, and the members of the company were deprived of its comforts, or admitted only on paying a pretty high rate for their berths, which they rarely could afford. The result was a great hardship for them. They were waked up at all impossible hours for the trains, sometimes they even had to change trains in the middle of the night. This way of travelling, especially in the rainy or freezing season, is most unpleasant, if not injurious to health, and the consequence of it is that the poor people are sometimes so tired and fagged that they neglect their appearance and become lazy and indifferent. No one can expect a good performance from a sleepy actor.

The introduction of private cars had some bad results. It tempted managers to book their stars in too many one-night stands, often causing unsatisfactory productions of the plays. The haste of putting up the scenery, and the constant wear and tear of it, soon makes it look shabby, or, if the stage is too small, local scenery is used instead of that carried by the company, and is usually ugly and unsuited to the plays. It is not inspiring to play "Marie Stuart" in a kitchen instead of a royal prison, or "Hamlet" in a room painted all over with cupids, or "Julius Cæsar" in some badly painted Gothic hall, — yet those things happen quite often, though carloads of fine scenery are awaiting outside.

I heard people saying, "What does it matter how the play goes in such a small town as this?" It is a great mistake. Men and women of culture can be found everywhere, even in the smallest corners of this country. With the constant fluctuation of this nation, often people move from the smaller places up to the metropolis or other large cities, and the impressions they get at first during these neglected performances spread around and create a bad reputation for the production.

CHAPTER XLII

In April, 1879, I made my second visit to Boston, with three plays, "Adrienne Lecouvreur," "Camille," and "Romeo and Juliet." I discarded "Peg Woffington," but "East Lynne" was added to the repertoire. I hated that play, and called it "Beast Lynne"; still, the managers insisted upon my playing it on Saturday nights, when a different class of people — fond of popular plays — formed the public; "East Lynne" being considered the most attractive of them, I was persuaded to put it into rehearsals — to please the Saturday-night audiences.

It was at my performance of "Romeo and Juliet" that I met Mrs. Annie Fields. She invited Longfellow and some members of his family to come to the theatre and see me in the part of Juliet, and the great poet answered as follows: —

"Cambridge, April 18, 1879.

"Dear Mrs. Fields:

"We shall be delighted to see Modjeska in Juliet, and will come four-strong, or on all-fours, as you kindly suggest.

"I suppose the 'lovely creature,' as a certain young artist would say, has not yet arrived.

"If you happen to know at what hotel she will stay, be kind enough to inform me by a postal card.

"Yours faithfully,

"Henry W. Longfellow."

This letter was sent to me as a Christmas present in 1906, by Mrs. Fields, and was accompanied by the following note: —

"148 Charles Street, Boston.

"Dear Madame Modjeska:

"Pray accept the enclosed letter, with my constant remembrance and appreciation.

"Yours,

"Annie Fields."

"Christmas, 1905.

"With my greetings also to Count Bozenta."

Then in a different kind of ink, Mrs. Fields added:—

"1906.

"Think of it! A whole year has gone, and I open this note (which could not go because I had no satisfactory address) to again send love and greetings."

I have been told that, after the performance of "Romeo and Juliet," Mr. Longfellow went to several newspaper offices to see what was written about me, and in case there were any antagonistic remarks, to try to moderate them. He knew the spirit of some critics, opposed to a foreigner's playing Shakespeare, and wished to ward off the blows. It was one of the kindest things ever done, and I never ceased to be thankful to the great poet and best of men for taking trouble to shield me against unkind remarks.

The critics were all fair, with the exception of one, who could not forgive my "foreign appearance" nor my accent. To criticise my accent was quite justifiable, but I wondered what my foreign appearance had to do with the matter. Was Juliet an American? Or must all Shakespeare's heroines look Anglo-Saxon, though they belong to different nationalities? Well, never mind that—my chief object was to act Juliet to the best of my ability, and I did so. It seems that the part was a success, for I kept it in my repertoire until the year 1888, just one year after the birth of my first grandchild.

Next day, after the play, we found Mrs. Fields's cards and an invitation to luncheon. There we met the poet-host,

Mr. James T. Fields, Henry Longfellow, Oliver Wendell Holmes, Aldrich, Celia Thaxter, and Edwin Booth, who came with his young, energetic-looking little wife.

Mr. Longfellow said many kind things to me about Juliet, and urged me to appear in London, where he said I was sure to succeed. His words made my heart swell with most delightful hopes. Play in London and play Shakespeare! The ambition of my whole life would then be satisfied! I tried not to think of it, for it made me too happy.

Both my husband and myself admired greatly Mr. Fields's library and different objects of art, as well as the view of the river from the back window; but most of all we admired Mrs. Fields's beautiful Dante Rossetti face, her intellect and distinction of manner. She and Mr. Fields did all they could to make our visit a pleasant one. Chopin's music was played for us, some interesting experiences related, Emerson's and Keats's verses quoted. Keats seemed to be a particular favorite in Mr. Fields's home. A cast of that youthful poet's head was placed on the writing-desk. I had quite a chat with Edwin Booth, whom I had always been anxious to meet since I first saw him on the stage. Though my knowledge of English was not yet sufficient for sustaining a long conversation, it was easy to talk to that great actor and lovely man, who met me half-way.

My attitude, however, towards the poets was mostly of a listener. This I could do to perfection, and with expression, too. I was quite a success in that capacity, it seems, for my listening to Chopin's music inspired Celia Thaxter with the following poem: —

"Deft hands called Chopin's music from the keys.
  Silent she sat, her slender figure's poise
Flower-like and fine and full of lofty ease;
  She heard her Poland's most consummate voice

From power to pathos falter, sink and change;
  The music of her land, the wondrous high,
Utmost expression of its genius strange, —
  Incarnate sadness breathed in melody.
Silent and thrilled she sat, her lovely face
  Flushing and paling like a delicate rose
  Shaken by summer winds from its repose
Softly this way and that with tender grace,
  Now touched by sun, now into shadow turned, —
  While bright with kindred fire her deep eyes burned!"

We paid another visit to Longfellow's home in Cambridge. I forgot my fan in the poet's house, and he sent it back to me with the following note:—

"CAMBRIDGE, April 25, 1879.

"DEAR MADAME MODJESKA:

"The English poet, Gay, once wrote a poem in three books on 'The Fan,' beginning—

'I sing that graceful toy, whose waving play
With gentle gales relieves the sultry day.'

"And Holmes, the American poet, has a charming piece on 'The First Fan,' in which he says:—

'Before this new Pandora's gifts,
  In slavery women's tyrant kept her,
But now he kneels her glove to lift,
  The Fan is mightier than the Sceptre.'

"Now, if I had a particle of the nimble fancy of these poets, I should not let your fan go back without a song. But as I have not, it returns to your hand unsung, though not unhonored.

"Thanking you for your, to us, delightful visit yesterday; congratulating you on your artistic success; imploring you not to kill yourself with overwork; wishing you a prosperous voyage across the Atlantic, and a safe and speedy return to us; with all these present participles, I am, dear Madame Modjeska,

"Yours faithfully,

"HENRY W. LONGFELLOW."

"P.S. I add a note of introduction to Lord Houghton in London, a poet and traveller, who I am sure will be glad to welcome you. I give his old address. You can easily ascertain if he has changed it."

My engagement in Boston was an uninterrupted chain of intellectual pleasure and artistic enjoyment. It would be difficult to find more congenial and inspiring circles in the whole world than those of Boston in 1879.

I closed my season there with "East Lynne," given on the last Saturday night of my engagement. I do not remember how I played that part I disliked so much,—badly, of course,—I only recollect that I replaced the song from the "Bohemian Girl," in the first act, by the recitation of one of Mrs. Browning's sonnets. I loved Mrs. Browning, and read and reread her poems.

I also remember that the Globe Theatre was so packed with people that there was no standing room, and the orchestra being sold out, the musicians were obliged to play on the stage. I had a curious sensation of walking on people's heads, the footlights being so close to the upturned faces. There was no art in that performance, though I was called repeatedly before the curtain. I was glad when it was over. Not everything that "pays" is necessarily artistic.

On the way south we met with an accident near Alabama. Our train went off the track. No one was killed, but we were shaken a good deal, and when the train stopped, our car tipped up considerably on one side. It was not pleasant to see that we were just within one yard of the brink of a precipice.

New Orleans was a joy. The two weeks we spent there were filled with many impressions. Every day we visited curious places, old, quaint houses and churches; we also took drives on the celebrated shell road, and went into ecstasies over the vegetation. The camellia trees growing everywhere were marvels. We even got up at five o'clock in the morning to go to the famous French market, bought some Indian trifles, and took a cup of bad coffee. The slave market was a point of great interest, especially when we went there accompanied by a native friend, who told us many blood-curdling stories about the old, happy days. There were, however, a few simple darkeys who told us they regretted the old times and the kind masters. In general, we met with many different opinions about the negro question, and the strange evolutions of that race were most amazing.

A few years later, in Boston, we had an opportunity to listen to speeches of some colored men, from a balcony where we sat, as in a gallery, and could see everything and hear every word spoken, through the open windows. It was a banquet in one of the prominent hotels, given by negroes, pure and mixed, on the occasion of the anniversary of Dumas' father's death. Many speeches of eulogy were delivered to the memory of that man of genius, who was related to them on his grandmother's side. One speaker, especially, displayed a great deal of energy in persuading his audience that, though the colored people had been kept for years in ignorance by their masters, they do not lack intelligence and even intellectuality, as was proved by the great writer of their race and also by Ira Eldridge, the famous actor, whose success in Europe and whose marriage with a white woman proved that it is not the race but the conditions in which that race was kept hitherto by their rulers that makes so vast a difference between them and the American people. "But," he went on, "the dawn of deliverance is at hand, and the day is not far distant when the people will vote for a colored President of the United States." It is easily imagined with what enthusiasm those words were received by the hot, impulsive hearers. Listening to those speeches, dictated by the inflamed hopes of the primitive people, put too rapidly in contact with culture, my memory carried me back to the abandoned slave market in New Orleans and the dreadful history of the past times of slavery, and I asked myself which would be preferable:

to have a pretty, dusky slavey to fan me on a hot day, or to be under the rule of an African President, and I decided that neither of those two alternatives were to my taste.

We spent several pleasant weeks in the South, and met many descendants of the aristocratic families of Virginia. They were all most charming and delightful in their hospitality.

In Memphis, Tennessee, we met Mrs. Sherwood Bonner, and were glad to renew the acquaintance (previously made in Boston) of that highly gifted woman.

We visited General Jackson's celebrated horse-breeding farm in Belle Mead, near Nashville, and were warmly welcomed by the host and hostess.

In many old houses, known for their opulence in the past, we noticed the reduced circumstances, verging on poverty, but borne with the dignity of high breeding. My heart went out to them in sympathy and admiration.

One day we were invited to a reception on a man-of-war in Norfolk, by Miss Mollie Seawell, who, being a granddaughter of an admiral, enjoyed a great popularity in the navy. Many congenial guests were present, and after a delightful and delicious luncheon we were shown all over the ship. At the close of our visit the pet of the crew was presented to us, — a very clean, pretty, pink and white pig with a ribbon around its neck. Miss Seawell informed me that the animal was so clever and performed so many stunts that they called it "Modjeska." I was very proud of my namesake, especially when I saw it dancing a hornpipe, which reminded me of my unfortunate jig in "Peg Woffington," and made me acknowledge the pig's superiority in the spirit of the dance, — that spirit I so sadly lacked.

After the regular, very successful season in the States, we returned to New York, where I played two weeks at the Grand Opera House, a popular house in those days.

On the first night, while in the dressing-room, trying to

bring the standing mirror to a certain angle, I pulled it a little too hard. It sprang out of its hinges and fell down with a great crash, strewing the floor with a flood of small pieces of glass. The expression on my maid's face was a study. She stood livid, and with white, trembling lips she said: "What have you done, Madame? Do you know that breaking a looking-glass means seven years of ill luck?" I laughed and ordered another mirror, but she remained gloomy and looked quite distressed. The superstition of the broken looking-glass is very deeply rooted among professional people, as are also such small things as the pinning of white stuff with a black pin, or the turning of your garment on the right side when you happen by mistake to put it on wrong side out, and so forth. Those omens of ill or of good luck are so numerous that it would take pages to describe them. It was interesting to study the effects of those different tricks of imagination. It happened frequently that when an actor who implicitly believed in omens met with a presage of ill luck, he would be affected by it to such an extent that he would act badly, forget his lines, and make silly mistakes all through the play. His only excuse was: "I knew I would have bad luck to-night."

Happily the bad omens were balanced by an equal number of good ones, and the effects of the latter were quite exhilarating. They mostly happened to young girls.

Against all precedents in points of "luck" the sad presage of my maid was not realized, for the next seven years and the seven more afterwards were the fullest and the most successful in my theatrical career.

My season being over, I visited the theatres of New York. I saw Clara Morris, and was amazed by the inborn talent of that actress, by her expression of passion and her gift of tears. I do not remember the title of the play; the plot did not interest me at all. I only saw her, and was

Photograph by Sarony.

Clara Morris.

fascinated. Art with its laws had no power over her, for her art was her own, apart from any rules and routine. She was a born actress, genuine, admirable, spontaneous, and powerful in her tragic moments, tender and gentle in the touching scenes, and always true to nature. I leave her deficiencies to the critics; we all have our deficiencies, have we not? But it is the fate of those who rise above others to be criticised severely, while some lesser talents are glorified above their merits.

SARAH JEWETT.

Joseph Jefferson was a rare treat. I only saw him then in "Lend me Five Shillings" at some benefit. The subtilty, the finish of details, were most admirable. He was simple, natural, and his roguish, irresistible smile immediately conquered the audience and brought them into sympathy with him. I had no need to see him in a larger part to judge how great an artist he was.

There was a charming actress in New York at that time. Her name was Sarah Jewett, and she played *ingénue* parts. Refined, genuine, subtle, and sympathetic, she appealed to me at once. The shade of sadness in her eyes when I met her made her interesting, and I watched her career. She died in the full bloom of her youth. Her loving and romantic soul met with great blows. Life with its realities smothered her ardent nature, and she died in an asylum,

Photograph by Sarony.

JOSEPH JEFFERSON.

leaving behind her nothing except the sweet memory of a few devoted friends and a little poem which tells the sad story of her heart.

WHY?

When love must bring regret,
  I would forget — and yet
For memories' rapturous pain,
  My heart would yearn again.
Ah me! Why would it be?

I know that love is blind,
  That so it is more kind.
And yet in my delight
  I long for perfect light.
Ah me! It must not be.

I wonder if love meant,
  To yield no full content,
And yet, for some reply
  That does not come, I sigh.
Ah me! It cannot be!

CHAPTER XLIII

Early in the spring of 1879 I received an invitation from a committee in Cracow to take part in the celebration of the fiftieth anniversary of the literary activity of the foremost Polish novelist, Kraszewski, which celebration was to last a week or more. The ceremonies of the Jubilee were to be combined with the opening of the recently restored "Sukiennice" (Draper's Hall), a public structure first built in the fourteenth century, and later on fallen into decay. The restoration was undertaken by the city of Cracow, and was accomplished under the supervision of our great national artist, Jan Mateiko. The dedication of that historic building was intended to add yet more splendor to the festivities inaugurated in honor of Kraszewski.

I was only too glad to participate in this national festival, and a few weeks after the end of my season I left for Poland, stopping a day or two in Paris to take my son with me.

Early in October we went to Cracow, where I was to take part in a few gala performances connected with the festivities of the occasion.

When we arrived in town I learned that I was announced for the next evening in the part of Adrienne. This was an unwelcome surprise, because, not having played the part in Polish since the spring of 1876, I was not sure of my lines. My husband had the same apprehension, for he asked me if I remembered my part. "Not at all," I replied, quite distressed. And, indeed, when I tried to recollect the Polish words, only the English text came to my mind. I sent to the stage manager for the manuscript, but it was too late; the theatre was closed that evening, and there was no one there.

It was very annoying, and there was nothing left but to plan a way of getting out of the performance. But how? To change the bill would be regarded as a slight to the occasion. It would surely place me in an unfavorable light, for no one would believe I ever could forget a part I had played so often. The only remedy left was to make a mental translation of the English words, and depend upon chance. This was against my principles; and then another difficulty arose — how could I deal in the same way with La Fontaine's fable, which Ladnowski had so charmingly translated for me?

I went to bed with my mind full of disastrous forebodings; fatigue, however, soon closed my eyes and I slept soundly. When I woke in the morning, the first thing that came to my mind were the Polish lines of my part. In my great joy I called my husband, told him I remembered every word of Adrienne, and began to recite it aloud to him.

"How did you do it?" he asked.

"I do not know; I must have read it in my sleep, for I dreamt I saw the manuscript on my dressing-table."

At the rehearsal I never stopped for a word; I knew my part to the smallest details.

There were many famous people at the occasion of the Jubilee; artists, poets, writers, men of political standing, in one word, the prominent citizens of all parts of Poland, prompted by the same desire to pay homage to Kraszewski.

The opening of the "Sukiennice" was inaugurated with a ball, and the president of the city (the mayor), Mr. Zyblikiewicz, selected me to lead the Polonaise[1] with him. He was a very remarkable man, one of our foremost legislators, both in the Assembly and in the Vienna Parliament, an eminent lawyer, a great patriot, and a man of wonderful activity, all together one of the most popular individualities

[1] The Polonaise is our national dance, of very ancient origin, and consists of a sort of march with divers figures. It usually opens the ball.

in Poland. He was the first to open the Polish schools to Hebrew children, and thus to bring them in contact with Christian boys. His wish was to destroy gradually the antagonism existing between the two races, and to widen the field for the young Israelites, who had hitherto been kept in the narrow circle of their antiquated Talmudic schools. They lived in perfect harmony with the Polish students, and never were allowed to be "insulted, beaten, and killed" by the Christians, as the erroneous report of some Prussian papers asserted. It is the old story of the wounded lion kicked even by the meanest animals. Our poor nation was and is repeatedly accused, slandered, condemned, punished, and robbed without any other reason but the greedy and malicious animosity toward the wounded lion.

At one of the public meetings, during the Jubilee, the question of building a new theatre was raised, and Siemiradzki, one of our most prominent artists, who was present at the meeting, promised to paint a curtain for it.

He kept his promise, and the beautiful painting he presented to the new theatre is one of the most artistic ornaments of the building, and excites the admiration of all foreign visitors, who cannot understand why such a beautiful work of art is used for a theatre curtain.

In my memoranda of those times I find a note referring to the Jubilee: —

"The Jubilee was a great success. Everybody who is anybody, in the three parts of Poland, came to Cracow to take part in it and to shake hands with Kraszewski. I feel so happy in this reunion of our people. Festivities follow festivities, and there is an enthusiasm in the air which makes the heart beat more quickly. The unanimity of all those people who came from the most remote nooks, with the same idea of offering their homage to our great writer, is the best proof of our vitality and patriotism.

"Oh! what is the use of saying that we have ceased to be a nation, when everything cries against that sentence! Are the great works of art and literature to be counted as non-existent? Can any political combination kill the spirit? No! A thousand times no! It lives and lives! And the more it is persecuted, the stronger it will become. They may suppress the individuals, rob them, exile them, but the national spirit cannot be destroyed. Enough! this is not a revolt, but the mere statement of truth as well as the outpouring of a heart filled to the brim with pride and love for my native land. My people may yet go through many trials, but the history of nations shows us strange evolutions, and it does not rest with the petty, persecuting policies of our oppressors to determine what part Poland will have to perform in the future.

"After the Jubilee performances, I played a regular engagement of several weeks in Cracow, which was followed by three series of appearances in the other Polish cities, Lwów (Lemberg), Posen, and Warsaw.

"It was very natural that my countrymen should be elated over my success in America. They imagined that I had helped to spread the fame of Polish art abroad. The result of this feeling on their part was a continued succession of ovations upon which I need not dwell. It will be sufficient to say that they appealed not so much to my ambition as to my heart. It was hard to part from those who showed me such love, but I thought that my favorable reception on the foreign stage — in America — ought to be crowned by success in the mother-country of the Anglo-Saxons — in England."

CHAPTER XLIV

In January, 1880, my husband went to London to visit his relatives in Herefordshire, Mr. and Mrs. Bodenham, and also to see the theatrical managers about an opening for me.

When he returned to Warsaw he told me that everyone he met in London advised me to come and wait patiently for a good opening. There were still two or three months before the beginning of the London season, and I could use that time to my advantage.

In February we crossed the ill-humored gray channel. The drizzling rain penetrated me to my bones, and I was sad, nervous, unstrung, and a limp sample of humanity when we stopped at Charing Cross. It took us some time to find a suitable apartment, but at last we succeeded in renting a suite of small but prettily furnished rooms in a street near Piccadilly.

The first person who called was Mr. Hamilton Aidé, whom my husband had met on his previous visit to London. Every one in the eighties knew Mr. Aidé, and I do not need to describe that ever-youthful man, a friend and patron of artists, an artist himself and dilettante in letters.

He at once, with his usual hospitality, arranged a reception for us in his handsome rooms, and asked me if I would like to recite before his guests, who were literary men and women, artists, and society people. I told him I had never recited in English, and informed him of my theory about recitations in a foreign language.

"Do you recite in Polish?"

"Of course I do."

"Then why not do so at the reception? The people I invited will be most desirous to hear your voice and see the expression of your face."

Another examination, I thought, but Mr. Aidé was so convincing that I succumbed to the charm of his persuasion and promised to recite my favorite poem, "Hagar in the Desert," by Ujejski.

When we entered the reception-room, I experienced, for the first time in my life, the most unpleasant sensation of being observed by some women as an interesting object of curiosity. Against all rules of good breeding and politeness, they looked me over from head to foot with their lorgnettes, and their supercilious smile was quite aggravating. When I knew the London society women better, I was glad to find that this behavior was not a fault of breeding, but of their desire to follow a silly old fashion, revived by some person of high rank and weak eyesight, who dreaded to put on honest, plain glasses.

I soon forgot my resentment toward the weaker sex, when Mr. Aidé presented to me men whose names were well known in artistic and literary circles. After a short musical program, I was asked to recite, and, oh! wonder! I saw the same ladies who had looked me over drop their lorgnettes in their laps and wipe their eyes. What made them cry? I asked myself, since they did not understand a word of my recitation. Was it because, moved by the inflections of my own voice, I really felt the intensity of that ancient tragedy? I could not tell. I was simply amazed, and happy to have removed the lorgnettes and moved the hearts, or, as that cynical person, Mr. Oscar Wilde, remarked, to have tickled with my voice the tendrils of their nervous system.

Among Mr. Hamilton Aidé's guests we met Lionel Tennyson and his exquisite wife, and a few days later we received an invitation to an evening reception at Alfred Tennyson's house.

My heart was beating fast when I entered the presence of the great man, and I could say but little when he greeted me with a cordial, strong grasp of his hand. I was looking for the hostess; he guessed my thought, and led me to the other end of the room, where a sweet, delicate-looking woman lay on her back, on a narrow couch. This was Mrs. Tennyson, to whom our host introduced me. There was something so appealing and touching in her frail person that when she extended her hand to me I instinctively knelt down beside her couch, as I would at the bedside of some dear, sick friend. I saw her smooth cheeks blush faintly, and I rose instantly, remembering that any sort of demonstration was regarded as out of place among English people. I said faintly, "Pardon me," and accepted Mr. Lionel's chair, which he had placed for me near his mother's couch.

Mrs. Lionel approached, and the acquaintance was soon made. There were many distinguished persons in the room: Sir Frederic Locker, Dean Stanley, Millais, the great artist, who invited us to his studio, and several others belonging to the aristocratic or diplomatic world. Hallam Tennyson, the elder son, was also present. He helped his father in receiving the guests, and seemed altogether to be his right hand.

The illustrious poet greeted all who came in with pleasant or jocular remarks.

When all his guests were in, he asked me a few questions about Poland. I could not speak calmly about my country. I preferred not to speak at all, and only told Mr. Tennyson I had read his poem, "Poland," and thanked him for the memorable words: . . . "Us, O Just and Good, forgive, who smiled when she was torn in three,"[1] which I recited, trembling all over. Seeing how stirred I was, he suddenly changed the subject.

[1] Allusion to the dismemberment of Poland into three parts, each subject to a different empire.

His tall figure dominated every other man in the room; his high forehead and the noble, proud, and far-away expression of his eyes made me think of some legendary god who had descended to earth, lived and moved among mankind, but whose spirit remained in his ancestral home.

The following extracts of letters, written to friends and to my mother, will best describe the impressions of my visit to London:—

Letter No. I

"I never yet felt so far from my country and my own people as I feel here. Everything seems to inspire me with an unexplained fear; the hastening and ever-pushing mob, the blackened walls of the buildings, the hissing of the engines, even the marvellous outlines of Westminster Abbey.

"Yesterday, standing at the foot of Nelson's statue, I looked up, and I imagined I saw on the lips of the great Englishman an ironical smile, as much as to say: 'What do you want here, little fly?' And, indeed, I seem to myself nothing but a fly, a poor fly with wilted wings. If I survive, it will be simply providential. I hope to play here in a few weeks, or months, who can tell? Oh, if I could sleep at least three months, study in dream, act in dream, and wake up, when all is over, somewhere in the Tatra Mountains or in the chestnut alleys of Cracow!"

Letter No. II

"GOOD FRIDAY.

"This day, which is a day of mourning in other countries, is celebrated here by a so-called 'bank holiday.' Everywhere jolly, laughing crowds, merry-go-rounds, hand-organs rattling hackneyed tunes, wrestling matches in the streets; and where there is a green hill in the outskirts of the city, grown-up girls and boys roll down the slopes with merry laughter and loud jokes.

"When we ask the people why, just on this day, they all seem so happy, the answer is more or less the same: 'Why should we not be happy? Was not our Saviour crucified, and did he not redeem us to-day?'

"A strange point of view — rational in a way — but strange — is it not?

"And now, something about my own person: I am engaged

for twelve performances by Wilson Barrett, the manager of the Court Theatre. We chose 'Diane de Lys' for the début. Charles Coghlan, of whom I wrote you, will play with me. The company is fairly well organized, and the production will be magnificent, as far as the small stage will allow.

"My first appearance will take place early in May. In the meantime I spend six or seven hours a day in studying English. I want to be worthy of myself and of the appreciation of the great Albion; I want to touch these people's hearts and see tears in their eyes, 'those drops of pity wrung out of the depths of the heart,' as Lamartine says.

"You see I am also quite jolly to-day — in spite of Good Friday. You would laugh to see my advertisements. Nothing but 'MODJESKA' in letters three feet long. We often stand near by to listen to the remarks of the passers-by. Some of them, having read the name, ask each other: 'What is it? Is it alive?' Others remark to their friends that it surely must be some new tooth-powder, or some sanitary cereal, or a medicine for rheumatism.

"My name is less known here than that of the ruler of the smallest of the Fiji Islands; still I have the audacity to brave the audience by giving them samples of my native art — and my individuality. Will any one care? I tremble at the prospect of my failure, yet, the stronger my fear, the stronger is my desire to reach the goal. And mind, I have no doubt concerning my value, only a dread of not feeling at home on the English stage. Had I been an Englishwoman, all would have been so easy!"

Letter No. III

"Here I am, closed in my gilded cage on Piccadilly. I beat my wings against the bars like a wild bird longing for space and air! but I study and wait, and dread to think that I shall have to wait seven more weeks, for my début has been delayed until the fifteenth of May.

"A certain gentleman with a monumental nose and strong white teeth (regular monkey's teeth) comes every morning, from eleven to one o'clock in the morning, to correct my accent. He says that under his tuition I shall speak perfect English, because I have no American accent, as should be expected, but a Russian one, which is far more easy to correct than a Yankee twang. When I told him I was not a Russian but a Pole, he only looked at

Henry Irving as Louis XI, from a Pastel by J. Bernard Partridge.

me blankly, thinking probably of the North Pole, and let escape a deprecating 'Oh!' from his screwed-up mouth.

"My dear little mother, do you know that I grow quite desperate when I see how little they know about us abroad, and how little they care. 'Poland? Where is it?' they ask. We are not on the map any more, — and therefore we do not exist. What a diabolical error!

"Last Sunday we went to the Polish church. I wanted to cry when I looked at that parody of a temple. The Mass was read by Father Bakanowski[1] in the basement of an Italian church. The altar was covered with soiled cloth, two candles, and thirteen wooden chairs. That was all. The poor priest brought in himself the wine, the Mass books, and other utensils. Some ragged individual lit up the candles, and the Mass began, quietly, sadly, oh! how sadly! I thought of the Catacombs, where the first Christians, had to hide their ceremonies. The sound of the organs and the roulades of an opera soprano, reaching our ears faintly from the upper church, augmented the painful impression."

My London début took place earlier than I expected. Mr. Barrett had at that time a successful play running at the Court Theatre, "A Banker's Daughter," if I am not mistaken, and he did not think it would be prudent to take it off the bills until he was quite sure of my success. Therefore he proposed to me to play six matinée performances first. I had no choice but to accept the suggestion, and we decided to open on Monday, May 1, in "La Dame Aux Camélias," under the title of "Heartsease."

This substitution of the flower happened this way: We had a great difficulty in passing through the censorship any of the French plays. Mr. Barrett thought it would be better not to touch Shakespeare until I made myself known in some easier literature. But the plays "Diane de Lys" and "La Dame aux Camélias" were on the index presented to the censorship. Both Mr. Barrett and myself were much annoyed by this obstacle, when a dramatist, Mr. Mortimer,

[1] A few weeks later Father Bakanowski was shot at by some fanatic anarchist and was wounded but not killed.

who had translated "La Dame aux Camélias," conceived the extravagant idea of changing its title and calling it "Heartsease."

He knew from Charles Coghlan about my performance of Camille; so did Mr. Barrett. Judging from Mr. Coghlan's statement, they were almost sure of my success in that play. They went to work and changed some objectionable features of the heroine's "profession," and then sent this remodelled version, under the title of "Heartsease," to the censor, and obtained his full sanction, as a modest production of Mr. Mortimer's pen.

The name of Dumas *fils* was not on the title-page, in order not to arouse suspicions, and thus "La Dame aux Camélias" was smuggled in and ready to be presented on the stage as the work of an English author. The audacity of it all was quite amazing.

Letter No. IV

"'Morituri te salutant.'

"With this quotation I had begun my letter last Friday, the fourteenth, but when I reread it, I found it was too morbidly sad, and I burned it up.

'To-day I can write without laments, for I have conquered. Do I feel happier now? I cannot tell. Life is strange, after all. Yesterday the public received me with more than approbation. After the last act many of them waved their handkerchiefs to me. The Prince and Princess of Wales also applauded warmly, and I?—I thought of you all, and regretted that Warsaw is so far and that it is impossible to drive from Hoza Street to London.

"My success surpassed all my expectations; every one here seems to think it quite extraordinary, and my manager already has numerous projects concerning my future. Perhaps I shall be obliged to keep playing the same part till the end of July.

"I also have letters from Russia. They want me to play there with a Polish company, but I don't think I shall have time to do so because I must be back in London next autumn, and remain here probably until Christmas. They speak of 'Romeo and Juliet,' 'Cymbeline,' and other Shakespearian plays. It is a great temptation.

Madame Modjeska in "Heartsease."

"I was very nervous before the first performance of 'Heartsease,' but when I was on the stage I was happy, and the play went on smoothly. I kept the reins of my part tight, and remained correct. There was a great deal of weeping in the audience during the third and the last act. My eyes also were moist, but I kept full control of my voice."

Mr. Coghlan did not play Armand, as it was decided at first, because Mr. Barrett and he did not agree as to the form of advertising his name. Mr. Dacre took his place. He was not as fine an artist as Mr. Coghlan, but he was young, handsome, and sympathetic.

During the first performance of "Heartsease" the Prince of Wales (the late king of England) came to my dressing-room with Count Jaraczewski, whom the Prince called by the pet name of Sherry Whiskey, though he, as became royalty, was trained to pronounce the most difficult foreign names with ease and the right inflection on the syllable. The Prince was grandly simple and cordial, very complimentary, and yet reserved; speaking of the play, in which he had at once recognized "La Dame aux Camélias," he wondered that it passed the censorship, while Sarah Bernhardt was refused the permission to play it. "I must look to it," he said.

Next season, 1881, the bills announced the great French actress in "La Dame aux Camélias."

The London actors and actresses spoiled me with their kindness. Mrs. Kendal came to my room with congratulations; the dear Mrs. Bancroft embraced me with tears in her eyes, saying that I had struck the right note and touched the people's hearts. Mr. John Hare and his beautiful wife, Johnston Forbes Robertson, Coghlan, Clayton, Cecil, and many others came to shake hands with me. All of them showed the most friendly disposition towards me and I was living in a blessed atmosphere of art, peace, and good-fellowship, never dreaming that those feelings might one day change their heavenly aspect.

Next day, after the performance, a box for the Lyceum Theatre was sent to us. Though I felt tired, I could not resist Mr. Irving's kindness, and we saw him in Shylock. I have described this visit to the Lyceum Theatre in one of the letters to my Polish friends:—

". . . the news of my success had already spread, and at the entrance to the theatre we met a gentleman in a most correct evening dress, with an exquisite bouquet of white flowers, which he offered me, with a hearty welcome in Mr. Irving's name.

"I was deeply touched by this delicate attention, yet you must not think that my judgment on his performance was in the least influenced by this courtesy. What I write now about him is my impartial opinion.

"When I saw this artist first as Van der Decken (in the 'Flying Dutchman'), his peculiarities suited his part. He was unusual, fantastic, and I liked him from the beginning to the end of the play. In the part of Shylock, however, it was different: the extravagant way of accentuation, the artificial gestures and gait, his breathless voice, and altogether the lack of simplicity made me wonder for a while why the English public admired this eccentric man. During the second act I began to be used to his ways, and in the Tubal scene a shiver ran through me when, after the outburst of hatred and anger, that stern Jew, apparently without any human feeling in his heart, buried his face in his hands and sobbed. When he looked up, his superb dark eyes were shining with ill-omened light, and a wonderful change transfigured his features. The painted lines of his face, the wretched delivery, the stiff countenance, the unpleasant, hollow voice, — all those deficiencies disappeared, and I saw only the Jew Shylock, — not a modern one, but Shylock of the sixteenth century, — the vision of the past, strange, but powerful and fascinating. Such is Irving.

"Those who judge him superficially, and cannot overlook his peculiarities, do not like him; but those who once are touched by his mental and occult powers must admire him without restriction.

"His exit in the court scene is very fine. No exaggeration, no contortions. He leaves the stage with one prolonged look at his enemies, — a look of despair, hatred, disdain, what you will; disdain, I believe, is predominant.

"The Jew at that moment looks more like an outraged lord than a money-lender, but the effect is most artistic."

I had stipulated with Mr. W. Barrett to play three weeks in matinées, but at the end of the second week he said to me that, owing to my success, he was willing, if I wished it, to

Photograph by Downey, London.

WILSON BARRETT AS "HAMLET."

take "The Banker's Daughter" off the bills and to put "Heartsease" on for the evening performances. He hoped it might run until the first of July, or longer.

I welcomed this arrangement with joy. He also advised

me to cut off the last week of the matinées and take a rest before the longer run of the play. We spent that week in Herefordshire, and after a delightful visit to Mr. and Mrs. Bodenham, and with our lungs filled with the balmy air of the country, we returned to London, and "Heartsease" was resumed to a splendid house, full of handsome faces and fine attire.

The play was a genuine success. The management was obliged to fill the pit with seats, and the ten-shilling tickets were sold for a guinea.

Heartsease became a fashionable flower.

The critics were very kind to me, especially the most important ones, as Labouchère, Joseph Knight, Sala, and Clement Scott.

London during the spring season has always been an international point of meeting for celebrities, and I had an opportunity of becoming acquainted with people of different nationalities, mostly French, France being such a close neighbor to England, and the trip to Calais and Dover only the matter of a few hours of seasickness.

One evening the great French critic, Francisque Sarcey, who happened to be in London at that time, came to my performance and wrote a flattering criticism about me. It was he who induced Sarah Bernhardt to see me, and the wonderful creature appeared in the box at the end of the second act. She was dressed in a cascade of black jet, and her small, cameo-like head, with its mass of golden hair, attracted every one's attention.

A bouquet of white camellias from her was brought to my dressing-room, and my husband went during the fourth act to thank her in my name. He told me afterwards that as soon as she saw me in my ball-dress, very much *decolletée* and without sleeves, according to the fashion of 1880, she exclaimed, "Mais votre femme est aussi maigre que moi!"

Sarah was, indeed, very thin at that time, and many

Photograph, copyright 1891, by Falk, Sydney.

SARAH BERNHARDT AS "PAULINE BLANCHARD."

amusing stories about her slender figure circulated among people. Some of them were told by herself.

After the play she came to my dressing-room, and said she cried during the last act. This was most flattering. We spoke of the play. She remarked, with her usual grace, that I made the third act interesting and dramatic. She never before liked that act, she said; it seemed to her tame. She also liked my letter-writing scene. Her talk was vivacious and interesting. She seemed to be filled with art to her finger-tips.

Among the French celebrities who visited London was Gustave Doré, a famous artist, yet simple and warm-hearted, loving his home, and speaking about his mother with adoration. "She comes first," he said, "and then my art." She was ill at that time, and he shortened his London visit to hasten to her bedside.

Bastien Lepage also came to see me after the performance. I was quite fascinated by his *espiègle* mood. He touched all the objects on my dressing-table, making amusing remarks, then suddenly stopped and looked straight in my face with his sharp, observing eyes, and smiled critically, I thought. I asked him if it was my make-up, or rather the absence of it, that amused him. He immediately took a blue and a brown pencil from the table and put a few lines around my eyes, nostrils, and cheeks.

The change was wonderful. "Now you are ready for the coffin," and he laughed. "But never mind; your acting was quite convincing without that," he added seriously.

One evening Mr. Wilson Barrett came in between acts and said there was a crazy man in front. He asked me not to be frightened if I saw any commotion or heard loud talking, for it was most probable the man would have to be removed from the theatre.

"What does he do?" I asked.

"He shows signs of great displeasure when the curtain

goes up, and only when you come on he listens quietly and applauds vigorously after each act, throwing satisfied glances at the audience. But as soon as the orchestra begins to play, he grows red with anger, springs up in his chair, and positively runs out of the hall, swearing in German. I heard him say 'Verflucht' and 'Verdammt,' while he rushed out into the street, where he remained till the beginning of the next act, walking up and down. He repeats this performance after each act, and grows more uncontrollable every time."

No one could tell me who that man was.

Next day the mystery was disclosed, when Hans von Bülow's card was brought up to our rooms. It was a happy and jolly meeting. His first words were congratulations and most hearty greetings, but immediately afterward there was an explosion:—

"Why do you allow that 'Esel' of a leader to murder Chopin between the acts? I know he does it to flatter your patriotic feelings, but the 'Schafskopf' has not the faintest idea of rhythm or harmony. It is a sacrilege,— a 'Katzenmusik.' My ears are sore from it even now. I was very angry last night, and were it not for you I would have left the theatre after the first notes of that stupid orchestra." At this point the man of the world came back to the surface, and he changed the subject with great skill. After a delightful chat, he said "Au revoir, in Warsaw."

"Heartsease" ran until the first of July; then we went for a few days to my husband's relatives, Mr. and Mrs. Bodenham. It was the second time we visited them, and I welcomed with pleasure the large brick mansion, with its hall ornamented by painted and gilded carvings, the spacious rooms arranged with great comfort, the beautiful park with ancient trees, and the small, cosy chapel where we used to pray together.

Mrs. Bodenham was a sister of my husband's mother.

She was a very handsome, rather fleshy woman past fifty, of aristocratic appearance and a certain air of unconscious and benevolent *hauteur*, inspiring respect. Her husband was

Photograph, copyright, by London Stereoscopic Co.

FORBES ROBERTSON.

a beautiful old gentleman with snow-white hair and beard and pink complexion. He loved to recite verses, and we spent a few evenings reviving poems and scenes from Shakespeare's plays. It was quite a novelty for me to read Juliet to that dear old Romeo. Most valuable was his information on the English traits, the peculiarities of the people, as well as their fine qualities and the difference existing between their opinions and the continental ideas. "We English are not satisfied with the Ten Commandments," he said once. "We invented one more, the Eleventh: 'Thou shalt not be found out.' No matter what people do, if they only keep up the appearances, they are never molested; but even the smallest, most innocent escapade, brought to light, creates a scandal which hurls down the victims into the pit of disgrace."

The rest of July and a part of August we stayed in a fishing-cove called Cadgwith, near Lizard Point, where we went in company of friends and my son Ralph, who came from Paris to spend his vacation with us.

This remote spot was suggested to us by Forbes Robertson, who also spent a few weeks there with his brother Ian, his sister, Mrs. Bromley, and her friend Mrs. Smith, Joseph Knight's daughter, both of them young and both widows.

In that congenial circle we lived free from conventionalities, taking long walks on the beach or attending the lawn-tennis games at the Rectory. Rector Jackson's and his wife's house was always opened to visitors, who were heartily welcomed by them at all hours of the day.

At this time I received the following letter from Henry Longfellow: —

"CAMBRIDGE, July 6, 1880.

"DEAR MME. MODJESKA:

"I am delighted to receive your letter — to know that you are well, and to have again your address, so that a kind greeting from me may reach you.

"My last was directed to the American Agency, Strand, London, so that it might meet you on your arrival; but I fear it never found you. It was in answer to yours from Léopol,[1] and told you

[1] French for Lemberg.

how heartily I rejoiced in your triumph at Cracow, during the fête in honor of Kraszewski.

"Now I can add my congratulations on your equally triumphal entry into London. How pleasant it is to be able to say, 'I told you so!' And did I not tell you so? Am I not worthy to be counted among the Minor Prophets? I cannot tell you how greatly rejoiced I am at this new success — this new wreath of laurel.

"But one thing in your letter saddens me. It is where you say that you have postponed your return to America till next year. As birds in Norway fly swiftest when the days are shortest, so swifter and swifter fly the years as we grow old, and life grows shorter. But when you *do* return, it shall be a holiday in this house.

"I am very glad that you have seen Mrs. Mackintosh and Lord Houghton, and that they have been kind to you. How could they be otherwise?

"Equally so will be Lord Rosebery, when he comes to town. He has come to town; he has been kind to you.

"Thanks for your kind thoughts of me, dear Mme. Modjeska; count me always among your best friends; always among your devoted admirers.

"My daughters join me in kind remembrance, and with best regards to your husband, I am,

"Ever yours,

"Henry W. Longfellow."

I cried for joy and gratitude when I read this kind message.

CHAPTER XLV

A contract for a year, with Mr. Barrett, was signed by me and, after a very short and prosperous provincial tour, we returned to London, where I played "Marie Stuart" for the opening of the winter season. The critic of the *Times* did not approve of me this time, neither did he of Schiller's play, — from a Protestant standpoint. But Joseph Knight gave me a splendid notice, calling my performance "an event in the history of the stage." Mr. Labouchère, Mr. Sala, and Clement Scott were also exceedingly kind. One organ cut me up very severely. I learned with a great deal of pain that it was a paper secretly supported by a prominent person belonging to the stage, and the most curious thing about it was that the criticism had been written by the same man who wrote a very laudatory article about me in another paper. What was my amazement when the critic who wrote the contradictory notices came to me and apologized, saying that he was on a salary for both papers, and that in one of them special orders had been given to attack my performances. He had a family, and could not afford to lose his place. The light dawned upon me. I had dared to touch the so-called "legitimate" repertoire.

In spite of those divided opinions, "Marie Stuart" reached very nearly one hundred performances.

The version of "Marie Stuart" played by me in London, and afterwards in America, is a combination of two translations from the German, one by Mellish, the second by Miss Fanny Kemble, — the whole arranged by Hon. Lewis Wingfield. The latter made the necessary cuts in the text

and improved it in several places. Particularly he introduced several lines in the final scene of the last act that are not in the original of Schiller. By a curious coincidence, Mr. Wingfield's ancestor, Sir Robert Wingfield, a high English official of the times, had been commissioned by Queen Elizabeth to be present at the execution of Mary. His report of the occasion, a very circumstantial one, is yet in the governmental archives, and it is from this description that a few details were added to the version.

The Prince of Wales came several times to the play. He was in sympathy with "Marie Stuart," and he found the quarrel between the two queens "rather refreshing."

Ellen Terry, who had returned from her provincial tour, and played with Henry Irving in some short play, came to see the last act of "Marie Stuart," and called at my dressing-room after the performance. She was accompanied by Charles Coghlan, who was then without engagement.

It seems that, hearing about a foreign actress playing "Marie Stuart," she took me for Madame Janauschek, who had played that part once or twice in London, and came with a preconceived idea that I was a stout woman. Her first movement when she entered my room and was introduced by Coghlan, was to feel my arm, and say, "I was told that you were stout; but I see you are not," and then she stepped back and looked at me again: "But perhaps you are; I cannot see your form under this voluminous garment."

Whoever has met Ellen Terry knows that she is irresistible, and I liked her from the start. We had quite a long chat, and parted friends.

During my London engagement I saw her in several parts, but I admired her most in "Much Ado About Nothing" and in the last act of "Merchant of Venice."

Her stage appearance was strikingly beautiful. The ease, the abundance of gestures, even the nervous restlessness which never leaves her, fitted the part, and her spirit,

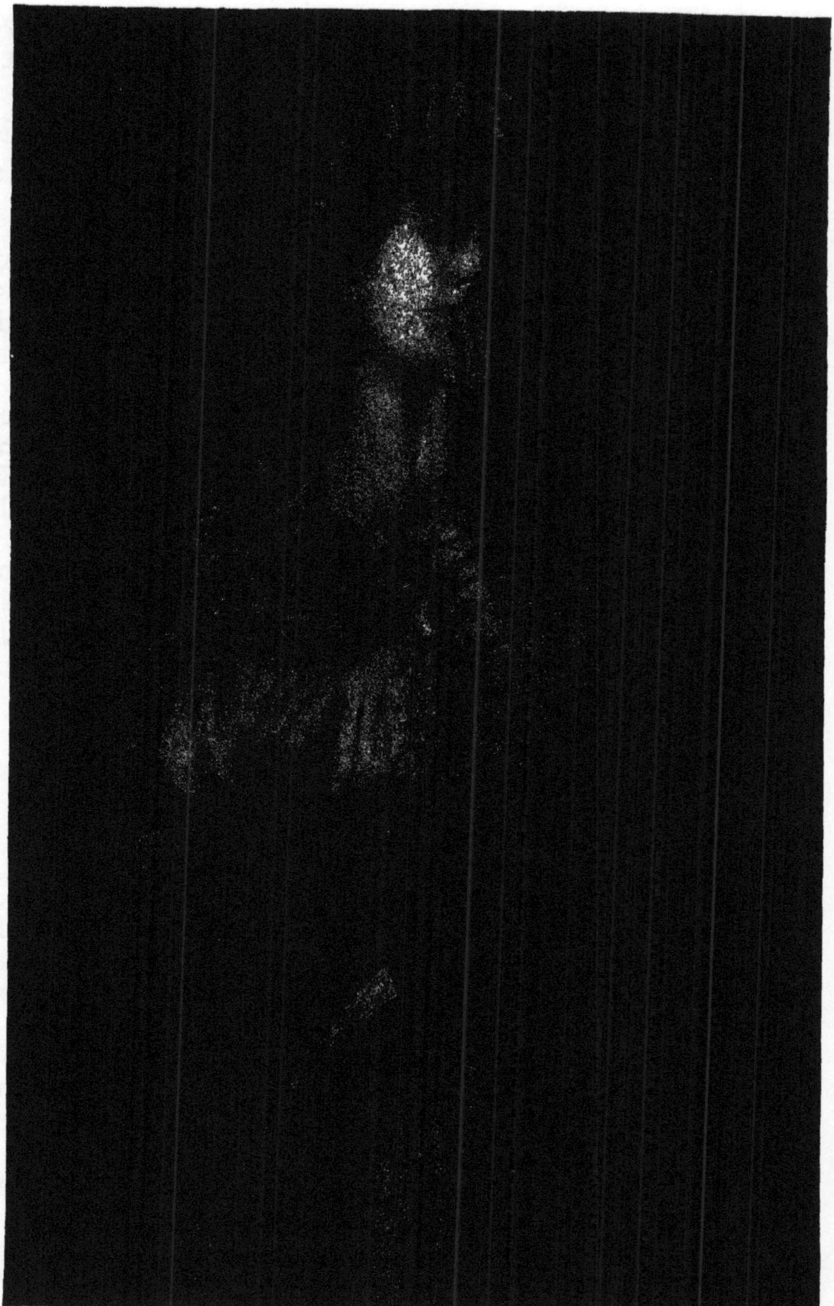

ELLEN TERRY AS "IMOGENE."

the sparkling repartees, the mischievous though good-natured fun, were captivating. I never saw a better performance; her Beatrice was perfectly fascinating.

In December "Adrienne Lecouvreur" followed "Marie Stuart." This is what I wrote about the performance in a letter to Poland:—

". . . Pray excuse my long silence. Adrienne swallowed my days and nights. I was obliged to study a revised version, because the one I played before was not good from the literary standpoint. A Rev. Mr. Harford, a canon of Westminster Abbey, translated the fable of 'La Fontaine' for me.

"Such mechanical work as restudying the lines is very tiresome and very difficult. Thank Heaven it is over now, and I came out of this new trial with 'triumph,' as my friends said; I could only say, 'safely,' when my manager told me that the play would run till the end of the season.

"The critics are unanimous this time, and those who like me are proud of me. I am neither proud nor happy; I am only tired. Last night I cried after the performance. I thought of you all. . . . Please excuse this shaky writing; the last act of Adrienne exhausts me."

Another letter:—

"Yes, I live and move; my heart aches, but my strength grows, for I want it for a still higher flight.

"I think they like me here, and that is an encouragement.

"Ah! if I could be satisfied and contented in the midst of applause and flattery, and not desire anything more of myself! If I could enjoy the present moments sincerely, foolishly, gather the flowers I find on my path of life, bind them up in a bouquet, drink in its perfume, and be glad and happy!

"But there is a saying that there are creatures in whose hands flowers wither at a touch. I belong to those. Every pleasure ceases to be a real pleasure the moment I begin to taste it; every ray of light grows dim when I smile at its radiance. There is nothing of interest to me save my work, and I am sure that even at the last moment of my life I will cry, not like Goethe, 'More Light!' but 'Work! work, more work!'

"This will seem to you like a touch of the contagious influence of 'Enfant du Siècle.' But you must not misunderstand me. I am contented with my *intime* life, to which I do not refer here. But I have two lives, and one is so different from the other that the transition oftentimes is puzzling, if not painful. My artificial life is too real at moments, and that is what makes the trouble. I take it sometimes too seriously, and then it is a burden.

A fragment of another letter to a Warsaw friend:—

"There was a snowstorm here a few days ago. The circulation and the traffic of the streets were stopped and all the theatres were empty. My manager says this may change the success of Adrienne, and he is thinking of substituting 'Romeo and Juliet.' That temptation lures and repels me. I see clouds gathering over my head and feel a fight in the air. Well, I must prepare for the next campaign. I have one consolation: my balcony scene I know and I love it. It is good and unconventional. After all, I am not afraid of anything except of my English pronunciation. But I will study the part with a competent person. More work! I suppose that's what keeps me alive."

Mr. Barrett asked me one day if I would like to play "Romeo and Juliet." He was indeed afraid that the spell of Adrienne's success had been broken by a few empty houses during the snowstorm, and that it would be rather difficult to bring back the audience with the same bill. He was mistaken, however, because as soon as the change was announced, the theatre became crowded again, but "Romeo and Juliet" was already advertised, and it had to be performed.

I went to Mrs. Sterling and asked her if she would correct my English. She consented, and for four weeks I worked with her. She gave me a great deal of encouragement. I needed it. Many failures are due to overconfidence or lack of confidence. I wanted to be sure that my English was not so bad as to mar my part, and I was told that it was not.

The rehearsals began, and I met with some unexpected difficulties:—

During the first rehearsal Mr. Ryder, who was cast for

Friar Laurence, told me that I spoke distinctly, but there were a few words he wished to correct, if I permitted it. I asked eagerly what those words were.

"One of them is the word 'direction'; you should pronounce it with a long 'i,' like this."

"Dairection?" I repeated.

"Yes; that is a proper pronunciation. The other word is 'either.'"

"Shall I say 'ayther'?" I asked.

"Yes, of course!"

There were some more words Mr. Ryder pointed to me as utterly wrongly pronounced which I omit here for fear of monotony.

When, in the afternoon, I recited my part to Mrs. Sterling, with Ryder's corrections, she stopped me, asking: "Who taught you that old-fashioned way of pronouncing? In the word 'direction' you must use the short sound of 'i.' It is not 'dairection'; it is written 'direction,' and the rhythm of the verse requires only one, not two syllables."

"Mr. Ryder corrected me this morning," I said.

"Oh, Mr. Ryder is a fine legitimate actor, but between us, he is an old fogy." And her sweet, slightly mischievous smile, as she said this, softened the severity of her judgment.

Next morning at the rehearsal I followed Mrs. Sterling's advice, but as soon as I uttered the sentence, "By whose direction foundst thou out this place?" Mr. Ryder, who sat in the stalls, spoke to me:—

"Madame, you forget; it is not 'direction' with a short 'i'; you must say 'dairection,' with a long 'i.' Excuse the interruption, but you should be reminded of the proper way of saying those words before you give the critics a chance to tell you so."

Mr. Ryder was a venerable gentleman and very friendly; therefore, though it was not quite polite nor right to interrupt the scene, I bore him no grudge. Besides, I wanted by all means to find out who was right, Mrs. Sterling or he. Leaning over my balcony, I told him, as gently as I could, that Mrs. Sterling insisted upon the word "direction" with a short "i." "Oh, Mrs. Sterling is a fine actress and a lovely woman, but she is no authority on pronunciation," he answered, with a shrug of his shoulders.

This began to amuse me. I turned to Mr. Barrett and asked him which he thought was the right way of pronouncing the word. "Well, I suppose," sounded his answer, "that the best way would be to pronounce it halfway, neither with a short nor a long 'i.'" Here I laughed aloud, and declared that I should follow Mrs. Sterling's ways, which seemed to me more simple and more euphonic.

The deed was done, and "Romeo and Juliet" was put on at the Court Theatre, and called forth many notices, some good, some adverse, as might have been expected by a foreigner "tackling Shakespeare"; but Mr. Sala wrote a most judicious account of my Juliet, pointing out my balcony scene. Mr. Labouchère, Mr. Joseph Knight, and Mr. Clement Scott dealt also most kindly with me, and all spoke of my improved English.

Forbes Robertson was an admirable Romeo, full of passion, poetry, and restrained pathos in the last scenes. Mr. Wilson Barrett had engaged him to play Maurice de Saxe in "Adrienne Lecouvreur," and retained him for Romeo. It was a very good choice, for there was no actor at that time in London who could even approach Robertson in the part of that typical lover, for which he was so admirably suited.

Mr. Ryder was an excellent Friar and Mr. Barrett a successful Mercutio.

Shortly after my first performance of the play, "Romeo and Juliet" was announced at the Lyceum Theatre, with Henry Irving as Romeo and Ellen Terry as Juliet.

London in winter is different from the spring London. It is more quiet, and for those who can endure occasional foggy days, more enjoyable. For my part I liked the fog. It was amusing to see the small red sun, so flat, so near, and so little imposing. The ugly chimney-pots disappeared in the mist, and the whole city became a phantasm. I used to take drives on such days and lose myself in dreams.

At the beginning of the winter season of 1880 we had changed our lodgings and moved to Sloane Street. When we were well established, we resumed the afternoon receptions we had left off in New York. We made many friends and also had opportunities of meeting the local celebrities.

I have rather a confused recollection of our social life in London. When I try to carry my thoughts back to that part of my existence, I only obtain a kaleidoscopic effect, a sort of moving picture. Sometimes a face or an incident comes to my mind, strong and clear, but most of the time they pass before me only in faint outlines. I shall try to speak of my clear impressions.

The sweet countenance of Mrs. Jeune is still present in my mind. At her five o'clocks we met Mr. Justin McCarthy, the celebrated historian, author and Home Ruler, the famous statesman, Mr. Chamberlain, and Sir Charles Dilke, whose striking intellect and extensive knowledge in matters of art and political conditions it was easy to recognize. I remember playing at Mrs. Jeune's house, for one of her charities, a one-act piece in French, with Mr. Pierre Berton, the well-known French actor and author. He became one of our friends, and in later years dramatized for me Balzac's novel called "Les Chouans."

I can see even now Mr. and Mrs. Jacob Bright, with whom we used to go to the Parliament, to hear Mr. Gladstone speak, and I remember clearly the impression the grand old man's beautiful language, convincing logic, and distinctness of utterance made on me. Mr. Jacob Bright was a brother of the great John Bright. While not so well known as his distinguished brother, he was much pleasanter personally; a man of high culture, he remained for many years a member of Parliament and was a great advocate of woman's suffrage. I also remember a happy week spent at Mr. and Mrs. Bright's home at Alderley Edge, near Manchester.

Another house that we frequented was that of Admiral and Mrs. Mayne, whom we had first known in New York. We passed most enjoyable days in their country home, and I recollect a great commotion about matches disappearing from the rooms, the catechising of the children, a great anxiety lest the latter might put the house on fire, and finally my interference in the matter, which greatly relieved the hostess, by the statement that all the missing matches must be in my husband's pockets, and so they were. In his absent-mindedness he picked them up instinctively everywhere, as a supply for his cigarettes when he went for a walk in the garden.

We met a great many distinguished people at the house of Lady Henniker, among them the celebrated General Wolseley, who asked me, in jest, I suppose, if I would like the English army to come over and fight for Poland against Russia. I told him that we were more afraid of our friends than of our enemies, to whom we had become more or less used, and I reminded him of the way in which the great Napoleon had played on the hopes of the Poles, only to frustrate them in the end.

We assisted at several gorgeous receptions at Lady Fricke's, but they left only a confused impression on me. But one figure stands out clearly, that of Mr. Gilbert (the playwright), leaning against the light background of the room, and looking picturesque, though he did not want to.

A very hospitable house was that of Mrs. Tennant, where I had an opportunity of hearing Monsieur Coquelin recite. His delivery of verses I regarded always as an unequalled

Photograph by Falk

perfection, and every time I heard this great artist I brought home the most delightful impression.

The most interesting party I assisted at was one given by

From a photograph, copyright by Aimé Dupont.

M. Coquelin.

Mr. Hamilton Aidé, — in honor of the Prince of Wales, — at which Mr. Aidé produced a short play from his pen in which I took part. Miss Genevieve Ward, who made such a hit in "Forget Me Not," also took part in the entertainment, after which supper was served. I was seated next to the prince, and had vis-à-vis the most beautiful Mrs. Lily Langtry. This gave me an opportunity to admire her

Photograph, copyright, 1882, by Sarony.

MRS. LANGTRY.

perfect neck and shoulders. I had met Mrs. Langtry several times before, and remember how, one evening, after "Romeo and Juliet," she came to my dressing-room and put on her head the wreath of small white roses I wore in the tomb scene; she also tried the skullcap I introduced in Juliet, and looked so bewitching in both that I asked her if she never had a tendency toward the stage. She smiled and said, "Yes; it would be nice to be an actress." But at that time she was not seriously thinking of the stage. The charming Mrs. Cornwallis West, with her miniature beauty, sat near by, and there were several other persons, some of them known and some unknown to me.

Genevieve Ward sat on the same side of the table with me, and between us was a Russian count whose name I forget. Count Jaraczewski was placed next to Mrs. Cornwallis West. The supper was animated. My husband, who, at the end of the play, had slipped away to smoke a cigarette, came in when everybody was seated. The prince perceived him, and said to me, "There is Monsieur Chlapowski." He pronounced the name perfectly, with a Polish inflection on the second syllable, and with the hard "l" so difficult to foreigners. I was amazed at the prince's memory of faces and names, for he had met my husband only once before.

Seeing him now approaching our table, the prince bowed slightly, waving his hand to him. Mr. Chlapowski, who is very near-sighted, thought that some one of his friends was greeting him, and sent back to the prince a most familiar wave of the hand. When he came nearer and recognized the prince, he apologized, and both had a good laugh over the mistake.

It was during that supper that the prince spoke to me about the drama. He said that dramatic art was not yet in its full development in England. I suggested the founding of an endowed national theatre, such as all other countries in Europe possess. His answer was discouraging: "Do you think there is enough love for art in the Anglo-Saxon race to make the theatre a state affair?" There was no answer to that. I was nonplussed, and did not know what to say next. Happily, at the same moment Count Jaraczewski

Photograph by Sarony.

GENEVIEVE WARD.

rose from his seat and came to say some amusing thing to the prince in German.

Other entertainments, big and small, flit across my mind in a state of great confusion. I remember being squeezed in a crowd through an enormous room, where fine music was played, but I had to come quite close to the instrument in order to hear it, for it seemed as though the first sounds of an orchestra, a solo, violin, or a 'cello, were a sign for the start of general loud conversation. The louder the music, the louder was the chatter. I never brought home from those parties any distinct recollection. Though numbers of people were introduced to me, I was not any the wiser, for the names were pronounced indistinctly, and often were drowned by the noise. Often the only thing I carried back with me was a headache.

Sometimes Signor Tosti commanded silence with his love-songs — sometimes Signor de Soria's beautiful baritone was heard without interruption, but even the best virtuoso could not stop the deafening, awful, jarring human voices.

In connection with this habit, Henry Wieniawski, the king of violinists, as he was once called, told me that once in London he was invited by some person of high rank to play at his house. When he stepped out to the front, all eyes and lorgnettes were on him, and there was not even a murmur in the audience; everybody was still and attentive; but he scarcely struck the first notes of Raff's cavatina, when all the people in the room began to talk. It was very provoking, and he was determined to teach them a lesson: knowing that every English man and woman had to rise and be silent when the hymn "God save the Queen" was played, he gave a wink to the accompanist, then passed cleverly from Raff to the tune of the hymn and played it fortissimo. To his great satisfaction, the people stopped talking, and those who were seated rose to their feet. But when he resumed the cavatina, they also instantly resumed their talk. He again intoned the hymn and gained a few minutes of silence, but the noise was stronger than ever when he changed the tune. He repeated the hymn trick five or six times. When he finished no one understood the hint; they only wondered at the strange composition in which the national hymn was so often repeated.

From time to time we met Americans. At Mr. and Mrs. Smalley's house we met the handsome Mr. Julian Hawthorne. Mr. Nadal, of the American Legation, whom we had known before in New York, introduced to me the poet Lowell, who was then American Minister. Our sincere admiration for Lowell's poems soon made us good friends, so much so that when, on one occasion, I introduced to him my son, then nineteen years old, he called me outright a "humbug." Could one expect a more friendly or more familiar compliment?

One sunny morning I was accosted in the street by a lady who exclaimed, "Why, how do you do, Madame Modjeska?" Her face was very familiar to me, but I could not place her, and I must have looked puzzled, for she exclaimed: "Well, I declare! Don't you remember Aunt Louisa?"

We nearly fell into each other's arms. I was truly glad to see Mrs. Eldridge, who was such an excellent Prudence in "La Dame aux Camélias," but remembering what a patriot she was, and how often she had repeated that she did not care a bit about London and the English, I chaffed her on account of her broken resolution of "never — never" going to England.

She interrupted me, saying quickly: "Don't you make any mistake; I am just as American as I ever was, and even more, if you please. Look here!" With these words she lifted her dress in front and advanced her foot to show me a most peculiar stocking — it was embroidered over the instep with the American flag in red, white, and blue. There was so much seriousness and also so much fun in the expression of her face as she thus exposed her loyalty to her native country, that it would puzzle many artists to paint it, or actors to imitate it. I saw only once a similar expression — in Joseph Jefferson's features when he played Bob Acres.

Our great pleasure was to visit the artists' studios, and we were often invited to parties at their homes.

I recollect Mr. and Mrs. Millais, both tall, finely built, and though youth had fled, the traces of beauty were still apparent in their features. In Millais's studio I admired greatly, among other pictures, Lord Beaconsfield's portrait.

I also remember the charming moments at Sir Frederick Leighton's sumptuous studio and his beautiful decorative works.

Of all artistic houses, Alma-Tadema's was the most attractive. We found both the great artist and his golden-haired wife most congenial and hospitable. Their evening receptions were ardently attended. The house was an attraction by itself, with its onyx windows, the wonderful pictures, the gilded and exquisitely painted piano, the small fountain among the tropical plants, the odd furniture, the rare vases, and all sorts of valuable bric-à-brac, all of them scrupulously clean. Gold is the predominant shade in Tadema's house. I heard him say that London atmosphere was so dull that he had to create an artificial sunshine in his house by putting in as much gold as he could, and indeed even on a dark winter day the onyx window flooded the living-room with a soft yellow light, making everything look bright and warm. The love for color, especially warm color, so characteristic of his exquisite pictures, was to be noticed everywhere.

As befits a son of Holland, his predilection for cleanliness is not only a remarkable feature of the house, but is also a distinctive trait of his works: there is no suggestion of sad, grayish, smutty tints in his clear landscapes, his blue skies, his white marbles (oh, how gloriously white!). But this cleanliness extends equally to his moral nature. One could not imagine him painting anything repulsive or suggestive.

One of the first living artists, Alma-Tadema was one of

From a photograph by Nulhinsh, London.

LAURENCE ALMA-TADEMA.

the most charming hosts. His home was open to all the foreign artists of note that came to London, not only painters, but sculptors, musicians, and occasionally actors.

It was my good fortune to meet this great artist and his

wife at the very beginning of my London engagement, and the happy hours spent in their hospitable home belong to my pleasantest memories of London.

I had a staunch friend at that time in the person of Ethel Coxon, who was a Ruskin, Burne-Jones, æsthetic girl, always picturesque, with her long limbs and soft draperies. Her intellectual qualities and inborn goodness of heart, however, were the strongest attractions, and we soon became great friends. She was always near me when I most needed her, consoling and encouraging me or correcting my English. She went with me to afternoon teas or accompanied me on my shopping trips. It was she who opened for me the gates of a woman's earthly paradise — Liberty's shop.

She also went to several studios with me. She knew almost every artist worth knowing in England, and she truly loved art.

We visited one morning Burne-Jones's simple rooms flooded with light. I was deeply impressed, and a feeling of veneration filled my heart when I stood before the pictures, known by me till then in reproductions only. His art satisfied the most exalted desires of my soul and imagination.

Whistler's pictures were on exhibition then, and we went to see them. They struck me as being exquisitely odd and most interesting. We met the artist. His appearance was very striking. With the celebrated white lock among his black waving hair, and his animated, nervous features, he looked almost mischievous. He came often to our house, and we listened with delight to his remarks about schools and styles of painting. His views on the subject proved his deep knowledge and most striking originality.

Mr. Watts, with his refined face and silver beard, lives still in my mind. We spent delightful afternoons in his studio, admiring his pictures and talking art. Ethel Coxon supplied a pigment to those conversations by her witty remarks.

It was there we met Matthew Arnold, the poet, and Mrs. Humphry Ward, who was then a very young girl. With her aureole of bright golden hair, she stood against the

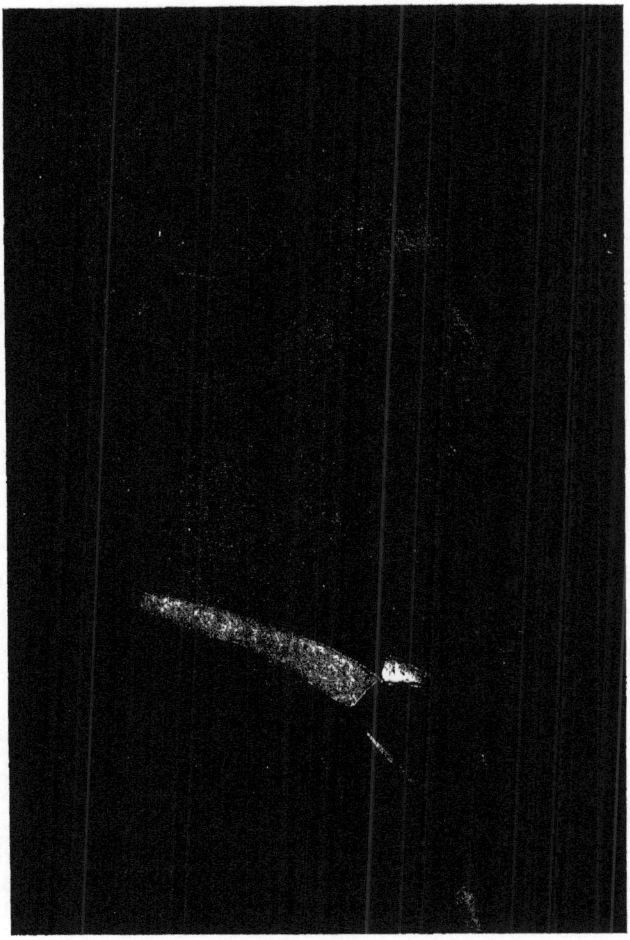

LORD LEIGHTON, FROM THE PORTRAIT BY G. F. WATTS.

picture of a multi-colored angel at such an angle that the wings seemed to belong to her. Mr. Arnold introduced her to me as his "niece who thinks she can write." There was, however, pride in his eyes when he uttered this joke.

Many charming hours in Mr. Boughton's house, with his

æsthetic wife and niece, come to my memory, with all their refreshing grace.

Mr. and Mrs. Labouchère we saw quite frequently. Mr. Labouchère's brilliant mind, his wit, and his intimate knowledge of English society and its foibles were most interesting. He always said the right thing at the right moment and to the right person; it was not diplomacy, but inborn tact. We met Mrs. Braddon in his house.

One of the eventful moments in London was my meeting Robert Browning. Before the introduction I took him for a retired French officer. He certainly looked French, with his pointed mustache, his imperial *à la* Napoleon the Third, and his vivacious manners. I never would have suspected him of being the author of "Andrea del Sarto" and "Fra Lippo Lippi." He spoke rapidly in French and English on all possible subjects with the same ease and knowledge. I do not believe I have ever met a man so versatile as he, so great and yet so simple; such a poet and yet so human.

Next I remember Bret Harte. When he was introduced to us, we greeted him as an old friend, for we knew him through his novels and poems. I believe that he was more appreciated on the continent than in either America or England.

When we spoke of his great fame in Europe, he said, smiling: "You could not say that about England; they do not appreciate me; they do not even know me." We protested against this judgment, and he replied with a story: —

"Some time ago I was to deliver a lecture in one of the English towns, and had to be introduced to the audience by some local authority. The man made quite a long speech, in which he praised my great qualities, my fame throughout the world, and my exceptional merits. He never mentioned my name, but wound up his words as follows: 'And now, let me introduce to you Mr. — er — Mr. . . .' Then, suddenly turning to me, he asked, in a furious whisper, 'What the deuce is your name?' This proved to me how well I was known in England.

In the month of May, 1881, when the grand opera opened, some of our Polish celebrities, together with other famous singers, arrived,—Sembrich Kochanska, Edward de Reszke, and Mierzwinski, the great tenor of the day.

Jan de Reszke did not sing at that time, but came to London with his brother. A peculiar thing in Jan de Reszke's career was that he began as a barytone. Once during the performance he drank a glass of ice-water and lost his voice. It was, as he thought, a paralysis of the vocal chords. A short time afterwards, however, he recovered from the shock, and his voice was stronger and better than ever, but it changed to a tenor — or rather, it was decided by one of the great singing teachers that his voice was never a barytone, but a heroic tenor.

There lay a great future before him, and yet, in spite of many offers, he hesitated to accept an engagement, so afraid was he of the repetition of the dreadful experience. When I met him in 1881, in London, he was still in this uncertain state of mind.

His voice was then in the best condition, and we encouraged him most urgently to accept an engagement, but he always answered the same: "I am afraid to appear on the stage, and my fear is greater than my desire for fame." It took him several years to overcome this dread, and then at last we read his name on the bills.

How can I ever forget the delightful Sunday evenings at our house in Sloane Street and later in Finchley Road, where those two glorious brothers sang many a time! We had a concert regularly every Sunday, for the De Reszkes said that since "Pani Helena" could not go to the opera, being occupied every evening herself, she must have her own opera performance at home.

Madame Sembrich Kochanska and her husband were also our guests. I had met this great artist before in Warsaw,

Photograph by Moro, New York.

MADAME SEMBRICH.

when she came from Dresden to bewitch her countrymen with her wonderful skill and voice.

The charming soprano and beautiful woman, Marie Rose, and her husband, Colonel Mapleson, frequently joined our Sunday parties, and we had the great joy of greeting Josephine de Reszke when she came from the Paris Grand Opera to London for a short engagement.

We also had instrumental music at our improvised concerts, — Joseph Wieniawski and Lovenberg, pianists, Reisenauer, Ondryczek, Natchez, violinists, and Holman, the exquisite 'cellist, who always brought with him his "wife," as he called his instrument, and never waited to be asked to play, but did so with pleasure.

The attraction lay in the congenial atmosphere of our receptions. Indeed our Sunday evenings could have been envied by many rich people, in whose houses our Polish artists declined to sing for high remuneration.

Almost every Sunday the De Reszkes, their friend, young Komierowski, quite a good amateur barytone, and Mierzwinski came to dinner; then the rest of the evening was spent in singing, which lasted sometimes until three o'clock in the morning.

We thought that the neighbors might object to the music at such hours — and, indeed, one evening a policeman knocked at our door. We were sure the object of his visit was to stop the music, and therefore great was our relief when he told us he came only to find out who sang the last air. We named Jan de Reszke, and asked him the reason of his inquiry.

"A man in the next house wanted to know," he said. "Go on; good night."

It seems that while these wonderful concerts were going on, every window was opened, and many people stood in the street listening.

I knew that our famous friends would not sing or play if we invited company, and we had to be very careful not to mention our concerts, lest some people should invite themselves.

The only persons our artists "adopted" were Mr. and Mrs. Bodenham, and Lord and Lady Denbigh, who came several times with their eldest daughter, Lady Clara. Johnston Forbes Robertson, as my leading man, and Mrs. Bromley, who lived in our house, were also with us.

But music was not the sole entertainment. We played charades and other games. All those artists were full of life, and enjoyed every minute with a childlike eagerness. Jests, *bon mots*, witty repartees, inventions of amusements, one more absurd than the other, were performed with the same light spirit and *insouciance*. I remember that one evening in 1882, when we lived in Finchley Road, I saw them put their heads together and whisper for a while. Then one of them announced the sextet of "Lucia di Lammermoor." The two De Reszke brothers, Mierzwinski, Marie Rose, Komierowski, and some one I do not remember, were to sing. Lovenberg, a young pianist of great talent and great mischief, sat at the piano.

We had heard but a few bars of the sextet when suddenly Lovenberg changed the tune to the "Merry War" waltz, which the singers took up, and after a while changed it again to the sextet, and so on and so on until the end. The effect was most tantalizing, and my Polish friend, Anna Wolska, who had just arrived from Paris, nearly cried with disappointment, and was disconsolate until Jan de Reszke sang the air of "Halka," and then she cried with emotion.

I had with me two nieces, who came from the convent for their vacation, and also my son Ralph, who had arrived from Paris.

The whole house rang with merry laughter and young voices. There was no end of practical jokes, and when our artists came on Sunday, we could not tell which was the youngest. The whole place was turned upside down.

Two years later we heard that Lovenberg died of consumption.

After "Romeo and Juliet" we played "Juana," by Wills. It was a tragedy in verse, based on the character of Jeanne la Folle, the queen of Spain, and was not a success. It was not a historic play. The queen was changed to a young girl of passionate temperament, and inclined to visions. Like the queen, she also was consumed by jealousy verging on madness.

The leading man's part was that of Friar John, a monk who formerly had loved Juana hopelessly, and to end his torment of unrequited love had buried himself in a monastery.

She loved and married another, a brute and a cad, and at the end of the second act, exasperated by his faithlessness and his cynical speeches, stabbed him with a dagger, which the señoras of Spain are supposed to wear always in their belt or garter. The bad man died on the spot.

Friar John, who happened to be at hand and who had witnessed the murder, took the crime on himself, and was tried, while Juana wandered in the woods, stark mad.

In the last act, led to the monastery, she confessed her crime and died quietly, comforted by the soothing words of the ever faithful Friar John.

I remember that the first performance of "Juana" was on Saturday, and the audience was very enthusiastic. I was called five times before the curtain after the murder scene. Others were applauded profusely also, and the author was called repeatedly before the curtain. We were sure of a long run for the play. The company congratulated me, and we were so happy that we planned an excursion to the country for a day, to stay over until next Monday. Some one suggested that there was a midnight train to —— and we could catch it.

"Let us go, too," said Ida Bromley to her elder brother, Johnston, "you, Norman, and myself."

"Bravo! we shall all go!"

MADAME MODJESKA AS "JUANA."

I sent my maid for the valise, and Mr. Chlapowski went home to fill his travelling-bag with toilet accessories and a large supply of cigarettes. The house we lived in was across the square, and he and my maid returned very soon. But the last act was very long. It was twenty-five minutes of twelve when the curtain went down, and our theatre was fifteen minutes from the station.

My husband and Ida lost hope of reaching the train, but I told them I would be ready in time. While taking off my make-up, I ordered my maid to pack my dress in the valise. I retained the costume of the last act, the nun-like garb of a penitent sinner: a dark brown cowl, a hood, and a white cord with tassels for a belt. Throwing over my shoulders a long cloak, I stood ready for departure.

My husband laughed when he saw me, but led me to the carriage, where Ida Bromley was already waiting. My maid followed with the bags, and we started on a sharp trot to the station. There we found Robertson and his brother Norman, who, having finished their parts in the third act, were waiting for us. When we arrived at ——, the hotel night-clerk was shocked to see a nun in such jolly company, but did not refuse to supply us with rooms.

We spent a delightful day in the country, not even dreaming that on our return we would find treacherous Dame Fortune grinning maliciously at our frustrated hopes. On our return we learned with dismay that the play was a total failure. The papers declared that it was altogether too gloomy, especially the last act, with its dark convent galleries, its procession of monks, and their lugubrious chant. One of the critics, after having praised my acting almost extravagantly, abused the play, and his criticism ended with these words: "If this play proves a success, then we may say that the English people take their pleasures sadly." I believe, though, that had Forbes Robertson played the poetic monk instead of Wilson Barrett, the play would have had a better chance.

It was a grave mistake, though it would be hard to blame an actor-manager for keeping the best part for himself.

The play was produced with great care and in best style, the scenery and costumes elaborate and handsome. Mr. Barrett did all he could to secure the success of the play, and it was a pity to take "Juana" off the bills after a two-weeks' run. Norman Forbes Robertson played with spirit the short comedy part, and Wiss Ward, from Australia, was the mischievous beauty. I spoke in former pages of actors' superstitions. This time I witnessed the realization of one: —

My husband and myself went to Mr. Barrett's office to find out what were his prospects for the remaining few weeks of the London season. We found the poor man almost buried in a pile of newspapers. He looked pale, though trying to smile at the bad luck. The first thing he said to me was: "I knew the play would prove a failure, because, just as I was leaving my house, a funeral appeared at the corner of the street, and being in a great hurry, I was obliged to cross it, and there it is!" He showed me the article I read before: "You see, they force you to take up the French repertoire again, and I am thinking of 'Frou-frou.'"

It was then that the lease of the Court Theatre expired, and we were moved to the Princess Theatre, where the atmosphere was not so congenial. With the change of house we changed the audience, which in that part of the city was quite different, used more to melodramas than to the modern plays. Mr. Barrett took the theatre in view of producing there his popular pieces, which, after the close of my engagement, he subsequently did with great success.

The stage of the Princess was very much higher than the one at the Court Theatre, and a little wider. In order to make the Court Theatre scenery fit, a frame narrow on the sides and very deep above was put in front of the stage, and the result was a fatal one, for the gallery audience could not see what was going on on the stage unless the actors were close to the footlights. All the action performed up stage was interrupted by the loud murmur of the angry gallery gods. It was very annoying, especially to me, who always avoided the glare of the footlights, and liked to move freely in all directions. I felt uncomfortable, and longed for the close of the season.

During the two last weeks I played my repertoire and at the end a benefit, to the success of which several prominent stars kindly contributed. Among them, Sarah Bernhardt played "Le Passant" with Madame Teissandier, Henry Irving recited, and Ellen Terry played Ophelia's scene.

In giving a benefit I followed my country's custom, and learned too late that in England such a thing was only allowed in case of retirement from the stage. I am sorry to say that no one told me so when I planned it.

Always faithful to Cadgewith, we spent a few weeks in that enchanting spot. This time we were rather numerous. Many friends came also, among them Mabel Cook, the novelist.

It was during that summer she wrote my biography, based on the information given her by Miss Wolska. I never was very communicative about my reminiscences, and therefore some of the facts in Mrs. Cook's book are erroneous.

We left Cadgewith in September, and then started on a short provincial tour under Wilson Barrett's management. It was my second visit to different English towns.

I have a few notes from that time, and here they are:—

"OCTOBER 2d, SHEFFIELD.

"In the afternoon we walked a long time in the country. Coming back, we met the procession of the Salvation Army. Their ministers call themselves Generals, and, as I hear, are doing a great deal of good, converting drunkards to soberness and commending pure life among the poor classes.

"Singing hymns, beating a drum, and playing tambourines, they march among hostile elements, for they are not liked here.

"We even witnessed a row; an old woman struck with her soiled broom the officer's face, and a skirmish ensued. The drum was broken, the banner torn to pieces; even some women who wanted to join the procession received quite serious blows.

"The English are demonstrative when they do not belong to the better classes."

"OCTOBER 3d.

"At ten o'clock in the morning we left for Birmingham, and opened with 'Heartsease.' The house was not very full because people were afraid the play was too *risqué*. They asked if it was the same play where the heroine dresses on the stage, getting up from her bed. We played it, however, three times, every time to better houses."

"OCTOBER 5th.

"Two days ago we rehearsed 'Marie Stuart.'

"It was a sad rehearsal. W. flirted with the dark-eyed Vivian, and paid no attention to his lines; the prompter snored in his chair, and Elizabeth could not read her part fluently, and said by way of excuse that she did not think it worth while to pay much attention to such an insignificant part.

"I am still reading the life of Ste. Jeanne Françoise de Chantal. Yesterday I had to put the book aside because I cried so much over the death of young Baron de Torrens and his wife, and over the silent resignation of Madame Chantal. Charles laughed, and said I would never grow old. I feel, indeed, as young at times as I was at twelve, and only when I look in the mirror the sad truth is revealed. But no matter, the older I grow the better I shall be, Anna says, 'like the old wine.'

"When shall I see the Carpathian Mountains again? When?

"Yesterday we were invited to supper by Mr. Rogers, the manager of the Prince of Wales Theatre. Mr. and Mrs. Kendal were there and also Mr. Hare.

"Mr. Rogers spoke a great deal of the brotherhood of actors. How optimistic!

"After the supper, Mrs. Kendal sang ballads, and was very eloquent and entertaining.

"Miss Rogers, who was in Poland, and knows a few Polish words, talked to me about our mutual friends and acquaintances."

"October 6th.

"We took a stroll in the city. A large place, but smoky.

"'Adrienne Lecouvreur' — a crowded house. Great applause after the fourth and fifth acts.

"Our little call-boy is awfully funny. He says he must marry one day a great lady, and as they call me here 'Countess,' he asked my maid if he could, when he grew up, and I became a widow, marry me — and how could he manage to do so. At twelve years of age, it seems so unnatural, but he follows me everywhere, carries the train of my dress, and always wants to treat me to a glass of lemonade. I wonder what will become of him. It is awful to say, but I have a feeling that he will become a very clever and prosperous business man."

"October 7th.

"The public here is not very demonstrative, but, as I had heard, it is quite an educated public.

"I met a man who tried to prove to me that the Birmingham audiences are very clever and good connoisseurs of art, because the manufactories of buttons here are the best in the world. I did not understand."

"October 8th.

"We played 'Marie Stuart,' and I was amazed at the reception. The applause in the third act was so genuine and prolonged that I could not say the final lines, but the curtain had to drop on my last words to Elizabeth. It is strange that this play is such a success in the country where Elizabeth is considered one of its greatest sovereigns."

"October 9th. Sunday.

"We went to see Lord and Lady Denbigh in Newnham Paddocks.

"There is a rare collection of pictures here. The five Van Dycks especially interested me.

"The English are conservative, and never part with their relics. Some of our Polish families could follow that praiseworthy custom.

"The bishop and the chaplain (who carried his arm in a sling because he had fallen from a bicycle) asked me to recite. I never refuse that pleasure to the clergy. I have already recited before ten bishops, at least.

"I took the balcony scene of 'Romeo and Juliet'; and Lady Clara read the lines of Romeo.

"There is no pleasanter home anywhere. The hostess and her daughters could serve as models to many women.

"It is very difficult to make acquaintances here, and foreigners often have erroneous opinions about the people. England is like a sea. If you know how to dive, and are allowed to do so, you will find pearls; but if not, you must float on the surface, and never see the riches hidden at the bottom of the depths."

"October 10th. 'Romeo and Juliet.'

"The fountain put by the obliging manager in the balcony scene interfered with the lovers' soft speeches, but it was pretty.

"The first act was spoiled by bad acting: W., in his beautiful boots, proved as clever as his footgear, and the poor L. delivered with such high falsetto the duke's speeches that the gallery boys imitated him. The part of Romeo is one of the best of Robertson's parts. B. was in his element in the part of the friar, but Lady Capulet walked sideways in the manner of crabs, and looked at everybody over her shoulder to prove her dignity."

"October 11th. 'Marie Stuart.'

"The lime-lights ordered by the stage manager in the third act, in view of brightening my scene with Elizabeth, made poor Shrewsbury look like an orange and Elizabeth like a strawberry ice-cream. At the moment when I have to kneel before my rival queen, the light went out with a snap. The stage manager nearly tore off one of his mustaches in a fit of vexation.

"They have good scenery here."

"October 12th. 'Frou-frou.'

"The house was not well filled. The play was too Frenchy, some one said. We were all in bad humor, which did not help the performance.

"It is my birthday. I received many presents and cards from friends and even strangers, but not one word from Poland. I must return, or else they will forget me entirely. This evening I formed a strong resolution to leave the stage in two or three years.

"I may succeed, because I have good work in view: to found schools for the mountaineers' children, and begin by Zakopane. I have no distinct plans, only a desire to do something good."

"OCTOBER 13th.

"Great joy! Ralph passed his examination for L'École des Ponts et Chaussées. The dear boy writes he was afraid, but was not thinking of himself, only of my disappointment in case of failure."

"OCTOBER 14th.

"We went to Stratford-on-Avon. The little house where the great William was born has been so often described that I already knew every corner in it. A strong emotion, however, thrilled me, when I entered that dwelling. When I looked around, this first impression was somehow dispelled by amazement at the human egotism and stupidity which prompt the people to put their own 'I' everywhere. Not only the walls, the window-panes, and the ceiling are covered with the names of visitors, but even the bust of the poet is defaced with them. What is the object of desecrating thus the sanctuary? Another proof of idiocy.

"In the first room there is a chair by the fireside where Shakespeare used to sit, as tradition tell us. Every person who comes to that room sits down in the chair. Is there any sense in that action?

"At the 'New Place' we saw an American couple, both young and handsome, kneel down and kiss the ground on which the great man walked. I wanted to do the same, but I had lived in England long enough to learn restraint, and limited my demonstrations to picking up some ivy leaves growing around the well. In church we saw the painted bust. I did not like it. The ruddy-cheeked and stout Shakespeare did not appeal to me."

"OCTOBER 16th.

"We spent Sunday very quietly. After the Mass we drove to the park like two commonplace citizens. The day was nice, though a little foggy. The weather is so changeable here that when the rain does not pour in streams, or the wind does not uproot the trees, or tear off the chimneys and roofs (as it did two days ago) the people call it a fine day.

"We told our coachman to follow us slowly, and we walked along the gravelled paths. Some children were jumping over a tree which had been broken by the storm. We were both silent, listening to the distant rhythm of horses' hoofs, children's laughter, and their piercing shrieks. The sand cracked under our feet. Charles smoked a cigarette and frowned. His thoughts were evidently not very bright. I was sending my soul to Poland, and walked along with him. After a long while I spoke: 'What are you thinking of?'

"'I am thinking of home — of course.'

"'Then we both had the same thoughts.'

"'Two months more, and we shall be there.'

"This hope made us forget the present monotony and solitude; for, after all, we shall always be solitary among strangers, and pass from their existence like two shadows.

"My name and fame will soon disappear and they will forget. There is only one link between us — art. Oh, but who understands its real meaning? Am I ungrateful, saying all this? I do not think I am; I only know that I long to go back, to plunge my soul in my native air. My people will find me unchanged, for I will bring nothing foreign in me, but the same warm and ever faithful heart.

"We arrived in Liverpool at noon. This time we stopped at a private house. The landlady wears curls on both sides of her ruddy cheeks, brimful with health. She is calm, discreet, and neat, and has two daughters. We are very comfortable here, for there are no other boarders. I grow so tired of hotels, though some one told me that the stars ought to stop in the first-class hotels, or they would have no success. Strange idea! I wonder what any one's value has to do with it. And yet, I fear there is some truth in that shoddy, popular conviction."

"OCTOBER 18th. 'Adrienne Lecouvreur.'

"The house was only half filled; the public was cold, and did not know where to applaud. We must go to the hotel."

"OCTOBER 20th.

"Yesterday I noticed among the audience a young couple sitting in the middle of the first row. The lady is white as marble, with black eyebrows and hair and very dark eyes. The oval of her face is classic. The young man looks very much like her, only his complexion is darker.

"She watches the acting with an expression of reverence in her face, intensely, and weeps during the emotional scenes; he has a nervous motion of the hands, biting his young mustache, or pulling his small beard. Who are they, I wonder? They do not look

English. Perhaps they are Jews. Whoever they are, I shall play only for them if they come again."

"OCTOBER 21st. 'Frou-frou.'

"My couple sat in the same seats. This time there was a stout man with them. I was so happy to see them again, and I played better than ever.

"'Frou-frou' was a success; the criticisms were splendid."

"OCTOBER 23d. 'Marie Stuart.'

"And my unknown friends were again in their seats.

"The house was very noisy that night. Shrieks, hurrahs, loud calls, and whistling were deafening. Here, when they whistle, it means that they are pleased, as in America.

"Sunday! the blessed, happy day of rest."

Here my notes stop. My mother was dangerously ill, and I neglected the diary.

We put on the bills "Juana," with Forbes Robertson in the part of Friar John. He played beautifully, and looked a saint to perfection.

After several other cities, as Leeds, Manchester, etc., we went to Scotland, and I went into ecstasies over Edinburgh. What a beautiful, interesting city, and what sad stories it contains!

At Edinburgh Castle I cried when I saw the tiny cold room in which Marie Stuart gave birth to her son, and at Holyrood I nearly quarrelled with the man at the door who was selling the fancy picture of Rizzio,—that contemptible picture, of some imaginative chap, with a pretentious mustache, curly hair, and pouting lips, while the real Rizzio was a homely man over fifty years old and a hunchback.

I asked the man if he believed that this was a real portrait of Rizzio, and he cynically answered: "Not at all; but people believe it is real and buy it."

I returned to Holyrood over and over again, and the whole life of Marie Stuart passed before my mind.

Poor, beautiful queen! They say she sinned, but had she time to sin much? If we consider her occupations,—the musical compositions, the verses, the abundant correspondence (for she wrote an enormous amount of letters), and many pieces of wonderful and most elaborate fancy work she left behind,—it is really hard to believe that she spent much time in dissipation.

But suppose she sinned, indeed, in the brief moments of her youth, had she not more than her share of expiation? And yet I hear that in some schools in America the lady teachers tell the children that even the name of Marie Stuart is odious — that she was the most horrible woman, with seven husbands and any number of illegitimate children.

Is it not strange that even in her grave she is persecuted? Yet it is only fair to state that she was treated most abominably, and I was glad when Andrew Lang's book came out, in which he proves most emphatically that the supposed casket letters to Bothwell were counterfeits. It was the devilish work of men who perjured themselves for money and honors.

Mr. Lang is an Englishman and not a Roman Catholic. No one can accuse him of partiality, for his object was only historic truth.

Please pardon this deviation; I learned to love Marie Stuart, not only from my part, but also from many books I read about her, and I am always slightly excited when I speak of her.

Walter Scott's statue was almost opposite our hotel, and I could say good morning and good night to the great Scotchman every day.

I was very kindly received by the Edinburgh audiences.

Of other Scotch cities I remember Glasgow, where I saw in a private house a very extensive collection of Marie

Stuart's portraits in print and etchings; also many works about her unhappy life.

The Glasgow people were very genuine in their approval, and we had a successful week, but we spent the dullest Sunday of our life in that city. Already Saturday afternoon, when I sat at the piano, I was informed by the chambermaid that music was not allowed in the hotel either on Saturdays or Sundays.

We had been told that the suburbs and the country around Glasgow were beautiful, and we planned a long drive on Sunday afternoon, but alas, there was no possibility of hiring a carriage. Our landlord told us proudly that people do not drive on the Sabbath in Glasgow, and we could not get a pair of horses for a million.

Just as he finished this respectful sentence, we heard the rattle of a vehicle and the horses' hoofs in the distance. My husband asked what was the meaning of this exceptional turnout, and the landlord's answer made us nearly uncivil with merriment. "Oh, that?" Then, after a moment's hesitation, he said it was only a cart hauling whiskey and beer about the city. New country, new customs! There was at least a human note in this— and it was rational, too; every other exercise being forbidden, what could the poor people do but seek consolation in drink, for surely no human being, not even a monk, could pray fifteen or sixteen hours in succession.

We gave up the afternoon drive, of course, and we thought that the next question my husband addressed to the landlord was at least quite respectable: he asked in what part of the city the Catholic church was. "I really cannot tell you that, sir," was the curt answer. A young lady behind the counter looked in the directory, and after a while she said there was nothing about it in the book.

We knew, however, of the existence of a Catholic church in Glasgow, and were determined to find it. But it was a difficult enterprise, since no one wished to inform us on the subject. "I don't know, I am sure," was all we got for our pains.

I saw a demure, pretty, middle-aged woman, with a large prayer-book in her hand, walking towards us, and I asked her politely to show us the way to our church.

"Not I!" exclaimed the woman, with fear and indignation in her face, and she walked away quickly and stiffly to the other side of the street. The poor creature looked really injured. We walked in all directions, not knowing where to go, and would have been obliged to return to the hotel, had we not chanced upon a jolly Irishman, who, seeing us look around, had the inspiration to ask where we wanted to go.

"To the Catholic church? Come along; I'll show ye where it is," he said, with a grin, and when we entered the poor, small church, he came in too.

On our return to London I made an engagement with Mr. Bancroft, the manager of the Haymarket Theatre, for the coming spring season to play "Odette," by Sardou — translated and somewhat localized by Clement Scott. All the persons of the play were turned into English people, with the exception of Odette and the wicked companion of her downfall in the fourth act.

A few weeks later I was in Poland, where I was greeted with enthusiasm. I proved quite competent now, after having passed the examination of two London seasons; I was also young again, and resumed Juliet, Ophelia, and Aniela, an *ingénue* part in Fredo's comedy. "Odette" was just translated, and I included it in my repertoire, getting better acquainted with the part before my London engagement.

I also created a great excitement among my friends and the critics by producing Ibsen's "The Doll's House." When I told my friends that I had to get under the table and bark, and leave my husband and children in the last act, they thought I was crazy to play such a part. They were all more or less conventional, and this too close approach to nature shocked them. On the night of the performance, however, they applauded, and said it was quaint, and the barking fitted the picture, and my leaving the unforgiving husband not so bad, after all.

The critics were simply puzzled. Some of them condemned the play, others lifted it to the skies. The result of these varied opinions was a long run of "The Doll's House," Polish, "Nora" for short.

Very sad news reached me and marred my Warsaw engagement: the great poet and best of my friends, Henry Wadsworth Longfellow, died.

Shortly after that our dear friend, Lucian Paprocki, lost his reason and was placed in an asylum. Such an end was predicted by those who knew the painful story of his imprisonment, and yet it was a great shock to us.

I went to Cracow, Lwów (Lemberg), and Posen, and played in each of those towns my repertoire. At the end of my short season I was more than usually tired, not because of the work, but because of our people's great hospitality.

In the spring of 1882 we returned to London.

While I was rehearsing "Odette" I went to see Mrs. Kendal's beautiful performance of "Coralie's Son," a French play by Delpit. I had seen her some time before in "Black-eyed Susan," and she was simple and touching and made me shed copious tears.

We went to the Gaiety Theatre one evening. Madame Chaumont played "Divorçons," and was quite irresistible.

Great pains were taken by Mr. and Mrs. Bancroft in the rehearsals of "Odette."

I remember Clement Scott sitting in the first balcony, giving advice, criticising, or approving. I liked those rehearsals, as I always liked the working out of the part even better than the performance.

The play was a great success, and was kept on the bills so long that I was sincerely tired of repeating the same lines and going through the same emotions.

After two months' run I used to groan every evening when I came to my dressing-room, and then dear Mrs. Bancroft would send her maid to ask if I were ill.

"Oh, no, no! I am quite well. Please give Mrs. Bancroft my thanks and tell her it is only 'Odette'!"

For change I got new dresses, but there was not much relief in that; besides, there was something worse in store for me. We had played "Odette" nearly three months. Such numerous repetitions of the same text caused the phonographic plates of my brain to be rubbed off in places, and I began to forget words of my lines. That was quite serious. I never really made a mistake, but was sometimes at the brink of an abyss, trying to keep my balance by a superhuman effort. To prevent serious accidents, I had to read my part every evening before going on. I grew a little nervous, losing at times my usual composure, or feeling uncomfortable, and when Mrs. Bancroft asked me if I would prolong my engagement until the middle of July, I declined politely to appear in the same part any longer than my contract called for.

Still, I parted with sincere regret from the pretty theatre and my cosy dressing-room which Mrs. Bancroft had given up for me, moving to the next floor; but most of all I regretted my kind manager and his charming, talented wife, dear Mrs. Bancroft. I have still the most vivid and grateful recollection of their courtesy.

Mr. Tennyson continued to be very kind to us, and we were often invited to meet him at luncheon time at his residence. I remember one day, after seeing the gorgeous performance of "The Cup," we talked about it, and Mr.

Tennyson praised Mr. Irving for the pains he took in giving such an elaborate production of the play.

Sometime later, after the end of my engagement, we were invited to visit him in his summer home in Surrey. We arrived in the evening. I shall never forget his figure in the dim light of his study. Mrs. Tennyson, who was still delicate, retired early, and we were led to the master's sanctum sanctorum. That room seemed to me filled with wonderful visions of his brain, and I felt hypnotized by the very atmosphere of it. There was a fire in the large fireplace. He sat in its light, and asked permission to smoke his after-dinner pipe, a very welcome proposition to my husband.

After talking for a while on different topics, he asked me if I had ever read his "Rizpah." I acknowledged my ignorance. "Would you like to hear it?" I could not believe my ears! What, will this great man read to us? He did, and it was a wonderful moment in my life.

I was told that Tennyson never could read his own poems with effect. I do not know what people meant by that, for I listened to his reading with great delight and with my face flooded with tears.

When I cooled off from my impression, he asked me if I would read a dialogue of his, together with Fanny Kemble. I had never met the lady, but I was afraid of reading with my accent against her perfect English.

When I communicated my fear to Mr. Tennyson, he smiled, and assured me that I could do so safely. I agreed then to the reading, which, however, for some reason or other, never took place.

Next day I remember walking in the garden by his side; in the afternoon we took leave and returned to London, my soul filled with the memories of the lofty moments spent in the great man's house.

During my London engagement I signed a contract with the American manager, John Stetson, for the season of 1882–

1883, to play thirty weeks in succession, with two intervals, the Christmas week and the Holy Week.

We rested a few weeks at the sea-shore and then went to Paris. Through my friends, who knew Victor Hugo quite well, we received an invitation to meet him.

The appointed hour was nine o'clock in the evening. We arrived a few minutes earlier, anxious to be on the spot when the great man left the dining-room. When we arrived the large reception hall was almost dark, being only scantily lit by a lamp, but soon a female servant came in with a taper mounted on a long stick, and proceeded slowly to light up the room. In the meantime we could take a good look at the hall. It was a stately reception hall, not unlike many others we saw in France. The arrangement of furniture, however, was a little puzzling: two rows of chairs, beginning at the fireplace and extending two-thirds the length of the hall, stood facing each other, with one arm-chair at the end of the right-hand row by the fire, which, on account of the warm weather, was not lighted.

Other visitors arrived, and sat discreetly on chairs and benches placed against the wall.

When the last candle was ablaze, both wings of the dining-room door opened, and a liveried footman walked in, and standing stiffly at one side, announced loudly: "Monsieur Victor Hugo." The poet came in, accompanied by his guests and "Madame," known to me only by that name. She was the great man's friend and his secretary.

We rose and stood before a man of medium size, with a flushed face and eagle eyes. His profuse white hair was cut an inch from his scalp, and stood erect. He bowed to all of us as he walked between the two rows of chairs to the fireplace, until he reached the goal — I mean the arm-chair. The seat next to him was empty. There was a long, silent moment, and the guests and inmates whispered to each other, with their eyes turned to the master.

It was very solemn. My husband suggested that we should kneel before the great man, say a prayer, ask for his benediction, and depart in peace. Soon, however, one of the visitors was brought into the presence of the host and was invited to sit in the empty chair. After a short talk, the person rose to yield the place to another.

The hall was still silent and solemn. This concentrated worshipping mood was suddenly broken by the entrance of a handsome middle-aged man with a *Légion d'honneur* in his buttonhole, who created quite a commotion. He spoke loudly, asking Hugo for a decisive answer to his letters. "Madame" was summoned to make an explanation, and this rather energetic intercourse lasted until the departure of the *Légion d'honneur* man.

Another solemn pause, and we were introduced. I was invited to sit in turn in the chair my predecessors had occupied.

No one can talk better than French people, and when a Frenchman is a great poet besides, the talk becomes stimulating.

I was told many things, and asked some questions about my country and America. I was also asked what parts I played. I mentioned some heroines of my repertoire, and then said that in Poland I also played Victor Hugo's plays a great deal.

"But have you good translations?"

"Quite decent ones, but they cannot be compared with the originals," I added, smiling; "for the language of the gods can only be translated by the gods themselves."

This seemed to please him, for he also smiled. I grew more communicative and slightly reckless, and when he suddenly asked me what parts I liked best to act, I answered, without hesitation, "Shakespeare's, of course."

In an instant realization of my mistake dawned upon me,

but it was too late to call back my words or to explain. Anything I could add would make it worse.

The great man sank deeper in his arm-chair and said nothing. It was time to say good-by. I rose, and Victor Hugo's great manners came to the front immediately. He kissed my hand and asked us to come often again.

"Ma maison est la vôtre," were his last words.

I thanked him effusively for this polite form of speech, and took my leave.

The poet addressed a few public sentences to the rest of us, and after a gracious good-night we departed.

The three weeks we spent in Paris were delightful. We went a great deal to the theatres, and it was then, if I remember rightly, I saw the adorable Madame Bartet at the Gymnase. Her subtlety, her mobile features, together with the sweet, melodious voice and her diaphanous figure, drew my attention at once, and I knew she would one day rise to a position worthy of her talent.

Excursions, parties, dinners, were showered upon us, and it was hard to leave the pleasures of the French metropolis, but the hardest of all was taking leave of my son. We parted with the promise on his part to spend his next vacation in California, where we intended to go next summer.

CHAPTER XLVI

We sailed on the steamer *Arizona* on the ninth of September, 1882.

In New York I met my manager, Mr. Stetson, and we arranged my repertoire for the season.

To "Adrienne," "Camille," "Juliet," "Marie Stuart," and "Frou-frou," I added "As You Like It," "Twelfth Night," and "Odette." I wanted to include also "The Doll's House," by Ibsen, but his name was utterly unknown in America, and the manager was afraid to take any risk of producing "them unpopular Dutchman's plays."

Of course it was out of the question to discuss Ibsen with John Stetson, and I put off "The Doll's House," hoping to introduce it to the audience next year.

We opened the season not in New York but in Boston, Mr. Stetson's home, where he had his own theatre, the "Globe." All my friends were at summer resorts — and Henry Longfellow was no more. The first and only visit I made during my stay in Boston was to his grave.

I threw myself feverishly into my studies, and allowed myself no time for anything else.

During the rehearsals I noticed that my stage manager was doing some guesswork, and that it would be necessary for me to take the direction of plays in my hands. Every scene had to be rehearsed and conducted by me, even the grouping of the people, the lights, and scenery. I also had to teach some young girls and boys how to deliver their lines and what to do with their too many hands and feet. I actually lived at the theatre, and that busy life absorbed me entirely.

I had a curious experience during my Boston engagement. At the first performance of "Romeo and Juliet" I noticed that the two stage-boxes were decorated with flags. To my inquiry as to the meaning of these festive adornments, I received the answer that President Arthur and General Ben Butler were coming to see the play.

"Why, how strange! have you two Presidents now?" I asked. The man who gave me the information smiled, and said: "No, of course not; but Ben Butler is the candidate for governor of Massachusetts, and his adherents have decorated his box for him as a mark of their devotion to his cause."

I thought that the wisest course was to be silent, and I said nothing, keeping my own counsel.

After the first act, a gentleman came behind the scenes with a very fine basket of flowers, which I naturally supposed was for me, but as I extended my hand he said, in subdued tones: "Will you please hand this to President Arthur at your first call after the next act?" "With pleasure, of course; only tell me in which box he is seated." "On the right of the stage, Madame." "And on the left from the audience — how funny," I thought.

The balcony scene over, I hastened to take the flowers, and while the applause was going on I made a curtsey before the President's box and handed him the basket, which he received with a slight bow to me and then to the audience, which cheered him most enthusiastically.

When I was waiting for the next scene, I heard ferocious cheers.

"What is that?" I asked.

"Ben Butler has just come," said the prompter.

Before the curtain had time to rise, another gentleman with another basket of flowers asked me, not in subdued tones of voice this time, but rather peremptorily, to hand it to General Butler.

I looked at my stage manager, then at my leading man, in a mute appeal for counsel, but at the same moment my acting manager, Fred Stinson, came in and said to the basket gentleman, "I will attend to it." Then he turned to me and said, "You are not supposed to belong to any party — and there is no harm in handing the flowers to General Butler." "Very well," I answered; so, after the act was over, the basket was transferred from my hands to those of General Butler. What was my amazement when he, quick as a flash, produced another much more gorgeous basket of flowers and handed it to me. The applause was simply deafening. I do not remember what happened next, but I know I was not a good Juliet that night.

Photograph by Bradley and Rulofson, San Francisco.

MAURICE BARRYMORE.

Of all the parts I played that season, Rosalind, in "As You Like It," was the one the public liked best, and we repeated the play so often that my manager, in order to add more weight to it, engaged John Muldoon, the well-known wrestler, who was, indeed, a valuable addition to the cast. He and Maurice Barrymore, who was of an athletic though slender build, made a splendid picture in the wrestling scene.

Maurice Barrymore was one of those handsome men who also have the rare gift of winning all hearts. He was much admired by women, but was too intellectual to be a mere matinée idol. He was equally liked by men and women. Sentimental girls used to send him flowers, to his great amusement. They went so far as to send him white lilies, which were always received with a roar of laughter. His best parts were Armand, Orlando, and Valreas in "Frou-frou."

Mr. Stetson was very proud to have engaged that "dandy leading man," as he called him, for me.

There are many anecdotes about John Stetson, who, though a shrewd and clever business man, never troubled his brain much with history or literature.

Here is an authentic story which happened during my engagement in New York:—

He had rented for eight weeks Booth's Theatre, and I had to close it, because it was already sold, and at the end of my engagement had to pass into its new owner's hands, to be transformed into a business building. Among other plays, I also played "Adrienne Lecouvreur."

Booth's Theatre, splendidly furnished with scenery and accessories for Shakespeare's productions, lacked the furnishings necessary for the French plays of past centuries.

Mr. Stetson always assisted at the scenery rehearsals, which was very good of him, and a great comfort to the company, because in case of any lack of appropriate pieces of scenery or furniture, the stage manager could apply directly to the highest authority. At rehearsal, when the stage was set for the fifth act of "Adrienne," I noticed a dark carved fireplace entirely unsuited to the light walls ornamented with Cupids' heads and garlands of flowers.

I asked the stage manager why he had allowed that sombre monument to be put in Adrienne's boudoir. He answered that there was nothing else but Elizabethan or modern English fireplaces.

Mr. Stetson, who was sitting in the first row of chairs, saw the embarrassment of the stage manager and my discontented countenance, and asked directly, "What is the matter?" I told him that the fireplace did not suit the scenes.

"It ought to be Louis Quinze."

"Wait a moment, Madame. What did you say — Louis who?"

"Louis Quinze," I repeated, distinctly this time. Upon that Mr. Stetson called the chief carpenter, who came before the footlights, waiting for orders.

"Where is that man Louis Kantz?" he asked peremptorily; "bring him to me immediately; I want him to give Madame another fireplace — he must have it ready for to-morrow's performance." The bewildered carpenter looked at me, the stage manager bit his lips, and Barrymore, highly amused, said to Mr. Stetson: —

"Louis Quinze is not here, poor man; he died and was buried some time ago."

"Confound it!"—that in a subdued tone of voice. "Never mind, Madame; we may find what you want in other theatres. I'll attend to it directly."

In New York "Odette" was liked the best, but I selected "Romeo and Juliet" for the closing of Booth's Theatre.

After the play I said a few words of farewell to the stage upon which Booth's Hamlet had walked. I also referred to his ambitious desire of building this perfect theatre with the hope that it would serve exclusively the purpose of producing what was highest and best in dramatic literature. Then I spoke of the sacrifices he had made in order to keep up the building, and how, in spite of all efforts, he was compelled to give up his pet dream.

CHAPTER XLVII

THE summer of 1883 we spent in California, where my son joined us. He brought excellent news. It was not easy to get along at the Ponts et Chaussées, and he was at the head of the class. We had a jolly good time together, visiting the Pleasants' homestead in San Iago Cañon. We were all three of us so enchanted with the place that at the end of our visit my husband went into partnership with the owner, and they planned for a large cattle-ranch.

Photograph by Aimé Dupont.

MARY SHAW.

When we returned to San Francisco, we opened the season under my husband's management, with Fred Stinson as acting manager.

This time, besides Maurice Barrymore, we had Mrs. Barrymore, Mr. Vandenhoff, William Owen (a most excellent Sir Toby Belch), and Mary Shaw, who was then a studious, intellectual young woman, with a great deal of talent. She never slighted even the smallest details in her parts, but always worked for improvement.

The two Barrymore children joined their parents on our return East. Lionel was four years old, and Ethel was one year younger. The boy was always busy painting ships and railroad trains, and Ethel was an actress. They composed some impossible dialogues and played them together. Lionel was always "Pap," and Ethel was Madame. She could not pronounce all the letters of the alphabet, but she acted with conviction. I often saw her eager eyes watching me from behind the scenes during the matinées.

I added to my repertoire "The Doll's House," which, I am sorry to say, was not relished by American audiences, and we had to take it off.

The play, however, inspired Mr. Barrymore, and he wrote the play called "Nadjezda," which bore not the slightest resemblance to Ibsen's, with the exception of the desperate dance he introduced, which had for its object the keeping the man from leaving the room. It was not a tarantella, however, but a waltz.

We produced the play, but it was so exhausting that, after the first three weeks' run, I had to take a rest.

In Boston "Nadjezda" was played to crowded houses, but Mr. Barrymore took it away from me because I did not consent to put it on every night. He also had an idea that the play would make a hit in London, where he produced it in 1884, but with no good result.

In 1884–1885 we stayed in Poland and England. We first went to Paris to pay a visit to my son, then to Zakopane in the Tatra Mountains, where we had built a villa. In that little house lived Mr. Calixte Wolski, with his daughter and my half-brother's daughter, Felice Benda, whom I had taken from the convent two years before and placed in the care of those dear friends of mine, Mr. and Miss Wolska.

Miss Wolska is half American and half Polish, for when

her father — forced by the unhappy results of the revolution of 1848 — was emigrating to America with his wife, she was born on the ocean. When her mother died, she was brought up by the Sisters in New Orleans. At the age of sixteen she returned with her father to Poland, and never crossed the ocean again. She is refined and witty, always

MADAME MODJESKA'S COUNTRY RESIDENCE, NEAR CRACOW.

jolly, and of the sweetest disposition; and Mr. Wolski was a highly educated man and a fine instructor. I believed myself very fortunate when those refined and kind friends consented to take care of my beloved brother's daughter.

As we neared Zakopane many friends and mountaineers, mounted on horseback, met and greeted us with cheers. We stopped our wagon, and a long while was spent in exchanging words of joy, embracing, and kissing. While we were thus engaged, another wagon came up to us and also stopped.

I heard a sweet voice from the depth of it, calling, "Madame Helena! how do you do?" and the beautiful face of Madame Gorska (the present Madame Paderewska) appeared between the white canvas of the wagon. New greetings, new exclamations.

The beautiful creature, whose name is also Helena, looked at me with her wistful eyes and said: "I envy your going to Zakopane; you are going to meet one of the most extraordinary young men you ever met." Then she sighed and said: "And I must go away." "I must," she repeated, lower. "Good-by," and she departed.

I never even had time to ask the name of that marvellous young man, but Anna knew whom she meant, and named Paderewski.

The very next day Dr. Tytus Chalubinski introduced us to a frail-looking young man of twenty-one, saying: —

"I want you to know and love Ignace Paderewski, our second Chopin," and then with a look of a loving father he squeezed the young man's hand.

At the piano Paderewski's head, with its aureole of profuse golden hair and delicate, almost feminine features, looked like one of Botticelli's or Fra Angelico's angels, and he seemed so deeply wrapped up in his music that this intensity was almost hypnotic. He also phrased with so much clearness and meaning that his playing made an effect of something new and quite unconventional.

Paderewski was married at nineteen, and became a father and widower at twenty. At eighteen he was already one of the professors of harmony at the Warsaw Music Conservatory, and at the time we met him he still held that position. He was a composer also, and many of his songs and piano pieces were published in Warsaw and Berlin.

ANTONIN DVOŘÁK.

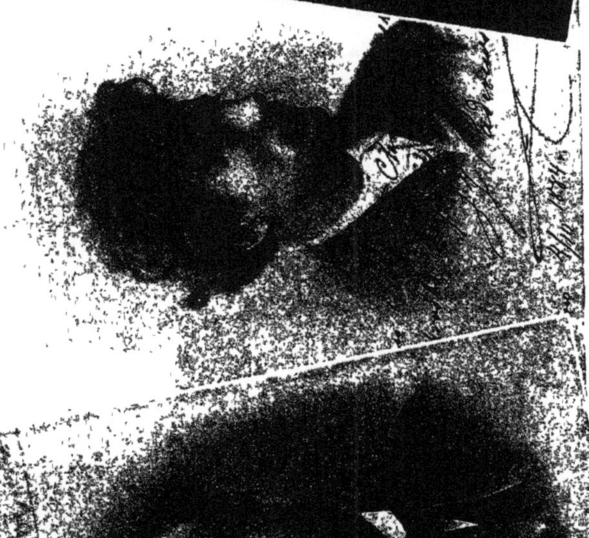

PADEREWSKI.

JOSEPH JOACHIM.

In private life he was witty, alert, most kind-hearted, always interesting, always having a ready answer.

When once a mature beauty chaffed him, saying that he was sentimental, he answered: —

"Why not, Madame; sentiment does not suit a gendarme; but will you not allow a little of it to an artist?"

He used to come often to our villa, and it was impossible to keep him away from the piano. Sometimes he played long after midnight, and had to be taken from the instrument by force when the refreshments were announced.

We had many chats, and I advised him to appear in public. I knew he would make a name and fortune. His poetic face, combined with his genius, was bound to produce brilliant results. He hesitated, but finally made up his mind to go to Vienna and study with Leschetitzky. That same summer, after leaving Zakopane, he gave a concert in Cracow, at which I had the great pleasure of reciting. Then he departed for Vienna.

I played short engagements in Cracow, Lemberg, and Posen, and we spent a few weeks in Prussian Poland, visiting my husband's relations. Then in the late autumn of 1884 I began a series of performances in Warsaw.

Warsaw! the city of my predilection and also the source of bitter experiences. It is an old saying that we love those the best who make us suffer the most. So it is with Warsaw.

I had scarcely played there a few weeks when a tragic accident marred my happy engagement.

Brandes, the celebrated Norwegian critic, in his "Impressions of Poland," writes about it as follows: —

"Even more dangerous to Polish nationality is that provision of the law which requires that all instruction in the schools shall be in Russian. Even the scanty instruction in the Polish language is given in Russian. And so strict is the prohibition against speaking Polish in playtime, or generally in the school grounds, that a boy of twelve years old was recently shut up for twenty-four hours in the dark because, coming out of school, he said to a comrade in Polish, 'Let us go home together.' But the régime to which the schools are subjected with regard to the suppression of the national peculiarities is not confined to the domain of language. In a family which I was invited to visit, the following incident happened. The son of the family, a boy of sixteen, the only son of a widow, one evening in the theatre had thrown a wreath to Helena Modrzejewska on behalf of his comrades. A few days after, in obedience to an order from the Minister of Education, the principal of the school called him up, and told him that he must not only leave the school, but that all future admission to any other school whatever was forbidden him; it was the punishment for having been guilty of a Polish demonstration. They boy went home and put a bullet through his head.

"We may perhaps wonder that provisions which in certain circumstances drive a half-grown lad to suicide are maintained, or that so innocent a thing as the throwing of a wreath is forbidden. But the answer is that, as a rule, everything which betrays a love for the language is forbidden in Warsaw."

The fact, as described by the famous critic, is correct; there are only some details accompanying this sad event to be rectified.

There were seventeen high-school boys who put together their pennies in order to buy a magnificent bouquet and offer it to me over the footlights. Artists and literary men had done the same thing before, and those young boys were only following their example.

They tied the bouquet with a pink ribbon (this detail is not without importance), ornamented with the inscription, in Polish, "To Helena Modrzejewska, from the high-school students," and when they brought their handsome gift to the theatre, they looked for the representative of police or some school authority in order to show it to them and ask permission to offer it to me. They perceived in one of the boxes Count Buturlin, the most kind and most popular chief of police that ever was in Warsaw. President Mouchanoff and my husband were with him.

Encouraged by the presence of Count Mouchanoff, who was a very popular man, two of them rapped at the door, and being admitted to the box, they explained the cause of their visit.

Count Buturlin, after having looked at the flowers and read the words printed on the ribbon, smiled indulgently, and said, "Yes, you may hand the bouquet to Madame Modrzejewska, only do it quietly," and when the happy boys were bowing themselves off, he added, "And mind, do not step on people's corns when you walk to the footlights." The boys did not know how to thank him for so much friendliness, and immediately selected one among them who had to hand me the bouquet. It was just the unfortunate boy Mr. Brandes speaks of.

The next day all the seventeen boys were expelled from the school by the Curator Apuchtin. They were accused as guilty of a "patriotic demonstration," for having tied the flowers with national Polish colors [1] and an inscription in the Polish language. This was not enough; they had not only to leave the school, but all future admission to any other school whatever was forbidden them.

The same evening they all met at the house of the boy who handed me the flowers, and there spent a few hours debating what course to take. Nothing but manual work was left to them, and they fully realized the failure of their lives.

At the end of the meeting the young host rose and said, "Be of good cheer; to-morrow you will all be re-admitted to the school." When they asked what he meant, he repeated his words and added, "Do not insist on explanation, but be of good cheer."

They parted. Some of them half believed in the prophecy; others treated it as an effervescence of a troubled brain. When they left the house the boy shot himself.

[1] Our national colors are red and white — not pink.

His prophecy became true, then, for his unexpected suicide alarmed the authorities, and the sixteen boys were called back to school.

These details come from one who was present at the meeting.

My husband asked all my friends, President Mouchanoff, as well as all the members of the company, not to tell me of it, knowing what a shock such news would give me. They all promised to be silent, and I lived in perfect ignorance of the fact.

On the day of the burial I had to recite at a charity concert. I remember that matinée so well. There was something in the air which made me sad and nervous.

Is it possible that there exists such a thing as an unconscious feeling of a misfortune passing by? I do not know, but during my recitation the tears flooded my face, and when I left the platform I had a good cry in the foyer.

I heard some one whisper, "She knows already," and at the same time a person entered hurriedly and the word "burial" struck my ears. I lifted my head and asked anxiously, "Whose burial?" The dear, faithful friend, Mademoiselle Emily, who sat near me, asked me in turn: "Did you not hear? a student fell down by accident from the third floor and died. It is his funeral they speak of."

Thus the truth remained unknown to me a few days longer, but one morning, when at the stage manager's office I was arranging the repertoire for the next week, some actors and actresses entered the room. I do not remember how it happened, but from them I suddenly learned the truth, without preparation and with all accompanying details. The knowledge that the boy was the only son of a widow was the most painful to me. To think of the tortures of that poor mother's heart, to know that I was the indirect cause of her son's suicide, made me disconsolate. Dismissing abruptly the question of the repertoire, I went home.

In spite of this painful experience, I had to go on playing, for I had signed a contract and had to fulfil its terms.

Some new Polish plays were added to my repertoire, and my time was taken up by constant rehearsals.

One day Cazimir Hofmann, formerly the leader of the orchestra in Cracow, and a friend of ours, asked if I could introduce to Louis Grossman his boy, then six or seven years old. He was anxious to hear Mr. Grossman's opinion about the little Joseph's talent.

I promised at once to comply with his wish, though it was not such an easy task as it seemed, for, though Louis Grossman was a very kind-hearted man, and many a young musician came to the front through his influence, yet I remembered that he had a strong aversion to small prodigies. He used to say that not one of the wonderful children he knew had amounted to anything. "The wonder disappears when they grow up, and nothing remains but the child."

In spite of this opinion and my knowledge of his prejudice, I did not hesitate to render Mr. Hofmann the slight service he asked of me, and I went directly to Grossman's house. After some hesitation he consented to hear the boy, and appointed an hour for the meeting.

I can even now see Joseph Hofmann's tiny figure wrapped up warmly from head to foot. When between Mr. Hofmann and myself we had taken off little Joseph's wraps and gaiters, I took him by the hand, and we entered the reception room, where Mr. Grossman was waiting to greet us.

I introduced father and son. The little artist never even looked at the host, but directed his eyes towards the upright piano. After having examined that instrument for a while, he looked at all four corners of the room, then at his father, and when Mr. Grossman asked him to play, he stood before the piano with his hands in his pockets, and after a moment's suspense, he said: —

"I will not play on that thing."

Our host was so surprised at that tiny person's pluck and impertinence that he forgot to laugh. He looked at me for a moment; then, with a loud outburst of merriment, said, "Well, I suppose I have to humor this little Mozart," and with "Come along, little man, I will give you your choice," he walked ahead and took us to his piano wareroom.

Little Joseph went from one piano to another, touching the keys lightly, and finally he sat in front of one of them and struck a few chords.

When Mr. Grossman heard the tone of the instrument, he said, smiling, "That brat chose my best Steinway," and he at once became interested in the boy. He let him play and improvise, and was so pleased with the abnormal knowledge of harmony in the child that he declared it was the first time in his life he had heard anything like it in a boy of seven.

While he was talking to Mr. Hofmann, giving his advice as to the future conduct of Joseph's studies, that diminutive personage was placidly eating chocolates offered him by Madame Grossman, who some moments before had quietly entered the hall.

The musical season was in its swing in Warsaw, and Hans von Bülow came to give one or two concerts. At the same time Brandes visited our country. I met him at one of Edward Leo's receptions. Hans von Bülow was also one of the guests.

I came late, for I played Feuillet's "Dalila" that evening, but I was told by my husband, who preceded me, that Bülow had delivered a panegyric about me before my arrival. He spoke with so much enthusiasm that our friends were afraid Mr. Brandes might resent it, because it is well known that every critic prefers rather to himself discover a genius than to be told to fall upon his knees before an acknowledged idol.

No one, however, could stop Mr. Bülow's laudatory mood, and he went so far as to say that he only knew two stars in Poland: one of them was Chopin, and the other — here he named me.

This was very erratic, indeed, but his words proved his appreciation and friendship.

I do not think this outburst of enthusiasm cooled off Mr. Brandes's judgment of me, for his criticism made me very happy. He praised not only my acting, but he also spoke in most flattering terms about my husband. No one could characterize Mr. Chlapowski better than the famous Dane did in his paragraph on the Warsaw Theatre: —

> "She is indebted to her present husband, an extremely artistic man of the world, Karol Chlapowski, for her taste for English poetry, as well as for her higher development as an artist generally."

Mr. Brandes's appreciation is quite correct, but what was ignored by him was my husband's influence over my inner self: the touch of a delicate nature and refined mind, never tired of instructing and polishing the rough edges of the too impulsive and somewhat violent disposition I brought with me to this world. The true Christian spirit which had always ruled his life had a great power over me, and the general improvement of my nature was due to his constant soul watching over mine.

I am bound, however, to correct Mr. Brandes's statement in one point. He says that my husband developed my taste for Shakespeare. Being brought up in France, Mr. Chlapowski was versed in French literature, and I learned a great deal from him. He read with me the French classics, the romantic and modern poets, but not Shakespeare, in whose masterpieces I had been deeply interested from my early days. His plays were introduced into the Cracow repertoire through Rapacki, Ladnowski, and myself. This fact I correct only because I have already spoken of my youthful craze for the Great William, and because this little error of the critic has nothing to do with my husband's refining influence upon my art.

CHAPTER XLVIII

BETWEEN 1884 and 1902 I visited Poland several times, and I had an opportunity of knowing many remarkable Polish men and women. Princess Sapieha was one of them. She was the mother of the Red Prince, of whom I spoke in the first part of my memoirs, Adam Sapieha, who inherited from her many qualities, among others the intense love of his country and great energy.

She was one of those women whom it was safe to compare with Volumnia in "Coriolanus," for her character bore a strong resemblance to the Roman matron. Exceedingly severe to herself, she could not help being so to others, and her judgment of people, though always just, was often slightly harsh. But her kindness to her friends and to the poor was unbounded, and she was loved and highly respected by many, though feared by others. She had no use for the weak-minded, and her hatred of them was equal to her hatred of the enemies of her country.

Justly proud of her ancestors and attached to her family traditions, she was free from silly, aristocratic prejudices, and disliked titles. On her visiting-card there was nothing but her name, without a prefix.

I consider myself very fortunate in being brought in contact with that remarkable lady. She was always affable, kind, brilliant, and most natural, a true *grande dame*.

We also had a glimpse of Princess Marceline Czartoryska, the famous amateur pianist, friend and pupil of Chopin, and recognized in Europe as one of his best interpreters.

The great poetess of recent days, Maria Konopnicka, we met in Lemberg. Her poems, like those of François Coppée, deal mostly with the poorer classes, and with our peasantry's miseries. They are written with deep feeling and art, and they won her the sympathy of the whole nation.

As Austrian Poland (Galitzia) is enjoying a perfect home-rule, the authorities are all Polish, and Lwów (Lemberg), its capital, is their chief residence. A great many young people whom I had known in Cracow in old times had risen to high dignities. The old acquaintance was not forgotten, and thus it happened that I was the recipient of many courtesies in the official spheres. The most remarkable career was achieved by two of our young friends, the brothers Badeni. The older Count Casimir Badeni became governor of the province, and his administration had such brilliant results that Emperor Francis Joseph called him to Vienna as the premier of the Austrian Cabinet. Representing the Polish nationality, as well as the Slavonic element of the empire, he was attacked violently by the German opposition, and had to resign after a term of most brilliant statesmanlike leadership.

Equally able, if not more so, is his brother, Count Stanislas Badeni, who has many times been the so-called marshal of the province — "Land Marshal." This office belongs only to Austria. It is somewhat parallel to the governorship, and the authority is divided between the two. While the governor represents the central government, the marshal is the chief of the home-rule authorities. Count Stanislas Badeni was always greatly interested in the theatre, and hence the special friendship with which he honored us.

Prince Eustache Sanguszko, for some time also marshal of the province, later on governor, was another one of those who entertained us during our stay in Lwów. His was a charming nature, not at all self-assertive, rather timid, but exceedingly sympathetic.

But the last one whom we met in the governor's chair

during our last visit to Poland (1902), and with whom we were bound most closely, is a man whose recent death by the hand of an assassin has shocked the whole civilized world, Count André Potocki, the son of Count Adam and the grandson of that grand and excellent lady, Madame Arthur, of whom I spoke in the first part of these memoirs, and who showed me such a marked partiality. It is almost impossible to realize that such a man could excite hatred. As governor of the province, he was probably the most conscientious official in the whole Austrian Empire; he worked continually for the welfare of all, and was renowned for his impartiality as well as for his reforming tendencies. Master of an enormous fortune, bearer of the greatest name in Poland, and without a blemish in his private life, a happy husband and father of a numerous family, he might have enjoyed a life of ease. But he was essentially a man of duty, believing in the old adage, "Noblesse oblige"; and in the hope of being able to do good to his countrymen he entered the public service.

Is it not a strange and terrible anomaly that the anarchists choose so frequently for their victims, not the oppressors, not the tyrants, but those who are doing their best to remedy the evils inherent to our present social system?

To-day it is the widow of the murdered Polish statesman, the Countess André Potocka, a representative of the highest type of Polish and Christian womanhood, she who has suffered the most by the crime, it is she who intercedes for the life of the assassin.

My last visit to Poland was made exceptionally pleasant through the kind attentions of both Count André Potocki and Count Stanislas Badeni. They both endeavored to keep me in the country, in order to take up the management and artistic direction of both our Galitzian National Theatres, the one in Lemberg and the one in Cracow. It was with a heavy heart that I refused the offer of this honorable position, which would have been such a beautiful crowning of my artistic career, but I did not think I could do justice to the task.

During these frequent returns to Poland I passed a great deal of time with the family of my husband, in the Duchy of Posen. I think it only fair to say a few words about those dear people, whom I cherish as my own. I am proud to say that few families in our country enjoy the respect with which the Chlapowskis are surrounded. And it is only just, for they deserve it in full. Conservative, though far from being reactionaries, broad-minded, and cultured, they are, before all, genuine Christians and ardent patriots.

There are only four of the immediate family left: my husband, his sister Anna, married to a cousin, Casimir Chlapowski, Doctor Francis, and Joseph.

Madame Anna I have already spoken of. Even in the best Polish society I did not meet many women of such gracious manners, such intellectual turn of mind, such affability and simplicity. Deeply interested both in letters and sciences, she charms one with her brilliant conversation. But all her best faculties are concentrated in her devotion to her husband and children.

Mr. Casimir Chlapowski, son of the great general, reminds one very much of his father. He is the man who, on account of his chivalrous disposition, has been called by one of the great French writers, Montalembert, "the last *gentilhomme* of Europe." Exceedingly simple and modest, with an infinite tact, he exerts a great influence in his province, and has been for many years selected as chairman of the great national meetings. Though practically the head of the Catholic Polish party, he is very popular with all the other Polish parties, on account of his moderation and impartiality. He is a member of the House of Peers in Berlin.

Doctor Francis Chlapowski's life has been devoted to

two aims, science and charity. For several years he was a member of the German Parliament, but lately has retired from political activity. Prince Bismarck, in his hatred towards Poles, did him the honor of singling him out during the time of his parliamentary service as an object of animosity. Eminent as a physician as well as a naturalist, he has been for years the chairman of the physical department of the main scientific society in Prussian Poland. But his chief characteristic is his activity in works of charity. He is the prime mover in this sphere, and his personal benevolence, as well as his disinterestedness, is proverbial through the whole country. He recently lost his wife, who was Countess Marie Lubienska, a woman of great heart and charming manners.

The youngest remaining member of the family is Mr. Joseph Chlapowski, eminently a man of action. He was very successful in the management of his estate; his wife is one of the sweetest and most modest women, the Princess Leonie Woroniecka, and they were blessed with an only son, an ideal boy, in whom they centred all their hopes and affections. At the age of nineteen the boy died. The lives of the father and mother were shattered. There seemed nothing left for them. Then it happened that the prominent people of the province selected Joseph Chlapowski for a hard task, but one of the most responsible ones in the country. Some time before a man of great character, Mr. M. Jackowski, had founded an organization called the Agricultural Circles. The latter were societies of peasant farmers, scattered all over the province, intended to develop their agricultural knowledge and thus improve their economic condition.

When Mr. Jackowski died, Joseph Chlapowski became his successor, with the title of "Patron."

Under the direction of both these men the organization increased in size, until to-day it is composed of from three to four hundred local societies, and the economic condition of the peasants has altered radically. Instead of eking out a miserable subsistence, deprived of almost the necessities of life, the present peasant-farmers of the province enjoy many comforts and are free from poverty. The change is wonderful.

The material betterment of this class had as a natural consequence the spread of general culture. Free from the fear of starvation, the poor peasant is becoming a citizen conscious of his duties, conscious of his rights.

To this work Joseph Chlapowski has devoted all his time, and his love for the Polish peasant has filled the void left in his life by his bereavement.

I beg to be excused for crowding together all my European recollections covering the space of nearly twenty years.

This makes my book more like a *scherzo*, if I may borrow Mr. De Morgan's expression, "in jerks and starts," but I would never finish my memoirs had I to make all the trips there and back and give my experiences in chronological order. It is not easy to describe over forty years of a theatrical and private career step by step, and I have to depend on a great deal of compassion and indulgence.

In the year 18 I played in Prague (Bohemia).

Mr. Schubert, who was at the head of the National Theatre, was one of the most courteous of managers, and also a most appreciative one, and he did everything to make my Prague début pleasant and artistic. He gave me an excellent cast and attended all the rehearsals.

It was at first difficult to play with Bohemian actors, but after a while I got quite used to it. Both languages, Polish and Czech, are very much alike and of the same Slavonic origin, and it was quite easy after a while to understand the words. Besides, the National Theatre in Prague possessed such fine and accomplished actors and actresses that it was a pleasure to work with them.

I never had a better Maurice de Saxe or a finer Benedict than the leading man of the Prague Theatre, Mr. Seifert. His manly appearance, his humor, combined with undoubted talent and skill, made all his impersonations stand out in clear outlines, and the whole gave the satisfaction of a finished picture, without being finicking, without muddy or blurred tints, but vigorous, fine in color, and true to nature.

I still remember some of his scenes in "Much Ado About Nothing," and the expression of his face when Beatrice invites him to dinner, for his acting depended mostly upon his expression, not upon the so-called "stage business."

The people in Prague received us very kindly, and we made many excursions with our new friends to the ancient buildings and churches, whose beauties are known to every one who ever visited Prague.

We had several artistic and literary reunions. At one of them the greatest poet of Bohemia, Vrhlicki, improvised and recited the following poem: —

To Helena Modrzejewska

"God looked at the poor down-trodden Poland.
Her brow was crowned with a wreath of thorns, in her side was a bleeding wound.
When He saw how unhappy she was,
He took pity and wanted to soothe her great sorrows:
He bent down from heaven, touched her forehead pale with pain,
Then upon the holy brow of Poland descended Strength and Beauty, and from them you were born.
Misery of the poor, fame, victory, songs of hope, flame of enchantment, smile of joy, — all the soul is longing for, all the heart can desire, — we find all in your art.
Oh! Queen of the beautiful! We greet you!"

Quite confused by the flattering words of the poem, I thanked the poet, and recited snatches from our great masters of thought and expression.

About that time we met Mr. Dvořák, and attended one of this wonderful man's concerts.

Prague seemed to me an unusually hospitable city.

I remember a dinner, given to us by a prominent citizen and his charming wife, which would have staggered any foreigner not acquainted with the local customs. The dinner began at six o'clock and ended at midnight.

There was a peculiar string orchestra in the next room playing during the meals, and after the dessert I wanted to see the instruments and went to look at them. There were such violas, guitars, violins, 'cellos, and bassos as I never saw before. They were of all imaginable sizes, from the tiniest toy-like ones to tremendously large ones, all of them made of some white polished wood. They looked as though they belonged to the same family, composed of ancestors, parents, and great-grandchildren. They also had names it would take any one a month to learn by heart, but when all those instruments were joined in one harmony, the effect was wonderful.

When I came back to the dining room, my amazement was great. I saw some new guests at the table, and the hostess invited me to sit down with them. The newcomers were those who could not come to the early dinner.

This dinner over, new people arrived, mostly prominent actors or musicians, who, being engaged early in the evening, could not come at the regular hour; but when they came after ten o'clock another dinner was served to them, beginning with soup, down to the dessert and black coffee.

We sat at the table six hours, watching the consecutive parties of diners, until we began to feel hungry again and ready for supper, which was, of course, provided in the same profusion.

The orchestra did not stop playing for a moment, although I saw many platters and bottles sent over to their room by the hospitable and thoughtful hostess.

All together, the month I spent in Prague was one of the most enjoyable in my career. It would be impossible to remember all the kind attentions showered on me. The welcome was extended both to the star and to the daughter of a nation akin to their own.

The last performance was, of course, an ovation, and after the curtain fell, the director of the theatre read from the stage a series of telegrams addressed to me, from about twenty or thirty town councils in Bohemia, full of congratulations and sympathy.

The extraordinary dinner described above reminds me of some original receptions our Polish actors arranged for me.

The most interesting one was a sleigh-ride with torches, on the occasion of our visit to Lemberg during the winter of 1882. The night was dark. Over twenty tiny sleighs were waiting at the entrance of the theatre, and at the side of each of them there was a man on horseback, with a torch in his hand, and this train of sleighs was headed by a small band of musicians. As soon as we started, a jolly air of Krakowiak resounded in the air, filling the hearts with merriment. Many windows opened to see our folly, many people in the street sent their laughing "Hurray" after us. When we left the city, the music stopped, and then a wild ride took place. We were almost flying in the air — at least it seemed so to me. My husband and myself could scarcely catch our breath; the snow sent up by the horses' hoofs was beating in our faces, and the men with torches looked like demons on their nocturnal ride in search for wicked souls.

It was all picturesque, refreshing, and jolly. After fifteen minutes of this extravagant pace, the horses slackened their gait, the musicians resumed their jolly airs, and in a few minutes we stopped at the door of a country house. The hospitable owner of the mansion and his wife greeted us warmly and invited us to come into their home. We found the large hall brightly lighted, and some refreshments served. The musicians came in; the air of a *valse* filled the hall, and dancing began.

Two hours later we were on our return to the city, where in an immense dining-room of a club the supper was served and speeches delivered. Some of them were in prose, some in rhymes, but all had only one object — art.

The whole character of that evening was purely Bohemian, and there was not one weary moment during the five or six hours we spent in the company of our congenial fellow-actors.

Another evening I remember, a few years later, Mr. Pawlikowski, the manager and director of the Cracow Theatre, together with the actors, gave us an original supper. When we entered the dining room, we were greeted by a chorus.

At each plate was placed a wreath of roses, which every one, men and women, had to put on their heads. The women looked pretty in them, so did the young boys; some faces with too many wrinkles and purple tints in their complexion looked sad, indeed, in those flowery ornaments, but to the men past thirty who were afflicted by a visible devastation of their foreheads, the wreaths were exceedingly becoming. Our manager looked twenty-five, and I thought that the renovation of the Roman fashion was a very ingenious one.

I never heard so many improvised witty toasts — all in rhymes — at any other banquet. There were poems recited, parodies, epigrams of all sorts, and the time flew so rapidly that it was almost daylight when we parted.

The manager and some of his guests offered to accompany us to the hotel. Our character actor liked his wreath so much that he left his hat behind, and went with us with that flowery halo on his head. When we passed before the church, there were a few women standing in front of it, waiting for the opening of the gate. We also wanted to go in and hear the early Mass, but we dared not on account of our garlanded companion. Besides, when those poor women looked at us they all turned their faces towards the gate and, no doubt, said a prayer for the wicked. We had to hasten away.

It was shortly before this that Mr. Tadeusz Pawlikowski had become the manager and lessee of the Cracow Theatre. A man of great culture and means, he saved the Cracow stage from utter decrepitude and lifted it up almost to the same high standard it had at the time of Stanislaw Kozmian. New forces were introduced, and most gorgeous productions took place upon that almost poverty-stricken stage, which, going from one hand to another, had lost gradually all its brilliancy and attraction.

Actors who had been kept in the background came in front, and many young talents found their way to success.

The most prominent actor was then, and is now, Ludwik Solski. He has a gift of making up his face in such a way that the paint cannot be seen at two steps' distance, and the range of his parts is enormous. He is intense, humorous, passionate, or light-hearted at will, and though all his parts have a stamp of strong individuality, they are true to nature and never conventional. He is at present the manager and stage director of the endowed theatre in Cracow.

Madame Solska, his wife, is a very talented woman of diaphanous appearance, poetic and original.

Kaminski is, above all, a character actor, very unique in his style. A great favorite of the public, he occupies the position of stage director in Warsaw.

There is also Madame Siemiaszko, called "Elemental." She is fine in passionate, primitive characters.

Since I mentioned our modern actors, it is essential that I should say a few words about the authors who provided them with new characters and gave them opportunity of showing the different sides of their talents.

I should have written about them in the first place, especially of the greatest one, who electrified the whole country with his acutely painful creations — Stanislaw Wyspianski, poet, artist, and dramatic author. His plays are entirely original, both in their themes and their construction — very often symbolical. After having written a few mythological plays in the style of the old Greek tragedies, he turned to national subjects. Though full of ardent patriotism, they are free from any tendency to flatter his country; on the contrary, all of his works are marked with a touch of pessimism, born from the grief of a desperate heart that feels intensely the wrongs of Poland. The most popular of his dramas is entitled "The Wedding."

Not only a writer but an accomplished artist, he ornamented many of our churches with his works. His frescos, and especially his stained windows, are of unusual beauty.

He died last year, 1907, at the age of thirty-five, and was conveyed to his grave on the Wawel [1] by an immense multitude of all classes of people, rich and poor, nobles and peasants.

Next to him, Lucian Rydel, another poet and playwright, though not of the same magnitude, yet highly endowed, made a great success in "The Enchanted Circle" and in "Jaselka," the latter in the style of old mystery plays.

Of a different stamp, but also very talented, is Madame Gabriela Zapolska. Her plays are realistic, and most of them represent scenes of Polish life under Russian despotism. Some of them treat of social questions. Her "Malka Schwarzenkopf," taken from the life of the poorest Jewish classes, has achieved the greatest popularity.

[1] The Kings' containing the graves of the Polish kings, also those of Kosciuszko and Mickiewicz.

CHAPTER XLIX

In the spring of 1884, after a few weeks in the Lyceum at London and in the English provinces, I played in Ireland, where I was greeted with an unusual courtesy. The Lord Mayor's carriage took us from the station to the hotel, and his private secretary, Mr. Cox, was appointed to show us the beauties of the city and the surrounding country places.

We owed this favor to our friend, Mr. Justin McCarthy, who was also a friend of the mayor. It was not the first nor the last proof of Mr. McCarthy's kindness to us.

Strange to say that such an innocent thing as driving in an official carriage would arouse suspicion, but the fact was that we were taken for political agitators, as it proved towards the end of my engagement. In the meantime, perfectly ignorant of our "dangerous" character, we enjoyed the beauties of the city and its surroundings.

Our "rainy" days, for it always rains in Ireland, were spent in the open. Always accompanied by Mr. Cox, who arranged excursions to the enchanting spots in the country, we passed the days in visiting the hills, rocks, meadows, and lakes, and in the evenings I played with pleasure before the impulsive, cheering audiences, for they *did* cheer as only Irish people can do. At the performance of "Marie Stuart" they grew almost frantic, and every sentence against Elizabeth and the English government called forth vehement acclamations.

After the last performance of my engagement in Dublin, the demands for a speech were so insistent that I was obliged to say a few words to the dear public. I believe I made a slight allusion to their sympathy for the daughter of an oppressed country, but it was said only in the way of explaining the great enthusiasm I was received with; it was a smiling and a modest "perhaps," rather than a statement, and I saw no harm in it.

When I was ready to return to the hotel, I looked for my husband, and seeing he was very busy talking to Mr. Cox and Mr. Redmond, — not wishing to interrupt their discourse,—I left the theatre with my maid. Our hotel was only at a short distance from the theatre, and I thought he would prefer to walk.

When I entered the brougham with my maid, I saw a man climbing quickly on the box, and we started on a very sharp trot in just the opposite direction from our hotel. My maid called to the coachman to turn back, but he was deaf to her entreaties, and proceeded on his own way until we were far away on a country road. The girl grew hysterical, and I also was very much frightened. Dreadful pictures of robbers, kidnapping, shooting, and I don't know what other horrors followed each other in my imagination. Suddenly we stopped short. Now, I thought, was the time for some catastrophe. But instead of that the brougham turned back, and we were trotting in the direction of the city. After a fifteen minutes' drive we came to the corner of our street, and stopped again for a moment to let the man on the box jump down and disappear in the gloom of the night.

My husband, who was very anxious about me, had looked in all directions for our brougham, and now, exhausted with running about, stood before the hotel, leaning against the pillar. Mr. Cox and Redmond were with him. When he saw the brougham, he exclaimed, "Here she is!" and I fairly fell into his arms descending from my treacherous conveyance.

When we all came to our drawing-room on the first floor, I learned that the man on the box was a detective.

Some enthusiasts wanted to honor me by taking the horses out of my carriage and putting themselves in harness, to bring me in triumph to the hotel. This project being overheard by the same detective, he was bound to spoil the fun by giving me a half-hour's drive. "But why?" I asked.

"God only knows," was the answer.

I had scarcely time to take off my hat and wraps when a *gendarme* entered the room without knocking, said "Good evening," and apparently took a mental note of the people in the room, for he looked from one to another and then left the room, wishing my husband and myself a good journey, for we had to leave next morning by the boat.

The crowd gathered before the hotel began slowly to disperse during my involuntary excursion with the guardian angel on the box, but some people still remained waiting for me. Seeing me coming, they brought back the brass band, and I was cheered again and called for. There was no means of escaping, for they saw me and knew I was in my room. I was advised to come to the window and thank the people for their truly Irish hospitality.

What was my amazement when next day I saw the same silly *gendarme* coming on the boat and saying that he wanted to see us safely off.

We could not thank Mr. Redmond and Mr. Cox sufficiently for their courtesies, and parted from them with the feeling of taking leave of old friends.

We knew many charming people in Dublin. One who has never met the real Irish society has no idea what fine specimens of true gentlemen and ladies are among them. Irish beauty and wit make a charming combination. There is more of French than Anglo-Saxon element in their composition, with one advantage—simplicity. They never are arrogant either, but their gentle wit is a powerful weapon against intruders.

We went for the summer months of 1885 to Zakopane, and then to our new home in Cracow, built with the hope of living in it after my retirement from the stage, in two or three years.

My son returned from Paris, having completed his studies, and directly became engaged to his cousin, Felicie Benda, my half-brother's daughter.

In September we all four sailed for America, as well as my two maids, and a little mountaineer boy whom we transformed into a "tiger," or, as they also called them, "buttons." His occupation on the steamer was to take care of my jewel-case, but my husband had often to dress or undress him, for he did not know how to manage his livery, having worn hitherto only a mountaineer's costume.

He was very tiny, though ten years old, and when he was seasick, Mr. Chlapowski had to carry him on deck. Finally he engaged a nurse to take special care of him.

I played the season of 1885–1886 under Daniel Frohman's management, and Mr. Vanderfelt, a very fine English actor, was my leading man. Mary Shaw was also engaged, and Charles Vandenhoff for heavy lead.

I added "Two Gentlemen of Verona" and "Cymbeline" to my repertoire; also a French play of short existence, called "Prince Zillah," was given occasionally.

My son obtained a position as a civil engineer directly after we arrived in New York through the intercession of our dear friend, Mr. Prescott Hall Butler, and departed immediately to Omaha, to take the place offered him by the bridge-builder, Mr. Morisson.

In December, 1885, during my engagement in New York, the affianced couple were married.

Nothing worthy of special comment happened during the remaining season. Mr. Frohman was very fond of "Adrienne

Lecouvreur." He wanted to give it everywhere, and as often as it was possible to do so without injuring the receipts of the box-office. He went so far with his hobby that even this consideration, so essential to the managers, was sometimes disregarded.

When we were going to St. Paul, I advised him not to

E. H. Vanderfelt.

give "Adrienne," but play a Shakespearian repertoire of three plays and "Marie Stuart." I had been in St. Paul before and knew the taste of the audiences, who disliked Scribe's play. I suppose not because it was French, for "Camille" was their favorite, but because no one liked to go to a play with an unpronounceable name, — at least to the majority of people.

A young lady once said to me: "I don't like those titles I cannot read fluently. If any one would ask me in what part I saw you, I would be obliged to blush and stammer, 'Oh, in that French actress, you know.' It is not comfortable at all."

Mr. Frohman consented to have Shakespeare, but wanted absolutely one performance of "Adrienne."

There was a good sale for every play but "Adrienne," and on the night of the performance I was chilled through when I saw the immense gap here and there studded with a human face. Not one of the boxes was taken, but there was a pale, smiling face looking at me from the stage-box, as much as to say, "Never mind, I am contented."

Needless to say, it was Daniel Frohman, who, like the celebrated king of Bavaria, had the performance all to himself.

Of all the managers I met in America, Mr. Frohman was certainly the kindest and most considerate one.

After we had our bungalow in California, we spent most of the summers in San Iago Cañon, and that was the reason I did not return to England any more.

Almost every two years we went to Europe, and usually spent a few months in Poland. I have written already about those visits, and will not dwell on them any more, but pass to my engagement with Edwin Booth.

My American tours were very exhausting, and my husband did not wish me to play during the spring London season after thirty or thirty-five weeks of mental and physical exertion.

In 1886 Mr. Chlapowski took again the management in his hands, with Fred Stinson as business manager, and we produced "Les Chouans," a play based on Balzac's novel of the same title, and written by Monsieur Pierre Berton, a very talented French actor and author. The play, how-

Madame Modjeska's California Residence.

ever, required such great production and so many people that we could not keep it long on the bills. The bulk of scenery and the number of extra men and women were very hard to handle and carry about the country. Besides that, we had our Shakespearian productions, requiring not only scenery but furniture and a great number of costumes.

Photograph by Sarony.

ROBERT TABOR.

Had we played but this one play, we could have managed to pull it through with fine results, but I would not give up Shakespeare, and preferred to lose "Les Chouans."

I introduced "Measure for Measure" to the public. It had not been given since Adelaide Neilson's time. My company that season was very numerous and fine: there was Maurice Barrymore, Mary Shaw, Charles Vandenhoff, who made a hit in "Les Chouans"; William Owen, Ian Robertson, brother of Forbes, stage-manager; and a very good actor; the dainty Hamilton Bell, Mrs. Grace Henderson, Mr. Carhart, etc.; and Robert Tabor, who was then a beginner, but who filled his parts with care and intelligence. In recent years he made a success of Macduff in London, but soon afterwards death put an end to his theatrical career.

When Mr. Lawrence Barrett was Booth's manager, I

received a letter from him, offering me an engagement as co-star with Edwin Booth. In reply to Mr. Barrett, I informed him that I was under contract, but willing to accept his proposal, provided the firm of Nixon and Zimmerman would release me.

I was released, to my great satisfaction, at the cost of $400 a week, which came off my salary to the firm of N. and Z. I much preferred to be with Edwin Booth than to play with insufficient support under a commercial management, and I did not think I made a sacrifice in giving up a few dollars for my artistic comfort.

I played with him Ophelia, Lady Macbeth, Portia, and Julie in "Richelieu." Besides these, we had two double bills; with Booth's "Fool's Revenge" I played "Dona Diana"; with his "Taming of the Shrew" I played "Marie Stuart." Those double plays were given usually on Saturday evenings or Wednesdays. The same was the case with the other double bill, — that of "Don César de Bazan" and "Marie Stuart" reduced to four acts.

The support was very fine, — Otis Skinner, Charles Hanford, Ben Rodgers, Owen Fawcett, Miss Annie Proctor, Lawrence Hanley, and other talented young men and women.

My season with Edwin Booth was delightful. I found him one of the kindest and pleasantest men of the profession. He also possessed what I considered a great quality — simplicity of manner.

Some stars have the idea that it is necessary to be haughty and inaccessible with the members of their companies. They put on airs, they like to crush the fellow-actor and pose as a kind of divinity before them. They even sometimes are most rude and insulting. I have heard of some who call women names, and behave altogether as slave-drivers.

Those may have fame and money, but they are not great,

Photograph by Sarony.

LAWRENCE BARRETT.

because true greatness means strength; and the strong like to fight only the equal, but do not take pleasure in abusing the weak.

That some managers are rude is another matter. No one looks for fine manners in them; all we expect is to find them good business men. But an actor who deals with subtilties of human nature is supposed to possess nobility of soul and refinement.

If they act upon the stage as though they possessed those qualities, it would do them good to practise them in real life. In Edwin Booth those qualities were inborn, and the result was that every one loved him, and all the remarks he made to the actors of his company were received as favors rather than reproofs.

I made a few notes on our life in the private car, which may throw more light upon the intimate character of that wonderful man and artist.

MILWAUKEE, April 22, Tuesday Night.

We played "Hamlet" last night.

Ralph and Félicie have gone — at 1.40 P.M. We did not cry at parting — we hope to meet again in Poland. Only when the train disappeared from the station the tears came to my eyes. I slept the whole afternoon in order to calm myself.

The audiences were cold and unsympathetic.

After the performance we went to the car and had supper. Edwin Booth was delightful. He told us some of his early experiences: how in Honolulu he was compelled to paste his own bills on the corners of the streets, and was surprised at that work by a fellow from New York who happened to be there just at the time. This happened, of course, some years ago, about thirty-five, I think.

I went to bed directly after supper, but I heard him talking to the ladies of the company for more than an hour. They all shrieked with laughter.

CEDAR RAPIDS, April 23.

We arrived about 1 P.M., and after breakfast Charles and I went for a walk. It was a bright morning, and we felt like students in

Photograph by Stein, Chicago

vacation time. Cedar Rapids is a regular country town, quiet and uninteresting.

At dinner Edwin Booth told more anecdotes about himself. He is a good talker; in fact, once started, he is a great talker.

We sat at the table in the following order: —

Edwin Booth at the head of the table, then I on his right, opposite Mr. Chase, our business manager, and Mr. Bromley, the treasurer. My husband sits next to me. Edwin Booth has no vis-à-vis but a mirror, so that he is not obliged to look at any one but himself. But this has not been arranged with premeditation, I am sure.

I am still reading Wagner's and Liszt's letters, and the sentence, "Do something new, new, and once more new" comes very often to my mind, and I long for some new parts again.

E. B. is just taking his nap, and I can hear in my stateroom his regular and sonorous breathing, commonly called "snoring." I am writing, and thinking how "treacherous all earthly blessings are." But I do not want to be despondent because some ideal persons will snore.

The day is beautiful, the birds are singing, and the chickens make quite a pretty picture on the fence.

Sophie just told me in secret that — but secrets are secrets, and I am not going to gossip. "This is spring, my child," I said, "and Nature is responsible for it."

"Oh! oh! oh!" I exclaimed, and put my handkerchief to my nose when we passed the threshold of the Cedar Rapids temple of art. "I wonder if there is in Hades a corner which smells as badly as that!" We learned later that a tannery was just back of the theatre. We burned pastilles, Chinese sticks, paper, and at last cotton in order to drown that terrible odor. I sprinkled the stage with eau de cologne, and smelt my bottle during the whole act in fear of fainting, but in the court scene I felt positively sick.

How I wished some of the stage-struck girls could have been here last night, that I could give them the pleasure of smelling the stage, which, in their imagination, is a heavenly ground strewn with roses. If any of them could see the dressing-room poor Portia occupied, they would shrink from this deceitful Paradise, go home, and thank Heaven and their good parents for a comfortable home. Of course, for those who have no home it may be better than to live in the open — just for a change of air. "Anything for change," some Frenchman said. Well, it is quite a French idea, superficial, as many French things are. I wish I could get him at the Cedar Rapids Theatre.

Last night we had a very interesting conversation about London and Henry Irving, and are both agreed that Irving is a "great man." "Not a great actor — but a great man," said Edwin Booth. "His knowledge of human nature — and his fibs are equally great."

We returned from our walk. I tried to induce E. B. to go out, but he would not. In fact, he never goes out. All exercise tires him and makes him unfit for the evening work. I noticed that his left arm is a little stiff. He showed us where it was broken. He broke it in falling from a dog-cart, and it never has been properly mended.

April 24.

Davenport is another uninteresting town, and dirty. We met some of the members of our company walking. Oh! the treacherous spring!

Peoria is another not highly interesting city. We took our usual walk, strolling about and stopping before the shops and posters of Madame Janauschek. What a strong, expressive face, and what genius! I wish I possessed half of her powers.

At dinner, or rather after dinner, E. B. told us many witty things — which also I do not recollect. I stopped writing my diary for a few days in order to make sketches. The consequence is that I made a few very bad sketches and forgot many nice things I heard. However, I remember that at supper we spoke of Shakespeare, and then I had the opportunity of learning how deeply and thoroughly Booth studies his parts. He says he has no ear for music, but any mistake in blank verse jars upon him as a false note. Of course he puts a great stress upon pronunciation, emphasis, and inflections of the voice, and he kindly pointed out some of my mistakes in pronunciation, which I gratefully accepted, and tried to correct myself at the next performance. They were all concerning Lady Macbeth. Then he said that at first he did not like Portia's putting her hand on Shylock's arm in the "Mercy" speech; but after a thought, I came to the conclusion that it was well conceived and a beautiful bit of business. He also said that my delivery of the "Mercy" speech was "admirable." I felt highly flattered, and happy, of course. It seems that the reason why he has not studied any new parts for a long time is that, whenever he put a new play on the bills, the audience kept away from it and were asking for "Hamlet," "Richelieu," etc. — plays which he has played for years. It is a very strange thing that people should be so conservative in their taste, but it is certainly the case with Americans, and the older the play the better "the draw."

He played "Richard III," studied "King John," played Cardinal Wolsey in "Henry VIII," and some other parts, but without success; not because they were criticised, but because the people liked the old favorites better.

"Merchant of Venice" was the play that night.

DECATUR, April 26.

"Hamlet" on the bills.

We had wretched weather. Everything looked gloomy and dirty, and the view from the car was sad enough to render melancholy even the poor pigs which were strolling slowly in the cool mud, grunting and sulky.

E. B. played Hamlet beautifully. I watched behind the scenes, and was deeply impressed. This put me on my mettle, and I played Ophelia better than usual. The pale face of Mrs. E., who recently lost her father, followed me through the play. A strange tenderness took possession of me when I sang, "White his shroud as a mountain snow," and tears came to my eyes because I felt her watching me from her box. Never have I understood the words of Liszt better. "We must become wise by means of feeling. Reason tells us 'so it is' only after feeling has told us 'so it must be.'"

After the performance we were chatting as usual about different matters, and again the conversation turned on the "shop."

E. B. says that Charlotte Cushman was really beautiful when she was old. Her face softened with age, and the pain she suffered gave her face an exalted look which she never had in her youth. She used to copy all Macready's peculiarities, even to his voice; having played with him for years, she involuntarily imitated him. Forrest used to call her Macready in petticoats, and she called him a brute, and they disliked each other profoundly.

The next day was Sunday. The birds woke me up. It was a glorious morning. I dressed and went out with Charles. There was something solemn and yet sweet and touching in this awakening of a spring day. We felt so happy that we wanted to embrace each other in the street.

The air had the same fragrance as it has in Poland. The day before last we received some letters from the old country and from my children.

Our hearts were full of home, and as we walked slowly side by side we were exchanging various recollections and making plans

Charlotte Cushman.

concerning our journey to Europe, or rather to Poland. I yearned for this journey with the eagerness of a child for the sight of his mother — and I dreaded it also. Will my friends be the same to me as before? I have not written to any one there since I left the country, — that is five years ago, — and they have a right to be angry with me.

Shall I play in Warsaw, and how will the audiences like me now, after all these years? When I last appeared before them, I was still called "the bewitching Madame Helena," and now I come back the grandmother of a grandson three years old.

I know I have not lost any of my powers, and my talent is now in its full vigor, but I fear the people will look for wrinkles on my face and, what is worse, they will find some. The wrinkles on a woman's face are a marvellous cooling agent in the stream of enthusiasm, although those on my own do not show on the stage, being not very numerous or very deep; yet I am afraid of the critical eyes of our countrymen. But, never mind! If I fail, I will kiss my little grandson, and find consolation in his blue eyes. My dear baby, he will in a few days be on the ocean with my older babies, his parents. May God bless you, my dear little crowd, and grant you a happy and quiet passage.

When we came home on Sunday, we found E. B smoking his cigar in the observation-room. He opened the door for us, and said, "Tickets," imitating the conductor. Then, of course, we all laughed and chatted until dinner-time. After dinner Mr. and Mrs. E. took us for a drive and then to their house.

A country house is always more or less attractive to me, and I spent my afternoon in the atmosphere of goodness, hospitality, and that little provincial *naïveté* which is so delightful in small doses, and then the children were so pretty. What did we talk about? Everything and nothing.

It was nearly eight o'clock when we came home, I mean to the private car. The name of the car is "Hazlemere." E. B. did not go out at all. I am afraid his health is failing rapidly. Yet he was in a splendid mood, and we sat until two o'clock in the morning, talking. How many things he remembers! It would be impossible to put down all I heard that evening; but I remember that we talked of spiritualism, art, and travel, and also a little about actors. When I say we talked, it means that he talked, and my husband a little; I only listened and marvelled at E. B.'s narrative gift, his impressionability, brightness, and intelligence, of which those who do not know him cannot have any idea. Very often

I heard people say: "He is getting old — he never talks;" or, "Is he interesting in private? Is his conversation original?" etc. Those are the individuals who do not know him sufficiently. His chief fault is indolence, and also that which his father described as a "bump of I-don't-care-a-damnativeness." He does not like to do anything for show either, and the result is that when he is with people it is only when he has confidence in them that he likes to open the valve of his eloquence, and then he is quite fascinating.

BLOOMINGTON, April 28.

"Macbeth."

Another queer little place. Nothing happened through the day. We took our usual walk. I brought down flowers to decorate the dining table; after dinner I wrote letters and at seven o'clock we went to the theatre.

What a queer little stage!

My dressing-room was painted with vermilion red, which made one's eyes smart.

Everything was trivial and common about the place, even to the inscriptions on the manager's notice, which usually is put in the dressing-rooms. On those notices there were remarks in pencil, apparently written by some disappointed actors, and I am sorry to say they were all of a startling vulgarity.

Otis Skinner wore his natural legs without fleshings in Macduff last night. They were painted with red, brown, and magenta — imitating the various cuts and wounds Macduff is supposed to have received in the battle. It was effective.

INDIANAPOLIS, April 29.

We arrived at 2 o'clock P.M.

We played "Macbeth," again, and this time Vroom and Hanley joined Otis Skinner in the bare-leg show. Skinner and Vroom's limbs were painted, and they looked natural, but Hanley's white and plump columns looked out of place. It was a cool night, and they were shivering, but proud of their appearance. The next morning a notice appeared in the paper: "Macduff, Malcolm, and Ross were more realistic than effective. A little less meat and a little more dressing would have been not only more artistic but more agreeable."

VINCENNES, April 30.

We played "Hamlet." The managers in small towns seem to have a mania for notices. This time it was placed on the tin

Photograph by Sarony.

Otis Skinner.

trough of a reflector inside of the footlights. When E. B. left the stage after the first scene, he said to me, "Just read that notice in the footlights." Otis Skinner, who played Laertes, and myself were just going on, and I nearly laughed aloud when I read the notice, "Do not spit in this trough." It was repeated three times, on each end and in the middle of the footlights. Of course it directly became the joke of the evening, and when Ben Rogers (Polonius) finished his advice to Laertes, he added in a low tone of voice, "and do not spit in this trough."

What a nice old man Ben is. I take real pleasure in talking to him behind the scenes. He is always cheerful, contented. I never heard him grumbling or complaining, and even when the company has to get up at 5 A.M. to catch the train, and when everybody looks lined and wornout in the evening, he is full of spirit and jolly as ever. I asked him once if the travelling did not tire him. "What?" exclaimed he, "a young man like me tired? Never!" He is over seventy years old. He is not only a nice man, but also a very excellent comedian. His father in "Garrick," his Gobbo, Polonius, and Dogberry are perfect types.

At supper E. B. was not feeling well, yet he was very interesting. He told us that once his brother Junius, who was a manager at that time, wanted him to play a part which was supposed to have been written especially to suit all his talents, and in which he had to play the fiddle, sing and dance. It seems, however, that the musical and terpsichorean capability of our tragedian did not inspire him with sufficient confidence to produce them before the public. Therefore fiddle, song, and dance were cast out of the part. He said also that most of the time he played comedy in his early days.

We had a special train, and the ladies were invited to the car. After supper E. B. went to the observation-room to smoke his cigar. There he found the ladies and Mr. Smith, who, being the husband of Mrs. Smith, enjoys also the privilege of being invited to the car. Otis Skinner and Ben Rogers — one because he is a leading man, and the other because of his age — are also invited usually.

The train was rattling along, making a dreadful noise. We chattered away about last night's performance, about the flowers Miss Proctor had gathered in the fields, dress, and other important matters, and E. B. was talking with Charles. I could not hear what he was saying, but I followed the movement of his hands, and nearly understood what he said. His hands and his eyes are remarkably expressive. He was describing some Indians and the way they shoot, and I could almost see the arrows fly in the air and the savage faces of the Indians. When the noise was less terrible, I heard him giving a very graphic description of his visit to the Mammoth Cave in Kentucky. He never says too much or too little, and that's what makes everything he says so interesting. I think that this is characteristic, even in his acting; that he always finds a right measure; even when situations might tempt one to exaggerate he very seldom oversteps the limits. There may be made an exception in one or two instances in "Richelieu," but in Shakespeare — never. He gives rather too little than too much sometimes, but for that only the state of his health is responsible. He often feels tired and ill. I heard him saying after some scenes, "I wish I had all my strength and vigor to play this as I ought to play it."

LOUISVILLE, May 1.

We left the car and stopped at the hotel that night.

When I came to the theatre, I found my dressing-room beautifully decorated with branches and flowers. A mysterious-looking red electric light shone through them on the table, and the walls were overhung with wild flowers and ivy. This was done on the occasion of the first day of May and at Miss Proctor's suggestion. She and four or five young people went to the woods and brought almost a car load of flowers and other plants, and they decorated E. B.'s and my room. Miss Proctor is full of pretty conceits and she loves flowers passionately. I used to give her flowers and wondered very often at the length of time she kept them fresh. It is the way she handles them that makes them live, I think.

We played "Macbeth," and I consulted Booth about the cuts we intended to make. In the banquet scene, my speech beginning with the words, "Oh, proper stuff!" seemed to us too long, and we agreed that it was far better to shorten it. It goes now as follows: —

"Oh, proper stuff,
This is the very painting of thy fear —
Shame itself — why do you make such faces?
When all's done you look but on a stool."

Also in the preceding speech: —

"Sit, worthy lords,
My lord is often thus and has been
From his youth. Feed and regard him not."

May 3.

"Hamlet," matinée; "Merchant of Venice" at night.

The performance of "Merchant of Venice" lasted until midnight. I thought that half of the audiences would go out, but they stayed until the last moment. When we came home it was nearly 1 A.M.

May 4, Sunday, on the road.

We have changed the car, and this one is called "Newport." It is not as pretty or comfortable as "Hazlemere" and not as clean, being an old car. We spent the whole day sitting in the observation-room — talking or reading. When it grew dark, I sat on the platform.

Mr. Booth looked pale and tired. We knew he was not well. He tried to read by the dim light of the car lamps. I went to our room, brought two candles, Charles carried the footstool, and we placed the candles on it and put the whole on the sofa at Booth's elbow. He turned to us with an angelic smile, and said, "How good you both are!" in a tone of voice which might have been interpreted as an expression of surprise.

After this he resumed his reading, and I went back on the platform to spin the thread of thoughts which were all flying towards the Atlantic Ocean, where my little crowd were seeking their way to Poland, and where my fancy preceded them.

How many times in the past did I sit, on such a cool evening, dreaming only of fame! How different my dreams are now. I would I had no fame, but a home full of loving creatures. The long winter evenings of my youth come to my mind, with their indescribable charm, when our mother sat at the table with her work and we sat around, one of us reading aloud and the rest busy with drawing or sewing. How far these evenings are from me now! Will they ever be repeated in my life? Shall I ever be free from care and this absorbing work? Perhaps.

DAYTON, May 5. "Merchant."

I spent the day reading in my room.

We played "Merchant of Venice," and after the play, at supper, we spoke about trees. I said that in Los Angeles there are two date palms standing together, a male and a female. They are both very tall, but the male is a great deal taller than the other, and they look like a pair of lovers. The smaller one is almost clinging to the other as with loving affection. People seem to have respect for them, for, in spite of a rage for building and cutting all the trees around, they left this pair untouched. Mr. Booth said: "I think the trees have feeling. I do not know what religion I have, but I believe that the trees love us when we treat them kindly. Why should we have so much affection for them, if they do not reciprocate it in some unfelt and unseen way? I planted once a grove of trees on my grounds. I sold the place long ago, but I never go to New York or back without stepping on the platform to look at them. They are as dear to me as children."

ZANESVILLE, May 6.

We arrived here at 3 P.M.

I stayed in bed until 1 P.M. I find that the most sensible thing is to lie down when we are not forced to get up. At least I could read at my leisure.

We played "Richelieu."

During the performance we had some amusement. A young man in our company who plays François has been born and brought up in this town. Previous to our coming, the editor of the local paper received a notice disparaging the company, but praising him highly. This notice was repeated in the paper. It is easily guessed who sent it.

The audience was thus prepared to see this wonder. In the first act, while Richelieu is on the stage, Mr. —— did not wait for his cue, but anticipated E. B.'s words, and walked on with quick steps and dignified demeanor,—a regular "star entrance." The friends in front gave him a round of applause which made everybody behind the scenes laugh. In the fourth act some one threw a bouquet to him, which he picked up gracefully, smiling and bowing — "à la Modjeska," some one said behind me.

Mr. Booth was amused, but said he did not like that sort of thing; they usually do more harm than good to the young men. He is right. Our friends are sometimes our worst enemies. This young man is already frightfully conceited. He exhibits his large photograph in the shop windows, flatters the critics to get good notices, and does many things that would be repulsive to any modest young actor. He may have talent, but if he does not take time to ripen, he may fall off the stem — decayed though green. The sun of flattery is hot and destructive.

WHEELING, May 7.

I read in the paper two or three days ago that there was a fight for tickets in Wheeling; the police interfered, and some people were bruised.

Last night we sat a long time after supper talking. We spoke of Shakespeare, Boucicault, Bacon, Donnelly, etc. Mr. Booth, of course, believes in Shakespeare, and laughs at the cipher cranks and those who try to deny him. As we all agreed, that subject was dismissed, but he spoke of how he studies Shakespeare. He says, "It is not enough to take one edition and study your part from it; you have to see as many as you can get to find the true meaning of a word sometimes." And then he quoted different readings of different people, and it is strange that the most far-fetched meaning is usually the most popular with the actors.

Then we spoke of blank verse and prose, and how difficult it is sometimes when we want to be natural not to fall into the commonplace.

His father was a splendid reader, being at the same time a great actor. He never allowed the little Edwin to look at him while he played. The boy, who used to go with his father in order to help him with the dressing, was kept in the dressing-room and supposed to learn his lessons, but he was all ears, and did not lose one word of his father's reading nor of the other actors, and thus, while still very young, formed his opinion and judgment. His father did not want him to acquire any of his own peculiarities. He used to say, "I want your ear to be educated first."

It seems that Edwin Booth has been three times a star and three times reduced to a position of an ordinary actor in a stock company. His salary while he was engaged at a Philadelphia theatre was six dollars a week, and after two weeks of trial he was discharged for incompetency.

He spoke a great deal about the right pronunciation of certain words on the stage. To make the blank verse sound well he changes the inflection of vowels. In "Hamlet" he pronounces "orisons" with the inflection on the letter "i" — or*i*sons, while it ought to be *or*isons with a short "i" and the inflection on the letter "o." He does it to suit the melody of the blank verse, to avoid the jerky sound which it would produce in the sentence. "In thy *or*isons" — the three first syllables of the verse with the emphasis on "o" would sound harshly.

WHEELING. "Merchant of Venice."

While Mr. Booth was taking his afternoon nap, I sat down to write. Suddenly I heard the voice of our waiter calling the porter to show him the crowd gathered on the shore (our car stopped at the bank of the river). I also looked out, but no one could tell me

Photograph by Falk

what it was. A few minutes later Mr. Chase came in and told me with a smile that a boat had been struck by a steamer and overturned. Twenty people went down — two of them drowned. He said it all with such cheerful expression and such a sweet smile that I thought he was telling me of some advertising trick he had arranged; but I turned to our negro waiter, and seeing his lower lip hanging with a dejected expression, I understood that it was a real accident. Some young people took a tiny boat to go on the other side of the river to a ball game, and coming home they were run into by a steamer. "Two children were drowned and an architect." On my way to the theatre I saw three elderly ladies crying in the street. I was not in a very cheerful mood when Sophie told me that Mr. Bromley had just received news of his mother's death. "What a sad day!" I exclaimed.

The play began as usual. The audience was large and very sympathetic, and I began in a good mood, when, before the third act, Mr. Skinner told me of Charles Vandenhoff's death. That dreadful news spoiled the rest of the evening for me, and I went through the third act with my face flooded with tears.

Charles Vandenhoff was one of those men who were bitterly disliked by some but dearly loved by others. He was the best friend I had in the profession, and both Charles and myself were very fond of him. It is dreadful to think that he, with all the refinement he possessed, all the delicate tastes, should die in a hospital in Washington Territory — a half-civilized country where the word "comfort" is almost unknown. Poor, dear man! What a generous, grateful nature he had! What pains he took to correct my English and instruct me in the meaning of obscure passages in Shakespeare! I did not even write to him lately; it is hard to think of the duties which we have not accomplished, and which we cannot accomplish, because it is too late!

We closed our season in Buffalo. The "Merchant of Venice" was given that night. When we took a call after the court scene, and I looked at Edwin Booth, I had a feeling that I should never see him again, and tears came to my eyes. He might have had a similar idea at the moment, for his eyes were almost moist when, after the falling of the curtain, he said "Good-by" to me. He looked weak and tired as he walked to his room.

We went to Poland that spring and remained there the whole year. When we returned he lived no more.

CHAPTER L

In 1893 I was invited by the Committee of the World's Fair Auxiliary Women's Congress, in Chicago, to take part in the theatrical section of the Congress and to say something about "Woman on the Stage." I dwelt a little on the history of Hroswitha, the so-called nun of Gandersheim, who in the tenth century wrote a series of most remarkable plays, and whose standing in the annals of dramatic literature is unique. Besides me, three other ladies of our profession addressed the Congress: Clara Morris, Georgia Cayvan, and Julia Marlowe. It may be remembered that one of the features of the Congress was a series of national women's delegations, each of them describing the position of women in their country. Among others, there was expected a delegation of ladies from Russian Poland, but none of them came to Chicago. Apparently they were afraid of the possible conflict with their government, and they limited their activity to sending a few statistical notes — ah! most poor, bashful notes!

In the face of this obstacle, wishing by all means to have a representative of our nationality, Mrs. May Wright Sewall, the Chairman of the Executive Board, appealed to me, requesting most urgently that I appear as the proxy of the Polish delegates and speak on their behalf. Mrs. Sewall, who for years has been my friend, put such pressure on me that I finally consented.

I had only half a day to get ready. I scrambled through some of the statistic material sent from Poland, and made a synopsis of the situation of our country.

The auditorium was packed, and I had some difficulty in reaching the platform. The beginning of my speech was an excuse for the absence of my countrywomen from the Congress. I explained that they could not do anything so independent as speaking freely upon the situation of Polish women under the Russian and Prussian government, and then I sketched a few pictures of our existence, such as I knew and had read about.

Warmed up by the subject, and trying to arouse the sympathy of the brilliant audience for our cause, I was probably not careful enough in the choice of my expressions, but I said such words as my heart prompted me at the moment. The people were moved by my words, and expressed in an emphatic way their approval of my feelings. Next day most of the Chicago papers, in big editorials, alluded to my address in a most flattering way, and added their own scathing comments upon the governments which had dismembered Poland, and especially upon Russia. Unfortunately for me, excerpts of the Chicago press were sent over to Europe and repeated both in the English, German, and Russian papers.

Two years later I happened to be in Poland, and immediately upon my arrival I concluded contracts for performances in the theatres of Posen, Cracow, Lemberg, and Warsaw. The president of the latter, a colonel whose name I do not remember, had to submit my contract to the Governor-General, the famous General Hurko, for his approval. When he told him of his errand, the latter remarked, "It will be all right; come back in two days." When the president returned in two days, Hurko upbraided him most violently: "How dare you engage for the Imperial Theatre such a revolutionary 'mateznitza' as this woman? Never as long as I live will she appear here."

Evidently during those two days some interested person had reported to the Governor-General my speech before the

NATIONAL THEATRE, CRACOW, WHERE MADAME MODJESKA LAST PLAYED.

Chicago Congress, and that, of course, had incensed him against me. The president sent me word that my engagement was impossible, relating his conversation with the governor. It was a grievous disappointment for me, because I loved my Warsaw audiences and I knew they loved me.

In the meantime I was negotiating with some St. Petersburg managers about a series of appearances there with a Polish company. The fact of my being prohibited to play in Warsaw would not interfere, they thought, with an engagement in the Russian capital, because the St. Petersburg local authorities were not half as stringent in Polish matters as those of Warsaw. Besides, I could rely there upon the support of a most influential official, General Wahl, whom I had known personally in old times in Warsaw, when he was *aide-de-camp* to the Lieutenant-General of Poland, Count Berg.

So the negotiations went on, and a contract on most favorable terms was signed for an engagement in St. Petersburg in the next spring.

In the meantime I went on playing in Cracow, Lemberg, Posen, and in February my husband and I started on a trip to Italy, with the idea of returning in time for the St. Petersburg appearance. The news I received from my managers was most encouraging: all the preparatory work was going on splendidly, the press wrote very complimentary notices of me, the company was selected and properly rehearsed, the advertising bills were posted, and at last the subscription for tickets was opened. Inside of a few days the seats for ten performances were sold out, and we were telegraphed to come on.

So, about ten days before the date of the beginning, we left Rome on our way to St. Petersburg. We stopped a day in Posen, at the house of my husband's brother, Dr. Francis Chlapowski, when a despatch arrived from General Wahl:

"Tell Madame Modrzejewska not to come to St. Petersburg —her performances have been forbidden." A subsequent letter from the managers told us that at the last moment an order came from the Minister of the Interior, Durnovo, prohibiting my appearances. Durnovo was a personal friend of General Hurko. The money was refunded to the public, and both the managers and myself suffered severe financial losses caused by the advance expenses.

This was the second misadventure caused by my Chicago address. But this was not the end.

Simultaneously with the fatal despatch from St. Petersburg, I received news from friends in Warsaw that, as there was a new Governor-General, Count Shouvaloff, in place of Hurko, and the new administration was much more liberal, there probably would not be any more objection to my Warsaw engagement. Count Shouvaloff had been approached on the subject, and did not see any difficulty in the way. At the same time a semi-official letter of the management reached me, proposing a renewal of the old contract.

Half hopeful and half dreading a new drawback, we went to Warsaw, and, as I remember, we arrived on Wednesday. Thursday morning, on the advice of friends familiar with the situation, we went to the Castle to see Count Shouvaloff. He was away at the time, but the same afternoon an *aide-de-camp* of his called at our hotel, bringing us word from the governor to come and see him next Monday. We saw the president of the theatre, and perfected plans for my appearance.

On Saturday afternoon my husband was called to the chief of police, General Kleigels. The latter, with the greatest courtesy, asked when we were going to leave. "I hope not for some time," Mr. Chlapowski replied — "not before my wife's engagement is over." "I am sorry to say that the engagement is cancelled, and I think it would be best for you to leave town at once." "Is this an advice or an order?" asked my husband. "I am sorry to say it, but it is an order — an order straight from St. Petersburg." "But we were bidden by the Governor-General to call on him next Monday." "This invitation is also cancelled." After some more conversation, he allowed us to remain twenty-four hours more, and when we went to the station next day, there were a number of *gendarmes* watching to see if we really would take the train.

During the conversation the General expressed his regret that "Madame Modrzejewska, who had been so much admired by the Russians living in Warsaw, had spoken so harshly of them." "In this you are mistaken, General; she did not say a word against the Russians themselves; she has not the slightest prejudice against the Russian nation, and has a great many friends amidst your countrymen. She only spoke of the government." "Of course, but she was so many years in our public theatre under the authority of the government that she had not the right to speak the way she did. Her address made a very bad impression, the more so as she is so much known."

My husband explained to him that I never was a Russian subject, that at present I was, through his own naturalization, an American citizen, and as such I enjoyed the rights of an American to express freely my opinion of my own government, and also of all foreign governments. "Besides, you know, General," added Mr. Chlapowski, "that she did not say anything more than the truth. All of you Russians, when you are abroad, say the same things, and even worse ones, about your authorities, than my wife did; and I dare say that you yourself, General, when you are in Paris, are not an exception to the rule and that you criticise severely those highest in rank in Warsaw or in St. Petersburg."

"Jamais en public" (never in public), was the characteristic reply of the chief of police.

Two weeks later there was published an imperial "ukase" (decree) forbidding "Helena Modrzejewska, the famous actress, and wife of Charles Bozenta Chlapowski, American citizen, to enter any part of the Russian territory."

The decree was repeated in all the papers. Several times later, when the wind blew differently in St. Petersburg, did influential friends of ours endeavor to have the decree rescinded, and to obtain permission for me to return at least to Warsaw, but up to the present time the order has been upheld, and I am still precluded from visiting Russian Poland.

From a photograph by Thors, San Francisco

CHAPTER LI

I HAVE already written about my impression when I first saw Edwin Booth's acting, and will say more now. Mr. William Winter, the celebrated critic of America, has sufficiently exhausted this subject, and all I could say would appear tame beside the eulogy of that eminent writer.

For my part I admire the great actor mostly in Hamlet, Benedict, Shylock, and I shall never forget his exquisite subtlety in the second act of "Richelieu," nor his banquet scene in "Macbeth."

Richard Mansfield came to the front a few years previous to Edwin Booth's death. He made his first hit in the "Parisian Romance." I saw him first in "Beau Brummel," in which part he was very remarkable. The critics did not like his Richard III, but I liked him. He had splendid moments, and was quite unconventional. In "Monsieur Beaucaire" he was simply exquisite. After Edwin Booth, Mr. Mansfield occupied the most prominent position on the American stage.

It would be a very difficult task to write about the present "stars" in America, for there are so many in the theatrical constellation that it would take too much time to enumerate them.

Some of them I have seen, and many I have only heard about.

Besides, I do not claim to be a critic; I only could praise those I like, and pass over the others in silence. That would never do.

It is true that I spoke of those who worked with me

and those who retired or are no more. I also spoke of some foreign actors and actresses, but when I made a list of the present "stars" in this country I succumbed. A vertigo seized me and I gave up.

RICHARD MANSFIELD.

I can only say in general that there is a great deal of talent on the American stage, and that many American actors and actresses have attained a high artistic level. In the younger generation I have noticed, however, a sad lack of proper training. It is not their fault; the evil lies in the unfortunate condition of the "star" system. There is little opportunity for beginners to learn much. They usually are shifted from one company to another, and often forced to play one single part all through a season. In most cases they are not allowed to present their own conception of the character, but are compelled to follow blindly the stage-manager's instructions.

In case they have to understudy the part, they must exactly imitate their predecessors, and woe to those who dare to do otherwise.

There are actors and actresses who cannot count more than five, and sometimes only three, parts during the five years taken out of their life's career.

There is no field for development under such a system, and the best schools of acting, after all, are the stock companies, though the latter have again another drawback: they change bills every week, and actors, being forced to study in a hurry, cannot pay much attention to details. Yet, at least, they gain experience.

It also happens that some young actors or actresses are raised suddenly to the dignity of a "star" before being quite ripe for the position. They are advertised and pushed until the public, bewildered by the extravagant advertisements, crowds the theatre and repeats after the clever theatrical manager, "Great! Great!"

The consequence is that the word "great" is not sufficient any more, if you do not add to it, "Genius!" In Europe the word "genius" is only applied to the greatest of the world, but here it has become an every day occurrence.

It is strange to say that some of those geniuses, after having quarrelled with their managers, suddenly cease to be great, and no one knows why. The public does not suspect the wires pulled by a cunning hand.

The reasons which several times before had made me anxious for retirement from the stage, and which decided my ultimate retreat, were, however, personal, and I cannot say that my decision was influenced by any special condition of the American drama. If it had been so, I should long ago have given up my professional career.

So much I have to confess, but this does not alter the fact that I do not admire the way in which theatrical matters are conducted here, and all along I have found fault with the present system in vogue.

Years ago I published an article in the *Forum* in which I pointed out the drawbacks of the so-called "star system." In those combinations it only too often happens that the chief actor or actress is surrounded by a poor company, and the lack of a good *ensemble* is frequently very painful. There are some notable exceptions to this rule.

I must in this connection say a few words of sincere appreciation for Mrs. Fiske, whose companies are remarkable for their entire cast; no part, however small, is slighted, and the result is a harmonious whole.

I believe that in the above-mentioned article I was the first to insist upon the necessity of establishing an endowed theatre which, being independent of the ticket office, might devote all its energies towards artistic and literary ideals. The hope is justified by the action and influence of the endowed theatres in continental Europe, especially in France, Germany, and Austria.

My dream is coming to life in New York, and though I have retired into privacy, I am sincerely happy to see the progress and expansion of the artistic atmosphere which has prompted and rendered possible the realization of this project, so long desired by numerous lovers of drama as well as by myself.

This idea of a national theatre, richly endowed by private or public donations, was taken up by Henry Irving,

Photograph by Dupont.

Minnie Maddern Fiske.

and recently by many influential people both in and out of the profession. It has started quite a movement, and has found favor with the intellectual theatre-goers.

I do not think that I ought to be accused of optimism if I look, in the near future, to the realization of this project.

Madame Modjeska.

Having spoken of several of my fellow-artists who have disappeared from the American stage, I would be glad to speak of those of my brothers and sisters in the dramatic profession who are at present in full activity. Unfortunately, there are a number of them with whose work I am not familiar. Some of the prominent ones I have not even seen, occupied as I was with my daily performances; others

I have seen only in one part, often not their best one. It would not be fair to mention a few and omit others. Therefore I think it best to refrain from expressing any opinion on the present American "stars," the more so that it would be based chiefly on impressions instead of on careful analysis. I have to deprive myself of paying a just tribute to those I admire, in order not to slight unwillingly those whom I cannot judge.

Of course I was obliged to speak of several of my fellow-actors with whom I was associated in common work, in order to describe my own experiences, but this could not be helped, and I suppose that I may make another exception in regard to some among the *foreign* artists who have temporarily appeared in American theatres. The first place belongs to Salvini, whom I consider the foremost tragedian of our times. The impression he made on me was akin to that I felt when I first came into the presence of the masterworks of Michael Angelo. In such moments we do not criticise; we bow in reverence. I am perfectly aware that my opinion runs counter to the judgments passed on him, and especially on his Shakespearian performances, by some of the most valued dramatic critics in this country. Nevertheless, I am bold enough to maintain my own opinion.

As to his rendition of Shakespearian parts, and above all, of Othello, there was raised a question which by implication touches all the foreign-born actresses, and consequently also applies to myself, and I shall return to it later on. But as to Salvini himself, I can only say that what impressed me most in him was that, while endowed with an unequalled tragic force, he never allowed himself to abuse it, and never took recourse to any unnecessary display of his wonderful powers. The most admirable thing, in my estimation, consisted in the psychological continuity of his personations, the subtlety of his transitions from mood to mood, the birth and gradation of passion, and the motiva-

Tommaso Salvini.

tion of the successive phases of the internal struggle — in one word, in the logical evolution of his characters, which seemed in his hands to be his own spontaneous creations, so closely were they linked with the author's conception. When seeing Salvini I was proud of my art.

Next to Salvini I place Madame Ristori, of whom I have spoken before, and then Eleonora Duse, their great country-woman. She came here as the exponent of the newest dramatic methods of the so-called realistic school of acting.

Generally speaking, I do not take great interest in all this talk about the different schools of acting. It seems to me that there are only two schools, one of good acting, the other of bad acting. Thus, in the case of Madame Duse, I cared much less for her particular modernistic methods than for her own self and her artistic powers. Whatever school she belongs to, she is a great actress. The intensity with which she abandons herself to the feelings and sufferings of the character she personates makes you forget all surroundings; you do not realize any more that you are at the theatre, that there is an actress on the boards; you cease analyzing; you only feel that you are in presence of terrible pain, despair, and agony. I shall never forget her wonderful last act in "Camille," nor the thrill that passed through me, at the very end of "Fedora," by a single phrase, "*E la Morte*" ("It is Death"), when she drinks the poisoned cup.

I regret exceedingly that I did not see Duse in comedy. One whose opinion in comedy acting cannot well be gainsaid, and who was not altogether an admirer of the Italian actress, Mr. Joseph Jefferson, told me that she was perfection itself in the "Locandiera."

Now, in regard to the often-discussed question of the innovations she brought on the stage, I am bound to acknowledge that her abstention from conventionality, from any kinds of stage tricks, could only gratify me. While she spoke very often in very low tones and in an accelerated

Photograph, Copyright 1896, by Aimé Dupont.

Eleanora Duse.

tempo, this did not interfere with the distinctness of her speech and did not diminish the impression, thanks to her beautiful mellow, clear voice, the play of her wonderful, expressive features, and the look of her glorious, lustrous eyes.

It is somewhat different with her imitators. Deprived of the advantage of her face and her voice, they mumble and whisper as one would in a private room; their words are not understood, and their intentions remain obscure to the public.

Another Italian actor, Novelli, has visited America last year, and it was my good luck to see him in several of his parts. The character in which I liked him best was Petruchio in "The Taming of the Shrew." I was familiar, of course, with the play, and had seen it performed by various actors, some quite prominent. He is different from all of them, and I daresay his conception of the part is entirely contrary to the old traditional one. Notwithstanding that, he seemed to me the most convincing one, the only one, in fact, who could have effectively tamed a "shrew." He was far from being boisterous; on the contrary, he had such a quiet, good-humored, chaffing way of treating Katherine, that it would have been impossible for the most stubborn and ill-tempered girl to hold out against him.

The above artists, as is well known, played always in Italian, and one of the best proofs of their greatness lies in the fact that, without knowing their language, one could follow them and feel with them.

In speaking of Salvini, I said that I would return to the question of foreign actors in the Shakespearian repertoire.

It has been often maintained, both in England and America, that in order to render faithfully Shakespeare's creations one must be of English stock, on the plea that the poet was himself an Englishman, and therefore could only bring forth personages endowed with English characteristics, which cannot be successfully grasped by any foreigners. This argument seems both narrow and disparaging to the genius of Shakespeare.

Many authors, either historians or poets, have perfectly understood, either by study and observation, or by intuition, sometimes better called "inspiration," the peculiarities of other nationalities or races. Why refuse this knowledge or intuition to Shakespeare?

We foreigners, born outside of the magic pale of the Anglo-Saxon race, place Shakespeare upon a much higher pedestal. We claim that, before being English, he was human, and that his creations are not bound either by local or ethnological limits, but belong to humanity in general.

One might as well say that Shakespeare could only be rightly comprehended and interpreted by his contemporaries, for certainly the English people of the Elizabethan Era are very different from their descendants of the twentieth century. If our poet was not able to reproduce truthfully Italians, Moors, or Spaniards, he certainly could not be well acquainted with the idiosyncrasies of those who were to be born a few hundred years after his time. And yet, are the sentiments and passions which animate the characters of his plays so different from those of our generation? Our argument is that when Shakespeare wanted to present English people he located them in England, or at least gave them English names (Sir Toby Belch, Sir Andrew Aguecheek, etc.); while, when he presents Romans, Greeks, Jews, Italians, or Moors, he does not mean them to be travestied Anglo-Saxons, but to have the characteristics of their own race and nation. It is evident to me that it was not without purpose that he made Othello a Moor, Romeo and Juliet Italians, and Coriolanus a Roman patrician. It is a southern sun that warms up the atmosphere of the romance of Verona; it is the fire of African blood that runs through the veins of Desdemona's lover; it is the cruelty inborn to his race that prompts him to murder; and it is the pride of the conquerors of the world which swells the bosom of Coriolanus.

The feelings and passions typified in Shakespeare's plays animate all humanity, and this is the reason why the bard of Avon is equally understood, admired, and loved all the world over, or at least everywhere where Christian civilization has penetrated.

Nobody could or would take away from England the glory of having given birth to the greatest poet and the greatest analyst of human souls, but nobody has the right to limit his creations by geographical frontiers. Personally I have admiration and respect for the greatness of the Anglo-Saxon race; but I think that the greatness of the human race ranks above it, and that to be the poet of humanity is a greater honor than to be the poet of a special country.

The attitude of those who claim that only English people, or their descendants, have the right to touch the laurels of Shakespeare, reminds me, speaking with all reverence, of the narrowness of certain disciples of Christ (see Acts of the Apostles), who claimed that salvation was restricted to Jews, and did not benefit converted Gentiles.

There is, however, I confess, one point in which the argument against foreign interpreters of Shakespeare is justified — it is the question of language, and this applies in two ways: if the plays are rendered in foreign idioms, even the best translations cannot exactly reproduce the beauty and force of the original, and hence a great deal of the poetic charm is lost. If the plays are rendered in English by foreign-born actors, their lack of familiarity with the acquired language may make their pronunciation defective, and thus imperil, if not the poetry of the sentence, at least the music of the verse.

The latter is my own case, and therefore, whenever my pronunciation was found fault with, I could do nothing but accept the criticism in all humility and endeavor to correct the errors of my tongue; yet I persisted without discouragement, and went on studying more and more Shakespearian

Photograph by Aimé Dupont.

MADAME MODJESKA AS MAGDA.

parts, conscious that their essential value consisted in the psychological development of the characters, and confident that I understood them correctly and might reproduce them according to the author's intentions.

It is a perfect intuition of the human soul and a perfect knowledge of its most secret springs and its intricate workings which makes Shakespeare the greatest creator in literature, and it is this analysis of human nature that we foreign interpreters have principally in view when we have to render the creations of the master.

Speaking of my personal experience, I want to add that among all the English writers it was Shakespeare with whose works I felt most at home. I never had this feeling with the other English playwrights of the past, and therefore did not attempt such standard plays as "The School for Scandal," "The Lady of Lyons," "The Hunchback," or "She stoops to Conquer." The characters seemed to me too much imbued with racial Anglo-Saxon sentiments, to which I thought myself unable to do justice. Once I tried "Peg Woffington," and I failed badly.

During my next American tour Mr. Otis Skinner was my leading man. His intellectuality, combined with a fine appearance, beautiful voice, and the most remarkable elocution, in the true sense of the word, qualified him to a higher position, which he easily reached in due time.

The second season he played with me he was announced as my companion star, and since that time has made a fine name for himself and has become one of the most respected exponents of the best of both classic and modern drama.

I produced during those two seasons "Henry VIII," in which Mr. Skinner played the king, and John Lane, a fine legitimate actor, was Cardinal Wolsey.

The second play I added to my repertoire was Sudermann's "Magda," which proved quite a success. Mr. Skinner played my father, and did not quite like the part.[1]

[1] Sudermann was the second foreign author that it was my honor to introduce to the American public. But "Magda" was more successful from the start than was Ibsen's "The Doll's House." Although the play was severely criticised by the press in several cities, it was received exceedingly

In 1894 I was in Europe, and returned in the fall of 1895 to go on my regular American tour.

For years I tried to get a play written by an American author, but my efforts in that direction proved always fruitless. I had produced two of them, "Countess Roudine" and "The Tragic Mask," and both these plays fell flat. Still I was again tempted to produce a play from the pen of an American, and added to my repertoire a new play by Clyde Fitch, "Mistress Betty Singleton," with the intention of making a feature of it. Unfortunately, the New York critics condemned the play, which, however, contained man charming scenes and touching moments. I had to take refuge in Shakespeare. "Measure for Measure," which we revived soon afterwards, proved a success, and I resumed the repertoire.

My season opened unfortunately this time: Miss Abell, my juvenile lady, was bitten in the face by a naughty little dog, and could not appear for several weeks.

A few days later another young talented actress, Miss Grace Fisher, fell ill with typhoid fever, and Mr. Wadsworth Harris had a grievous family loss.

That was not all. With the resuming of my legitimate repertoire I had to change my leading man, who, having been selected for the new piece, was not adapted to Shakespeare or Schiller, and all the plays had to be rehearsed over again.

All these contrarieties were taken by the members of my company as so many strokes of bad luck; they began to look for a "Jonah," and I am sorry to say they found one in an inoffensive character actor. Forebodings floated in

well in others, and acknowledged as a masterpiece of dramatic literature. As for myself, I found in the title part one of my favorite and most successful personations. That which appealed to me was not so much the Bohemianism, the plea for woman's rights, as Magda's enthusiasm for art, the consciousness of the high mission of an artist.

the air and were whispered around until they really proved true.

For some time everything went well. The young ladies recovered, one from her wound, the other from typhoid fever, and the company, thoroughly rehearsed, was in good trim, when suddenly, one January morning, in Cincinnati, I woke up dangerously ill. My illness was caused by cold-water baths every morning. The Kneipp system was in fashion then, and I stupidly followed it. The system is good in itself, but it becomes dangerous when followed without prescribed exercises and proper care. My disease, called thrombophlebitis, was of a very serious character, as it has often a fatal ending when, as in my case, it settles not far from the heart.

I did not recover until late in the summer. In the meantime I was transported from Cincinnati to Chicago to be with my son and his family, and later on I was advised by the doctors to return to our California home.

Most of the physicians thought I would never recover, but thanks partly to my constitution and partly to the restful, balmy climate of our mountain home, I came back to my usual state of health.

I even tried to act in the winter, and started on a short tour on the Pacific coast under Mr. Al. Hayman's management, but after two weeks in San Francisco and three days in the south, I fell ill again in Los Angeles.

This time the doctors thought it was the fashionable disease, appendicitis, that held me in its grip. For a week six physicians deliberated if I was to be operated on or not, until there came a turn in my state, and the sword of Damocles was removed.

After an interval of ill health I returned to the boards in the fall of 1897, under my husband's management, who, mindful of my health, had arranged a very short tour of twelve weeks, with intervals, to prevent my being overworked. I had a very successful engagement of a few weeks at the New York Fifth Avenue Theatre, and other leading cities, and the tour was prolonged to twenty-three weeks.

Joseph Haworth was my leading man. I watched that talented actor, and was sometimes surprised by his great resources, combined, however, with a certain lack of keeping up the same diapason from the beginning to the end of his parts. These drawbacks, however, all disappeared when he played the father in "Magda." He gave a perfect performance. His Macbeth was well characterized and his banquet scene very effective, but the following acts were indifferent, until he came to the fight with Macduff, and then he was fine.

He was the best example of a wrongly conducted genius. He used to put me out sometimes by unexpected stage business or attitude, and surprises of that kind are not welcome, and ought not to happen in a well-trained company. Yet I have no doubt that, had he lived longer, he would have overcome all those deficiencies. The news of his sudden death was a great shock to both my husband and myself, for we had a true friendship for that talented and erratic actor.

I played afterwards two seasons with Mr. John C. Fisher as manager, from 1898 to 1899 and from 1899 to 1900.

I kept some of my old plays,—"As You Like It," "Magda," "Camille," "Marie Stuart," and "Macbeth,"—but the chief attraction of the first season was Shakespeare's "Cleopatra." The cast was good, the production fine, without being gorgeous, and above all, correct. My nephew, Wladyslaw Benda, who had just arrived from Vienna, and was on a visit to our mountain home, made the sketches for the scenery, accessories, and costumes.

Since then he made his way to New York, where he found his Mecca, but in spite of success he never stopped improving

his art. His activity is simply stupendous, and his imagination so great that I saw him composing four large-sized charcoal sketches in one day, with wonderful ease, whistling or humming some Polish airs.

Returning to "Cleopatra," I am glad to say that this time, as before, Shakespeare proved a good friend to me. The play was a success, and I loved my part.

I had actually two leading men that season. The first and principal one was Charles Herman, and he was fine as Antony. The second one was the young and handsome Mr. Lonegan, who was then at the start of his career. He played juvenile lead, — Armand, Orlando, etc.

John Lane was also with us, as well as a promising young actor, Spencer. Miss Annie Proctor, who had been several seasons my leading lady, was reëngaged. Stately, handsome, and experienced actress, she possessed, besides, the most winning manner, which was the result of her pure nature and kind heart.

Mrs. Sargent, the widow of Harry Sargent, my first American manager, was a splendid Aunt Francisca in "Magda."

The feature of my second season with Mr. Fisher was "Marie Antoinette," and John Kellard was my leading man, a very talented, intellectual actor, who distinguished himself in many parts in New York and other large cities.

I had not given up my desire of producing plays of American authors. "Marie Antoinette" was written by Clinton Stuart, and we produced it first in San Francisco.

The play was severely criticised, but we kept it in the repertoire and brought it to Boston and New York, where it received the final blow, due partly, I am bound to confess, to some intrigues which caused the dismissal of two members of the company, who were replaced at the last moment before the production of the play.

One of those substitutes was an improvement, for it was

John Malone who stepped into the part, but he had not sufficient time to learn his part, and made some slight mistakes which were quickly taken up by the critics.

The other substitute was quite incompetent, and the first act fell flat.

I could not interfere with those matters, for Mr. Fisher was quite absolute and would not give in. There was a slight misunderstanding between us about these and other things, and we parted at the end of the season.

In 1900–1901 and 1902 I was under the management of Wagenhals and Kemper. We produced "King John," with MacLean in the title part and Odette Tyler as Prince Arthur.

The next season's feature again was "Henry VIII," with Mr. Louis James in the part of Cardinal Wolsey. We were announced as companion stars, Modjeska and Louis James. He was very fine in the part of Wolsey and also in Shylock. Besides "Henry VIII" we had "Marie Stuart," "Macbeth," and "Merchant of Venice" always ready for a change.

Between the two seasons with Wagenhals and Kemper we went in summer to Europe and, of course, visited also Poland, where we spent happy moments in family circles, and where we had the good fortune to witness the performance of Paderewski's opera, "Manru," and greet the famous man and his charming wife.

In 1902 we visited Paderewski at his beautiful château in Morges, Switzerland. Those were delightful days spent on the shores of Lake Leman in view of all the glory of Mont Blanc. There also I could witness what a busy life Paderewski led. He was never seen before luncheon, but we could hear the piano constantly. He was both composing and practising. After lunch he retired for a short rest, and then the piano was again sending up its brilliant notes. He reappeared at dinner, fresh, jolly, a brilliant

Views on Madame Modjeska's California Estate.

man of the world, and stayed with his guests until late at night.

In the late summer of 1903 we crossed the ocean for the last time, probably, and settled down quietly in our mountain home in California.

Our place was removed ten miles from the railroad and

THE LIBRARY OF MADAME MODJESKA'S CALIFORNIA RESIDENCE.

twenty-three from the nearest town, Santa Ana. It was really a very peaceful retreat, far from the turmoil of the world. Access to it was not easy, and we had no visits except from those who really cared for us. Yet we did not suffer from lack of society, for during the many returns to California we had won a great many dear friends, too numerous to be mentioned here.

The residence itself was a bungalow of modest dimensions, but in harmony with the surroundings, and designed by Stanford White. The scenery was magnificent, at least we thought so, and there was a small park in front of the house and a rose garden we took great care of, as well as of the lawn. But all our improvements had for their main

INTERIOR VIEW OF THE LIBRARY IN MADAME MODJESKA'S CALIFORNIA RESIDENCE.

object not to spoil what nature had provided, and we left all the old oaks around the house, and the pretty, wild shrubs on the terrace.

Every time I came to "Arden" my thoughts were far away from the stage. It was an ideal place for rest — and

I needed rest. After almost a year and a half of quiet, '*Villegiatura*,' one day we received a telegram from Australia announcing Paderewski's arrival in California, with a promise of visiting our house.

The news was greeted with rapture, and we anticipated the pleasure he and his wife would take in driving up the cañon which bears such strong resemblance to some nooks in our Tatra Mountains, with its rushing brooks and waterfalls. We thought they would be glad to be far away from the noise for a few days, and above all to breathe the pure and fragrant air of the California hills.

It was the month of December, and the weather was still warm and mild when my husband went to meet our friends at the station. Trusting to the blue sky, he ordered a half-open conveyance in order to show them all the scenic beauties.

Hardly had they started on the twenty-three mile ride when the sky turned its color from pure blue to gray, clouds gathered, and a drizzling rain, the first of the season, began to fall. The hills and rocks were shut off from view, and what was worse, our passengers were not well protected from the moisture. The bad weather prolonged the trip, and they were shivering with cold when they arrived at "Arden."

Notwithstanding this unfortunate trick of nature, the days which Mr. Paderewski and his lovely wife spent in our house belong to our pleasantest reminiscences. Paderewski, besides being one of the greatest in art, is also the most delightful companion. Gifted with a brilliant wit, fascinating in conversation, posted on every subject, he is a perfect entertainer either as host or guest.

But it was not all perfect harmony. He scolded me fearfully at bridge whist, but this was not all: he found other reasons for blaming me. Almost from the start he upbraided me for my seclusion, for retiring into what he called a wilderness. He could not be reconciled to the idea that

Library in Madame Modjeska's California Residence. The Portrait on the Easel is by Bastien-Lepage.

I had given up the profession and was shrinking from a return to public life.

In vain I pleaded advanced years and fatigue. He pooh-poohed all my arguments, and he especially objected to my retiring so quietly without more ado.

When he insisted upon my returning to the footlights I was obliged to tell him that I was not a favorite with the so-called Theatrical Trust, and that it would be difficult to arrange a satisfactory season, as the syndicate managers would shut me out of the best cities.

Of course he was indignant, but said that this might be overcome.

Besides this, he implored us most earnestly to sell the ranch and live among "human beings." In this respect we agreed with him, and we then determined to sell the property, which had been a white elephant on our hands, for it did not yield any income and was too expensive to keep up. He was so pleased with this resolve that he did not scold me that evening when I made mistakes at bridge.

As to my return to the stage, we did not come to any conclusion, but his parting words were: "You will soon hear from me."

A month or two later I received the following paper, signed by some of the most prominent people in New York, by many of the distinguished authors and artists, and a number of my brothers and sisters in the dramatic profession.

TO MADAME HELENA MODJESKA

The undersigned, your friends and admirers, with many others whose names do not appear here, desire to tender you a public testimonial in recognition of your services to the stage, and as an expression of our appreciation of your genius and our regard for your character. We feel, dear Madame, that all that we can do must be an inadequate attempt to discharge the great debt we owe you. In you the art of acting in our day has rejoiced in one of its loftiest exponents. Shakespeare has found in you an interpreter worthy of his most exquisite and thrilling imaginations, and in the range of modern tragedy and comedy the refinement and charm of your every impersonation have ennobled the original.

If agreeable to you, the performance, in which we hope for your personal coöperation, will take place at the Metropolitan Opera House on May 2.

New York, April, 1905.

This document was accompanied by an explanatory letter from my old manager and friend, Daniel Frohman.

I was deeply touched by that high proof of appreciation, and accepted the testimonial.

I knew that the idea was inspired by Paderewski, who was joined in his efforts by several of our old friends, and Daniel Frohman, who took on his shoulders all the practical details.

When I arrived in New York, a few days previous to the date fixed for the occasion, I learned with dismay that Paderewski, who was to take part in the program, had been injured in travelling, and would not be able to appear. It was like a blow of fate. The performance lost its chief attraction.

The testimonial was given in the afternoon of May 2, 1905, before a brilliant audience. Many of the prominent artists then present in New York took part in it,—Mrs. Patrick Campbell, Miss Ada Rehan, Miss Mary Shaw, Mr. Bispham, Mr. Louis James, Mr. O'Neill, Mr. John Kellard, and many more excellent actors and actresses who consented to take even small parts in order to give brilliancy to the occasion.

Paderewski's absence was in part alleviated by a letter which was read from the stage.

After the second act of "Macbeth," Mr. Clarence Stedman delivered a speech to which I responded.

This performance was my farewell to New York, and

Photograph, copyright, by Aimé Dupont.

ADA REHAN AS "PORTIA."

it had the same character as my greeting in this city almost twenty-eight years before.

I thought it would be my farewell to the American stage altogether, but Daniel Frohman and Paderewski urgently advised me to make another tour through the United States. They were both very persuasive, and I followed their advice.

Photograph by Sarony.

JAMES O'NEILL.

The tour was prolonged for two years, up to April, 1907, and was conducted by Jules Murry.

I played my old repertoire only, mostly "Macbeth" and "Marie Stuart."

There is nothing of special interest to note in these last seasons, except a great ovation, arranged by our friends in Los Angeles, during which a speech was delivered by one of the most brilliant men of California, Joseph Scott, a prominent lawyer and great friend of ours.

The reception that evening, the shower of flowers thrown from the boxes by the prettiest young girls of Los Angeles, and the hearty applause made me feel that I was at home.

We had thought many times of returning for our last days to our native country, but for many reasons we decided to remain in the United States.

The part of Poland under Russian dominion we are forbidden to enter. In the German provinces we are looked upon with suspicion by the authorities, and we are too old to be of much use in the strenuous struggle of the present times.

Another strong motive for remaining here is that most of my family settled in the United States. My son has achieved a great career in his profession of civil engineer and bridge-builder; two of my nephews, Louis Opid and Ludomir Tomaszewicz (called Thomas for short), both talented musicians, were married here and established in this country.

Another nephew, Wladyslaw Benda, has achieved a fine reputation as an artist and illustrator.

My grandchildren and my grandnieces and nephews were all born here, and we count already over twenty members of my family settled in the United States.

Through living in California, I can only at rare intervals see those nearest to my heart; yet the fact that in four and even less days I can come to Chicago makes the distance very short in comparison with crossing the Atlantic Ocean.

To all those reasons I will add another. Both of us have become Americanized in many ways. The long years we spent in this country have exerted a great influence upon our way of looking at things.

We have met many fine men and women and learned to love them.

While we have not become blind to the blemishes of American civilization, to some faults and defects of its inhabitants, yet we have learned not to look at them with the eye of indifferent observers. We have learned to suffer from them as from injuries affecting ourselves, and are anxious for their removal.

On the other hand, we have become very sensitive to the grandeur of our adopted country; its possibilities dazzle us, and its wonderful growth and progress excite our enthusiasm.[1]

[1] It seemed to us that both on the European and American horizon there were many dark clouds, but the difference was that while in Europe

Photograph, copyright 1891, by Schumacher, Los Angeles

This new love does not injure our old love for Poland. It only broadens our feelings and knowledge. We still remain the same ardent patriots, for the attachment to the mother-country could not be extirpated from our souls; we are always stirred by its misfortunes to the very depth of our hearts, and we always watch with the most vivid interest and pain the oppression of that most injured part of our land remaining under the Prussia-German rule.

In the autumn of 1906 we sold our ranch in San Iago Cañon, and a year later, in spring, I left the stage for good. We were looking for some quiet corner in the country to build our nest, but we finally decided to remain somewhere near the sea, where the air is purer and more invigorating than in the valley. After a few months' search, we found a little island inhabited by a club of eighteen families, and there we made our new residence.

I am often asked if I do not long for the footlights again, and my answer is that even in the deepest corner of my heart I cannot find that desire any more.

Very often during my long theatrical career I asked myself if I had done right in devoting my life to the stage, and could not find a satisfactory solution of the question. I certainly did not become an actress to make a fortune. In our country actors never get rich, and besides, I never attached much value to money. When I was young I yearned for fame, but later on all other considerations paled against the enthusiasm of the work itself. I fell in love with my art. To get out of myself, to forget all about Helena Modjeska, to throw my whole soul into the assumed character, to lead its life, to be moved by its emotions, thrilled by its passions, to suffer or rejoice, — in one word, to identify myself with it and reincarnate another soul and body, this became

it was hard to foresee a happy solution of the present difficulties, the conditions of life in America, as well as its institutions, made it possible to obviate the evils of the day and to escape the dangers of the future.

Madame Modjeska, Mr. and Mrs. Ralph Modjeska, Count Bozubs.

A FAMILY BREAKFAST PARTY.

my ideal, the goal of all my aspirations, and at the same time the enchantment and attraction of my work. I was very often misjudged and misunderstood, oftener yet appreciated beyond my merits, — and yet none of the comments upon my value made me deviate from my aim, which was always the grasping for my ideal, so far as it could be attained, — which at the end proved a struggle for the impossible.

Friends who are familiar with my work claim that I have some right to say a few words about "dramatic art." "Is it an art, indeed?" asked once a sceptical acquaintance of mine, who had seen a comic-opera singer, a person he knew to be without any training, with no artistic instincts, and of a very commonplace turn of mind, achieve a success in a serious drama. I was myself puzzled, but I watched carefully the performer, and discovered that the acting, though effective, was purely mechanical, the impression produced by old stage tricks, while the supposed talent acclaimed by the critics and applauded by the public consisted of a remarkable gift of imitation. When I think of this incident, I cannot help observing that the correct interpretation of a part is not always *ipso facto* a work of art. Something else is needed, something which ought to lie in the very depth of the actor's soul, the suggestion of which has much more value than even the most laborious study. I do not know well how to define this something, but it seems to me to be an irrepressible desire of expression, together with the riches of feeling, which one can open to the world. Those who are endowed with this sense of expression, and moreover can enhance it with the color of their imagination and the intensity of emotional temperament, achieve what a mechanical though excellent performer can never do. They thrill the audience, which will carry home some of the actor's inmost treasures and live on them for a while. The richer his nature, the better the influence.

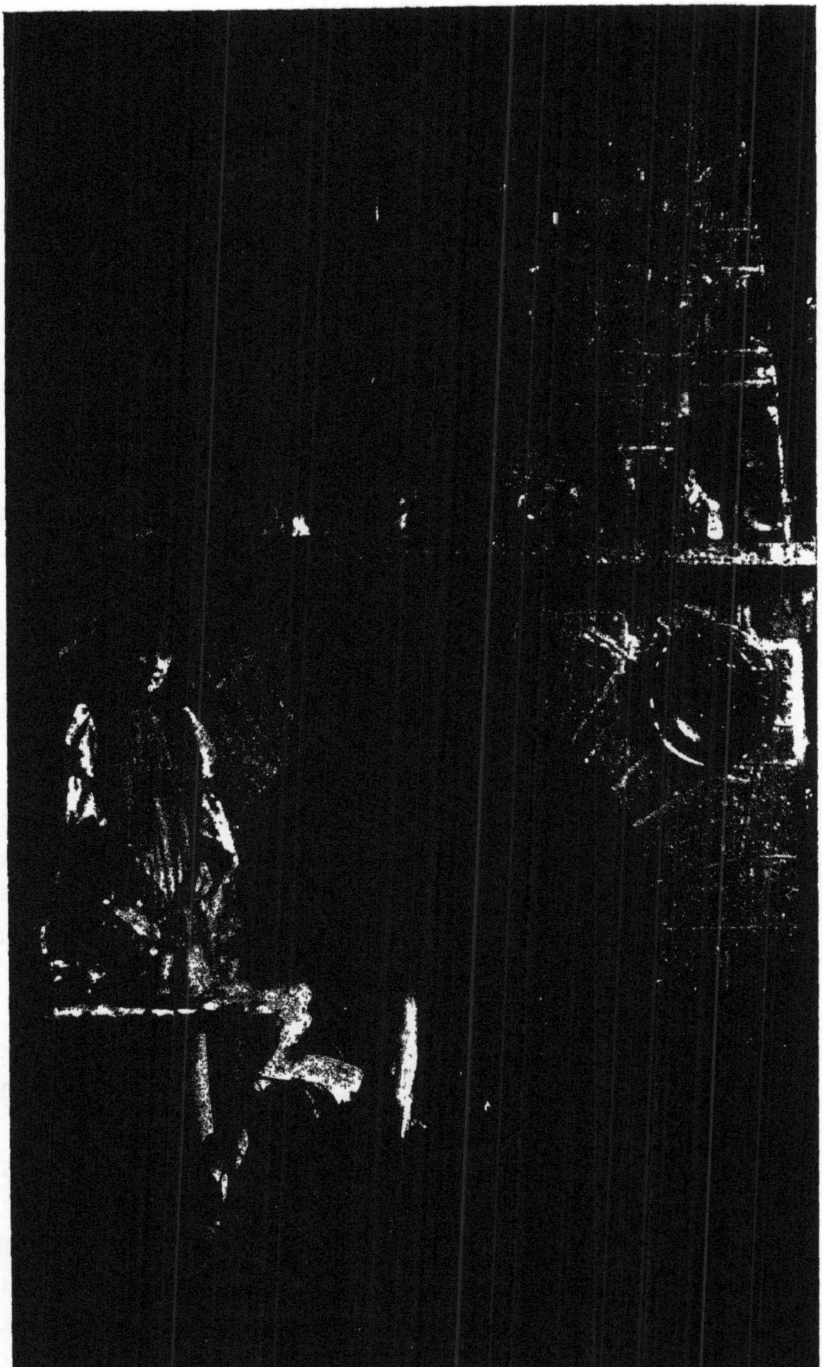

Fireplace in Madame Modjeska's Library in "Arden."

"The more I give, the more I have," says Juliet. To give and to give is our task.

This does not mean that actors get nothing from the outside world. On the contrary, a keen sense of observation will help them to store their minds and give back to people the very thing they got from them in a different form. Some of the prominent comedians possess a gift of close observation and analysis which might be envied by many psychologists.

But in personating dramatic or tragic parts one cannot depend solely on the documents furnished even by the closest observations. While tragic situations abound around us, the emotions produced by them are usually concealed and hidden before outsiders; the ludicrous features of men, on the contrary, are most often exposed to our view. It is therefore in his own soul and in his imagination that the tragic or emotional actor must look for inspiration; it is to his own power of expression that he must trust to reproduce the reality of the feeling.

The actor who is not impressionable, who is not stirred within himself, has to rely on elocution and conventional methods, but his work will be cold and mechanical in spite of his assiduous and meritorious efforts. All theatrical devices, all the display of lung power, will not give life to a dead-born personation.

The artist who feels makes the public feel. Coldness cannot produce heat, and it is the latter only which can produce life, or at least the illusion of life.

Of course control and good taste are imperative in every artistic work. We have often to curb the exuberance of our temperament in order to avoid exaggeration, which may lead even a talented person into the pit of "ranting." The ideal actor, it seems to me, must possess intelligence, quick perception, originality, impressionability, and imagination enough to allow him to identify himself with an assumed character, and above all, a store of emotion and passion. Besides those, he has to possess many physical attributes, as, for instance, an expressive face, a fine figure, and a sympathetic voice, which can carry the tones without strain. If a person possesses all these qualities, or at least a good part of them, he or she may start on their apprenticeship and hope for success. It happens, however, very often that really talented individuals are outdone in their struggles by those quick, business-like ones, who do not trouble their brains by trying to do original work, but simply imitate others, get hold of somebody else's stage business and attitudes, etc. They do all this with so much assurance and so much self-confidence that they dazzle the innocent managers, who supply them with situations often denied to the more retiring and less self-assertive, though talented, candidates.

A pretty doll-like face in the case of women is almost always a winner, while a plainer but expressive and intellectual one is left in the shade until some one who knows finds her out.

As a rule the way to enter the stage profession is a harder one for women than for men. A bold, dashing creature counts for more than one truly qualified for the boards. In the present state of affairs, where tuition is so expensive, and where all depends upon the good-will of those who direct the theatrical world, it is exceedingly hard for a poor and modest girl to obtain an engagement.

In several European countries, and especially in France, there are so-called dramatic conservatories, public institutions usually closely connected with the national theatres, where aspirants for the stage can find an adequate training gratis. Of course these conservatories accept only students who appear best adapted for the career, and they do not keep them unless they show genuine talent. After having finished the proper course and passed examination, the pupils of these institutions receive positions in stock companies, either in the capital or in some provincial theatres.

There is nothing of the kind here. The dramatic schools in America, such as they are (and a few of them are very good, indeed), are very expensive, and only those who can afford to pay the required sum can receive tuition and a subsequent engagement. Such a system presents two drawbacks:—

First, young people who have talent and no money are deprived of the advantages the school could give them.

Second, those schools being planned on a business basis, every one who pays is admitted to them. The result is that they produce aspirants for the dramatic career without the slightest qualification for it, who only increase the number of bad actors and actresses.

Therefore I welcome with joy the advent of the National Theatre in New York, which will, like the Théâtre Français, have in connection with it a dramatic school, where only students who give indication of talent will be accepted, and where the tuition and training will be offered without pay.

The establishment of the National Theatre is in itself a great event in the annals of the American stage, and will undoubtedly have a beneficent influence on the development of dramatic art in the United States.

I cannot refrain from mentioning that years ago I published an article in the *Forum* upon the advisability of founding endowed theatres in this country.

I began these general considerations by quoting the query of a pessimist: "Is dramatic acting an art?" In my own estimation it is as high an art as painting, sculpture, architecture, or music. All of them are based on brain-work, and are inspired by imagination perfected by æsthetic sense. In common with painting and sculpture, the object of drama is to represent nature through the artist's temperament. It may be true that the other branches require a more assiduous training, as the artistic execution depends, in a great measure, upon perfect manual skill, or the deft use of the tools.

Is the actor's task less hard because his only tool is his own personality? Has he not to master and moderate his voice, rule his motions and gestures, graduate and control his feelings, watch over the inflection of every word and over the expression of his face, and do all this without showing the effort, so that art be concealed and appear like reality? Has he not to throw away his own nature and put himself into the character he represents, to identify himself with it, to shed tears or to laugh, to rage, to hate, to love, and doing this maintain the illusion of life before hundreds of strangers, while perhaps his own heart is trembling lest in the heat of passion he lose control over his part?

I often hear people complain of the number of bad actors, but nobody who has not been connected with the stage can realize how difficult it is to be really a good actor and what amount of work and experience it takes to form a psychologically true conception of a character, and how much nervous power it needs to create an impression of reality.

I have endeavored here to prove why I consider the drama entitled to take rank among its sister arts; it remains only now to say a few words about its influence over the outside world.

Nobody, surely, tries to deny the strong impression it can produce when well presented. Acting through the medium of both senses, sight and hearing, like plastic art and music combined, it brings the audience in closer contact than either with the reality of life and the beauty of poetry, and therefore impresses itself also more strongly and quickly upon man's mentality and imagination. In the same way as literature its effects can be good or bad.

There is no question that when it is treated purely as an object of commercial speculation the drama is apt to

LAST HOME OF MADAME MODJESKA, ON BAY ISLAND IN EAST NEWPORT, CALIFORNIA, WHERE SHE HAD SETTLED A FEW MONTHS PREVIOUS TO HER DEATH ON APRIL 8th, 1909.

degenerate by becoming an appeal to the grosser instincts of humanity, to be a purveyor of coarseness and immorality. This fact explains, in some way, though it does not entirely justify, the prejudice against the theatre which exists, even to-day, among many serious and respectable though narrow-minded people, who are apt to condemn the highest effort of true art, because at some theatres indecent plays are produced, and so-called "leg shows" are still in existence. They forget that the theatre, if true to its mission and properly conducted, may be one of the most refining and wholesome influences.

All these thoughts have been often expounded in a much abler way than I can presume to do, but whilst I do not know how far my apology may convince others, I can state that these considerations always formed the essence of my belief.

I began this article with a query as to whether I have done right in devoting my life to the stage. Now that I have retired, and can look over my past calmly, I do not regret my choice. Of course the road I travelled was not an easy one, the obstacles were numerous and difficult, the work was hard, indeed, and many pangs did my career cost me, but I was amply rewarded. My life became richer through the experience I gained, through the many associations it was my good fortune to form; but the best reward of all was the artistic satisfaction, the joy that I found in the work itself, also the hope that my achievements may have been of some use, and in any case that they did not exert an unwholesome influence upon my audiences; for the keynote of my conceptions was always founded on human sympathy, and I persistently tried to find a redeeming side to the weaknesses and errors of my heroines, whilst, on the other hand, I endeavored in the execution never to lose sight of the æsthetic objects of art. Another advantage I reaped, which I value most highly, was the privilege I shared with several illustrious countrymen of mine in proving to the outside world that our unfortunate and much-maligned nation, Poland, is always alive, and cannot be relegated to oblivion, as its civilization and art are undeniable tokens of its vitality.

I have done what I could do for art and myself; I certainly could not do it over again, and as for the excitement and applause, I never attached much value to either. What I loved best in my profession was the work, but the moment I realized I was losing my buoyancy and my quick perception, I left the stage without regret.

Every age has its rights, and I am only taking a due advantage of them when I allow myself to rest.

The writing of my "memories and impressions" was rather a pleasure than a work, and I could not occupy my time better than in sharing some of my thoughts and feelings with those who in the past have seen me act.

When I sit on the porch of our cottage, looking at the purple hills of Santa Ana and the peaks of Sierra Madre, or at the blue waters of the bay, I feel calm and contented. The love for my dearest ones fills my heart to its very brim, and though my thoughts are often visited with the images of the glorious moments of my stage life, yet no regret, no bitterness, disturbs my mind, but gratitude for all I received from God and men.

ORATION OF MICHAEL TARASIEWICZ AT FUNERAL OF MODJESKA[1]

CRACOW, July 18, 1910.

"Hail to thee upon thy return to the country the earth of which is to be thy last resting-place. Welcome thou, who might say of thyself as did Countess Idalia: —

"'I am here as a passing angel. I have let thee see the lightning and disappeared upon the firmament of the sky.'

"Welcome, thou, for passing like an angel upon the Polish firmament of art and genius and showing the lightning of it to both hemispheres.

"Be blessed for thy unbounded heart, for thy sweetness, goodness, charm, and grace; for having carried generations to the highest summits of ecstasy by pointing towards the sublime in the field of art and forcing thy public to forget the misery and grayness of everyday life.

"Be blessed, thou unforgotten, who disappeareth like 'a golden dream' ineffaceable in the memory of those who had the happiness of seeing thee, and those who, never having seen thee, will know of thee by tradition.

"For thy art, for thy constant work, for that thou hast never become renegade to thy ideal, and that, in perfecting thy soul, thou hast been perfecting the soul of humanity — be blessed.

"Depart in the name of those who cannot bow to the reality that they will never see thee again — in the name of the throng thirsting for beauty not satiated, the hungry not to be nourished, and in the name of the thankful and sincere, the sad and the unhappy.

[1] Translated by Félicie Modjeska.

"Depart in the name of those to whom thy heart gave itself in particular and for which it had to suffer.

"In the name of those to whom thou wert an example unreached, an unparalleled mistress, an exquisite friend, and a sincere colleague, accept our homage and good-by.

"Let Cracow receive thee in its cemetery, where so many great hearts have been laid away — where the great spirit of Matejko lies.

"Thou queen of dramatic art and queen of the beautiful, rest in peace after thy work, thy battles, and thy triumphs. May the breeze of weeping willows bring thee the murmurs of thy beloved stage's poetry, to soothe thy spirit and please thy heart.

"And in return let thy genius be the guardian of the Polish stage and keep it in the light it hath attained, and may the pilgrim artists visiting thy grave drink as they would from the spring of Castal, — faith, strength, example, — so that the thankful hearts of generations accompany thee to the land of eternity and the Pantheon of immortality."

INDEX

Princess Helene von Racowitza

An Autobiography

Translated from the German by CYRIL MAR

$3.50 net

"A special interest cannot but attach to the recollections of a woman of the world who has possessed exceptional beauty and charm and has turned these gifts to the fullest social account, always provided, of course, she has had the intellegence to appreciate her advantages and is equipped with the literary capacity for self-expression. Helene von Racowitza was in her day one of the most famous and fascinating women in Europe, and she met and was admired by all sorts of world-renowned persons, — statesmen, authors, princes, artists, social reformers, musicians. Endowed with an eager and passionate temperament, ever ready to warm both hands at the fire of life, fond of and able to hold her own with the exceptional people who crossed her path, she kept her eyes and ears open amidst all her pleasure-hunting and conquests. At the same time she preserved a certain instinctive candor, and it is this quality that has helped her so immensely now that in the autumn of her career she has sat down to record her impressions and experiences. Records of love-passages, detailed with the most startling frankness, memoirs in which figure names so familiar as those of Hans Andersen, Bulwer Lytton, Meyerbeer, Louis Napoleon, and the Empress Eugenie, Bismarck, Liszt, Paul Lindau, Mme. Blavatsky, and Bjornson — these of themselves would make a remarkable book. But the author and her autobiography have another and a supreme claim on our attention. Helene von Racowitza was the heroine of almost the strangest and most tragic romance the nineteenth century had to show, and it is because she now supplies in full her version of that love story which had so fatal a termination for Ferdinand Lassalle that readers all the world over will turn to her pages with keen anticipation. What that story was and how it ended, those who are acquainted with George Meredith's 'Tragic Comedians' will not need to be reminded."

— *London Times.*

Lightning Source UK Ltd.
Milton Keynes UK
UKHW010803290720
367358UK00001B/143

9 781406 735727